Barron's Regents Exams and Answers

English

CAROL CHAITKIN, M.S.
Former Director of American Studies, Lycée Français de New York
Former English Department Head, Great Neck North High School,
Great Neck, New York

BARRON'S

Barron's Educational Series, Inc.

All inquiries should be addressed to:
Barron's Educational Series, Inc.
250 Wireless Boulevard
Hauppauge, New York 11788
www.barronseduc.com

ISBN-13: 978-0-8120-3191-1
ISBN-10: 0-8120-3191-1
ISSN 1069-2924

PRINTED IN THE UNITED STATES OF AMERICA
9 8 7 6 5 4 3 2 1

Contents

Reading and Writing About Literature 84

CHAPTER 5 Reviewing Literary Elements and Techniques

Glossaries of Terms 92

A Guide to Proofreading for Common Errors 107

Appendices: 111
The New York State Learning Standards for English Language Arts

Regents Examinations and Answers 117

Introduction

QUESTIONS AND ANSWERS ABOUT THE REGENTS COMPREHENSIVE EXAMINATION IN ENGLISH

WHAT IS THE ENGLISH REGENTS EXAM?

This is an exam designed to assess New York State students' ability to perform a broad range of reading, critical thinking, and writing skills. It represents a rigorous level of expectation reflected in the State's *Learning Standards for English Language Arts*, and a passing score on this exam is a requirement for a high school diploma.

WHAT DOES THE EXAM LOOK LIKE?

The exam is in **four parts** or "tasks," and **each includes an essay response.** The first three parts require you to listen to or read extended passages of informational text or literary passages, answer multiple-choice questions on those passages, and write an essay for a particular purpose and audience. The fourth part is an essay of critical analysis and an evaluation of two works of literature you have read. All written responses require effective use of language and standard written English.

HOW AND WHEN IS THE EXAM GIVEN?

The English Regents exam is administered over two days of three-hour sessions each, with two tasks per session. It is offered in January, June, and August of each year. Students must be present on both days of the examination, and a student who misses one of the two days must retake the entire exam when it is next administered. Students may take the exam more than once if needed to meet the graduation requirement.

WHY IS THE EXAM SIX HOURS LONG?

Each of the four tasks on the English Regents exam is designed to take most students about one hour to complete. The additional time gives you the opportunity to do your best work. For many students, this means there is time to plan, outline, and even draft an essay response.

HOW CAN THIS BOOK HELP YOU?

This book shows you exactly what each part of the exam looks like. The answers to the multiple-choice questions are explained, and there are several sample student essays with analyses. Each chapter gives you specific tips on how to prepare, what to review, and offers sample tasks for review. Each chapter offers guides to writing the essays and explanations of how they will be scored. In addition, you will find a detailed Glossary of Literary Terms and Techniques and a Guide to Proofreading for Common Errors. In the Appendices, you will find a comprehensive outline of the New York State *Learning Standards for English Language Arts*, and ten actual Regents Exams, with essays and answers explained, are included.

TERMS TO HELP YOU UNDERSTAND THE REGENTS COMPREHENSIVE ENGLISH EXAMINATION

assessment You may hear teachers and other educators using the term **assessment** instead of test or examination. An **assessment** is more than a simple test (in arithmetic, say) because it seeks to measure a number of skills at one time. Although we continue to refer to the English Regents as an exam or test, its goal is to be a valid **assessment** of a broad range of listening, reading, thinking, and writing skills outlined in the *Learning Standards*.

audience In talking about writing, we use the term **audience** to mean the intended readers. Session One, Parts A and B of the Regents exam require that you write an essay or report for a particular group of readers and for a particular purpose.

conventions This term is found in the **rubrics** and refers to conventional standards for spelling, punctuation, paragraphing, capitalization, grammar, and usage. You are expected to follow the **conventions** of standard written English in all four parts of the examination.

critical lens This term is used in Session Two, Part B of the exam and will be a quote about a particular way of "looking at" and evaluating works of literature. You will use your interpretation and response to the **critical lens** to compose the literary essay.

guidelines The **guidelines** follow the description of each **task** and list the specific steps you must take to write a successful essay. The scoring **rubric** details how each part of the guidelines is to be assessed.

performance indicators This is the technical term educators use to identify what it is students should be able to do in order to demonstrate they have the listening, reading, thinking, and writing skills outlined in the **standards**. The map on page 7 shows how many of the activities and skills developed by high school students are related to the **tasks** on the Regents exam.

rubric A **rubric** is a descriptive guide to scoring or evaluating an essay, examination, or other **task**. Many teachers now use **rubrics** in their own courses to show students how their work is assessed or evaluated. You will find a **rubric** for each part of the Regents exam at the end of each chapter. Be sure to review these carefully.

situation Session One, Parts A and B of the English Regents include a **situation**, a specific context, purpose, and **audience** for the essay, article, or report that you will write.

standards For students in New York State, *The Learning Standards for English Language Arts* establish four broad categories of language skills, state general goals for each, and then outline **performance indicators** for each. The English Regents exam reflects the emphasis on performance—specific expectations for what intellectual habits you must develop and skills you must exercise on a habitual basis. (The *Standards* are outlined in the map on page 7 and reprinted in the Appendices)

task The **task** is what you must actually do on each part of the exam. The exam is composed of a series of **tasks** because you are expected to demonstrate how well you comprehend, analyze, and write.

THE ENGLISH REGENTS EXAM—AN OVERVIEW

Session One, Part A: Listening and Writing for Information and Understanding

You will listen to a lecture or a speech, answer 6 multiple-choice questions about key ideas in the passage, and **write an extended response**. The lecture or speech will be read twice. You may take notes at any time during the readings, and you may use your notes in answering the multiple-choice questions. These questions also may help you choose ideas and details for the written response.

The written response is based on a situation related to the passage, for a specific purpose and audience. One example might include a report to classmates on the views of the speaker in preparation for a class project. Another example might require that you compose a letter to the editor of a newspaper or the local school board in support of a particular position.

Session One, Part B Reading and Writing for Information and Understanding

You should expect to **read an informational article accompanied by a chart, diagram,** or other graphic presentation, **answer 10 multiple-choice questions** on basic comprehension of main ideas, vocabulary, and interpretation, and **write an informative or persuasive piece** expressing a point of view and recommendation based on the information in the reading.

This part incorporates many of the skills you use in doing research. Like Part A above, it first requires that you interpret and analyze information. You must then compose a clear argument based on sound interpretations and selection of relevant details.

Note: The informational texts in Session One, Parts A and B are likely to come from subjects across the curriculum; sources might include texts from history and social sciences, the arts, or technical and scientific subjects. Session Two, Parts A and B, however, are literature based.

Session Two, Part A Reading and Writing for Literary Response

You will **read two literature selections** (from fiction, poetry, memoir, or literary non-fiction), **answer 10 multiple-choice questions** on key ideas, details, vocabulary, and you will **write an essay** that discusses the ways in which the two passages reveal the subject and that shows how specific literary elements and techniques convey the meaning of the selected passages. The essay must be organized in a unified and coherent manner and must follow the conventions of standard written English.

Session Two, Part B Reading and Writing for Critical (Literary) Analysis and Evaluation

In this part, you are required to **write a critical essay** in which you discuss **two** works of literature you have read from the particular perspective of a statement that is provided as a "critical lens." Your interpretation of the "lens" and response to it become the controlling idea for your essay.

Here you must interpret a sophisticated prompt, develop a critical point of view in response to that prompt, and develop that critical point of view with detailed reference to two works. You must also use specific references to appropriate literary elements to show how the chosen works support your opinion.

HOW IS THE ENGLISH REGENTS SCORED?

Your final score is based on the total number of correct answers to the multiple-choice questions and the rating of the four essays. All papers are read by at least two English teachers and may be reviewed by a third reader. They will evaluate your essays for meaning, development, organization, language use, and conventions. The scoring rubrics for the essays are outlined later in this chapter and discussed in detail in the chapters on each part of the exam.

Does a Regents examination score of 65 indicate that 65 percent of questions were answered correctly? No. The passing score of 65 is not intended to indicate answering 65 percent of questions correctly. The score for a total of 26 points in the multiple-choice questions and a possible 24 points for the four essays is converted to **a final score that signifies a level of achievement of the State *Learning Standards*.** The conversion of these two scores to a final grade is determined during standard setting for each exam. In the "Regents Exams and Answers" section you will find the conversion chart for each of the ten exams included in this book.

Understanding the Rubrics

Rubrics are descriptive guidelines for how teachers will score the essays you write. Understanding the language of the rubrics will help you understand what is expected in each task and show you what makes the difference between a high and a middle score, or between a middle and a low score on an essay.

The essay response for each part of the Regents exam is scored on a scale of 1–6 for the same five qualities. Essays rated 5 or 6 are considered high scoring essays; 3–4 are middle range; 1–2 are low scoring and are not likely to result in a passing score.

What are the Five Qualities in the Rubrics?

Meaning The extent to which the response exhibits sound understanding, interpretation, and analysis of the task and text(s).

Development The extent to which ideas are elaborated using specific and relevant evidence from the text(s).

Organization The extent to which the response exhibits direction, shape, and coherence.

Language Use The extent to which the response reveals an awareness of audience and purpose through effective use of words, sentence structure, and sentence variety.

Conventions The extent to which the response exhibits conventional spelling, punctuation, capitalization, grammar, and usage.

When you review the rubric for each task, you will see that the definition of each Quality is the same for all four parts of the exam. The descriptions of scores for Meaning and Development vary with each task; the descriptions for Organization vary slightly for Session Two, Part B. The descriptions for Language Use and Conventions are the same in all four tasks.

You will see that the **guidelines** for each task are not only statements of what the Regents exam expects you to be able to do, they are also outlines of the rubrics for assessment.

A MAP TO THE ENGLISH LANGUAGE ARTS STANDARDS AND PERFORMANCE INDICATORS

	Task	Standard	Performance Indicators
SESSION ONE, PART A	(a) Extended written response to a speech (b) Multiple-choice questions on key ideas (6)	Listening and writing for information and understanding	Interpret and analyze complex informational texts and presentations... Use a combination of techniques to extract salient information from texts... Make distinctions about the relative value and significance of specific date, facts, and ideas Write...research reports, feature articles, and thesis/support papers on a variety of topics... Present a controlling idea that conveys an individual perspective and insight into the topic Use a wide range of organizational patterns... Support interpretations and decisions... Use standard English skillfully...
SESSION ONE, PART B	(a) Extended written response to informational materials (text and visual) (b) Multiple-choice questions on basic comprehension (salient information, vocabulary, and interpretation) (10)	Reading and writing for information and understanding	Interpret and analyze complex informational texts and presentations... Use a combination of techniques to extract salient information from texts... Make distinctions about the relative value and significance of specific date, facts, and ideas Write...research reports, feature articles, and thesis/support papers on a variety of topics... Present a controlling idea that conveys an individual perspective and insight into the topic Use a wide range of organizational patterns... Support interpretations and decisions... Use standard English skillfully...
SESSION TWO, PART A	(a) Extended written response to two linked passages of different genres (b) Multiple-choice questions on key ideas, details, and vocabulary (10)	Reading and writing for literary response	Read...independently and fluently across many genres of literature Identify the distinguishing features of different literary genres...and use those features to interpret the work Recognize and understand the significance of a wide range of literary elements and techniques... and use those elements to interpret the work Produce literary interpretations that explicate the multiple layers of meaning Use standard English skillfully...
SESSION TWO, PART B	Extended written response to literature read for school	Reading and writing for critical analysis and evaluation	Analyze, interpret, and evaluate...a wide range of...texts... Evaluate the quality of texts...from a variety of critical perspectives Make precise determinations about the perspective of a particular writer... Present...well-developed analyses of issues, ideas, and texts... Make effective use of details, evidence, and arguments... Use standard English skillfully...

Test-Taking Techniques

The following pages contain several tips to help you achieve a good grade on any examination you have to take at any time, including your English Regents exam. Specific suggestions and tactics are also given in each of the chapters of this book.

TIP 1

Be Confident and Prepared

SUGGESTIONS

- Try to relax: you have been preparing by doing the work assigned in your English courses as well as in many other courses throughout high school.
- Review the essays you have written, noting your teachers' comments.
- Use a clock or watch and take previous exams at home under examination conditions (i.e., don't have the radio or television on).
- Review sample Regents tasks your teachers have provided.
- Get a review book. (The preferred book is Barron's *Let's Review*: *English*.)
- Visit www.barronseduc.com for the latest information on the Regents exams.
- Talk over your answers to questions with someone else. Use Barron's web site to communicate directly with subject specialists.
- Use your classroom teacher as a resource and don't hesitate or be afraid to ask questions about material you do not understand or answers that do not make sense to you.

- Try to be as good a student as possible: (a) finish all of your homework assignments; (b) take class notes carefully, (c) answer and ask questions in class; (d) review your notes and homework assignments before any test.
- Be aware that the people who make up the Regents exams want you to pass. The English Regents exam represents standards all students should be able to meet.
- On the night before the exam, prepare all the things you will need: admission card, pens, watch, and comfortable clothing.
- Go to bed early. Set your alarm to wake you up in plenty of time.
- Get to school early, at least a half hour before the start of the exam.
- Keep your eyes on your own paper; do not let them wander over to anyone else's paper. The penalties for cheating are severe and can include losing credit for every Regents exam taken and barring from admission to any New York State university.

TIP 2

Read Directions, Tasks, Questions, and Guidelines Carefully

SUGGESTIONS

- Be familiar with the test directions ahead of time. If you are uncertain about anything, raise your hand and ask the proctor in the examination room. Proctors will try to help you by providing any general information—not, of course, any specific answers to questions.
- Understand the rubric for scoring each section of the exam. In each chapter of this book you will find detailed discussion of the rubrics and analysis of how the essays are scored.
- Remember to answer all questions. There is no penalty for wrong answers.
- If you have to guess, do so intelligently by first eliminating answers that are clearly incorrect. This will raise your chance of guessing correctly.
- Review the guidelines and be sure to do all parts of each task.

TIP 3

Budget Your Test Time in a Balanced Manner

SUGGESTIONS

- No one is admitted to a Regents examination 45 minutes after the start of the test. This is the state rule adhered to by your school no matter what caused the lateness.
- Arrive early; leave your home earlier than usual to allow for possible delays.
- Bring a watch to the test.
- Be aware of the passing of time. You have a total of 3 hours to complete two tasks on each of the two days of the exam.
- Take time to plan your essays. The 3 hours allotted for each day are intended to give you time to do your best work. The teachers who score your essays expect you have done this.
- Don't get "hung up" on a question that is proving to be very difficult. Go on to another question and return later to the difficult one.
- Plan to stay in the room for the entire three hours. If you finish early, read over your work. Use the additional time to:
  1. check to see that you have answered all the multiple-choice questions;
  2. make an intelligent guess for those questions you did not know the answer to so that every answer space is completed;
  3. make sure your essays address all parts of the task: in Session One, Part B, be sure you write about the text and the graph or chart; in Session Two, Part A be sure you write about both texts; in Session Two, Part B be sure you write about two works of literature you have read.
  4. proofread your essays carefully.
- Examine every word in your essays to make certain they can be read. Remember neatness does not count; correctness and legibility do. It is better to cross out a word and rewrite it than to have the reader not understand it.

TIP 4

Use Your Test-Taking Skills on the Multiple-Choice Questions

SUGGESTIONS

- In general, go with your first answer choice. Use the texts and your notes to confirm your answers.
- Eliminate obvious incorrect answers.
- There is no penalty for guessing; answer all questions. An omitted answer gets no credit.

TIP 5

Use Your Classroom Experiences in Writing the Essays

SUGGESTIONS

- Use the skills you developed in social studies, science, and other courses for analyzing and understanding informational texts, graphs, diagrams, and charts.
- Try to recall your class discussions, especially about literature, for the Session Two, Part A task, and about the works you chose for the Session Two, Part B essay. Recall the paragraphs, exams, and class essays you wrote on those works. Recall the comments your teachers made in class and on your written work.
- Try to visualize essays you have written in the past to "see" the need for revision or corrections your teacher indicated. Review your exam essays to see if any of those errors or weaknesses are present and try to implement teachers' past suggestions.
- Review your essays to see that the language you have used is appropriate for the task and audience indicated.

SUMMARY OF TIPS

1. Be Confident and Prepared.
2. Read Directions, Tasks, Questions, and Guidelines Carefully.
3. Budget Your Test Time in a Balanced Manner.
4. Use Your Test-Taking Skills on the Multiple-Choice Questions.
5. Use Your Classroom Experiences in Writing the Essays.

Strategy and Review for Session One, Part A of the Examination

CHAPTER 1
Listening and Writing for Information and Understanding

WHAT DOES THIS PART OF THE EXAM REQUIRE?

In this part of the Regents exam, you will listen to a speech or a lecture on a topic of general interest to students. You will take notes as you listen, then answer multiple-choice questions on what you have heard. Finally, you will write an article, report, or informational essay for a particular situation and audience. The task in Part A requires more than a summary or simple report. You may have to take a position on a particular issue; that is, you may have to write in order to inform *and* persuade.

WHAT DOES THIS PART OF THE EXAM LOOK LIKE?

SAMPLE TASK I
Directions: For this part of the test, you will listen to a speech about being well educated for today's world, answer some multiple-choice questions, and write a response based on the situation described below. You will hear the speech twice. You may take notes anytime you wish during the readings.

> **The Situation**: As a representative of your high school you have been asked to write an article for the junior high or middle school newspaper to help eighth-graders select the courses and

activities to pursue in high school in order to be well educated for today's world. In preparation for writing your article, listen to a speech given by J. Peter Kelly, president of a steel company, to an audience of science students. Then use relevant information from this speech to write your article.

Your Task: Write an article for the junior high or middle school newspaper in which you offer advice and suggestions to eighth-graders about what courses and activities to pursue in high school in order to become well educated for today's world.

Guidelines:
- Tell your audience what they need to know to help them select appropriate courses and activities to pursue in high school
- Use specific, accurate, and relevant information from the speech to support your discussion
- Use a tone and level of language appropriate for an essay for a junior high school newspaper
- Organize your ideas in a logical and coherent manner
- Be sure to indicate any words taken directly from the speech, by using quotation marks or referring to the speaker
- Follow the conventions of standard written English

As you can see, **this task requires more than simple recall of information;** it requires that you understand the subject of the speech you have just heard, appreciate its point of view and purpose, and have the ability to distinguish key points and significant details in order to present them to the audience described in the **Situation.**

Here is the speech for the Part A Task outlined above, followed by the multiple-choice questions. Remember: on the Regents exam, *you are expected to take notes* as you listen.

Listening Passage

A quote I heard many times when I was your age and which I now know traces back to Sir Francis Bacon, one of our earliest scientists, or philosophers as they were then called, is the statement, "Knowledge Is Power." Today I believe that the fuller, more correct statement is: "the application of knowledge is power." As you pursue your math, science, or engineering studies, I'd like you to keep in mind a few things on the application side of these pursuits. Yes, we need mathematicians, scientists, and engineers, and we need people with exceptional levels of capability who will earn Ph.D.'s in these disciplines. You should also know that we need many more people who will be what I call scientifically and technically literate. These people will not necessarily acquire Ph.D.'s in the sciences, but they will be highly successful in fields as diverse as sales, finance, law, manufacturing, and business management. In fact, the list is virtually endless. I hope you get the idea. The study of science, math, and technology subjects will broaden your opportunities in life, not narrow them. However, a failure to be scientifically literate will greatly limit your future opportunities.

My point is, do not stop pursuing an interest in the sciences, math, or technology areas simply because you may decide you do not want to be a scientist, a mathematician, or an engineer. A solid foundation in these disciplines will be an excellent foundation for an extraordinarily broad range of career choices.

But now let me broaden this discussion a little bit more and address two areas of personal concern. Again, to the students, I assume that at this point in time you have high personal aspirations. You should, and your presence here this evening says that you do. But, unfortunately, we as human beings tend to focus on what we enjoy and find easy and comfortable, and too often we are tempted to ignore the rest.

Well, if you truly aspire to be something more than a star, solo performer, that is, to effectively participate in a group activity; to lead an entire organization or even lead a small part of one; or to play a significant role in your community, then you must also develop your communication skills. You must be able to write effectively, and you must be able to speak effectively. And now at your present age is when you should be developing these competencies. Surfing the Internet may be fine and it has its own jargon, but you must be able to move away from the keyboard and speak effectively. If you are to be a leader, you must be able to explain, persuade, and, in short, communicate your vision to others. You must develop the ability to make others share your vision, and help you realize your dream. If you are not comfortable speaking to a group, or if you know that you are not effective when you speak or write, then I urge you in the strongest terms possible, to address these issues as vigorously as you would pursue any other learning discipline. Effective communication skills can be developed.

Let me be very clear about this subject. You do not have to do this, but let me also be clear, if you do not do it, if you are not a good communicator, you will not achieve your full potential, and, there will be many, many opportunities that you will not be able to realize.

My second concern is this: as a scientific and technical society, we have done a much better job of answering the question of "how can we do something?" than we have of answering the much deeper question of "should we do something?" We know how to make weapons of awesome, destructive power; we know how to efficiently perform abortions and euthanasia; and we know how to use technology to support life almost indefinitely. We know how to do an endless array of amazing things, but knowledge, scientific or otherwise, does not necessarily imply wisdom.

The greater question is, do we know whether we should do any of these things at all? And do we even know how we should go about developing answers to those higher questions, and who is it that should be answering these questions.

So to the students I urge, yes, study science, math, and technology, but make time to read some history, study some philosophy, enjoy some Shakespeare, grow in your understanding of whatever you believe about your maker and your reason for being here in this world at this time. Do not educate yourself so narrowly that you are excluded from those greater considerations of "should we?"

Let me give you an example. Today there is technology available, for exorbitant sums of money, to reduce by incredibly small amounts various pollutants in the air. But that same amount of money might enable large numbers of our population to simply eat regularly, enjoy decent housing, or receive proper medical care. Well, how should that money be spent? Who should decide? Too often today the majority of the scientific community, which has a real grasp of the technical or economic merits of a subject, sit by silently while those with a particularly strong social agenda and little appreciation of the technical merits are most communicative and have the greatest influence upon the decision makers. Tonight I am urging you to equip yourself to intelligently participate in the whole dialogue to help us make the best decision, the right decision. We will need your balanced, reasoned, and educated involvement. But you will have to decide whether you will educate yourself so as to be a worthy participant and valuable contributor to the dialogue.

Directions: Use your notes to answer the following questions about the passage read to you. The questions may help you think about ideas and information you might use in your writing. You may return to these questions anytime you wish.

1 According to the speaker, the power of knowledge lies in its

1 accumulation	3 use	
2 accuracy	4 limits	1 _____

2 The speaker assumes that the members of his audience
  have studied

  1 math and technology   3 business and manufacturing
  2 history and philosophy 4 writing and speaking   2 _____

3 According to the speaker, communication skills are necessary for an individual to

  1 achieve stardom   3 earn money
  2 accomplish goals   4 use technology   3 _____

4 The speaker implies that the answer to "How can we do
  something?" depends on a knowledge of

  1 philosophy   3 literature
  2 history   4 science   4 _____

5 The speaker uses the examples of weapons and life support to illustrate a need for

  1 locating cheaper energy
  2 developing better technology
  3 asking deeper questions
  4 inventing safer procedures   5 _____

6 The speaker uses rhetorical questions in order to

  1 raise doubts about the future of science
  2 stimulate thinking about ethical issues
  3 challenge assumptions about the value of education
  4 avoid providing obvious answers   6 _____

7 The speaker criticizes members of the scientific community for their lack of

  1 concern for financial matters
  2 appreciation for art and music
  3 patience toward nonscientists
  4 involvement in social issues   7 _____

8 The speaker implies that the question of how to spend public money can best be answered by people with a

1 broad base of knowledge
2 strong social agenda
3 bold financial plan
4 high level of intelligence   8 _____

Note: The actual examination includes only 6 questions on Session One, Part A. Additional questions are included here to suggest a fuller range of possible question types.

Answers

(1) **3**   (2) **1**   (3) **2**   (4) **4**   (5) **3**   (6) **2**   (7) **4**   (8) **1**

At the end of the multiple-choice questions, you are directed as follows:

> Review **The Situation** and read **Your Task** and the **Guidelines.** Then write your response.

> **The Situation:** As a representative of your high school, you have been asked to write an article for the junior high or middle school newspaper to help eighth-graders select the courses and activities to pursue in high school in order to be well educated for today's world. In preparation for writing your article, listen to a speech given by J. Peter Kelly, president of a steel company, to an audience of science students. Then use relevant information from this speech to write your article.

Your Task: Write an article for the junior high or middle school newspaper in which you offer advice and suggestions to eighth-graders about what courses and activities to pursue in high school in order to become well educated for today's world.

Guidelines:
- Tell your audience what they need to know to help them select appropriate courses and activities to pursue in high school
- Use specific, accurate, and relevant information from the speech to support your discussion
- Use a tone and level of language appropriate for an essay for a junior high school newspaper

- Be sure to indicate any words taken directly from the speech, by using quotation marks or referring to the speaker
- Organize your ideas in a logical and coherent manner
- Follow the conventions of standard written English

Here is an example of a student response that would receive a high score[*].

Sample Essay

As eighth-graders, the time has come for you to start planning for your future. The next step is high school; after that, college. Going into the new millennium, there is a great challenge at hand. That challenge demands students, in today's educational system, to be equipped with a well-balanced education. As your time in middle school comes to a close, choices have to be made. A schedule needs to be determined upon entering high school. However, as eighth-graders, the commonality between peers is the feeling of uncertainty in selection of high school courses. As students venturing into an undetermined path, it may be confusing when trying to find one's way. The best way to be prepared for college, and the business world, is to have a well-balanced education. Having a broad education will allow you to speak coherently with different people, from all walks of life. The ability to apply knowledge with effective communication can give you power and influence.

It was Bacon who said that "Knowledge is Power." However [it is] a businessman by the name of J. Peter Kelly who said that the "application of knowledge is power." If Mr. Kelly hit it any more on the nose, it would be broken. The application of knowledge is key in today's society. One could have a college degree in math or science. However, a person with only a high school diploma, who has better communication skills and a stronger presence in community action, will have more to say in the social scene, than the person with the science or math degree who cannot communicate effectively. The ability to express ideas vocally, and literally, is the only way to convey the full amount of knowledge you have inside. However, it is also necessary to have a strong scientific and mathematical background. The technologically advanced society in which we live, demands it. The only way to fully meet the technological standards is to effectively communicate with peers, and the social community.

As you make decisions in choosing courses for high school, I do suggest taking a science and math course each year. But I also suggest that one take a sufficient amount of literature and history courses.

[*]You will find a detailed discussion of the scoring rubric beginning on page 31.

*Being educated in the four core studies will allow a fluid-like flow be-
tween all walks of life. Don't limit education. Also take business
courses, computer literacy courses, drama, art, music, all of these
courses will allow communication skills to develop greatly. It's also
important to take a language besides English. In the next millennium,
the world will grow closer to becoming one. Having a well-balanced
education is a necessity. However, the ability to communicate, and
convey thoughts in the social and political scene, is the only way to
make an impact on an exponentially developing society.*

Note: The original of this essay contained some spelling errors, which have
been corrected; errors in the use of comma or semicolon remain from
the original.

This would be a high-scoring essay because the writer demonstrates good
understanding of the speech and of the task. Although it is not perfect in
composition, and not all the efforts to create metaphors are successful, the
writer has good command of the ideas and how to organize them. (A detailed
analysis of the rubric for Part I begins on page 31.)

Here is how one rater might use the rubric to comment on this essay:

Analysis

Meaning—This paper shows an obvious understanding and
analysis of the text, and it establishes a clear connection between
Kelly's speech and the task of conveying its ideas to eighth-
graders. Although not consistently well phrased, the introduction is admirable in outlining the main points of the essay.

Development—The writer uses a wide range of details to develop ideas, has chosen specific examples, and understands
their relative importance.

Organization—The writer maintains a clear and appropriate
focus—an important part of the rubric—and keeps the response "on task" throughout. Repeated use of "however,"
lacks variety but gives the essay the transitions it needs.

Language Use—The writer makes an admirable effort at
sophistication in style, with some effective use of metaphor and
high-level vocabulary. Not all metaphors or word choices are apt,
however. The writer shows awareness of audience by addressing

---

them directly, but vocabulary is not always at appropriate level. The sixth sentence in the introduction, for example, uses unnecessarily formal and awkward language. The writer also uses passive voice: "choices have to be made . . ." "a schedule needs to be determined," when the active voice is better: "you must make choices . . . you must determine a schedule . . ."

Conventions—Demonstrates overall control of the conventions. Misuse of the semicolon and comma is evident but does not seriously hinder meaning.

STRATEGIES FOR TAKING THE EXAM

- Review the guidelines. Be sure you understand and complete all parts of the task.
- Listen carefully and take notes on the passage

The directions for Session One, Part A Tasks on the English Regents exam include a statement about the subject of the passage you will hear and identify a specific purpose for the essay you will write. This information is meant to guide you in your listening and note taking.

As the reading begins, you should be able to answer the following important questions for good listening:

What is the speech or passage about? What is its main idea and purpose? What is the purpose of the essay I will write?

During the first reading, keep the following question in mind and use your notes to "answer" it for yourself.

What does the author say? In other words, how would you summarize the speaker's subject and his attitude toward it?

As you listen to the passage the second time, use the terms below to help you clarify your general understanding and shape your notes for the essay.

For passages that develop ideas and opinions, consider the following:

What does the author

advise	challenge	propose
agree or disagree with	claim	question
argue	conclude	recommend
assert	emphasize	suggest
believe	explain	

For passages that share a significant experience, consider the following:

What does the speaker
describe	recall	reveal
illustrate	remember	value

Using some of these terms in your own essay will make your discussion specific and persuasive.

* Understand the multiple-choice questions

Because the main idea of the passage is indicated in the directions and in the Task, you are not likely to be asked about that directly. Instead, you will find that the multiple-choice questions are primarily about recall of specific information or about what inferences (conclusions) you should draw. You will also see questions that refer to how the speaker develops ideas.

You can expect examples of the following kinds of questions.

Questions about specific details

According to the speaker
The speaker states, indicates, believes, criticizes, associates...
The speaker assumes . . .
The speaker describes . . .
The main reason that . . .

Questions about making inferences, drawing conclusions from information in the text

The speaker implies . . .
The speaker suggests . . .
The speaker most likely means . . .
The speaker mentions . . . in order to . . .
When he refers to . . . the narrator means . . .
The purpose of the speech is . . .

Questions about language and literary devices

The expression symbolizes . . .
The phrase . . . implies
The use of the word . . . has the effect of . . .
The word . . . emphasizes . . .
The opening lines serve to . . .
The speaker uses examples to . . .

You will not see the questions until after the second reading of the passage, so they cannot serve as clues for listening; they should, however, help you plan your essay.

- Be sure that you understand and do all parts of the task. If you are directed to take a position or choose a point of view, do it; do not straddle the issue.
- Plan your essay

In the first sample in this chapter, the task requires you to write an article for a junior high or middle school newspaper, *advising* students. This is not a summary, or even a report; it is a persuasive essay using ideas and information from the speech to support what will be *your* opinion.

In the second sample you will listen to a speech by an author, in which she offers advice on how to use dialogue to improve writing. Your task will be to share this advice in a writing manual prepared for classmates.

- Write a good introduction

The introduction to your essay serves many purposes. On the Regents exam, the introduction will signal to the readers how well you understand the task, and this is very important! That first impression can affect the way the rest of your essay is read.

Another important purpose of the introduction is to help *you* clarify the topic and how you will develop it.

Review the introductions in the model essays for examples of how to do this well.

- Use a structure and length that fits your topic

Not all well-written essays must have five paragraphs—or three, or four. You will see that the sample essays vary in number of paragraphs. The Regents guidelines do not specify a minimum length, but the strongest essays require at least one full page for adequate development; most high scoring essays will be at least one and a half to two pages long.

Maintain the focus of the essay. Organize your paper so your reader can *follow* your argument. It is not enough to get where you are going. The reader must see how you got there!

- Use a wide range of specific and relevant details

Passages in this section are lengthy and rich in detail. Use as much of the information as you can—not simply to repeat, but to show that you have made an "in-depth analysis" of the text. Citing only one or two examples will not result in a high score on the essay.

• Use what you know, but stay on task

The best and most fully developed essays may include examples of the writer's own opinions or experiences, but they must not lead you away from the specific task, which is to make connections between information and ideas *in the text* and the task. The connection between the text(s) and your essay must always be evident.

SAMPLE TASK II

Overview: For this part of the test, you will listen to a speech about writing effective dialogue, answer some multiple-choice questions, and write a response based on the situation described below. You will hear the speech twice. You may take notes on the page allotted anytime you wish during the readings.

> **The Situation:** As a member of a class on fiction writing, you have been asked by your teacher to prepare an instructional manual for your classmates on the reasons and techniques for using dialogue to improve their writing. In preparation for writing the manual, listen to a speech by published writer Anne LaMott. Then use relevant information from the speech to write your instructional manual.

Your Task: Write an instructional manual for your classmates in which you give some reasons and techniques for using dialogue to improve their writing.

Guidelines:
Be sure to
• Tell your audience what they need to know about the reasons for using dialogue to improve their writing
• Discuss some techniques for writing effective dialogue
• Use specific, accurate, and relevant information from the speech to support your discussion
• Use a tone and level of language appropriate for a manual for high school students
• Organize your ideas in a logical and coherent manner
• Indicate any words taken directly from the speech by using quotation marks or referring to the speaker
• Follow the conventions of standard written English

Note: For this portion of the examination, the teacher will read a passage aloud. You will not actually see the passage reprinted below. Therefore, you are encouraged to have someone read the passage to you, in order to simulate the examination as closely as possible.

Listening Passage

Good dialogue is such a pleasure to come across while reading, a complete change of pace from description and exposition and all that writing. Suddenly people are talking, and we find ourselves clipping along. And we have all the pleasures of voyeurism because the characters don't know we are listening. We get to feel privy to their inner workings without having to spend too much time listening to them think. I don't want them to think all the time on paper. I have to think all the time.

On the other hand, nothing can break the mood of a piece of writing like bad dialogue. My students are miserable when they are reading an otherwise terrific story to the class and then hit a patch of dialogue that is so purple and expositional that it reads like something from a childhood play by the Gabor sisters. Suddenly the piece is emotionally tone-deaf and there's a total lack of resonance. I can see the surprise on my students' faces, because the dialogue looked okay on paper, yet now it sounds as if it were poorly translated from a foreign language. The problem is that the writer simply put it down word by word; read out loud, it has no flow, no sense of the character's rhythm that in real life would run through the words.

In nonfiction, the hope is that the person actually said the words that you have attributed to him or her. In fiction, though, anything goes. It is a matter of ear, just as finding the right physical detail is mostly a matter of eye. You're not reproducing actual speech—you're translating the sound and rhythm of what a character says into words. You're putting down on paper your sense of how the characters speak.

There is a real skill to hearing all those words that real people—and your characters—say and to recording what you have heard—and the latter is or should be more interesting and concise and even more true than what was actually said. Dialogue is more like a movie than it is like real life, since it should be more dramatic. There's a greater sense of action. In the old days, before movies, the dialogue in novels was much more studied, ornate. Characters talked in ways we can't really imagine people talking. Later, good dialogue became sharp and lean. Now, in the right hands, dialogue can move things along in a way that will leave you breathless.

There are a number of things that help when you sit down to write dialogue. First of all, sound your words—read them out loud. If you can't bring yourself to do this, mouth your dialogue. This is something you have to practice, doing it over and over and over. Then when you're out in the world—that is, not at your desk—and you hear people talking, you'll find yourself editing their dialogue, playing with it, seeing in your mind's eye what it would look like on the page. You listen to how people really talk, and then learn little by little to take someone's five-minute speech and make it one sentence, without losing anything. If you are a writer, or want to be a writer, this is how you spend your days—listening, observing, storing things away, making your isolation pay off. You take home all you've taken in, all that you've overheard, and you turn it into gold. (Or at least you try.)

Second, remember that you should be able to identify each character by what he or she says. Each one must sound different from the others. And they should not all sound like you; each one must have a self. If you can get their speech mannerisms right, you will know what they're wearing and driving and maybe thinking, and how they were raised, and what they feel. You need to trust yourself to hear what they are saying over what you are saying. At least give each of them a shot at expression: sometimes what they are saying and how they are saying it will finally show you who they are and what is really happening. Whoa—they're not going to get married after all! And you had no idea!

Third, you might want to try putting together two people who more than anything else in the world wish to avoid each other, people who would avoid whole cities just to make sure they won't bump into each other. Maybe there is someone like this in your life. Take a character whom one of your main characters feels this way about and put the two of them in the same elevator. Then let the elevator get stuck. Nothing like a supercharged atmosphere to get things going. Now, they both will have a lot to say, but they will also be afraid that they won't be able to control what they say. They will be afraid of an explosion. Maybe there will be one, maybe not. But there's only one way to find out. In any case, good dialogue gives us the sense that we are eavesdropping, that the author is not getting in the way. Thus, good dialogue encompasses both what is said and what is not said. What is not said will sit patiently outside that stuck elevator door, or it will dart around the characters' feet inside the elevator, like rats. So let these characters hold back some thoughts, and at the same time, let them detonate little bombs.

Dialogue is the way to nail character, so you have to work on getting the voice right. You don't want to sit there, though, trying to put the right words in their mouths. I don't think the right words exist already in your head, any more than the characters do. They exist somewhere else. What we have in our heads are fragments and thoughts and things we've heard and memorized, and we take our little ragbag and reach into it and throw some stuff down and then our unconscious kicks in. This is where the creating is done. We start out with stock characters, and our unconscious provides us with real, flesh-and-blood, believable people.

The better you know the characters, the more you'll see things from their point of view. You need to trust that you've got it in you to listen to people, watch them, and notice what they wear and how they move, to capture a sense of how they speak. You want to avoid at all costs drawing your characters on those that already exist in other works of fiction. You must learn about people from people, not from what you read. Your reading should confirm what you've observed in the world.

Directions (1–6): Use your notes to answer the following questions about the passage read to you. Select the best suggested answer and write its number in the space provided. The questions may help you think about ideas and information you might use in your writing. You may return to these questions anytime you wish.

1 According to the speaker, good dialogue is a pleasure to read because it

  1 identifies the theme   3 quickens the pace
  2 explains the setting   4 simplifies the plot   1 _____

2 According to the speaker, the act of reading dialogue allows the reader to

  1 eavesdrop   3 interrupt
  2 criticize   4 fantasize   2 _____

3 According to the speaker, her students first realize they have written bad dialogue when they

  1 see it   3 analyze it
  2 translate it   4 hear it   3 _____

4 The speaker suggests that fiction writers should view dialogue as being

  1 a reproduction of actual speech
  2 an extension of the characters
  3 the outline of the plot
  4 the insights of the author   4 _____

5 According to the speaker, a writer should prepare for writing dialogue by

  1 listening to ordinary conversations
  2 analyzing famous speeches
  3 reading classical literature
  4 talking to published authors   5 _____

6 In comparing "what is not said" to rats that "dart around the characters' feet," the speaker suggests that dialogue has the ability to

  1 reveal motive
  2 predict outcome
  3 create tension
  4 establish organization   6 _____

Answers

(1) **3** "quickens the pace." The first few sentences of the speech emphasize the point that dialogue offers "a change of pace...and we find ourselves clipping along [when people are talking]." The speaker concludes the first section of the speech by saying that "...dialogue can move things along in a way that will leave you breathless." She makes no direct connection of dialogue with setting, theme, or with simplification of plot.

(2) **1** "eavesdrop." In the opening section, Ann LaMott says that dialogue offers us "...all the pleasures of *voyeurism* because the characters don't know we are listening." Toward the end of the speech, in the anecdote about characters stuck in an elevator, she says, "good dialogue gives us the sense that we are eavesdropping, that the author is not getting in the way."

(3) **4** "hear it." LaMott says that her students are surprised when "dialogue [that] looked okay on paper...now sounds as if it were poorly translated from a foreign language...read out loud, it has no flow, no sense of the characters' rhythm...."

(4) **2** "an extension of the characters." The speaker says, "You're not reproducing actual speech...you're putting down on paper your sense of how the characters speak." LaMott expands on that point later when she says, "...you should be able to identify each character by what he or she says....each one must have a self." The author is not so much revealing her own insights as she is learning to listen and to hear what the characters are saying "over what you are saying."

(5) **1** "listening to ordinary conversations." LaMott says writers must "listen to how people really talk.... If you are a writer...you spend your days listening, observing, storing things away...." She does not mention analyzing speeches, reading classical literature, or talking to published authors (although she does hope the listeners heed her own advice).

(6) **3** "create tension." The anecdote about two characters who want only to avoid each other being stuck in an elevator describes a situation in which there would be great tension but not an outright "explosion." Rather,

in pointing out that good dialogue also encompasses what "is not said," LaMott urges the writer to let characters "hold back some thoughts" in order to create tension.

Sample Student Response Essay

"Dialogue is the way to nail character" states well-known author Ann LaMott. She believes that it's a lucky reader who, while moving through pages of writing, comes upon a flavorful burst of conversation between characters. While dialogue can be wonderful when used correctly, it can be drab and monotonous when used incorrectly. Ms. LaMott reveals that there are many reasons to use dialogue, and there are techniques to practice in order to make it good.

Adding dialogue can enliven any piece of writing. You can create a change of pace by adding a witty conversation to a slowly moving passage, or really stir things up by adding a sudden outburst from a quiet character. Using dialogue allows the reader to eavesdrop on the characters without being interrupted by the author. Let the reader learn about the characters through the conversations they're involved in. It's like eavesdropping while standing in a line waiting to purchase something. Listen to the conversations of customers, cashiers, and announcers.

Writing dialogue allows you to expand both your writing skills and your imagination, two excellent reasons to make dialogue a part of your practice. However, to achieve success at writing realistic speech for a character, you must train yourself to listen, observe, use, and store information from all around you. As I stated earlier, when standing in a check-out line, listen to random conversations of others and develop them in your head, mold them, play with them. After writing a dialogue down, read aloud what you have written: does it sound like a realistic way of speaking or a roughly translated document of a foreign language?

Another technique for writing good dialogue is to imagine putting together characters who would not want to talk to each other. Author Ann LaMott uses the example of placing such people in an elevator, and then having the elevator get stuck. When a situation like this occurs, the characters would have a lot to say and a lot they wouldn't want to say. Let them hold back some thoughts. This will create tension and uncertainty, and the excitement will improve the dialogue. Often, what is not said is as important as what is said.

Use simple, but concise and realistic writing to let your reader feel as if he or she were actually there, listening.

In conclusion, if you are looking for a way to liven up your stories, add a dash of dialogue. Learn to turn a five-minute speech into a single line and still retain the same meaning. Learn to suggest what characters are like and reveal their thoughts through the words they speak. Then you will have taken a big step in mastering the world of fiction writing.

Analysis

This is a very good essay because it not only reveals excellent understanding of the speech but also conveys the important ideas to the intended audience—student writers. The writer very skillfully introduces the essay with a quote, a bit of dialogue. The introduction also states very well the subject and purpose of the essay. The essay is quite fully developed in illustrating the advice LaMott offers with specific examples.

This writer has organized the essay clearly, moving from discussion of why writing dialogue is important to offering advice on the techniques for developing that skill. Transitions are clear and effective: The third paragraph begins with a restatement of the subject, paragraph 4 begins with "another technique...." "In conclusion" is unimaginative, but the sentence ends cleverly with the advice to "add a dash of dialogue." The language and tone are consistently appropriate for the subject and intended audience; the writer is speaking directly to the reader. The essay also reveals excellent command of the conventions. This essay would rate a high score. (See pp. 31–35 for a detailed explanation of the rubric for this part of the examination.)

Beginning on page 117, you will find 10 full Regents exams, with all answers explained and with examples of student essays. Each essay is followed by a detailed analysis of why it meets the criteria for a high score. Reviewing the tasks, essays, and analyses for this part of the exam should be a key part of your preparation.

Summing Up

While the passage is being read:
- Concentrate! Do not be distracted by others in the room. Do not worry about how much time you have.
- Listen to what is *said;* do not rely on what you may already know about the subject.
- Keep the task and situation in mind.
- Highlight the *relevant* details in your notes.

When you write the essay:
- Be sure you understand, and *do* all parts of the task.
- If you are directed to take a position or choose a point of view, do it; do not straddle the issue.
- Write a good introduction, one that states clearly the purpose of the essay.
- Review the questions for key ideas and relevant details.
- Develop *several* examples; mentioning only one or two details from the text will not be sufficient for a high score.
- Use a structure and length that fits your topic. Keep the essay focused on the topic and organized so your reader can *follow* your argument.
- Use what you know, but *stay on task;* the connection between the text and your essay must be evident.

KNOW THE RUBRIC

Here is the information from the chart on page 35. The key terms have been highlighted to show you how the teachers who read your essays might explain the difference between a 5 and a 6, for example, or between a 3 and a 4. Readers are directed to consider all five qualities equally and then give you an overall score of 1 to 6.

SCORING RUBRIC FOR SESSION ONE, PART A

Meaning: The extent to which the response exhibits sound understanding, interpretation, and analysis of the task and text.

High Scores

6—papers reveal an **in-depth analysis** of the text *and* make **insightful connections** between information and ideas in the text **and** the assigned task

5—papers convey a **thorough understanding** of the text *and* **make clear and explicit connections between** information and ideas in the **text and the assigned task**

Middle Scores

4—papers convey a **basic understanding** of the text *and* make **implicit connections** between information and ideas in the text and the assigned task

3—papers convey a **basic understanding** of the text *but* make **few or superficial** connections between information and ideas in the text and the assigned task

Low Scores

2—papers convey a **confused or inaccurate understanding** of the text *and may* allude to the text but make **unclear or unwarranted connections** to the task

1—papers provide **minimal or no evidence** of textual understanding *and/or* make **no connections** between information in the text and the assigned task

---

Development: The extent to which ideas are elaborated using specific and relevant evidence from the text.

High Scores

6—papers **develop ideas clearly and fully,** making effective use of a **wide range of relevant and specific details** from the text

5—papers **develop ideas clearly and consistently,** using **relevant and specific** details from the text

Middle Scores

4—papers **develop some ideas more fully than others,** using relevant and **specific details** from the text

3—papers **develop some ideas briefly,** using **some details** from the text

Low Scores

2—papers are **incomplete or largely undeveloped, hinting at ideas,** but references to the text are **vague, irrelevant, repetitive, or unjustified**

1—papers are **minimal,** with **no evidence of support**

> **Organization:** The extent to which the response exhibits direction, shape, and coherence.

High Scores

6—papers maintain a **clear and appropriate focus** *and* **exhibit a logical and coherent structure** through **skillful use** of appropriate devices and transitions

5—papers maintain a **clear and appropriate focus** *and* **exhibit a logical sequence** of ideas through **use** of appropriate devices and transitions

Middle Scores

4—papers **maintain a clear and appropriate focus** *and* exhibit a **logical sequence** of ideas *but* **may lack internal consistency**

3—papers establish, but **fail to maintain, an appropriate focus;** exhibit a **rudimentary structure** *but* may include some **inconsistencies or irrelevancies**

Low Scores

2—papers **lack an appropriate focus** but suggest **some organization,** *or* **suggest a focus** but **lack organization**

1—papers show **no focus or organization**

> **Language Use:** The extent to which the response reveals an awareness of audience and purpose through effective use of words, sentence structure, and sentence variety.

High Scores

6—papers are **stylistically sophisticated,** using language that is **precise and engaging,** with a **notable sense of voice** and **awareness of audience and purpose** *and* **vary structure** and length of sentences to enhance meaning

5—papers use language that is **fluent and original,** with **evident awareness** of audience and purpose *and* **vary structure** and length of sentences **to control rhythm and pacing**

Middle Scores

4—papers use **appropriate language,** with **some awareness of audience and purpose** *and* **occasionally** make effective use of sentence structure or length

3—papers rely on **basic vocabulary,** with **little awareness** of audience or purpose *and may* exhibit **some attempt to vary** sentence structure or length for effect, but **with uneven success**

Low Scores

2—responses use **language that is imprecise or unsuitable** for the audience or purpose *and* reveal **little awareness of how to use sentences** to achieve an effect

1—responses are **minimal** *and/or* use language that is **incoherent or inappropriate**

Conventions: The extent to which the response exhibits conventional spelling, punctuation, capitalization, grammar, and usage.

High Scores

6—responses **demonstrate control** of the conventions with **essentially no errors,** even with sophisticated language

5—responses **demonstrate control** of the conventions, exhibiting **occasional errors only when using sophisticated language**

Middle Scores

4—responses demonstrate **partial control,** exhibiting **occasional errors that do not hinder comprehension**

3—responses demonstrate **emerging control,** exhibiting **occasional errors that hinder comprehension**

Low Scores

2—responses demonstrate a **lack of control,** exhibiting **frequent errors** that make comprehension difficult

1—responses are **minimal,** making assessment of conventions unreliable *or* may be **illegible or not recognizable as English**

SCORING RUBRICS

SESSION ONE, PART A: LISTENING AND WRITING FOR INFORMATION AND UNDERSTANDING

QUALITY	6 Responses at this level:	5 Responses at this level:	4 Responses at this level:	3 Responses at this level:	2 Responses at this level:	1 Responses at this level:
Meaning: the extent to which the response exhibits sound understanding, interpretation, and analysis of the task and text(s)	—reveal an in-depth analysis of the text —make insightful connections between information and ideas in the text and the assigned task	—convey a thorough understanding of the text —make clear and explicit connections between information and ideas in the text and the assigned task	—convey a basic understanding of the text —make implicit connections between information and ideas in the text and the assigned task	—convey a basic understanding of the text —make few or superficial connections between information and ideas in the text and the assigned task	—convey a confused or inaccurate understanding of the text —allude to the text but make unclear or unwarranted connections to the assigned task	—provide no evidence of textual understanding —make no connections between information in the text and the assigned task
Development: the extent to which ideas are elaborated using specific and relevant evidence from the text(s)	—develop ideas clearly and fully, making effective use of a wide range of relevant and specific details from the text	—develop ideas clearly and consistently, using relevant and specific details from the text	—develop some ideas more fully than others, using specific and relevant details from the text	—develop ideas briefly, using some details from the text	—are incomplete or largely undeveloped, hinting at ideas, but references to the text are vague, irrelevant, repetitive, or unjustified	—are minimal, with no evidence of development
Organization: the extent to which the response exhibits direction, shape, and coherence	—maintain a clear and appropriate focus —exhibit a logical and coherent structure through skillful use of appropriate devices and transitions	—maintain a clear and appropriate focus —exhibit a logical sequence of ideas through use of appropriate devices and transitions	—maintain a clear and appropriate focus —exhibit a logical sequence of ideas but may lack internal consistency	—establish, but fail to maintain, an appropriate focus —exhibit a rudimentary structure but may include some inconsistencies or irrelevancies	—lack an appropriate focus but suggest some organization, or suggest a focus but lack organization	—show no focus or organization
Language Use: the extent to which the response reveals an awareness of audience and purpose through effective use of words, sentence structure, and sentence variety	—are stylistically sophisticated, using language that is precise and engaging, with a notable sense of voice and awareness of audience and purpose —vary structure and length of sentences to enhance meaning	—use language that is fluent and original, with evident awareness of audience and purpose —vary structure and length of sentences to control rhythm and pacing	—use appropriate language, with some awareness of audience and purpose —occasionally make effective use of sentence structure or length	—rely on language from the text or basic vocabulary, with little awareness of audience or purpose —exhibit some attempt to vary sentence structure or length for effect, but with uneven success	—use language that is imprecise or unsuitable for the audience or purpose —reveal little awareness of how to use sentences to achieve an effect	—are minimal —use language that is incoherent or inappropriate
Conventions: the extent to which the response exhibits conventional spelling, punctuation, paragraphing, capitalization, grammar, and usage	—demonstrate control of the conventions with essentially no errors, even with sophisticated language	—demonstrate control of the conventions, exhibiting occasional errors only when using sophisticated language	—demonstrate partial control, exhibiting occasional errors that do not hinder comprehension	—demonstrate emerging control, exhibiting occasional errors that hinder comprehension	—demonstrate a lack of control, exhibiting frequent errors that make comprehension difficult	—are minimal, making assessment of conventions unreliable —may be illegible or not recognizable as English

Strategy and Review for Session One, Part B of the Examination

CHAPTER 2

Reading and Writing for Information and Understanding

WHAT DOES THIS PART OF THE EXAM REQUIRE?

You will read an informational article accompanied by a chart, diagram, or other graphic presentation, answer 10 multiple-choice questions on basic comprehension of main ideas, vocabulary, and interpretation, and write an informative or persuasive piece expressing a point of view and recommendation based on the information in the reading.

This part assesses many of the skills you use when you do research. Like Part A, it first requires that you interpret and analyze information. You must then compose a clear argument based on sound interpretations and selection of relevant details. As in Part A, you may have to take a position on a particular issue; that is, you may have to write in order to inform *and* persuade.

The informational texts in Session One, Parts A and B come from subjects across the curriculum: sources might include documents from history and social sciences, the arts, or technical and scientific subjects.

WHAT DOES THIS PART OF THE EXAM LOOK LIKE?

SAMPLE TASK I

Directions: Read the text and study the graph on the following pages, answer the multiple-choice questions, and write a response based on the situation described below. You may use the margins to take notes as you read and scrap paper to plan your response.

The Situation: The planning team in your school is interested in developing a school-to-work program in connection with businesses in your community. As a member of the career guidance class, you have been asked to write a letter to the school planning team in which you describe the benefits of school-to-work programs and the conditions needed to make such programs successful.

Your Task: Using relevant information from *both* documents, write a letter to the school planning team in which you describe the benefits of school-to-work programs and the conditions needed to make such programs successful. *Write only the body of the letter.*

Guidelines:
Be sure to
- Tell your audience what they need to know about the benefits of school-to-work programs and the conditions needed to make such programs successful
- Use specific, accurate, and relevant information from the text *and* graph to support your discussion
- Use a tone and level of language appropriate for a letter to the school planning team
- Organize your ideas in a logical and coherent manner
- Indicate any words taken directly from the text by using quotation marks or referring to the author
- Follow the conventions of standard written English

School-to-Work Programs

Several years ago, faculty at Roosevelt High in Portland, Oregon, recognized that many of their students went directly from high school to low-paying, dead-end jobs. No wonder the school's dropout rate was 13 percent. Kids didn't see a reason to stay in school.

(5) Determined to make school more relevant to the workplace, the faculty developed "Roosevelt Renaissance 2000." In their freshman year, students explore six career pathways: natural resources, manufacturing and engineering, human services, health occupations, business and management, and arts and communications. The following year, each student chooses one of the pathways *(10)* and examines it in depth. The ninth and tenth graders also participate in job shadow experiences, spending three hours a semester watching someone on the job.

During their junior and senior years, Roosevelt students participate in internships that put them in the workplace for longer periods of time. Internships are *(15)* available at a newspaper, a hospital, an automotive shop, and many other work sites. "One student did an internship with the local electrical union," says business partnership coordinator Amy Henry, "and some kids interested in law have been sent to the public defender or the district attorney's offices."

Win-Win Partnerships

For many schools, the school-to-work initiative is built around a series of part- *(20)* nerships. For example, Eastman Kodak, a major employer in Colorado, introduces elementary students to business by helping them construct a model city using small cardboard structures. "The children use the models to decide on the best place to locate lemonade stands," says Lucille Mantelli, community relations director for Eastman Kodak's Colorado Division. Kodak representatives intro- *(25)* duce math concepts by teaching fifth graders to balance a checkbook. They also provide one-on-one job shadowing experiences and offer internships for high school juniors and seniors. "Students come to the plant site two or three hours a day," explains Eastman Kodak's Mantelli. "They do accounting, clerical, or secretarial work for us. We pay them, and they get school credit. We also give them *(30)* feedback on their performance and developmental opportunities."

In these partnerships, everybody wins. The participating students tend to stay in school and to take more difficult courses than students in schools that don't offer such programs. Business benefits by having a better prepared workforce. "It's a way for us to work with the school systems to develop the type of workforce
(35) we'll need in future years," continues Mantelli. "We need employees who understand the basics of reading and writing. We need them to be proficient in math and to be comfortable working on a team."

The Middle Years

While some schools start as early as elementary school, and others wait until high school, it's in the middle grades where schools really need to catch students.
(40) Middle school is the time when many students lose interest in school, explains Jondel Hoye, director of the National School-to-Work Office. "Middle schools need to reinforce exploration activities within the community at the same time they're reinforcing math and reading skills in the classrooms."

In Texas, weeklong internships in the business community are currently
(45) offered to seventh graders in the Fort Worth Independent School District. The Vital Link program involves nearly 300 companies which offer students experiences in banking, accounting, hotel management, engineering, medicine, government, the arts, communications, education, nonprofit agencies, retailing, legal services, and printing.

(50)   "We target middle school students because research shows that at age 12 kids start making choices that will affect them for the rest of their lives," explains coordinator Nancy Ricker. Students are placed in internships that match their skills and interests. Business people come to the school to talk with the kids before the internships begin. "They tell them about the business and what the people who
(55) work there do and what their salaries are," Ricker explains. "They ask the students to fill out job applications and explain why that's required."

When the students get to the job site, they are given the same introduction any new hire receives. After a morning of "work," they return to their classrooms to talk about their experiences. Their teachers reinforce the link between skills
(60) they have used in the workplace and those learned in the classroom. Vital Link students take harder courses, perform better on state-mandated tests, and have better attendance and discipline records than students who are not part of the project.

In Milwaukee, Wisconsin, a school-to-work project introduced middle school
(65) students to the intricacies of city planning. "Representatives from the city came
into the classroom and showed our students how math, science, writing, and communication skills relate to building new structures," reports Eve Maria Hall, who
oversees the school-to-work initiative for the Milwaukee Public Schools.

Learning Reignited in High School

In Maryland, students can apply to the Baltimore National Academy of
(70) Finance, a school-within-a-school located at Lake Clifton Eastern High School.
In addition to courses in history, English, math, science, and computer skills, students study financial careers, economics, accounting, security operations, international finance, financial planning, and banking and credit. "Every Friday,"
explains Kathleen Floyd, who directs the academy, "we have a personal develop-
(75) ment day, when we teach interview skills, résumé writing, business etiquette, how to
dress for success, and how to speak to adults."

"Our philosophy is that they can learn as much outside the classroom as in,"
says Floyd. "It helps them see how classes relate to what's happening in the real
world."

(80)   "All students have the ability to change the world, not just to live in it," comments Milwaukee's Eve Maria Hall. "To do that, they have to know how to solve
problems and use critical thinking skills, and they have to be able to work in
teams. They also have to develop transferable skills because it's predicted that they
may have to change jobs six or seven times in their lifetime."

(85)   From the time students enter school, "We need to encourage them to dream
about careers that go beyond what they see today," concludes National School-to-
Work's Hoye, noting that "a majority of our kindergarten students will have jobs
that don't even exist today."

— Harriett Webster

Graph

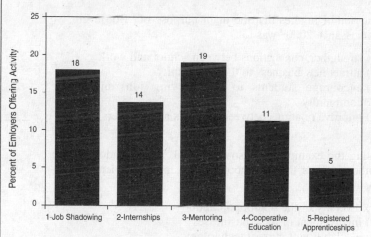

**Work-Based Activities Offered
by Employers Participating in School-to-Work Programs**

1 A student follows an employee for one day or more to learn about a particular occupation or industry.

2 For a specified period of time, students work for an employer to learn about a particular occupation or industry. This may or may not include financial compensation.

3 An employee is assigned to guide a student and serve as a liaison with the school on behalf of the student and the firm.

4 Students alternate or coordinate their academic and vocational studies with a paid or unpaid job in a related field.

5 Formal programs registered with the U.S. Department of Labor or with an approved state apprenticeship agency. Registered apprenticeships are typically paid work experiences.

Source: *National Employer Survey*,
U.S. Bureau of the Census, 1994

Directions (7–16): Select the best suggested answer to each question and write its number in the space provided. The questions may help you think about ideas and information you might want to use in your writing. You may return to these questions anytime you wish.

7 The author implies that the main purpose of "Roosevelt Renaissance 2000" was to

    (1) strengthen connections between school and work
    (2) attract new business to the community
    (3) encourage students to take paying jobs in the community
    (4) improve relations between students and teachers   7 _____

8 Using the example of Eastman Kodak in Colorado, the author implies that a school-to-work program depends partly on the

    (1) diversity of the school population
    (2) involvement of local businesses
    (3) availability of current technology
    (4) cooperation of government agencies   8 _____

9 According to Nancy Ricker (lines 50 through 52), the middle school years are appropriate for career internships because middle school students begin to

    (1) experience physical growth
    (2) form strong friendships
    (3) develop academic skills
    (4) make significant decisions   9 _____

10 Lines 60 through 63 imply a correlation between internships and a student's

    (1) behavior at school
    (2) salary at work
    (3) choice of college
    (4) relationship with parents   10 _____

11 In lines 64 through 68, Eve Maria Hall implies that Milwaukee students learned that city planning involves knowledge of

(1) economic systems   (3) academic subjects
(2) social structures   (4) political strategies   11 _____

12 The term "transferable skills" (line 83) refers to skills that are

(1) easily learned by new workers
(2) likely to result in high wages
(3) highly technical in nature
(4) useful in different situations   12 _____

13 Hoye's comment about kindergarten students (lines 87 and 88) implies that

(1) jobs will be scarce in the future
(2) young children learn quickly
(3) society's needs change rapidly
(4) teachers' skills are out of date   13 _____

14 The author develops the text primarily by

(1) providing illustrations of existing programs
(2) examining advantages and disadvantages
(3) comparing opinions of proponents and
    opponents
(4) explaining ways to develop programs   14 _____

15 From the graph, a reader can determine which activities are most likely to be

(1) successful   (3) difficult
(2) available   (4) expensive   15 _____

16 According to the footnotes below the graph, which example illustrates an internship?

(1) Tamika follows a physical therapist for a day.
(2) José writes a research paper about law-related careers.
(3) Sue alternates 3 hours in class with 3 hours at a restaurant job.
(4) Tim works at a newspaper office for 2 weeks.   16 _____

Answers

(7) **1** "strengthen connections between school and work." Lines 5–6 declare that the purpose of "Roosevelt Renaissance 2000" was to "make school more relevant to the workplace." Details in the two paragraphs on this project show how connections between school and work are offered to students throughout high school.

(8) **2** "involvement of local businesses." The activities offered to students through the Eastman Kodak partnership (outlined in the paragraph beginning at line 19) could be offered only through the cooperation of local businesses. Other examples in the article show how access to local workplaces gives students the opportunity to learn through direct experience outside the classroom. The Eastman Kodak example makes no reference to diversity, availability of technology, or to government agencies.

(9) **4** "make significant decisions." The term "significant" captures the meaning of Nancy Ricker's assertion that "students start making choices [in middle school] that will affect them for the rest of their lives." These lines make no reference to physical growth, friendships, or to development of academic skills.

(10) **1** "behavior at school." These lines [60–63] assert that students involved in internships "take harder courses . . . perform better on state-mandated tests, . . . have better attendance and discipline records. . . ." All these are examples of behavior at school. The passage makes no reference to salaries, choice of college, or relationships with parents.

(11) **3** "academic subjects." The passage states that representatives from the city showed how "math, science, writing, and communication skills" relate to the work of city planning. This passage makes no reference to economic systems, social structures, or political strategies.

(12) **4** "useful in different situations." The need for "transferable skills" is here linked to the prediction that as workers in the future, these students "may have to change jobs six or seven times in their lifetime." They must have skills that they can take with them when they change jobs or employers.

(13) **3** "society's needs change rapidly." Hoye says in the preceding two lines that students must be encouraged to "dream about careers that go

beyond what they see today. . . ." Preparing students for work in the future cannot be limited to the skills and occupations we know today; the world of work and professions is continually changing.

(14) **1** "providing illustrations of existing programs." This is the most accurate description of how the article is developed. The author does not include discussion of any disadvantages or opponents to such programs. While one could use the examples as guidelines for developing similar programs, that is not the point of the article.

(15) **2** "available." The only information the graph offers concerns what percentage of work-based activities is *offered*, that is, "available." The graph offers no information on success, difficulty, or expense involved in these activities.

(16) **4** "Tim works at a newspaper office for 2 weeks." Note 2 defines "Internships" as working "for a specified period of time . . . for an employer to learn about a particular occupation or industry." Tim's activity best fits that definition. Sue's example is one of an actual job, not an internship as defined here. Tamika is observing but not actually working, and José is not directly involved in the activity he is writing about.

Sample Student Response Essay

In today's quickly changing, career-oriented world, it is easy for some students to be disillusioned or impatient with their high school education. Dropout rates have increased, yet students enter the work world without the skills they need. To combat this problem, many schools have turned to school-to-work programs. These programs provide a viable option for students looking for an education that will give them real-life skills while also giving them the necessary academic background.

The benefits of a school-to-work program that allows students to participate in businesses in and around classroom time are multifold. Some schools that have used such programs, such as the Fort Worth Independent School District, report that students who participate in school-to-work actually work harder in school. Teachers at the school indicate that they "take harder courses, perform better on state-mandated tests, and have better attendance and discipline records." These programs stimulate the interests of those who may be bored with traditional schooling while also showing them that an academic background is useful.

Kathleen Floyd, director of the Baltimore National Academy of Finance, a school-within-a-school program, says that a program that includes study of all aspects of careers in finance "helps [students] see how classes relate to what's happening in the real world." Students in these programs obtain skills that can be applied to any work environment, such as dealing with senior staff, workplace etiquette, and business interaction. Our students could benefit from programs like these in many ways.

Once the decision to have a school-to-work program has been made, the logistics can be worked out by examining the successes of other programs. Jondel Hoye, director of the National School-to-Work Office, recommends beginning with middle school students. Career exploration at this age is valuable, says Hoye, because ". . . research shows that at age 12 kids start making choices that will affect them for the rest of their lives." The actual program elements can be worked out in different ways. A U.S. Bureau of the Census National Employer Survey in 1994 indicated that mentoring, job shadowing, and internships are the most popular programs. Mentoring features students working one-on-one with a worker; shadowing features a student following a worker for a period to observe the nature of the industry; and in an internship, a student would actually work at the company for a period of time. Programs such as cooperative education, where a student alternates between the classroom and the workplace, and registered apprenticeships, where a student works at an apprenticeship registered with the U.S. Department of Labor and is paid, are less widely used.

The types of programs a school may offer will mainly depend on the participation and support of industries and businesses in the area. Businesses are generally eager to participate in these programs because they see them as excellent public relations and as an opportunity to train future employees. Lucille Mantelli, community relations director for Eastman Kodak's Colorado Division, indicates that their participation in a school-to-work program is ". . . a way for us to work with the school systems to develop the type of workforce we'll need in future years." This willingness to work with schools is what makes these programs so successful. In addition, cooperation from the entire school system, including the students, is necessary. Teachers have to be willing to give up a portion of class time, and students must be willing to give up a portion of personal time.

Meeting these conditions is worth the effort, however, when we look at the large picture. School-to-work programs will make school more relevant to the workplace, improve academic standards, and provide students with useful experience. As a member of the career guidance class, I strongly urge you to consider this proposal and to research it further. Bear in mind that today's students are the future, and they should be provided with every available opportunity.

Analysis

This is an excellent essay because it offers an in-depth analysis of the documents as well as insightful understanding of the implications of the proposal to the school planning committee.

There is full discussion of the examples of successful school-to-work programs to demonstrate their benefits. The details are relevant, illustrated with quotes, and are drawn from both documents. The writer is particularly skillful in addressing the intended audience by recognizing the need for "cooperation from the entire school system," and by concluding with the assertion that it "is worth the effort" to explore school-to-work programs.

The essay maintains a clear focus, and the organization is clear as the writer moves from recognition of a problem to discussion of a possible solution. The conclusion is persuasive because of the strength in the development of the essay. This writer demonstrates control of the conventions and uses variety of sentence structure and awareness of audience especially well. This essay meets the criteria for a high score. (See pp. 49–53 for a full discussion of the rubric for this part of the examination.)

STRATEGIES FOR TAKING THE EXAM

- Review the guidelines. Be sure that you understand and complete all parts of the task.
- Read carefully. Take notes on the text and on the graph, chart, or diagram. You may use the text itself and the margins to highlight relevant details and useful quotes.
- Understand the multiple-choice questions.

As in Part A of Session One, you will find that the questions are primarily about the significance of specific information or about what inferences can be drawn.

Questions about comprehension
  According to the article or chart . . .
  Line . . . refers to . . .
  The text mentions. . . . as an example of . . .
  The author develops the text primarily by . . .
  This paragraph explains . . .
  The main purpose of the text . . .
  A main idea of the text is . . .
  The graph shows . . .
  A word or phrase is used to signify . . .
  The example of . . . illustrates

Questions about interpretation
  The author implies . . .
  The information suggests . . .
  From the graph, the reader can determine . . .
  The effect of the anecdote is . . .

Beginning on page 117, you will find 10 full Regents exams, with all answers explained and with examples of student essays. Each essay is followed by a detailed analysis of why it meets the criteria for a high score. Reviewing the tasks, essays, and analyses for this part of the exam should be a key part of your preparation.

KNOW THE RUBRIC

Here is the information from the chart on page 53. The key terms have been highlighted.

Important Note: Responses that refer to only one of the documents can be scored no higher than a 3, regardless of how well written.

SCORING RUBRIC FOR SESSION ONE, PART B

> **Meaning:** The extent to which the response exhibits sound understanding, interpretation, and analysis of the task and documents.

High Scores

6—papers reveal an **in-depth analysis of the documents** *and* make **insightful connections** between information and ideas in the documents **and** the assigned task

5—papers convey a **thorough understanding** of the documents *and* **make clear and explicit connections** between information and ideas in the documents and the assigned task

Middle Scores

4—papers convey a **basic understanding** of the documents *and* make **implicit connections** between information and ideas in the documents and the assigned task

3—papers convey a **basic understanding** of the documents *but* make **few or superficial** connections between information and ideas in the documents and the assigned task

Low Scores

2—papers convey a **confused or inaccurate understanding** of the documents *and may* allude to the documents but make **unclear or unwarranted connections** to the task

1—papers provide **minimal or no evidence** of understanding *and/or* make **no connections** between information in the documents and the assigned task

> **Development:** The extent to which ideas are elaborated using specific and relevant evidence from the documents.

High Scores

6—papers **develop ideas clearly and fully,** making effective use of a **wide range of relevant and specific details** from the documents

5—papers **develop ideas clearly and consistently,** using **relevant and specific** details from the documents

Middle Scores

4—papers **develop some ideas more fully than others,** using relevant and **specific details** from the documents

3—papers **develop some ideas briefly,** using **some details** from the documents

Low Scores

2—papers are **incomplete or largely undeveloped, hinting at ideas,** but references to the documents are **vague, irrelevant, repetitive, or unjustified**

1—papers are **minimal,** with **no evidence of support**

> **Organization:** The extent to which the response exhibits direction, shape, and coherence.

High Scores

6—papers maintain a **clear and appropriate focus** *and* **exhibit a logical and coherent structure** through **skillful use** of appropriate devices and transitions

5—papers maintain a **clear and appropriate focus** *and* **exhibit a logical sequence** of ideas through **use** of appropriate devices and transitions

Middle Scores

4—papers **maintain a clear and appropriate focus** *and* exhibit a **logical sequence** of ideas *but* **may lack internal consistency**

3—papers establish, but **fail to maintain, an appropriate focus;** exhibit a **rudimentary structure** *but* may include some **inconsistencies or irrelevancies**

Low Scores

2—papers **lack an appropriate focus** but suggest **some organization,** *or* **suggest a focus** but **lack organization**

1—papers show **no focus or organization**

> **Language Use:** The extent to which the response reveals an awareness of audience and purpose through effective use of words, sentence structure, and sentence variety.

High Scores

6—papers are **stylistically sophisticated,** using language that is **precise and engaging,** with a **notable sense of voice** and **awareness of audience and purpose** *and* **vary structure** and length of sentences to enhance meaning

5—papers use language that is **fluent and original,** with **evident awareness** of audience and purpose *and* **vary structure** and length of sentences **to control rhythm and pacing**

Middle Scores

4—papers use **appropriate language,** with **some awareness of audience and purpose** *and* **occasionally** make effective use of sentence structure or length

3—papers rely on **basic vocabulary,** with **little awareness** of audience or purpose *and may* exhibit **some attempt to vary** sentence structure or length for effect, but **with uneven success**

Low Scores

2—responses use **language that is imprecise or unsuitable** for the audience or purpose *and* reveal **little awareness of how to use sentences** to achieve an effect

1—responses are **minimal** *and/or* use language that is **incoherent or inappropriate**

Conventions: The extent to which the response exhibits conventional spelling, punctuation, capitalization, grammar, and usage.

High Scores

6—responses **demonstrate control** of the conventions with **essentially no errors,** even with sophisticated language

5—responses **demonstrate control** of the conventions, exhibiting **occasional errors only when using sophisticated language**

Middle Scores

4—responses demonstrate **partial control,** exhibiting **occasional errors that do not hinder comprehension**

3—responses demonstrate **emerging control,** exhibiting **occasional errors that hinder comprehension**

Low Scores

2—responses demonstrate a **lack of control,** exhibiting **frequent errors** that make comprehension difficult

1—responses are **minimal,** making assessment of conventions unreliable *or* may be **illegible or not recognizable as English**

SCORING RUBRICS

SESSION ONE, PART B: READING AND WRITING FOR INFORMATION AND UNDERSTANDING

QUALITY	6 Responses at this level:	5 Responses at this level:	4 Responses at this level:	3 Responses at this level:	2 Responses at this level:	1 Responses at this level:
Meaning: the extent to which the response exhibits sound understanding, interpretation, and analysis of the task and document(s)	—reveal an in-depth analysis of the documents —make insightful connections between information and ideas in the documents and the assigned task	—convey a thorough understanding of the documents —make clear and explicit connections between information and ideas in the documents and the assigned task	—convey a basic understanding of the documents —make implicit connections between information and ideas in the documents and the assigned task	—convey a basic understanding of the documents* —make few or superficial connections between information and ideas in the documents and the assigned task	—convey a confused or inaccurate understanding of the documents —allude to the documents but make unclear or unwarranted connections to the assigned task	—provide no evidence of understanding —make no connections between information in the documents and the assigned task
Development: the extent to which ideas are elaborated using specific and relevant evidence from the document(s)	—develop ideas clearly and fully, making effective use of a wide range of relevant and specific details from the documents	—develop ideas clearly and consistently, using relevant and specific details from the documents	—develop some ideas more fully than others, using specific and relevant details from the documents	—develop ideas briefly, using some details from the documents	—are incomplete or largely undeveloped, hinting at ideas, but references to the documents are vague, irrelevant, repetitive, or unjustified	—are minimal, with no evidence of development
Organization: the extent to which the response exhibits direction, shape, and coherence	—maintain a clear and appropriate focus —exhibit a logical and coherent structure through skillful use of appropriate devices and transitions	—maintain a clear and appropriate focus —exhibit a logical sequence of ideas through use of appropriate devices and transitions	—maintain a clear and appropriate focus —exhibit a logical sequence of ideas but may lack internal consistency	—establish, but fail to maintain, an appropriate focus —exhibit a rudimentary structure but may include some inconsistencies or irrelevancies	—lack an appropriate focus but suggest some organization, or suggest a focus but lack organization	—show no focus or organization
Language Use: the extent to which the response reveals an awareness of audience and purpose through effective use of words, sentence structure, and sentence variety	—are stylistically sophisticated, using language that is precise and engaging, with a notable sense of voice and awareness of audience and purpose —vary structure and length of sentences to enhance meaning	—use language that is fluent and original, with evident awareness of audience and purpose —vary structure and length of sentences to control rhythm and pacing	—use appropriate language, with some awareness of audience and purpose —occasionally make effective use of sentence structure or length	—rely on language from the documents or basic vocabulary, with little awareness of audience or purpose —exhibit some attempt to vary sentence structure or length for effect, but with uneven success	—use language that is imprecise or unsuitable for the audience or purpose —reveal little awareness of how to use sentences to achieve an effect	—are minimal —use language that is incoherent or inappropriate
Conventions: the extent to which the response exhibits conventional spelling, punctuation, paragraphing, capitalization, grammar, and usage	—demonstrate control of the conventions with essentially no errors, even with sophisticated language	—demonstrate control of the conventions, exhibiting occasional errors only when using sophisticated language	—demonstrate partial control, exhibiting occasional errors that do not hinder comprehension	—demonstrate emerging control, exhibiting occasional errors that hinder comprehension	—demonstrate a lack of control, exhibiting frequent errors that make comprehension difficult	—are minimal, making assessment of conventions unreliable —may be illegible or not recognizable as English

*If the student addresses only one document, the response can be scored no higher than a 3.

Strategy and Review for Session Two, Part A of the Examination

CHAPTER 3

Reading and Writing for Literary Response

WHAT DOES THIS PART OF THE EXAM REQUIRE?

It is on the second day of the Regents exam that your study of literature in high school is most specifically assessed. In Session Two, Part A you will show how well you comprehend, appreciate, and write about different genres of literature.

WHAT DOES THIS PART OF THE EXAM LOOK LIKE?

You will read two passages that develop a common theme. The passages will be of different literary genres. For example, you may read a poem and a selection from a novel or story; or you may read passages from nonfiction, such as memoirs, journals, or reflective essays. Your task is to appreciate how these two works of literature develop a common theme using various literary elements and techniques. After answering 10 multiple-choice questions on the passages, you will compose a **unified essay** in which you use evidence from both passages to develop your **controlling idea** and show how each author uses specific literary elements or techniques to convey ideas.

Guidelines:

- Use ideas from **both** passages to establish a controlling idea about the central idea or theme revealed in the passages
- Use specific and relevant evidence from **each** passage to develop your controlling idea

- Show how each author uses specific literary elements (for example: theme, characterization, structure, point of view) or techniques (for example: symbolism, irony, figurative language) to convey ideas
- Organize your ideas in a logical and coherent manner
- Use language that communicates ideas effectively
- Follow the conventions of standard written English

LOOKING AT THE GUIDELINES

These guidelines should now be quite familiar to you because they are similar to the guidelines for Session One, Parts A and B. The first three state what is expected for this particular task; the last three are the expectations for good writing found in all four tasks. Remember, too, that they are an outline of the **rubric** used to score your essay. (See page 68 for a full discussion of the Session Two, Part A rubric.)

Why is *both* emphasized?
This is a reminder that you must write about two passages. If you were to write about only one, your paper would receive no more than a **3** overall—no matter how well you wrote about that passage.

What is meant by a *unified essay*?
This means that your response provides evidence from both literary passages and that this evidence is woven together in a way that supports and develops the controlling idea. Linking both passages with the controlling idea in your introduction and in your conclusion also makes your essay unified.

What is a *controlling idea*?
This is the significant generalization that is drawn from both passages and provides the focus for the essay. In the sample tasks offered below, you will find several examples of what is meant by controlling idea. In your own courses, you may also use the terms *topic* or *thesis* to express the central purpose of an essay. The term "controlling" is useful because it is a reminder that your controlling idea determines what details you choose to develop and what method you use to organize.

What is the difference between *literary elements* and *literary techniques*?
In general, literary **elements** are the essential components of literary works; for example: plot, setting, theme, characterization, point of view, structure, and tone. Literary **techniques** are the devices a writer uses to develop those elements; for example: irony, imagery, symbolism, and figurative language. These categories occasionally overlap, and the Regents exam does not expect you to make this distinction. The most skillful readers and writers will, however, appreciate the relationship of techniques to basic elements of literature and be able to express that relationship in their essays.

Are the literary elements and techniques listed in the task the ones I must write about?
No. It is important to understand that the examples offered in the guidelines are meant as *reminders* of what the terms mean; they are not necessarily the examples you are meant to use, and not all those examples will be evident in every Session Two, Part A passage.

Which literary elements and techniques do I need to know?
Begin with the examples listed in the Guidelines. You are expected to be familiar with them and recognize their importance in developing the meaning of literary works.

(You will find a detailed review of literary elements and techniques on pages 84–91.)

SAMPLE TASK
Directions: Read the passages on the following pages (a memoir and a poem). Write the number of the answer to each multiple-choice question in the space provided. Then write the essay on separate sheets of paper as described in **Your Task.** You may use the margins to take notes as you read and scrap paper to plan your response.

Your Task:

> After you have read the passages and answered the multiple-choice questions, write a unified essay about the experience of visiting libraries as revealed in the passages. In your essay, use ideas from *both* passages to establish a controlling idea about the experience of visiting libraries. Using evidence from *each* passage, develop your controlling idea and show how the author uses specific literary elements or techniques to convey that idea.

Guidelines:
Be sure to
- Use ideas from *both* passages to establish a controlling idea about the experience of visiting libraries
- Use specific and relevant evidence from *each* passage to develop your controlling idea
- Show how each author uses specific literary elements (for example: theme, characterization, structure, point of view) or techniques (for example: symbolism, irony, figurative language) to convey the controlling idea

- Organize your ideas in a logical and coherent manner
- Use language that communicates ideas effectively
- Follow the conventions of standard written English

Passage I

From the nearest library I learned every sort of suprising thing—some of it, though not much of it, from the books themselves.

The Homewood Library had graven across its enormous stone facade: FREE TO THE PEOPLE. In the evenings, neighborhood people—the men and
(5) women of Homewood—browsed in the library and brought their children. By day, the two vaulted rooms, the adults' and children's sections, were almost empty. The kind Homewood librarians, after a trial period, had given me a card to the adult section. This was an enormous silent room with marble floors. Nonfiction was on the left.
(10) Beside the farthest wall, and under leaded windows set ten feet from the floor, so that no human being could ever see anything from them—next to the wall, and at the farthest remove from the idle librarians at their curved wooden counter, and from the oak bench where my mother waited in her camel's-hair coat chatting with the librarians or reading— stood the last and darkest and most
(15) obscure of the tall nonfiction stacks: NATURAL HISTORY. It was here, in the cool darkness of a bottom shelf, that I found *The Field Book of Ponds and Streams*.

The Field Book of Ponds and Streams was a small, blue-bound book printed in fine type on thin paper. Its third chapter explained how to make sweep nets,
(20) plankton nets, glass-bottomed buckets, and killing jars. It specified how to mount slides, how to label insects on their pins, and how to set up a freshwater aquarium.

One was to go into "the field" wearing hip boots and perhaps a head net for mosquitoes. One carried in a "ruck-sack" half a dozen corked test tubes, a smat-
(25) tering of screwtop baby-food jars, a white enamel tray, assorted pipettes and eye-droppers, an artillery of cheesecloth nets, a notebook, a hand lens, perhaps a map, and *The Field Book of Ponds and Streams*. This field—unlike the fields I had seen, such as the field where Walter Milligan played football—was evidently very well watered, for there one could find, and distinguish among, daphniae, planaria,
(30) water pennies, stonefly larvae, dragonfly nymphs, salamander larvae, tadpoles, snakes, and turtles, all of which one could carry home.

That anyone had lived the fine life described in Chapter 3 astonished me. Although the title page indicated quite plainly that one Ann Haven Morgan had written *The Field Book of Ponds and Streams*, I nevertheless imagined, perhaps

(35) from the authority and freedom of it, that its author was a man. It would be good to write him and assure him that someone had found his book, in the dark near the marble floor at the Homewood Library. I would, in the same letter or in a subsequent one, ask him a question outside the scope of his book, which was where I personally might find a pond, or a stream. But I did not know how to

(40) address such a letter, of course, or how to learn if he was still alive.

I was afraid, too, that my letter would disappoint him by betraying my ignorance, which was just beginning to attract my own notice. What, for example, was this substance called cheesecloth, and what do scientists to with it? What, when you really got down to it, was enamel? If candy could, notoriously, "eat through

(45) enamel," why would anyone make trays out of it? Where—short of robbing a museum—might a fifth-grade student at the Ellis School on Fifth Avenue obtain such a legendary item as a wooden bucket?

The Field Book of Ponds and Streams was a shocker from beginning to end. The greatest shock came at the end.

(50) When you checked out a book from the Homewood Library, the librarian wrote your number on the book's card and stamped the due date on the sheet glued to the book's last page. When I checked out *The Field Book of Ponds and Streams* for the second time, I noticed the book's card. It was almost full. There were numbers on both sides. My hearty author and I were not alone in the world,

(55) after all. With us, and sharing our enthusiasm for dragonfly larvae and single-celled plants, were, apparently, many adults.

Who were these people? Had they, in Pittsburgh's Homewood section, found ponds? Had they found streams?

Every year, I read again *The Field Book of Ponds and Streams*. Often, when I

(60) was in the library, I simply visited it. I sat on the marble floor and studied the book's card. There we all were. There was my number. There was the number of someone else who had checked it out more than once. Might I contact this person and cheer him up?

For I assumed that, like me, he had found pickings pretty slim in Pittsburgh.

(65) The people of Homewood, some of whom lived in visible poverty, on crowded streets among burned-out houses—they dreamed of ponds and streams. They were saving to buy microscopes. In their bedrooms they fashioned plankton nets. But their hopes were even more vain than mine, for I was a child, and anything might happen; they were adults, living in Homewood. There was neither pond

(70) nor stream on the streetcar routes. The Homewood residents whom I knew had little money and little free time. The marble floor was beginning to chill me. It was not fair.

—Annie Dillard

Passage II
Maple Valley Branch Library, 1967

For a fifteen-year-old there was plenty
to do: browse the magazines,
slip into the Adult section to see
what vast *tristesse*[1] was born of rush-hour traffic,
(5) décolletés[2], and the plague of too much money.
There was so much to discover—how to
lay out a road, the language of flowers,
and the place of women in the tribe of Moost.
There were equations elegant as a French twist,
(10) fractal geometry's unwinding maple leaf;

I could follow, step-by-step, the slow disclosure
of a pineapple Jell-O mold—or take
the path of Harold's purple crayon through
the bedroom window and onto a lavender
(15) spill of stars. Oh, I could walk any aisle
and smell wisdom, put a hand out to touch
the rough curve of bound leather,
the harsh parchment of dreams.

As for the improbable librarian
(20) with her salt and paprika upsweep,
her British accent and sweater clip
(mom of a kid I knew from school)—
I'd go up to her desk and ask for help
on bareback rodeo or binary codes,
(25) phonics, Gestalt theory,
lead poisoning in the Late Roman Empire;
the play of light in Dutch Renaissance painting;
I would claim to be researching
pre-Columbian pottery or Chinese foot-binding,
(30) but all I wanted to know was:
Tell me what you've read that keeps
that half smile afloat
above the collar of your impeccable blouse.

---

[1]sadness
[2]low-cut necklines

So I read *Gone with the Wind* because
(35) it was big, and haiku because they were small.
I studied history for its rhapsody of dates,
lingered over Cubist art for the way
it showed all sides of a guitar at once.
All the time in the world was there, and sometimes
(40) all the world on a single page.
As much as I could hold
on my plastic card's imprint I took,
greedily: six books, six volumes of bliss,
the stuff we humans are made of:
(45) words and sighs and silence,
ink and whips, Brahma and cosine,
corsets and poetry and blood sugar levels—
I carried it home, five blocks of aluminum siding
and past the old garage where, on its boarded-up doors,
(50) someone had scrawled:

    I CAN EAT AN ELEPHANT
    IF I TAKE SMALL BITES.

Yes, I said to no one in particular: *That's
what I'm gonna do!*

                      —Rita Dove

Directions (1–10): Select the best suggested answer to each question and write its number in the space provided. The questions may help you think about the ideas and information you might want to use in your essay. You may return to these questions anytime you wish.

Passage I (the memoir)—Questions 1–5 refer to Passage I.

1 The author's repeated references to *The Field Book of Ponds and Streams* has the effect of emphasizing the book's

   (1) age   (3) unpopularity
   (2) significance   (4) size   1 _____

2 Lines 23 through 31 are developed primarily through the use of

   (1) listing   (3) metaphor
   (2) definition   (4) analogy   2 _____

3 The narrator implies that *The Field Book of Ponds and Streams* was a "shocker" partly because it revealed to her the

   (1) cruelty of nature
   (2) capabilities of women
   (3) existence of a different way of life
   (4) importance of preserving the environment   3 _____

4 In lines 59 through 63, the narrator implies that studying the book's card gave her a sense of

   (1) commitment   (3) privacy
   (2) order   (4) community   4 _____

5 At the end of the passage, the narrator implies that she is chilled by both the coldness of the floor and her awareness of

   (1) dishonest people
   (2) unequal opportunities
   (3) unworthy goals
   (4) irresponsible behavior   5 _____

Passage II (the poem)—Questions 6–10 refer to Passage II.

6 In lines 9 and 10, equations and geometry are depicted as being

    (1) difficult   (3) ancient
    (2) beautiful   (4) useful   6 _____

7 The images in lines 11 through 15 are used to suggest two different

    (1) historical eras
    (2) character types
    (3) book genres
    (4) architectural elements   7 _____

8 According to the narrator, the list of topics in lines 24 through 29 was

    (1) an excuse   (3) a symbol
    (2) an assignment   (4) an apology   8 _____

9 The expression "my plastic card's imprint" (line 42) refers to

    (1) copying books   (3) signing out books
    (2) buying books   (4) writing in books   9 _____

10 In line 51, the narrator most likely uses the expression "eat an elephant" to mean

    (1) gain knowledge   (3) be patient
    (2) achieve fame   (4) banish fear   10 _____

Answers

    (1) **2** "significance." Repetition is one of the most common and effective forms of emphasis. In this passage, the repetition of the full title shows the importance of this book in Annie Dillard's childhood. While she does refer to the book's age and size, repetition of the title does not serve to emphasize those details.

    (2) **1** "listing." This too is one of the most common forms of elaboration. The paragraph begins with a list of what one might carry going into "the

field"; the paragraph closes with a list of many things one might find there. There are no examples of figurative language (metaphor, analogy) in this section; nor is there the sense of something being "defined."

(3) **3** "existence of a different way of life." In lines 32–47, Dillard shows her astonishment and wonder; she is even reluctant to reveal her ignorance by writing to the author. In line 49, she tells us that "The greatest shock came at the end." She discovers that there are many adults who have checked out this book and wonders who they are and whether they had found such ponds and streams. The passage does not raise questions about cruelty in nature, the capabilities of women, nor of the importance of preserving the environment.

(4) **4** "community." In this section, Dillard tells us that when she was in the library, she would often "visit" the *Field Book* to look at the card with the numbers of all the other readers; she even thinks about contacting "this person [to] cheer him up." The emphasis is on how she feels part of a group of people who have shared this book.

(5) **2** "unequal opportunities." The passage closes with Dillard's understanding that for those who live in a poor, urban neighborhood, the opportunity and the means to explore life in the ponds and streams are remote. She even feels the "unfairness" in being a child who can have hopes, while for the adults of Homewood, many hopes are in vain. The passage makes no reference to dishonest people or unworthy goals, nor to irresponsible behavior.

(6) **2** "beautiful." The word "elegant" and the phrase "unwinding maple leaf" convey a sense of beauty in the equations and geometry. While these may be complex, the poet does not suggest that they are "difficult" here, nor do the images suggest something that is ancient or useful.

(7) **3** "book genres." These lines are images evoking a cookbook and a fanciful tale for children, works with very different purposes, styles, and content, or "genres."

(8) **1** "an excuse." These lines are framed by the "confession" that she would ask the librarian for help in her research when "all I wanted to know was" what the librarian has found interesting or satisfying.

(9) **3** "signing out books." The poet is telling us that she was permitted to sign out only six books at a time.

(10) **1** "gain knowledge." Having signed out her six books "greedily," the poet suggests the range of everything that is in them. Just as she might eat an elephant by taking many small bites, she will learn everything there is to know about "the stuff we humans are made of " by reading these books.

Sample Student Response Essay

The two passages, a memoir and a poem, are about childhood visits to a library. The experiences are somewhat different, but for each child the experience is exhilarating, even surprising. The books they find there provide glimpses of new and unexpected worlds, or offer a wealth of additional knowledge. Both the memoir and the poem reveal significant and powerful childhood experiences.

Through the first-person point of view, the author of the memoir depicts the adult section of the Homewood Library as ". . . an enormous silent room with marble floors . . . [and] leaded windows set ten feet from the floor." We feel Dillard's awe not only at the architecture but also at the wealth of knowledge she might discover.

In The Field Book of Ponds and Streams, *she discovers the wonders of nature. The only field she had known before was the ballfield where Walter Milligan played football. She discovers there is world of creatures and things that can be found in ponds and streams. She learns how she might create "sweep nets" and "killing jars"; she imagines a world of "planaria" and "tadpoles." The author presents all this information in a series of lists, which emphasize how much she has discovered. But there is something else to be learned from the card in the back of the book. The card on which are recorded the names of the people who have borrowed this book is full. This is a surprise to her because the library is in Pittsburgh, which has no streams or ponds nearby. She realizes that she is one of a community of readers and wonders about the others. She even thinks that they might be frustrated or disappointed because they can't find ponds or streams. Her most poignant realization, however, is that for her "anything might happen," but for the adult residents of Homewood there are only dreams among the "burned-out houses."*

For the poet, the visit to the library is also a voyage of discovery. In free verse, the writer reveals the wonders the library held for her. Metaphorically, the speaker can "smell wisdom" and "touch . . . the harsh parchment of dreams." The poem alternates between vivid images—"salt and paprika upsweep"—and eclectic lists to suggest the range of what she is fascinated by. The poem ends with the speaker "greedily" checking out the limit of six books. A slogan scrawled on an old garage—"I can eat an elephant if I take small bites"—assures her that she can indeed learn <u>everything there is to know</u>, one book at a time.

Both authors enter the library with a sense of wonder and emerge richer for what they have found.

Analysis

This is an excellent essay. The writer demonstrates an in-depth understanding of the two passages and links them in the controlling idea: "Both the memoir and the poem reveal significant and powerful childhood experiences." The examples are briefly but skillfully developed, and references to various literary techniques—point of view, images, lists, metaphor—are also relevant observations about the meaning of the passages. This meets one of the most important guidelines for this task.

The essay maintains the focus on the power of the experiences for each writer, and the organization in two sections is a logical one for this task. The final, single sentence links the two passages in a new expression of the controlling idea. The language is especially good here, precise and engaging, as it is throughout the essay. Finally, this writer shows excellent control of the conventions. This essay meets the criteria for a high score. (See pp. 68–71 for a detailed review of the rubric for this part of the examination.)

REVIEWING FOR SESSION TWO, PART A OF THE EXAM

What do I need to know about *literary elements* and *techniques*?
As noted on page 84, literary **elements** are the essential components of literary works; for example: plot, setting, theme, characterization, structure, and tone. Literary **techniques** are the devices a writer uses to develop those elements; for example: point of view, irony, imagery, symbolism, and figurative language. You should be able to recognize and write about the following in both Parts A and B of Session Two of the Regents. (See Chapter 5 for a review of these terms. There are also extensive Glossaries of Terms, beginning on page 92.)

Character/Characterization
   traits, motivation, conflicts (internal and between characters), dialogue

Plot
   incidents, conflict, resolution

Setting
   time and place, influence on characters, cultural features, historical context

Theme
> major ideas, significant human experiences, moral observations

Point of View
> first person, detached, or omniscient narrator; relationship to story

Tone/Mood
> language, word connotation, irony, the full range of human emotion and attitudes that literature may express

Structure
> significant patterns of organization, use of repetition, parallel elements

Poetic and Literary Techniques
> pattern of lines, rhythm and meter, alliteration, personification, metaphor and simile, stanza, symbolism, imagery

STRATEGIES FOR TAKING THE EXAM

- Review the Guidelines. Be sure that you understand and complete all parts of the task.
- Read carefully and take notes on the passages.

As you read, underline key ideas and mark those parts that most directly relate to the task. You should also make notes in the margins to identify literary elements and techniques you see as significant.

If one of the passages is a poem, read it several times to discover what it says. Who is the speaker? What is the subject, the dramatic situation? How does the poem reflect the theme identified in the task? What is the tone or mood? Try to summarize or paraphrase the poem as a whole. Then, note the formal details: What is the pattern of organization: what is the movement of ideas and feeling? of images and metaphors? How do stanzas or arrangement of lines relate to the meaning? How do rhyme, meter, and rhythm contribute to the experience and meaning of the poem?

In prose passages, one of the first things to note is the narrative point of view and the sense of time or chronology. If this is a memoir or personal narrative, is the writer recounting a long past or a current experience? How does that affect the tone of the passage? If there is dialogue, how does that contribute to the effect of the passage? Is there significance in the overall organization? If this is a work of fiction, how are character and incident revealed?

- Understand the multiple-choice questions.

You can expect examples of the following kinds of questions.

Questions about tone
The mood conveyed . . .
The dominant mood is . . .
The tone is best described as . . .
The author's attitude is . . .

Questions about form and structure
The repetition establishes a feeling of . . .
The organization is characterized by . . .
The passage is developed primarily through . . .
The primary effect of short, broken lines is . . .

Questions about literary elements and techniques
The following lines are an example of . . .
    alliteration, metaphor, allusion, personification, onomatopoeia, or oxymoron

The development of the passage is characterized by use of . . .
    metaphor and simile, allusion, repetition, or irony

The dominant figure of speech is . . .
    alliteration, metaphor, allusion, personification, onomatopoeia, or oxymoron

Questions about the meaning of specific details
The author feels . . .
The variety of . . . reflects . . .
The word . . . is used to mean
Lines . . . suggest
The statement refers . . .

- Plan your essay.

In addition to the texts and your notes, you will have scrap paper to plan your response. Do not leave this step out! Those who score Regents exams expect that students have used the allotted time to plan and do their best work. Remember: a good introduction is essential. You must compose a controlling idea that expresses how the two passages convey the common subject or theme given in the task.

- Use a wide range of specific and relevant details.

Good development is crucial for a high score on this part of the exam. A simple summary of the passages will yield a minimally passing score at best. Use the multiple-choice questions as guides to the important ideas and the significant literary elements in the passages.

Do not make the mistake of writing about the common theme only—you are writing about the *texts*. The controlling idea shapes the essay, but it is not its only subject. Your essay must be about how the texts express the controlling idea, how literature achieves its meaning and effect.

As for the first two tasks, be sure to review the 10 full Regents exams, with answers explained and examples of student essays. Reviewing the Session Two, Part A tasks will give you several examples of the poems, personal essays, and passages of fiction or memoir that appear on this part of the exam. Reviewing the student essays should also be a key part of your preparation.

KNOW THE RUBRIC

Important Note: If you write about only one work of literature, the response can be scored no higher than a 3—regardless of how well that response is written. The key terms for this part of the exam have been highlighted. See page 71 for the complete rubric.

SCORING RUBRIC FOR SESSION TWO, PART A

> **Meaning:** The extent to which the response exhibits sound understanding, interpretation, and analysis of the task and text.

High Scores

6—papers **establish a controlling idea** that reveals an **in-depth analysis** of both texts *and* make **insightful connections** between the controlling idea and the ideas **in each text**

5—papers establish a **controlling idea** that conveys a **thorough understanding** of both texts *and* **make clear and explicit connections** between the controlling idea and the ideas in each text

Middle Scores

4—papers establish a **controlling idea** that conveys a **basic understanding** of the texts *and* make **implicit connections** between the controlling idea and the ideas in each text

3—papers establish a **controlling idea** that conveys a **basic understanding** of the texts *and* make **few or superficial connections** between the controlling idea and the ideas in the texts

Low Scores

2—papers convey a **confused or incomplete understanding** of the texts *and* make a **few connections** but **fail to establish a controlling idea**

1—papers provide **minimal or no evidence** of textual understanding *and/or* make **no connections** between the texts or among ideas in the texts

> **Development:** The extent to which ideas are elaborated using specific and relevant evidence from the text.

High Scores

6—papers **develop ideas clearly and fully,** making effective use of a **wide range of relevant and specific details** from both texts

5—papers **develop ideas clearly and consistently,** using **relevant and specific** details from both texts

Middle Scores

4—papers **develop some ideas more fully than others,** using relevant and **specific details** from both texts

3—papers **develop some ideas briefly,** using **some details** from both texts and **may rely primarily on plot summary**

Low Scores

2—papers are **incomplete or largely undeveloped, hinting at ideas,** but references to the texts are **vague, irrelevant, repetitive, or unjustified**

1—papers are **minimal,** with **no evidence of development**

> **Organization:** The extent to which the response exhibits direction, shape, and coherence.

High Scores

6—papers **maintain the focus established by the controlling idea** *and* **exhibit a logical and coherent structure** through skillful use of appropriate devices and transitions

5—papers maintain a **focus established by the controlling idea** *and* **exhibit a logical sequence** of ideas through **use** of appropriate devices and transitions

Middle Scores

4—papers **maintain a clear and appropriate focus** *and* exhibit a **logical sequence** of ideas *but* **may lack internal consistency**

3—papers establish, but **fail to maintain, an appropriate focus;** exhibit a **rudimentary structure** *but* may include some **inconsistencies or irrelevancies**

Low Scores

2—papers **lack an appropriate focus** but suggest **some organization,** *or* **suggest a focus** but **lack organization**

1—papers show **no focus or organization**

The rubric for Language Use and Conventions is the same as for Session One, Parts A and B and Session Two, Part B. See chart on the following page.

SCORING RUBRICS

SESSION TWO, PART A: READING AND WRITING FOR LITERARY RESPONSE

QUALITY	Responses at this level: 6	Responses at this level: 5	Responses at this level: 4	Responses at this level: 3	Responses at this level: 2	Responses at this level: 1
Meaning: the extent to which the response exhibits sound understanding, interpretation, and analysis of the task and text(s)	—establish a controlling idea that reveals an in-depth analysis of both texts —make insightful connections between the texts —convey the ideas in each text, and the elements or techniques used to convey those ideas	—establish a controlling idea that reveals a thorough understanding of both texts —make clear and explicit connections between the controlling idea, the ideas in each text, and the elements or techniques used to convey those ideas	—establish a controlling idea that shows a basic understanding of both texts —make implicit connections between the controlling idea, the ideas in each text, and the elements or techniques used to convey those ideas	—establish a controlling idea that shows a basic understanding of the texts* —make few or superficial connections between the controlling idea, the ideas in the texts, and the elements or techniques used to convey those ideas	—convey a confused or incomplete understanding of the texts —fail to establish a controlling idea —allude to the texts but give no examples of literary elements or techniques	—provide minimal evidence of textual understanding —make no connections between ideas in the texts and literary elements or techniques
Development: the extent to which ideas are elaborated using specific and relevant evidence from the text(s)	—develop ideas clearly and fully, making effective use of a wide range of relevant and specific evidence from both texts	—develop ideas clearly and consistently, using relevant and specific evidence from both texts	—develop some ideas more fully than others, using specific and relevant evidence from both texts	—develop ideas briefly, using some evidence from the texts	—are incomplete or largely undeveloped, hinting at ideas, but references to the text are vague, irrelevant, repetitive, or unjustified	—are minimal, with no evidence of development
Organization: the extent to which the response exhibits direction, shape, and coherence	—maintain the focus established by the controlling idea —exhibit a logical and coherent structure through skillful use of appropriate devices and transitions	—maintain the focus established by the controlling idea —exhibit a logical sequence of ideas through the use of appropriate devices and transitions	—maintain a clear and appropriate focus —exhibit a logical sequence of ideas but may lack internal consistency	—establish, but fail to maintain, an appropriate focus —exhibit a rudimentary structure but may include some inconsistencies or irrelevancies	—lack an appropriate focus but suggest some organization, or suggest a focus but lack organization	—show no focus or organization
Language Use: the extent to which the response reveals an awareness of audience and purpose through effective use of words, sentence structure, and sentence variety	—are stylistically sophisticated, using language that is precise and engaging, with a notable sense of voice and awareness of audience and purpose —vary structure and length of sentences to enhance meaning	—use language that is fluent and original, with evident awareness of audience and purpose —vary structure and length of sentences to control rhythm and pacing	—use appropriate language, with some awareness of audience and purpose —occasionally make effective use of sentence structure or length	—rely on language from the text or basic vocabulary, with little awareness of audience or purpose —exhibit some attempt to vary sentence structure or length for effect, but with uneven success	—use language that is imprecise or unsuitable for the audience or purpose —reveal little awareness of how to use sentences to achieve an effect	—are minimal —use language that is incoherent or inappropriate
Conventions: the extent to which the response exhibits conventional spelling, punctuation, paragraphing, capitalization, grammar, and usage	—demonstrate control of the conventions with essentially no errors, even with sophisticated language	—demonstrate control of the conventions, exhibiting occasional errors only when using sophisticated language	—demonstrate partial control, exhibiting occasional errors that do not hinder comprehension	—demonstrate emerging control, exhibiting occasional errors that hinder comprehension	—demonstrate a lack of control, exhibiting frequent errors that make comprehension difficult	—are minimal, making assessment of conventions unreliable —may be illegible or not recognizable as English

*the student addresses only one text; the response can be scored no higher than a 3.

Strategy and Review for Session Two, Part B of the Examination

CHAPTER 4
Reading and Writing for Critical Analysis and Evaluation

WHAT DOES THIS PART OF THE EXAM REQUIRE?

The final part of the Regents exam also assesses your ability to show how literary elements and techniques reveal theme (see Chapter 5 and Glossaries of Terms for a comprehensive review), but it requires that you first interpret and respond to a general statement about literature, called a "critical lens." You will then choose from works you have read and use those works to compose an essay on a thesis you have developed from the critical lens. For many students, this will be the most challenging part of the exam. A closer look at the different parts of this task, however, will show you how the reading, discussion, and writing about literature you have done in high school has prepared you for it.

WHAT IS A *CRITICAL LENS*?

A *critical lens* does much of what the lenses in a pair of glasses or the lens in a camera does: it brings what we are looking at into focus—and, like the lens of a camera, it directs our attention to something worth looking at. In literary terms, critical lenses express a point of view about how to evaluate literature. The critical lens statements are likely to focus on what literature "is about"; and they are meant to prompt your thinking about how authors achieve the meaning and effect of their works. Your task is to respond to such a point of view and then express it as your own for purposes of developing a critical essay on works you know and appreciate.

WHAT DOES THIS PART OF THE EXAM LOOK LIKE?

Here for review is a familiar example, which the developers of the Regents exam have offered as a model:

Your Task: Write a critical essay in which you discuss **two** works of literature that you have read from the particular perspective of the statement that is provided for you in the **Critical Lens.** In your essay, provide a valid interpretation of the statement, agree **or** disagree with the statement as you have interpreted it, and support your opinion using specific references to appropriate literary elements from the two works.

> **Critical Lens:** According to author Joseph Conrad, the task of a writer is "by the power of the written word, to make you hear, to make you feel—it is, before all, to make you see."

Note that there are three parts to this task: first, you must *interpret* the statement, say what it means to you; then, you must state how you agree or disagree with the statement; finally, you must choose two literary works for a discussion that supports your position. Now, look at the Guidelines for this task.

Guidelines:
Be sure to
- Provide a valid interpretation of the critical lens that clearly establishes the criteria for analysis
- Indicate whether you agree or disagree with the statement as you have interpreted it
- Choose two works you have read that you believe best support your opinion
- Use the criteria suggested by the critical lens to analyze the works you have chosen
- Avoid plot summary; instead, use specific references to appropriate literary elements (for example: theme, characterization, setting, point of view) to develop your analysis
- Organize your ideas in a unified and coherent manner
- Specify the titles and authors of the literature you choose
- Follow the conventions of standard written English

STRATEGIES FOR TAKING THE EXAM

• Be sure that you understand the critical lens and consider fully its implications.

Be able to paraphrase it in a sentence that begins, "Another way to say this is . . ." Then, state how you agree or disagree with the lens as you have interpreted it. The terms "agree" or "disagree" may seem limiting at first, but they allow you to adapt the critical lens statement so that you have a critical point of view you are comfortable with and can develop convincingly.

> **Critical Lens:** According to author Joseph Conrad, the task of a writer is "by the power of the written word, to make you hear, to make you feel—it is, before all, to make you see."

To interpret what Conrad means here, you must first look at the key terms. He is talking about the power of the written word to make us re-create the experience of hearing, feeling, and seeing, and the power to make us understand—to see in the figurative sense. Remember: to interpret means to state what you think Conrad means, then state your response to it.

To agree with Conrad's statement, you might choose works of literature that are particularly vivid in imagery and show how they are effective in re-creating experience for the reader. This would be a literal but perfectly valid interpretation of the quote. A more sophisticated discussion would emphasize Conrad's final point—the power of literature to make us understand character and theme in new and powerful ways. This is an example of what the rubric (see page 81) means by an interpretation that is "faithful to the complexity of the statement . . ."

To disagree with Conrad's statement, if you feel that the greatest power of literature is to make us feel, for example, you would choose works of literature whose effect on the reader is primarily emotional or affecting. This too would be a valid response to the task.

• Choose two works that support your opinion.

Remember that these must be works that you have read. This does not include film, but it does include poems, short stories, literary essays, and memoirs, as well as novels and plays. Before you write, consider more than the first two works that come to mind; try sketching brief notes for four or five works you might choose from. This will help you select the most effective examples for your discussion. If you can think of only one or two examples from a particular work to support your opinion, you should consider others with more examples to choose from. Remember: adequate development of ideas is one of the most important parts of a highly rated essay. Minimum development will give you only a minimal score.

- Use the criteria suggested by the critical lens.

In this example, the criteria are the ideas and literary qualities that Conrad claims are the basis of judging what constitutes "the power of the written word" and the "task of the writer."

- Avoid plot summary.

Because many critical observations about the power and effect of literature are also about the subjects of literature, you will certainly have to refer to the characters and plot of the works you discuss. Remember that the rubric for Development in this part includes discussion of "appropriate literary elements from both texts." The most effective essays do not simply summarize what happens; they show how the meaning of a work of literature is revealed.

(See Chapter 5 for a detailed review of literary elements and techniques.)

- Remember to specify the titles and authors of the works you discuss
- Be sure you understand and complete all parts of this task

SAMPLE TASK I
Here, with sample essays, is another example of a Part B Task.

Your Task: Write a critical essay in which you discuss **two** works of literature you have read from the particular perspective of the statement that is provided for you in the **Critical Lens.** In your essay, provide a valid interpretation of the statement, agree **or** disagree with the statement as you have interpreted it, and support your opinion using specific references to appropriate literary elements from the two works.

Critical Lens: "The best literature is about the old universal truths, such as love, honor, pride, compassion, and sacrifice."
—William Faulkner (adapted)

Guidelines:
Be sure to
- Provide a valid interpretation of the critical lens that clearly establishes the criteria for analysis
- Indicate whether you agree or disagree with the statement as you have interpreted it
- Choose two works you have read that you believe best support your opinion
- Use the criteria suggested by the critical lens to analyze the works you have chosen
- Avoid plot summary; instead, use specific references to appropriate literary elements (for example: theme, characterization, setting, point of view) to develop your analysis
- Organize your ideas in a unified and coherent manner
- Specify the titles and authors of the literature you choose
- Follow the conventions of standard written English

Sample Essay

It is often said that in literature the classics are those which focus on universal topics. This is what William Faulkner means when he says that "The best literature is about old universal truths, such as love, honor, pride, compassion, and sacrifice." This means that the best literature, or the literature that has the most meaning for readers, is that which covers topics that are universally of interest. These topics, including love, honor, and compassion, when explored with thought and insight, make the best literature. Two novels, by Thomas Hardy and by Harper Lee, show how these universal truths define characters and heighten plot.

One of Thomas Hardy's novels, The Return of the Native, *explores two of the universal truths Faulkner mentions. The main theme in this novel is about love and honor. Hardy creates many characters whose lives are changed by decisions they make based on their love for certain other characters. Hardy shows how love affects each character and the overall community of a small town. He also shows the internal struggle of characters torn between honoring their marriage vows and pursuing the love for another they desire. Hardy's depiction of these characters and the struggle they undergo offers the reader insight into human nature. It is because of this universal theme that Hardy's text is among one of the best in literature.*

In Harper Lee's novel To Kill a Mockingbird, *the character of Atticus Finch, who is a very proud man, shows compassion for a black man by defending him against charges of murder. The fact that the story is set in a small town in the segregated South makes Atticus's decision especially heroic. In doing what he knows is right, Atticus also teaches his children the importance of compassion for others. Because this novel is told from the point of view of a child, we feel we are part of the Finch family and that we are learning about overcoming prejudice just the way Scout does. The universal truths Faulkner speaks of are depicted in the conflicts of the plot and in the characters of Atticus Finch and Scout.*

Both these novels show characters who portray the emotions of everyday people. Although they often face situations that we may never have to face, we can still relate to them. These characters and stories illustrate what Faulkner means by "universal truths."

Analysis

This is a good introduction because the opening paragraph makes a thoughtful interpretation of the critical lens, and the several sentences in which the writer restates the meaning of the critical lens make it clear that the writer agrees with it. The writer also establishes several criteria for evaluation of the works to be discussed: literature offers "thought and insight"; "universal truths define characters and heighten plot."

The development that follows is not extensive in use of detail, but it is clear and consistent and makes reference to specific evidence and literary elements from both texts. The writer maintains the focus on "universal truths," and the organization is clear and logical. The writer also demonstrates control of the conventions. This essay would receive a high score.

SAMPLE TASK II

Your Task: Write a critical essay in which you discuss **two** works of literature you have read from the particular perspective of the statement that is provided for you in the **Critical Lens.** In your essay, provide a valid interpretation of the statement, agree **or** disagree with the statement as you have interpreted it, and support your opinion using specific references to appropriate literary elements from the two works.

Critical Lens: "Fiction is truer than history, for it is only in fiction [and drama] that we can understand the hidden life of the characters . . ."

—E. M. Forster

Sample Essay

E. M. Forster once said, "Fiction is truer than history, for it is only in fiction and drama that we can understand the hidden life of the characters." This statement can be interpreted to mean that in fiction, unlike history, the reader can often see the secret thoughts of the characters and better understand why they act as they do. This statement is true for many works of literature, including The Crucible, *by Arthur Miller, and* Macbeth, *by William Shakespeare. In both plays, the innermost thoughts or motives of the characters are revealed.*

The motives of the girls in The Crucible *are fully understood through revelation of the girls' real thoughts. Led by Abigail, a group of girls accuses several residents of Salem of associating with the devil. Their reasons for acting in this manner are revealed in scenes where only the girls are present. With no one else present, there is no reason that they should lie to each other. The reader learns that the girls, who had danced in the woods, were trying to avoid punishment by claiming that they had been bewitched by Tituba, a black slave. The rest of the town does not know the motives behind the accusations with the exception of John Proctor, whose guilty relationship with Abigail makes it nearly impossible for him to reveal what he knows, even though Abigail told him the "truth." In the course of the drama we understand many of the inner feelings and conflicts in characters that others in Salem cannot. In the drama, Arthur Miller offers an understanding of events that history cannot fully explain.*

In the play Macbeth, *just as in* The Crucible, *the hidden thoughts of the central character are shown. Macbeth is faced with a moral dilemma as he questions whether he should kill King Duncan in order to become king himself. Macbeth has to decide whether his ambition is greater than his loyalty. In numerous soliloquies, Macbeth thinks out loud, exposing the struggle between his conscience and his ambition only to the audience. Those thoughts reveal how he is convinced, with his wife's urging, to commit the murder. The later soliloquies show how Macbeth understands the consequences of what he has done. The causes of historical events can never be completely comprehended the way events can be comprehended in literature. In* The Crucible *and* Macbeth, *the authors are able to give clear motives for the characters' actions by showing the secret thoughts of those characters. In history we read about human events, but in literature we can actually experience them. I think that is what E. M. Forster means in this quote.*

Analysis

This is a good essay on a rather sophisticated critical lens. The writer at first interprets it narrowly to mean actual history, but the conclusion suggests a more complex interpretation of the statement.

Though there is not a wide range of evidence from either work, the writer does make effective use of literary elements of drama, incident, and soliloquy in particular. The writer's decision to use examples from drama only limited the possibilities for development.

The paper maintains the focus and is clear in its organization; the language is fluent and there is effective variety in sentence structure. The writer also demonstrates control of the conventions. This essay would receive a high score.

How can I review for this part of the exam?

- Review the literary essays you have written in high school. The papers in which you have written about themes or character, plot or setting are good examples. This part of the exam is a "proxy" for much of the thinking and writing you have done in your literature courses. Your reading of secondary sources, such as critical essays and reviews, has also prepared you for this part of the exam.

- Make up a list of 6 to 10 works that you know well. List authors and titles, names of main characters, key details of setting and plot, and important themes. Then, for each, make notes on which literary elements are particularly significant for that work. This is a very important part of your preparation! For novels, these might include narrative point of view or structure, as well as conflict within characters and within plot. For plays, literary elements might include dramatic incidents, use of dialogue, monologue, and soliloquy. For memoir and other works of nonfiction, consider use of chronology, point of view, and incident. (See the discussion beginning on page 84 for a detailed review of literary elements and techniques.)

- Consider the examples of critical lens statements; think about how you would interpret them. Your interpretation must reveal that you have understood what the statement suggests, but the critical lens statements are chosen to suggest a variety of thoughtful interpretations. You are not assessed on "getting the right answer."

- Remember the purpose of the task: it is to show that you have a sound grasp of what literature "does" and that you can write about how authors achieve the effect and meaning of their works. How you agree or disagree with Faulkner, or Conrad, or Forster, for example, is only a **prompt,** a way of provoking ideas and suggesting a thesis.

Critical Lens Statements for Reflection and Practice

"A work of literature must provide more than factual accuracy or vivid physical reality . . . it must tell us more than we already know."

"Good literature appeals to our intelligence and imagination, not merely to our curiosity."

—E. M. Forster

"A writer should aim to reach all levels of society and as many levels of thought as possible, avoiding democratic prejudice as much as intellectual snobbery . . ."

—Saul Bellow

"I am interested in making a good case for distortion because I am coming to believe that it is the only way to make people see."

—Flannery O'Connor

"If literature is nebulous or inexact, this inexactness is the price literature pays for representing whole human beings and for embodying whole human feelings."

—Donald Hall

Here are two examples of statements that might provoke strong agreement or disagreement:

"Knowing about the life and times of an author is irrelevant to appreciating the full meaning of a literary work."

"A work of literature is limited by the dominant attitudes and ideas of the time period in which it was written."

In the "Regents Examinations and Answers" section, you will find 10 examples of the **critical lens** tasks on actual Regents exams. Be sure to review these and the student essays. The analysis that follows each essay shows why it merits a high score.

KNOW THE RUBRIC

Here is the information from the chart on page 83. The key terms for this part of the exam have been highlighted. As you have seen in previous examples, the rubrics for Language Use and Conventions are the same for all four tasks.

Important Note: If you write about only one work of literature, the response can be scored no higher than a 3—regardless of how well that response is written.

SCORING RUBRIC FOR SESSION TWO, PART B

> **Meaning:** The extent to which the response exhibits sound understanding, interpretation, and analysis of the task and text.

High Scores

6—papers provide **an interpretation** of the "critical lens" that is **faithful to the complexity** of statement and **clearly establish the criteria** for analysis *and* they use the criteria to make an **insightful analysis** of the chosen texts

5—papers provide **a thoughtful interpretation** of the "critical lens" that **clearly establishes the criteria** for analysis *and* they use the criteria to make a **clear and reasoned analysis** of the chosen texts

Middle Scores

4—papers provide **a reasonable interpretation** of the "critical lens" that **establishes the criteria** for analysis *and* they **make implicit connections** between the criteria and the chosen texts

3—papers provide **a simple interpretation** of the "critical lens" that **suggests some criteria** for analysis *and/or* they **make superficial connections** between the criteria and the chosen texts

Low Scores

2—papers convey a **confused or inaccurate interpretation** of the "critical lens" *and* may allude to the "critical lens" but **do not use it to analyze** the chosen texts

1—papers **do not refer to the "critical lens"** and reflect **minimal or no analysis** of the chosen texts

> **Development:** The extent to which ideas are elaborated using specific and relevant evidence from the text.

High Scores

6—papers **develop ideas clearly and fully,** making effective use of a **wide range of relevant and specific evidence and appropriate literary elements** from **both** texts

5—papers **develop ideas clearly and consistently,** using **relevant and specific evidence and appropriate literary elements** from **both** texts

Middle Scores

4—papers **develop some ideas more fully than others,** using **relevant and specific evidence** and appropriate literary elements from both texts

3—papers **develop some ideas briefly,** using **some evidence** from both texts *and* **may rely primarily on plot summary**

Low Scores

2—papers are **incomplete or largely undeveloped, hinting at ideas,** but references to the texts are **vague, irrelevant, repetitive, or unjustified**

1—papers are **minimal,** with **no evidence of development**

Organization: The extent to which the response exhibits direction, shape, and coherence.

High Scores

6—papers **maintain the focus established by the critical lens** *and* **exhibit a logical and coherent structure** through skillful use of appropriate devices and transitions

5—papers maintain a **focus established by the critical lens** *and* **exhibit a logical sequence** of ideas through **use** of appropriate devices and transitions

Middle Scores

4—papers **maintain a clear and appropriate focus** *and* exhibit a **logical sequence** of ideas *but* **may lack internal consistency**

3—papers establish, but **fail to maintain, an appropriate focus;** exhibit a **rudimentary structure** *but* may include some **inconsistencies or irrelevancies**

Low Scores

2—papers **lack an appropriate focus** but suggest **some organization,** *or* **suggest a focus** but **lack organization**

1—papers show **no focus or organization**

See chart on page 83 for the complete rubric.

SCORING RUBRICS

SESSION TWO, PART B: READING AND WRITING FOR CRITICAL ANALYSIS

QUALITY	6 Responses at this level:	5 Responses at this level:	4 Responses at this level:	3 Responses at this level:	2 Responses at this level:	1 Responses at this level:
Meaning: the extent to which the response exhibits sound understanding, interpretation, and analysis of the task and text(s)	—provide an interpretation of the "critical lens" that is faithful to the complexity of the statement and clearly establishes the criteria for analysis —use the criteria to make an insightful analysis of the chosen texts	—provide a thoughtful interpretation of the "critical lens" that clearly establishes the criteria for analysis —use the criteria to make a clear and reasoned analysis of the chosen texts	—provide a reasonable interpretation of the "critical lens" that establishes the criteria for analysis —make implicit connections between the criteria and the chosen texts	—provide a simple interpretation of the "critical lens" that suggests some criteria for analysis —make superficial connections between the criteria and the chosen texts	—provide a confused or incomplete interpretation of the "critical lens" —may allude to the "critical lens" but do not use it to analyze the chosen texts	—do no refer to the "critical lens" —reflect minimal analysis of the chosen texts or omit mention of texts
Development: the extent to which ideas are elaborated using specific and relevant evidence from the text(s)	—develop ideas clearly and fully, making effective use of a wide range of relevant and specific evidence and appropriate literary elements from both texts	—develop ideas clearly and consistently, with reference to relevant and specific evidence and appropriate literary elements from both texts	—develop some ideas more fully than others; with reference to specific and relevant evidence and appropriate literary elements from both texts	—develop ideas briefly, using some evidence from the texts	—are incomplete or largely undeveloped, hinting at ideas, but references to the text are vague, irrelevant, repetitive, or unjustified	—are minimal, with no evidence of development
Organization: the extent to which the response exhibits direct, shape, and coherence	—maintain the focus established by the critical lens —exhibit a logical and coherent structure through skillful use of appropriate devices and transitions	—maintain the focus established by the critical lens —exhibit a logical sequence of ideas through the use of appropriate devices and transitions	—maintain a clear and appropriate focus —exhibit a logical sequence of ideas but may lack internal consistency	—establish, but fail to maintain, an appropriate focus —exhibit a rudimentary structure but may include some inconsistencies or irrelevancies	—lack an appropriate focus but suggest some organization, or suggest a focus but lack organization	—show no focus or organization
Language Use: the extent to which the response reveals an awareness of audience and purpose through effective use of words, sentence structure, and sentence variety	—are stylistically sophisticated, using language that is precise and engaging, with a notable sense of voice and awareness of audience and purpose —vary structure and length of sentences to enhance meaning	—use language that is fluent and original, with evident awareness of audience and purpose —vary structure and length of sentences to control rhythm and pacing	—use appropriate language, with some awareness of audience and purpose —occasionally make effective use of sentence structure or length	—rely on basic vocabulary, with little awareness of audience or purpose —exhibit some attempt to vary sentence structure or length for effect, but with uneven success	—use language that is imprecise or unsuitable for the audience or purpose —reveal little awareness of how to use sentences to achieve an effect	—are minimal —use language that is incoherent or inappropriate
Conventions: the extent to which the response exhibits conventional spelling, punctuation, paragraphing, capitalization, grammar, and usage	—demonstrate control of the conventions with essentially no errors, even with sophisticated language	—demonstrate control of the conventions, exhibiting occasional errors only when using sophisticated language	—demonstrate partial control, exhibiting occasional errors that do not hinder comprehension	—demonstrate emerging control, exhibiting occasional errors that hinder comprehension	—demonstrate a lack of control, exhibiting frequent errors that make comprehension difficult	—are minimal, making assessment of conventions unreliable —may be illegible or not recognizable as English

*If the student addresses only one text, the response can be scored no higher than a 3.

Reading and Writing About Literature

CHAPTER 5

Reviewing Literary Elements and Techniques

ELEMENTS OF FICTION AND DRAMA

When we speak of fiction, we are generally speaking of narrative works—works in which events are recounted, are *told*, and which have been imagined and structured by the author. Although not narrative in form, drama shares many of the essential characteristics of fiction.

Plot and Story

The primary pleasure for most readers of narrative fiction is the story. If we become involved in a novel or short story, it is because we want to know how it turns out; we want to know what is going to happen to those characters. An author creates a plot when he or she gives order and structure to the action: in a plot, the **incidents** or **episodes** of the story have a meaningful relationship to one another. A story becomes a plot when we not only understand *what happened* but also *why*. In good fiction we are *convinced* of the causal relationship among incidents and we are convinced by the relationship of characters' motives and feelings to the action.

Plot and Conflict

At the end of any meaningful story, something has *happened*; something is significantly different in the world and lives of the characters from what it was at the beginning. **Conflict** in the most general sense refers to the **forces** that move the action in a plot. Conflict in plot may be generated from a search or pursuit, from a discovery, from a deception or misunderstanding, from opportunities to make significant choices, or from unexpected consequences of an action. Although the term conflict connotes an active struggle between opposing or hostile forces, conflict in fiction may refer to any progression, change, or discovery. The **resolution** of conflict in a plot may be subtle and confined to the inner life of a character or it may be dramatic and involve irreversible change, violent destruction, or death.

Conflict may identify an actual struggle between characters, for anything from dominance or revenge to simple recognition or understanding. A plot may also focus on conflict between characters and the forces of nature or society. These are essentially *external conflicts*. A work may center on *internal conflict*: characters' struggle to know or change themselves and their lives. Most works of fiction and drama contain more than one aspect of conflict.

In Shakespeare's *Romeo and Juliet*, the most dramatic conflicts are external, vivid, and literal: the street brawls between followers of the rival Capulets and Montagues and the fatal fight with Tybalt that leads to Romeo's banishment and the tragic deaths of the young lovers. In *Macbeth*, the primary interest is in the internal conflict between Macbeth's ambitious desires and his understanding of the moral consequences of the actions he takes to achieve those desires.

The action in Edith Wharton's most famous story, "Roman Fever," is ironically serene and pleasant: two middle age women, long-time friends now both widowed, sit on a terrace overlooking the splendors of Rome and reflect on their common experiences and lifelong friendship. At the end of the conversation—and the story—their actual feelings of rivalry have come to the surface, and one of the two learns something that reveals how little she truly knew her husband or understood her marriage or the life of her friend. The conflict between the two women emerges almost imperceptibly and its meaning is only fully understood in the completely unexpected revelation of the last line.

Structure/Plot and Chronology

Narrative is not necessarily presented in chronological order, but it does have chronology. That is, incidents may be presented out of the order in which they actually occurred, but by the end of the work the reader does understand their order and relationship and appreciates why the story was structured as it was. Plots that are narrated in flashback or from different points of view are common examples.

The Great Gatsby by F. Scott Fitzgerald and *Ethan Frome* by Edith Wharton are novels in which the narrator first introduces himself and his interest in the story, then tells it in a narrative flashback whose full significance to the narrator (and reader) is revealed only at the end. Tennessee Williams's play *The Glass Menagerie* has a similar structure, in which the character of Tom serves both as a narrator in the present and as a principal character in the series of memory scenes that make up the drama. The memory scenes in Arthur Miller's play *Death of a Salesman*, however, are not flashbacks in the same way. Willy Loman relives incidents from the past while the other characters and action of the play continue in the present. As the play progresses, the shifts in time occur only within Willy's mind.

Shakespeare's tragedies are dramas in which normal chronology is preserved, as it is in such familiar novels as William Golding's *Lord of the Flies* and Mark Twain's *Huckleberry Finn*.

Narrative Point of View

The narrator of a work is the character or author's *persona* that tells a story. Point of view is the standpoint, perspective, and degree of understanding from which the narrator speaks. For many students and scholars, the question of how a story is told is one of the most interesting questions. What is the narrative point of view? Is the narration *omniscient,* essentially the point of view of the author? Or, who is the narrator? What is the narrator's relationship to the story? What is the narrator's understanding of the story? How much does the narrator really know? Appreciating how, or by whom, a story is told is often essential to understanding its meaning.

One of the most easily discerned narrative points of view is the **first person** (*I*) in which either the central character or another directly involved in the action tells the story. J. D. Salinger's novel *Catcher in the Rye* is a vivid and popular example of such narration. Fitzgerald's *The Great Gatsby* is also told in the first person. In each of these works, the fundamental meaning of the novel becomes apparent only when the reader understands the character of the narrator. In each of these works, what the narrator experiences and what he learns about himself and the world are the novel's most important themes.

In **first-person narration,** the incidents of the plot are limited to those that the narrator himself experiences. First-person narrators can, however, report what they learn from others. In Wharton's *Ethan Frome*, the engineer who narrates tells us that he has "pieced together the story" from the little he has been able to learn in the town of Starkfield, from his limited conversations with Frome himself, and from his brief visit to the Frome house. Wharton's method, of course, dramatizes Frome's inability to express or fulfill the desires of his heart and reveals the reluctance of the people of Starkfield to fully understand the lives of those around them.

Authors may also use first-person narration to achieve an ironic or satiric effect. In Ring Lardner's story "Haircut," a barber in a small midwestern town narrates a story about a local fellow who kept the town entertained with his practical jokes on people. As the story progresses, the reader understands how cruel and destructive the fellow's pranks were, but the barber does not. The narrative method in this story reveals, indirectly, a story of painful ignorance and insensitivity in the "decent" citizens of a small town. Mark Twain's masterpiece, *Huckleberry Finn*, is told by Huck himself. Through the morally naive observations of Huck, Twain satirizes the evils of slavery, fraud, hypocrisy, and nearly every other kind of corrupt human behavior. Edgar Allan Poe's story "The Tell-Tale Heart" is the confession of a cunning madman.

In **third-person** narration (*he, she, it, they*), a story is reported. The narrative voice may be *omniscient* and, therefore, able to report everything from everywhere in the story and also report on the innermost thoughts and feelings of the characters themselves. In many novels of the eighteenth and nineteenth centuries, the omniscient narrator even speaks directly to the reader, as if taking him or her into the storyteller's confidence. In Nathaniel Hawthorne's *The Scarlet Letter*, the narrator pauses from time to time to share personal feelings with the reader. Nick Carraway, the narrator of *The Great Gatsby* also does this, but the method is not common in contemporary fiction.

A widely used narrative method is the *limited omniscient* point of view. The narrative is in the third person but is focused on and even may represent the point of view of a central character. The actions and feelings of other characters are presented from the perspective of that character. Hawthorne's short story "Young Goodman Brown" is an excellent example.

Some third-person narration is dramatically **objective** and detached; it simply reports the incidents of the plot as they unfold. This narrative method, too, can be used for intensely **ironic** effect. Jackson's "The Lottery" is one of the best examples. The real horror of the story is achieved through the utterly detached, nonjudgmental telling of it.

In some plays, too, there is a character who serves a narrative role: the Chorus in Shakespeare's *Henry V*, the character of Tom in Williams's *The Glass Menagerie*, and the Stage Manager in Thornton Wilder's *Our Town* are familiar examples.

In each of the works discussed here, narrative method is not simply a literary device; it is an intrinsic part of the meaning of the work.

Setting

The setting of a work includes the time and places in which the action is played out; setting may also include significant historical context. In drama, setting may be presented directly in the set, costumes, and lighting. In narrative fiction, setting is usually presented directly through description. In some works, the physical setting is central to the plot and developed in great detail; in other works, only those details necessary to anchor the plot in a time or place will be developed. Regardless of detail, responsive readers re-create images of setting as they read.

In addition to the physical and natural details of the fictional world, setting also includes mood and **atmosphere.** In some works, social or political realities constitute part of the setting. *The Scarlet Letter* is not only set in Puritan Boston, it is also *about* that society; and *The Great Gatsby* presents a vivid picture of life in New York during Prohibition and the roaring twenties.

For some works, the author may create specific details of setting to highlight a theme. In Golding's novel *Lord of the Flies*, the island on which the story takes place has everything essential for basic survival: there is food and water, and the climate is temperate. In order to explore the moral questions of the boys' regression into savagery, Golding carefully establishes a setting in which survival itself is not a primary issue. In *Ethan Frome*, details of the harsh winter and of the isolation of a town "bypassed by the railroad" intensify the story of a man's desperately cold and isolated life.

Character and Characterization

We understand characters in fiction and drama as we do the people in our own lives, by what they say and do, and by what others say about them. Because characters are imagined and created by an author, we can even understand them more reliably and fully than we can many of the people around us. Many students find their greatest satisfaction in reading works about characters to whom they can relate, characters whose struggles are recognizable and whose feelings are familiar.

Understanding character in fiction means understanding a person's values and **motivation,** beliefs and principles, moral qualities, strengths and weaknesses, and degree of self-knowledge and understanding. To fully appreciate a work, the reader must understand what characters are searching for and devoting their lives to.

Literature also seeks to account for the forces outside individuals that influence the direction and outcome of their lives. These "forces" range from those of nature and history to the demands of family, community, and society. The response of characters to inner and outer forces is what literature depicts and makes comprehensible.

In literature courses and on examinations, discussions of character are the most common. That is because any meaningful or convincing plot stems from human thought, motive, and action. Depending on the narrative point of view (see page 86) a character's thoughts and feelings may be presented directly through **omniscient** narrative or first-person commentary. In "Young Goodman Brown," the narrator tells us directly what the title character is thinking and feeling; in "Roman Fever," the most important revelations of character are discovered by the reader simultaneously with the two central characters. Character in drama is revealed directly in dialogue and action, but it may be expanded through soliloquies and asides. In Shakespeare's *Othello*, for example, the full extent of Iago's evil is revealed through the variety of methods he uses to manipulate different characters and through the soliloquies.

In some works, the author's primary purpose is to reveal character gradually through plot; in others, the author establishes understanding of character from the beginning in order to account for what happens. In the opening pages of *The Great Gatsby*, the narrator, Nick, who is also a character in the novel, introduces himself and declares his judgment of the moral quality of the people and events he is about to narrate. With Nick's own character and motives clearly established, the reader then shares his gradual discovery of the truth about Gatsby and his life.

Theme

The subjects of literature may come from any aspect of human experience: love, friendship, growing up, ambition, family relationships, conflicts with society, survival, war, evil, death, and so on. **Theme** in a work of literature is the understanding, insight, observation, and presentation of such subjects. Theme is what a work *says about* a subject. Themes are the central ideas of literary works.

One way to think about theme is to consider it roughly analogous to the topic or thesis of an expository essay. If the author of a novel, story, or play had chosen to examine the subjects of the work in an essay, what might be the topic assertions of such an essay? The student is cautioned, however, not to overinterpret the analogy. Themes in literature are rarely "morals," such as those found at the end of a fable, but neither are they "hidden meanings." Although scholars and critics often express thematic ideas in phrases, students are often required to express themes in full statements. In the next paragraph are some examples of statements about theme.

Macbeth is a play about the temptation to embrace evil forces and about the power of ambition to corrupt; Macbeth himself makes one of the most important statements of theme in the play when he says, "I do all that becomes a man/who does more is none." *Ethan Frome* and Lardner's "Haircut" both illustrate that people in small towns do not truly understand the innermost needs and desires of people they think they know. William Golding's novel *Lord of the Flies* illustrates the bleak view that human beings' savage nature will prevail without external forces of authority, that human beings are not civilized in their fundamental natures. In contrast, in *Adventures of Huckleberry Finn*, Twain presents civilization as the source of corruption and finds truly moral behavior only in the runaway slave, Jim, and the ignorant boy, Huck.

ELEMENTS OF NONFICTION

Fiction and nonfiction share many common elements; they also make similar demands and offer comparable rewards to the thoughtful reader. In broad contrast to fiction, where characters and plot are imaginative creations of the author, nonfiction is about actual persons, experiences, and phenomena. Nonfiction also speculates on abstract and philosophical questions of history and politics, ethics and religion, culture and society, as well as the natural world. In biography and autobiography, the writer focuses on what is meaningful and interesting in the life of an individual.

On the Regents exam you will listen to or read more than one piece of nonfiction. The Part A Listening section of Session One is likely to be taken from a speech, memoir, or informative talk. You will note that the sample Part A task of Session Two includes a reading from a memoir. This is a good example of **narrative** and **characterization.** Authors of literary nonfiction also make imaginative use of **structure** and **chronology.** The literary elements reviewed above are often found in nonfiction. Be sure to observe and write about these in your essays.

ELEMENTS OF POETRY

Part A of Session Two of the English Regents exam may include a poem for close reading and discussion with a piece of prose. The multiple-choice questions are designed to measure your skill at reading for the meaning; they also expect you to recognize and identify the elements of poetry. You are encouraged to include poetry among the works you choose to write on in Part B of Session Two.

Poetry and Experience

In poetry, we are meant to sense a structure and to feel the rhythm (see **meter and rhythm,** page 103). The structure and rhythm of poetry may be formal, informal, even "free." Poetry is also characterized by its directness of effect and by its concentration—ideas and feelings are expressed in relatively few words. Karl Shapiro says, "Poems are what ideas feel like." Where the writer of prose may seek immediate clarity of meaning above all, the poet often seeks **ambiguity,** not to create "confusion," but to offer multiplicity of meaning: in single words, in images, in the meaning of the poem itself.

The experience of poetry is conveyed in vivid **imagery,** which appeals to the mind and to the senses. It is often expressed in **figurative language;** that is, through imaginative use of words and comparisons that are not literal but which create original, vivid, and often unexpected images and associations. (See **metaphor,** page 102, and **simile,** page 104.) Finally, in poetry there is particular significance in the way words and lines sound. The story or experience is enhanced through musical effects. A poem must be felt and heard!

Theme in Poetry

Some poems may assert a belief. Others may be a comment on the nature of human experience—love, death, loss or triumph, mystery and confusion, conflict and peace, on the humorous and the ironic, on the imagined and the unexpected in all its forms. Some poems reflect on the nature of time, of existence. Many poems are about poetry itself. These aspects of human experience are what we refer to as the **themes** of poetry.

Tone

Tone in poetry, as in prose and all forms of human communication, expresses the *attitude* of the speaker toward the reader or listener and toward the subject. Tone in literature is as varied as the range of human experience and feeling it reflects. When we speak of the *mood* of a piece of writing, we are also speaking of tone, of an overall feeling generated by the work.

Here are some terms to help you recognize and articulate **tone** or **mood** (see also Structure and Language in Poetry, beginning on page 100):

ambiguous	insistent	reconciled
amused	**ironic**	reflective
angry	melancholy	regretful
bitter	mournful	reminiscent
celebratory	mysterious	satiric
elegiac	nostalgic	sorrowful
grateful	optimistic	thoughtful
harsh	**paradoxical**	**understated**
humorous	questioning	

Note: Terms in bold are included in the glossary.

Glossaries of Terms

STRUCTURE AND LANGUAGE IN PROSE

abstract In contrast to the *concrete*, abstract language expresses general ideas and concepts apart from specific examples or instances. Very formal writing is characterized by abstract expression. As a noun, *abstract* denotes a brief summary of the key ideas in a scientific, legal, or scholarly piece of writing.

analogy An expression of the similarities between things that are not wholly alike or related. (See *metaphor* in Structure and Language in Poetry, page 102.)

anecdote A very brief, usually vivid story or episode. Often humorous, anecdotes offer examples of typical behavior or illustrate the personality of a character. Writers of biography and autobiography make extensive use of anecdote to reveal the lives of their subjects.

antithesis In formal argument, a statement that opposes or contrasts a *thesis* statement. Informally, we use the term to refer to any expression or point of view completely opposed to another. In literature, even an experience or a feeling may be expressed as the *antithesis* of another. (See also *thesis*.)

argument In persuasive writing or speaking, the development of reasons to support the writer's position; it is the method of reasoning used to persuade. Informally, we may use the term to describe the development of a topic in any piece of expository writing. Historically, it has also denoted a summary of a literary work's plot or main ideas.

atmosphere Closely related to *tone* or mood, it refers to a pervasive feeling in a work. Atmosphere often stems from setting and from distinctive characters or actions. The atmosphere in many of Poe's stories is mysterious, troubling, even sinister. Hawthorne's "Young Goodman Brown" reflects the threatening and morally ambiguous world of its Puritan setting.

autobiography A formally composed account of a person's life, written by that person. Although we must trust, or be skeptical of, the reliability of the account, we often appreciate the firsthand narration of experience. Autobiography is also a rich source of information and insight into a historical period or into literary or artistic worlds. Autobiography, like the novel, has *narrative* and chronology. (See also *journal, memoir.*) We describe literary works that are closely based on the author's life as **autobiographical.** Eugene O'Neill's *Long Day's Journey into Night* and Tennessee Williams's *The Glass Menagerie* are plays that reflect many details of their authors' lives.

biography A narrative, historical account of the life, character, and significance of its subject. Contemporary biography is usually researched in detail and may not always be admiring of its subject. A critical biography of a literary figure includes discussion of the writer's works to show the writer's artistic development and career. Biographies of figures significant in history or public affairs also offer commentary on periods and events of historical importance.

character The imagined persons, created figures, who inhabit the worlds of fiction and drama. E. M. Forster distinguished between *flat* and *round* characters. Flat are those, like stereotypes, who represent a single and exaggerated human characteristic. Round are those whose aspects are complex and convincing, and who change or develop in the course of a work. In good fiction, plot must develop out of character. It is the desires, values, and motives of characters that account for the action and conflict in a plot.

characterization The method by which an author establishes character; the means by which personality, manner, and appearance are created. It is achieved directly through description and dialogue and indirectly through observations and reactions of other characters.

concrete The particular, the specific, in expression and imagery. That which is concrete can be perceived by the senses. Concrete also refers to that which is tangible, real, or actual, in contrast to *abstract,* which is intangible and conceptual.

conflict In the most general sense, it identifies the forces that give rise to a plot. This term may identify an actual struggle between characters, for anything from revenge to simple recognition or understanding. A plot may focus on conflict between characters and the forces of nature or society. These are essentially external conflicts. A work may also center on internal conflicts: characters' struggles to know or change themselves and their lives. Most works of fiction and drama contain more than one aspect of conflict. (See Plot and Conflict, page 84.)

denouement A French term meaning "untying a knot," it refers to the way the complications or conflict of a plot are finally resolved. It also refers to what is called the "falling action" in a drama: that part of the play that follows the dramatic climax and reveals the consequences of the main action for minor characters; it also accounts briefly for what happens in the world of the play after the principal drama is resolved. In Arthur Miller's *Death of a Salesman*, the "Requiem" may be considered a denouement: it accounts for the response to Willy's death of his wife, sons, and only friend. In Shakespeare's *Macbeth*, the climax is in the scene following the death of Lady Macbeth in which Macbeth understands that he has destroyed all capacity for feeling and has rendered his life meaningless; the denouement occurs in the battle scene in which Macbeth comprehends the treachery of the witches and is killed by Macduff, thus restoring the throne to the rightful heir, Malcolm.

determinism The philosophical view that human existence is determined by forces over which humans have little or no control. The concept that fate predestines the course of a character's life or a tragic figure's downfall is a form of determinism.

episode A series of actions or incidents that make up a self-contained part of a larger narrative. Some novels are structured so that each chapter is a significant episode. Fitzgerald's *The Great Gatsby* and Mark Twain's *Huckleberry Finn* are good examples. A *scene* in a play is often analogous to an episode in a narrative. Many television series are presented in weekly episodes.

essay Denotes an extended composition, usually expository, devoted to a single topic. Essays may be composed to persuade, to reflect on philosophical questions, to analyze a subject, to express an opinion, or to entertain. As a literary form, the essay dates from the sixteenth century and remains a popular and widely practiced form. The origin of the term is the French word *essai*, which means an attempt, a trying out of something. (See *formal/informal essay*.)

exposition Writing whose purpose is to inform, illustrate, and explain. In literature, exposition refers to those passages or speeches in which setting, offstage or prior action, or a character's background is revealed. In *The Great Gatsby*, Nick Carraway pauses in the narrative to give the reader additional information about Gatsby's background. The prologue to Shakespeare's *Romeo and Juliet* is an example of exposition.

flashback A presentation of incidents or episodes that occurred prior to the beginning of a narrative itself. When an author or filmmaker uses flashback, the "present" or forward motion of the plot is suspended. Flashback may be introduced through the device of a character's memory, or through the narrative voice itself. William Faulkner's "Barn Burning" and *Light in August* include vivid passages of memory and narrative flashback. Jack

Burden's recounting of the Cass Mastern story in Robert Penn Warren's *All the King's Men* is also a form of flashback.

foreshadowing Establishing details or mood in a work that will become more significant as the plot progresses. Thoughtful readers usually sense such details and accumulate them in their memories. In one of the opening scenes of *Ethan Frome*, Ethan and Mattie talk about the dangers of sledding down Starkfield's steepest hill. In the second paragraph of Shirley Jackson's well-known story "The Lottery," the boys stuff their pockets with stones and make piles of them on the edge of the square.

form The organization, shape, and structure of a work. Concretely, form may refer to *genre* (see below); for example, the sonnet form, the tragic form. More abstractly, form also refers to the way we sense inherent structure and shape.

formal/informal essay In contrast to the formal essay, which emphasizes organization, logic, and explication of ideas, the informal essay emphasizes the voice and perspective of the writer. In the informal essay, also called a *personal essay*, the reader is aware of the author's *persona* and is asked to share the author's interest in the subject. Examples of a personal essay might appear as Part A listening passages of Session One or in the Part A literary passages of Session Two of the Regents exam.

genre A type or form of literature. Examples include *novel, short story, epic poem, essay, sonnet,* and *tragedy.*

image Although suggesting something that is visualized, an image is an expression or recreation through language of *any* experience perceived directly through the senses. (See also Structure and Language in Poetry, page 100.)

irony In general, a tone or figure of speech in which there is a discrepancy— a striking difference or contradiction—between what is expressed and what is meant or expected. Irony achieves its powerful effect indirectly: in satire, for example, to ridicule or criticize. We also speak of dramatic irony when the narrator or reader understands more than the characters do.

journal A diary or notebook of personal observations. Many writers use journals to compose personal reflection and to collect ideas for their works. The journals of many writers have been published. Students are often urged to keep journals as a way to reflect on their reading, compose personal pieces, and practice writing free of concern for evaluation.

melodrama A plot in which incidents are sensational and designed to provoke immediate emotional responses. In melodrama, the "good" characters are pure and innocent and victims of the "bad" ones, who are thoroughly evil. The term refers to a particular kind of drama popular in the late nineteenth century and, later, in silent films and early Westerns. A work becomes melodramatic when it relies on improbable incidents and unconvincing characters for strong emotional effect.

memoir A form of autobiographical writing that reflects on the significant events the writer has observed and on the interesting and important personalities the writer has known. The passage by Annie Dillard, on pages 57–58 is a good example of memoir.

monologue In a play, an extended expression or speech by a single speaker that is uninterrupted by response from other characters. A monologue is addressed to a particular person or persons, who may or may not actually hear it. In Ring Lardner's short story "Haircut," a barber tells (narrates) the story to a customer (the reader) who is present but does not respond. (See also **dramatic monologue** in Structure and Language in Poetry, page 100.)

motivation The desires, values, needs, or impulses that move characters to act as they do. In good fiction, the reader understands, appreciates, and is convinced that a character's motivation accounts for the significant incidents and the outcome of a plot.

narrative point of view The standpoint, perspective, and degree of understanding from which a work of narrative fiction is told. (See *omniscient point of view, objective point of view.*)

narrator The character or author's *persona* that tells a story. It is through the perspective and understanding of the narrator that the reader experiences the work. In some works, the narrator may inhabit the world of the story or be a character in it. In other works, the narrator is a detached but knowledgeable observer.

naturalism Closely related to *determinism*, naturalism depicts characters who are driven not by personal will or moral principles but by natural forces that they do not fully understand or control. In contrast to other views of human experience, the naturalistic view makes no moral judgments on the lives of the characters. Their lives, often bleak or defeating, simply *are* as they are, determined by social, environmental, instinctive, and hereditary forces. Naturalism was in part a reaction by writers against the nineteenth-century Romantic view of man as master of his own fate. It is important to note, however, that none of the Naturalistic writers in America (Crane, Dreiser, London, Anderson, and Norris chief among them) presented a genuinely deterministic vision. Several of these authors began their careers in journalism and were drawn to the Naturalistic view of life as a result of their own experience and observation of life in America. (See also *realism.*)

objective point of view In fiction or nonfiction, this voice presents a story or information without expressed judgment or qualification. A fundamental principle of journalism is that news *reports* should be objective. Ernest Hemingway's short story "The Killers" is an example of fiction rendered in a completely detached, objective point of view.

omniscient point of view Spoken in third person (*she, he, they*), this is the broadest narrative perspective. The omniscient narrator speaks from outside the story and sees and knows everything about the characters and incidents. Omniscient narration is not limited by time or place. In *limited omniscient* point of view, the author may choose to reveal the story through full understanding of only one character and limit the action to those incidents in which this character is present.

persona A term from the Greek meaning "mask," it refers in literature to a narrative voice created by an author and through which the author speaks. A narrative persona usually has a perceptible, even distinctive, personality that contributes to our understanding of the story. In Nathaniel Hawthorne's *The Scarlet Letter,* the omniscient narrator has a distinctive persona whose attitudes toward Puritan society and the characters' lives are revealed throughout the novel.

plot The incidents and experiences of characters selected and arranged by the author to create a meaningful story. A good plot is convincing in terms of what happens and why.

poetic justice The concept that life's rewards and punishments should be perfectly appropriate and distributed in just proportions. In Ring Lardner's short story "Haircut," Jim Kendall's ironic fate is an example of poetic justice: he is a victim of one of his own crude and insensitive practical jokes. The short story "They Grind Exceeding Small," by Ben Ames Williams, is also a vivid example of what is meant by poetic justice.

point of view In nonfiction, this denotes the attitudes or opinions of the writer. In narrative fiction, it refers to how and by whom a story is told: the perspective of the narrator and the narrator's relationship to the story. Point of view may be *omniscient,* where the narrator knows everything about the characters and their lives; or, it may be *limited* to the understanding of a particular character or speaker. Point of view may also be described as *objective* or *subjective. Third-person* narrative refers to characters as "he, she, they;" *First-person* narrative is from the "I" point of view. J. D. Salinger's *Catcher in the Rye* and Mark Twain's *Huckleberry Finn* are told in the first person. *Second person,* the "you" form, is rare but is found in sermons addressed to a congregation or in essays of opinion addressed directly to a leader or public figure: "You, Mr. Mayor (Madame President), should do the following . . ." Political columnists occasionally write pieces in the second-person voice for the Op-Ed pages of newspapers.

prologue An introductory statement of the dramatic situation of a play. Shakespeare's *Romeo and Juliet* begins with a brief prologue. The first two pages of Fitzgerald's *The Great Gatsby* are a prologue to the story Nick Carraway will tell.

prose Most of what we write is prose, the expression in sentences and phrases that reflect the natural rhythms of speech. Prose is organized by paragraphs and is characterized by variety in sentence length and rhythm.

protagonist A term from ancient Greek drama, it refers to the central character, the hero or heroine, in a literary work.

realism The literary period in America following the Civil War is usually called the Age of Realism. Realism depicts the directly observable in everyday life. Realistic writers seek to *present* characters and situations as they would appear to a careful observer, not as they are imagined or created by the author. After 1865, American writers became increasingly interested in the sources of power and force, and in the means to survival and success, in an increasingly materialistic society. For writers of this period, realism was a literary mode to express a *naturalistic* philosophy. (See also *naturalism, verisimilitude.*)

rhetoric From Ancient Greece, the art of persuasion in speech or writing achieved through logical thought and skillful use of language.

rhetorical question A question posed in the course of an *argument* to provoke thought or to introduce a line of reasoning.

romance A novel or tale that includes elements of the supernatural, heroic adventure, or romantic passion. Hawthorne's *The Scarlet Letter* is a romance, not because it is a love story but because it goes beyond *verisimilitude* in dramatizing elements of demonic and mystical forces in the characters and their lives.

satire A form or style that uses elements of irony, ridicule, exaggeration, understatement, sarcasm, humor, or absurdity to criticize human behavior or a society. All satire is **ironic** (see *irony*) in that meaning or theme is conveyed in the discrepancy between what is said and what is meant, between what is and what should be, and between what appears and what truly is. Although satire is often entertaining, its purpose is serious and meant to provoke thought or judgment. The verses of Alexander Pope and many poems by e. e. cummings are satiric. In prose, much of the writing of Mark Twain is satire; *Huckleberry Finn* is the most striking example. Other American writers of satire include Sinclair Lewis, Edith Wharton, Aldous Huxley, Joseph Heller, Veronica Geng, and Tom Wolfe. Popular television programs such as *The Daily Show*, *South Park*, and *The Simpsons* are also good examples of satire.

short story This form is distinguished from most novels not simply by length but by its focus on few characters and a central, revealing incident. In stories, however, there is as much variety in narrative point of view, subject, and technique as there is in novels. Edgar Allan Poe characterized the short story as "a short prose narrative, requiring from a half-hour to one or two hours in its perusal."

soliloquy A form of *monologue* in which a character expresses thoughts and feelings aloud but does not address them to anyone else or intend other characters in the work to hear them. In essence, the audience for a play is secretly listening in on a character's innermost thoughts. Macbeth's reflection on "Tomorrow, and tomorrow, and tomorrow . . ." is the best-known soliloquy in the play.

speaker The narrative voice in a literary work (see *persona*). Also, the character who speaks in a *dramatic monologue*.

symbol Most generally, anything that stands for or suggests something else. Language itself is symbolic: sounds and abstract written forms may be arranged to stand for virtually any human thought or experience. In literature, symbols are not Easter eggs, or mushrooms—they are not "hidden meanings." Symbols are real objects and *concrete* images that lead us to *think about* what is suggested. They organize a wide variety of ideas into single acts of understanding. They embody not single "meanings" but suggest whole areas of meaning.

theme Roughly analogous to *thesis* in an essay, this is an observation about human experience or an idea central to a work of literature. The *subject* of a work is in the specific setting, characters, and plot. Theme in a work of fiction is what is meaningful and significant to human experience generally. Themes are the ideas and truths that transcend the specific characters and plot. Shakespeare's *Macbeth* is about an ambitious nobleman who, encouraged by his equally ambitious wife, murders the king of Scotland in order to become king himself. The themes in *Macbeth* include, the power of ambition to corrupt even those who are worthy and the mortal consequences of denying what is fundamental to one's nature. Many of the critical lens statements in Session Two, Part B of the Regents exam are about the themes of literature.

thesis The central point, a statement of position in a formal or logical argument. Also used to refer to the topic or controlling idea of an essay. Use of the term *thesis* implies elaboration by reasons and examples.

tone The attitude of the writer toward the subject and toward the reader. (See the discussion in Chapter 5, page 91, and a glossary of Terms for Writing, page 92.)

transition A link between ideas or sections in a work. In prose arguments, single words such as *first, second, moreover,* and *therefore* or phrases such as *in addition, on the other hand,* and *in conclusion* serve as transitions. In fiction, a brief passage or chapter may serve as a transition. In *The Great Gatsby*, the narrator pauses from time to time to "fill in" the reader and to account for the passage of time between the dramatic episodes that make up the novel's main plot.

turning point In drama and fiction, the moment or episode in a plot when the action is moved toward its inevitable conclusion.

verisimilitude A literal quality in fiction and drama of being "true to life," of representing that which is real or actual. Verisimilitude in fiction is often achieved through specific, vivid description and dialogue; first-person narration also creates the effect of verisimilitude. In drama, it may be achieved through means of set, costumes, and lighting that are realistic in all their details.

STRUCTURE AND LANGUAGE IN POETRY

allegory A narrative, in prose or verse, in which abstract ideas, principles, human values, or states of mind are **personified.** The purpose of the allegory is to illustrate the signficance of the ideas by dramatizing them. *Parable* and *fable* are particular kinds of allegory, in which a moral is illustrated in the form of a story.

alliteration The repetition of initial consonant sounds in words and syllables is one of the first patterns of sound a child creates; for example, "ma-ma; pa-pa." The stories of Dr. Seuss are told in alliteration and **assonance.** Poets use alliteration for its rich musical effect: "Fish, flesh, and fowl commend all summer long/Whatever is begotten, born, and dies" (Yeats); for humor: "Where at, with blade, with bloody, blameful blade/He bravely broached his boiling bloody breast" (Shakespeare); and to echo the sense of the lines: "The iron tongue of midnight hath told twelve" (Shakespeare).

allusion A reference to a historical event, to Biblical, mythological, or literary characters and incidents with which the reader is assumed to be familiar. Allusion may, with few words, enrich or extend the meaning of a phrase, idea, or image. Allusion may also be used for ironic effect. In his poem "Out, out . . ." Robert Frost expects the reader to recall from Macbeth's final soliloquy the line, "Out, out brief candle!" Such expressions as "a Herculean task" or "Achilles heel," are also forms of allusion.

ambiguity Denotes uncertainty of meaning. In literature and especially in poetry, we speak of intentional ambiguity, the use of language and images to suggest more than one meaning at the same time.

assonance The repetition of vowel sounds among words that begin or end with different consonants.

ballads Narrative poems, sometimes sung, that tell dramatic stories of individual episodes and characters.

blank verse Unrhymed *iambic pentameter*, usually in "paragraphs" of verse instead of stanzas. Shakespeare's plays are composed primarily in blank verse. For example, from *Macbeth* (Act I, Scene 5):

> Your face, my Thane, is as a book where men
> May read strange matters. To beguile the time,
> Look like the time; bear welcome in your eye,
> Your hand, your tongue; look like the innocent flower,
> But be the serpent under't . . .

connotation The feelings, attitudes, images, and associations of a word or expression. Connotations are usually said to be "positive" or "negative."

couplet Two lines of verse with similar meter and end ryhme. Couplets generally have self-contained ideas as well, so they may function as stanzas within a poem. In the English (Shakespearean) *sonnet*, the couplet serves as a conclusion. You will also discover that many scenes in Shakespeare's plays end with rhymed couplets: "Away, and mock the time with fairest show/False face must hide what the false heart doth know." (*Macbeth* Act I, Scene 7)

denotation That which a word actually names, identifies, or "points to." Denotation is sometimes referred to as "the dictionary definition" of a word.

dramatic monologue A poem in which a fictional character, at a critical or dramatic point in life, addresses a particular "audience," which is identifiable but silent. In the course of the monologue, we learn a great deal, often ironically, about the character who is speaking and the circumstances that have led to the speech. Robert Browning is the best-known 19th-century poet to compose dramatic monologues; "My Last Duchess" is a famous example. In the 20th century, such poets as Kenneth Fearing, E. A. Robinson, T. S. Eliot ("The Love Song of J. Alfred Prufrock"), Robert Frost, and Amy Lowell composed well-known dramatic monologues.

elegy A meditative poem mourning the death of an individual.

epic A long narrative poem often centering on a heroic figure who represents the fate of a great nation or people. *The Iliad* and *The Odyssey* of Homer, *The Aeneid* of Vergil, and the Anglo-Saxon *Beowulf* are well-known epics. Milton's *Paradise Lost* and Dante's *Divine Comedy* are examples of epic narratives in which subjects of great human significance are dramatized. *Omeros*, by Derek Walcott, is a contemporary example of an epic poem.

figurative language The intentional and imaginative use of words and comparisons that are not literal but that create original, vivid, and often unexpected images and associations. Figurative language is also called *metaphorical language*. (See *metaphor* and *simile*.)

free verse A poem written in free verse develops images and ideas in patterns of lines without specific metrical arrangements or formal rhyme. Free verse is distinguished from prose, however, because it retains such poetic elements as assonance, alliteration, and figurative language. The poetry of Walt Whitman and e. e. cummings offers striking examples. The poem by Rita Dove on pages 59–60, is also an example of free verse.

hyperbole An exaggerated expression (also called overstatement) for a particular effect, which may be humorous, satirical, or intensely emotional. Hyperbole is the expression of folktales and legends and, of course, of lovers: Romeo says to Juliet, "there lies more peril in thine eye/Than twenty of their swords." Hyperbole is often the expression of any overwhelming feeling. After he murders King Duncan, Macbeth looks with horror at his bloody hands: "Will all great Neptune's ocean wash this blood/Clean from my hand . . . ?" In her sleepwalking scene, Lady Macbeth despairs that "All the perfumes of Arabia will not sweeten this little hand." And everyone of us has felt, "I have mountains of work to do!"

iambic pentameter The basic meter of English speech: "I think I know exactly what you need/and yet at times I know that I do not." Formally, it identifies verse of ten syllables to the line, with the second, fourth, sixth, eighth, and tenth accented. There is, however, variation in the stresses within lines to reflect natural speech—and to avoid a "sing-song" or nursery rhyme effect. It is the meter in which most of the dialogue in Shakespeare's plays is composed (see *blank verse*).

image Images and imagery are the heart of poetry. Although the term suggests only something that is visualized, an image is the re-creation through language of *any* experience perceived directly through the senses.

internal rhyme A pattern in which a word or words within a line rhyme with the word that ends it. Poets may also employ internal rhyme at irregular intervals over many lines.

irony In general, a tone or figure of speech in which there is a discrepancy— a striking difference or contradiction—between what is expressed and what is meant or expected. Irony may be used to achieve a powerful effect indirectly. In satire, for example, it may be used to ridicule or criticize.

metaphor A form of analogy. Metaphorical expression is the heart of poetry. Through metaphor, a poet discovers and expresses a similarity between dissimilar things. The poet uses metaphor to imaginatively find common qualities between things we would not normally or literally compare. As a figure of speech, metaphor is said to be implicit or indirect, in contrast to simile where the comparison is expressed directly. In his final soliloquy, which begins "Tomorrow, and tomorrow, and tomorrow . . ."

Macbeth creates a series of metaphors to express the meaninglessness of his own life: "Life's but a walking shadow, a poor player . . . it is a tale told by an idiot . . ." And in the poem on pages 59–60, Rita Dove tells us that she "studied history for its rhapsody of dates . . ."

meter and rhythm Rhythm refers to the pattern of movement in a poem. As music has rhythm, so does poetry. Meter refers to specific patterns of stressed and unstressed syllables. (See *imabic pentameter*.)

ode A meditation or celebration of a specific subject. Traditional odes addressed "elevated" ideas and were composed in elaborate stanza forms. Keats's "Ode to a Nightingale" and "Ode to Autumn" are particularly fine examples. Modern odes may address subjects either serious or personal. One well-known contemporary ode is Pablo Neruda's "Ode to My Socks."

onomatopoeia The use of words whose sound reflects their sense. "Buzz," "hiss," and "moan" are common examples.

oxymoron Closely related to *paradox*, oxymoron is a figure of speech in which two contradictory or sharply contrasting terms are paired for emphasis or ironic effect. Students' favorite examples include "jumbo shrimp" and "army intelligence." Poets have written of the "wise fool," a "joyful sadness," or an "eloquent silence."

paradox An expression, concept, or situation whose literal statement is contradictory, yet which makes a truthful and meaningful observation. Consider the widely used expression, "less is more," for example. Shakespeare's play *Macbeth* opens with a series of paradoxes to establish the moral atmosphere in which "foul is fair." John Donne's famous poem "Death Be Not Proud" ends with the paradox "Death thou shalt die."

personification A form of metaphor or simile in which nonhuman things—objects, plants and animals, forces of nature, abstract ideas—are given human qualities. Examples include "Pale flakes . . . come feeling for our faces . . ." (Owen), "Time . . . the thief of youth," (Milton); and "Blow winds, and crack your cheeks! Blow! Rage!" (Shakespeare).

prose poem This form appears on the page in the sentences and paragraphs of prose yet its effect is achieved through rhythm, images, and patterns of sound associated with poetry. The poetry of Karl Shapiro offers many excellent examples.

quatrain A stanza of four lines. The quatrain is the most commonly used stanza form in English poetry. Quatrains may be rhymed, *abab, aabb, abba,* for example, or they may be unrhymed.

rhyme In general, any repetition of identical or similar sounds among words that are close enough together to form an audible pattern. Rhyme is most evident when it occurs at the ends of lines of metrical verse.

rhyme scheme A regular pattern of end rhyme in a poem. The rhyme scheme in Shakespeare's sonnets, for example, is *abab/cdcd/efef/gg*.

satire A form or style that uses elements of irony, ridicule, exaggeration, understatement, sarcasm, humor, or absurdity to criticize human behavior or a society. All satire is **ironic** in that meaning or theme is conveyed in the discrepancy between what is said and what is meant, between what is and what should be, between what appears and what truly is. Although satire is often entertaining, its purpose is serious and meant to provoke thought or judgment. The verse of Alexander Pope is often extended satire, and many poems by e. e. cummings are satiric.

simile An expression that is a direct comparison of two things. It uses such words as *like, as, as if, seems, appears*. For example, "A line of elms plunging and tossing like horses" (Theodore Roethke); "Mind in its purest play is like some bat" (Richard Wilbur); "I wandered lonely as a cloud" (William Wordsworth).

soliloquy A form of monologue found most often in drama. It differs from a dramatic monologue in that the speaker is alone, revealing thoughts and feelings to or for oneself that are intentionally unheard by other characters. In Shakespeare's plays, for example, the principal characters' reflections on how to act or questions of conscience are revealed in their soliloquies. Hamlet's "To be, or not to be . . ." is probably the most famous of dramatic soliloquies.

sonnet A poem of fourteen lines in *iambic pentameter* that may be composed of different patterns of stanzas and rhyme schemes. The most common forms are the English, or Shakespearean sonnet, which consists of three quatrains and a closing couplet, and the Italian sonnet, which consists of an *octave* of eight lines and a *sestet* of six lines.

speaker The narrative voice in a poem. Also, the character who speaks in a *dramatic monologue*.

stanza The grouping of lines within a poem. A stanza reflects the basic organization and development of ideas, much as paragraphs do in an essay. Many stanza patterns may have a fixed number of lines and a regular pattern of rhyme. Poets, however, often create stanzas of varying length and form within a single poem. A stanza that ends with a period, completing an idea or image, is considered "closed," whereas a stanza that ends with a comma or with no punctuation is called "open," indicating that there should be very little pause in the movement from one stanza to another.

symbol Most generally, anything that stands for or suggests something else. Language itself is symbolic: sounds and abstract written forms may stand for virtually any human thought or experience. Symbols are real objects and *concrete* images that lead us to *think about* what is suggested. Symbols organize a wide variety of ideas into single acts of understanding. They embody not single "meanings" but suggest whole areas of meaning.

understatement Expression in which something is presented as less important or significant than it really is. Understatement is often used for humorous, satiric, or *ironic* effect. Much of the satire in *Huckleberry Finn* stems from Huck's naive and understated observations. One particular form of understatement, actually a double negative, includes such expressions as "I was not uninterested," which really means "I was interested"; or "He was not without imagination," which really means "He had some imagination."

TERMS FOR WRITING

anecdote A brief story or account of a single experience, often biographical, that illustrates something typical or striking about a person. Anecdotes, like parables, are effective as vivid, specific examples of a general observation or quality.

argument The development of reasons and examples to support a thesis; narrowly, to outline a position on an issue or problem with the intent to clarify or persuade. Argument is also used in a broad sense to refer to the way a writer develops any topic. The speech by J. Peter Kelly in Chapter 1, pages 15–16 is a good example of argument.

audience For the writer, this term refers to the intended reader. Awareness of an audience determines, for example, what the writer may assume a reader already knows, the level of diction, and the tone. The Situations in Parts A and B of Session One of the exam specify an audience for the essay you will write.

coherence A piece of writing has coherence when the logical relationship of ideas is evident and convincing. In a coherent discussion, statements and sections follow one another in a natural, even inevitable way. A coherent discussion hangs together; an incoherent one is scattered and disorganized.

description The expression in words of what is experienced by the senses. Good description recreates what is felt, seen, heard—sensed in any way. We also use the term describe to mean *identify, classify, characterize,* even for abstract ideas. Description permits readers to re-create the subject in their own imaginations.

diction Refers to word choice. Diction may be formal or informal, complex or simple, or elegant or modest, depending on the occasion and the audience. The language used in casual conversation is different from the language used in formal writing. The good writer uses language that is varied, precise, and vivid. The good writer has resources of language to suit a wide range of purposes. In the rubrics for the Regents exam, Language Use is the term for diction.

exposition The development of a topic through examples, reasons, and details that explain, clarify, show, and instruct—the primary purpose of exposition is to convey information. Much of the writing assigned to students is referred to as expository writing. Through exposition, you can demonstrate what you have learned, discovered, understood, appreciated. The Tasks for Parts A and B of Session One of the Regents exam are good examples of what is meant by expository writing.

focus Refers to the way a writer concentrates and directs all the information, examples, ideas, and reasons in an essay on the specific topic.

narrative Because it tells a story, a narrative has chronological order. The narrative method is commonly used in exposition when examples are offered in a chronological development.

prompt A set of directions for a writing task; may also be a quote or passage meant to stimulate a piece of writing.

tone Refers to the attitude of the writer toward the subject and/or toward the reader. Tone may range from *harsh and insistent* to *gentle and reflective*. There is as much variety of tone in writing as there is in human feeling. Some pieces, essays of opinion for example, usually have a very distinct tone. Other works, especially in fiction or personal expression, may be more subtle and indirect in tone.

transition Words or phrases used to link ideas and sections in a piece of writing. Common transitions include *first, second . . . in addition . . . finally; on the other hand, moreover, consequently, therefore.* Transitions make the development of an argument clear.

unity In the narrowest sense, unity refers to focus: the ideas and examples are clearly related to the topic and to one another. In the largest sense, unity refers to a feature of our best writing. All elements—ideas, form, language, and tone—work together to achieve the effect of a complete and well-made piece.

A Guide to Proofreading for Common Errors

THE BASICS

Review your essays to make sure that you have begun sentences with capital letters and ended them with a period! Carelessness in this basic use of the conventions could lower your score if the test raters feel that you have not mastered this aspect of formal writing.

PUNCTUATION

COMMA USE

There is one general guideline to keep in mind for comma use: The primary function of the comma is to prevent confusion for your reader. The comma shows how separate parts of sentences are related to one another.

Introductory clauses and phrases need a comma. This makes it clear where the introduction ends and the main clause begins. Note the following examples:

> *"Though I have traveled all over the world, it is the smell of the tides and marshes of Beaufort County that identifies and shapes me."*

> *"Because I came to Beaufort County when I was a boy, my novels all smell of seawater."*
>
> —Pat Conroy

Use the comma in compound sentences with coordinating conjunctions *and, but, yet, so, or, for.* A compound sentence joins two or more independent clauses that could be expressed separately as simple sentences. *Note that the comma precedes the conjunction:*

> *"I walked slowly,* for *the detail on the beach was infinite."*
> —Ernie Pyle

> *"The luncheon hour was long past,* and *the two had their end of the vast terrace to themselves."*
> —Edith Wharton

A final suggestion: Use a comma only where you *hear* a clear need for one.

THE APOSTROPHE
Remember, the most common use of the apostrophe is to show possession.

> The *novel's* major themes = The major themes **of the novel**
> Fiction reveals *characters'* motives and actions = The motives **of the characters**
> Shakespeare dramatizes *Macbeth's* struggle with his conscience and ambition.

Avoid the increasingly common error of using the apostrophe to show the plural.

> Mark Twain wrote several **novels;** he did not write "novel's."
> Holden Caulfield spends several **days** (not day's) in New York before going home.
> Students in New York State are expected to read at least 25 **books** (not book's) per year.

GRAMMAR

SUBJECT/VERB AGREEMENT
Be sure to match subjects and verbs. Agreement is a form of consistency and is one of the most basic elements of grammar. When you learn to conjugate verbs, for example, you are applying the concept of agreement. Singular subjects take singular verbs; plural subjects take plural verbs.

> He speaks/they speak; One is/many are

PRONOUN/ANTECEDENT AGREEMENT
Because pronouns replace nouns or other pronouns, they must agree with their singular or plural antecedents.

> *Evelyn* is very grateful to *her parents* for *their* constant support and encouragement.

Most pronoun/antecedent errors arise when we use the indefinite pronouns *anyone, anybody, everyone, everybody, someone, somebody, no one,* and so on. These pronouns are singular because they refer to *individuals:*

Everybody is responsible for *his* own work.
Someone has left *her* books on the floor.
If *anyone* calls while I am out, please tell *him* or *her* that I will call back after lunch.

The common practice of replacing *him/her* with *them,* or *her/his* with *their,* solves the problem of choosing gender, but it is ungrammatical and illogical. The careful writer (and speaker) avoids these errors, or rewrites:

Please tell *anyone who calls* that I will return at noon.
Someone's books have been left on the floor.
Everyone has individual responsibility for the assignments.

SPELLING

You are, of course, expected to spell correctly common words, the key terms of your essay, and the names of authors, titles, and characters. An occasional misspelling in an on-demand piece of writing should not lower your score if all other elements are good. The Part A Listening Passage of Session One may have unfamiliar terms, names for example. If those names appear in the multiple-choice questions, you should check the spelling there in order to use them in your essay. If not, test raters are not likely to consider misspelling of an unfamiliar name as a significant error on your part.

Be especially careful to proofread for these very common errors—they mar the overall impression that your essay makes on the reader.

accept/except
To *accept* is to receive, take willingly, agree to:
I *accept* your offer, apology, invitation
To *except* is to exclude, to separate out:
I will *except* you from the requirement.
Except is also a preposition:
Everyone *except* him will be leaving on Tuesday.

affect/effect
To *affect* (v.) means to move, influence, or change.
To *affect* also means to put on an artificial quality of personality or character; an exaggerated or artificial person may be called *affected.*
The *effects* (n.) are the consequences or results.
To *effect* (v.) means to put into action, to complete—a plan or a change, for example.

could of/should of
You mean *could have/should have*.
Do not make this unfortunate confusion in the way words sound!

hear/here
You may put your things *here* on the table.
I cannot *hear* you with all the noise outside.

its/it's
it's = a contraction for *it is*
its = a possessive form; do not add an apostrophe

loose/lose
Be careful not to *lose* your ticket; it cannot be replaced.
The dog ran *loose* when the leash broke.

principal/principle
Lack of effort is often the *principal* reason for failure.
Many consider honesty a fundamental *principle* in their lives.

than/then
My sister is several years younger *than* I am.
You will answer multiple-choice questions, *then* complete your essays.

there/their/they're
There he goes! It is over *there*.
Students should bring *their* books to class everyday.
They're = *they are*

to/too/two
You will have *two* weeks *to* complete the reading assignment; do not put
it off until it is *too* late.

who's/whose
Who's (who is) that coming down the hall?
Whose books are these lying on the floor?

See Barron's *Let's Review: English, Third Edition* for a comprehensive review
of punctuation, grammar, and usage.

Appendices

The New York State Learning Standards for English Language Arts

APPENDIX A: INTRODUCTION

Building on the Board of Regents goals that call for using language skillfully in different contexts, the English language arts standards set forth four broad areas for curriculum, instruction, and assessment: Language for Information and Understanding, Language for Literary Response and Expression, Language for Critical Analysis and Evaluation, and Language for Social Interaction. The ELA Standards are expressed in terms of what students must be able to do, and each requires reading, listening, speaking, and writing. These standards are given in their entirety in Appendix B, followed by the performance indicators in Appendix C.

APPENDIX B: THE ENGLISH LANGUAGE ARTS LEARNING STANDARDS

The standards are identified as four broad areas of language experience, each requiring reading, listening, speaking, and writing.

STANDARD 1: LANGUAGE FOR INFORMATION AND UNDERSTANDING

Listening and reading to acquire information and understanding involves collecting data, facts, and ideas; discovering relationships, concepts, and generalizations; and using knowledge from oral, written, and electronic sources. **Speaking and writing** to acquire and transmit information requires asking probing and clarifying questions, interpreting information in one's own words, applying information from one context to another, and presenting the information and interpretation clearly, concisely, and comprehensibly.

STANDARD 2: LANGUAGE FOR LITERARY RESPONSE AND EXPRESSION

Listening and reading for literary *response* involves comprehending, interpreting, and critiquing imaginative texts in every medium, drawing on personal experiences and knowledge to understand the text, and recognizing the social, historical, and cultural features of the text. **Speaking and writing** for literary *response* involves presenting interpretations, analyses, and reactions to the content and language of a text. Speaking and writing for literary *expression* involves producing imaginative texts that use language and text structures that are inventive and often multilayered.

STANDARD 3: LANGUAGE FOR CRITICAL ANALYSIS AND EVALUATION

Listening and reading to analyze and evaluate experiences, ideas, information, and issues requires using evaluative criteria from a variety of perspectives and recognizing the difference in evaluations based on different sets of criteria. **Speaking and writing** for critical analysis and evaluation requires presenting opinions and judgments on experiences, ideas, information, and issues clearly, logically, and persuasively with reference to specific criteria on which the opinion or judgment is based.

STANDARD 4: LANGUAGE FOR SOCIAL INTERACTION

Oral communication in formal and informal settings requires the ability to talk with people of different ages, genders, and cultures, to adapt presentations to different audiences, and to reflect on how talk varies in different situations. **Written communication** for social interaction requires using written messages to establish, maintain, and enhance personal relationships with others.

APPENDIX C:
PERFORMANCE INDICATORS

For teachers, as well as students and parents, the English Language Arts Learning Standards are most meaningfully expressed in what are called **performance indicators,** descriptions of what students are required to do, do habitually, and do on demand. Below are some of the required performance indicators at commencement (Regents exam) level for each standard.

ELA STANDARD 1: LANGUAGE FOR INFORMATION AND UNDERSTANDING

Students are expected to:

Interpret and analyze complex informational texts and presentations, including technical manuals, professional journals, newspaper and broadcast editorials, electronic networks, political speeches and debates, and primary source material, in their subject courses.

Synthesize information from diverse sources and identify complexities and discrepancies in the information.

Use a combination of techniques to **extract salient information** from texts.

Make distinctions about the relative value and significance of specific data, facts, and ideas. **Make perceptive and well-developed connections** to prior knowledge. **Evaluate** writing strategies and presentational features that affect interpretation of the information.

Write research reports, feature articles, and thesis/support papers on a variety of topics. **Present a controlling idea** that conveys an individual perspective and insight into a topic. **Support** interpretations and decisions. **Use** a wide range of organizational patterns.

Revise and improve early drafts by restructuring, correcting errors, and revising for clarity and effect. **Use standard English skillfully,** applying established rules and conventions for presenting information and making use of a wide range of grammatical constructions and vocabulary to achieve an individual style that communicates effectively.

ELA STANDARD 2: LANGUAGE FOR LITERARY RESPONSE AND EXPRESSION

Students are expected to:

Read and view independently and fluently across many genres of literature from many cultures and historical periods. **Evaluate** literary merit based on an understanding of the genre, literary elements, and the literary period.

Identify the distinguishing features of different literary genres, periods, and traditions and use those features to interpret the work. **Read aloud** expressively to convey a clear interpretation of the work.

Recognize and understand the significance of a wide range of literary elements and techniques (including figurative language, imagery, allegory, irony, blank verse, symbolism, stream-of-consciousness), and use those elements to interpret the work.

Understand how multiple levels of meaning are conveyed in a text. Produce literary interpretations that **explicate** the multiple layers of meaning.

Write original pieces in a variety of literary forms, using the conventions of the genre and using structure and vocabulary to achieve an effect.

Use standard English skillfully and with an individual style.

ELA STANDARD 3: LANGUAGE FOR CRITICAL ANALYSIS AND EVALUATION

Students are expected to:

Analyze, interpret, and evaluate ideas, information, organization and language of a wide range of general and technical texts . . . across subject areas, including technical manuals, professional journals, political speeches, and literary criticism.

Evaluate the quality of the texts . . . from a variety of critical perspectives within the field of study. **Make precise determinations** about the perspective of a particular writer.

Present well-developed analyses of issues, ideas, and texts . . . . **Make effective use** of details, evidence, and arguments . . . to influence and persuade an audience.

Use standard English, a broad and precise vocabulary, and the formal conventions of formal oratory and debate.

ELA STANDARD 4: LANGUAGE FOR SOCIAL INTERACTION*

Students are expected to:

Engage in conversations and discussions on academic, technical, and community subjects, anticipating listeners' needs and skillfully addressing them.

Express their thoughts and views clearly with attention to the perspectives and voiced concerns of others in the conversation. **Use** appropriately the language conventions for a wide variety of social situations.

Use a variety of print and electronic forms for social communication with peers and adults. **Make effective use** of language and style to connect the message with the audience and context.

---

*This standard is not formally assessed in the English Regents Exam.

Regents Examinations
and Answers

Examination
June 2003
English

Session One

Part A

Overview: For this part of the test, you will listen to a speech about effective speech writing, answer some multiple choice questions, and write a response based on the situation described below. You will hear the speech twice. You may take notes on the page allotted anytime you wish during the readings.

> **The Situation:** Your English class intends to publish a handbook for incoming freshmen, advising them on skills needed for high school. Your assignment is to write an article on techniques for effective speech-writing. In preparation for writing your article, listen to a speech by Jane Tully, a professional speechwriter. Then use relevant information from the speech to write your article.

Your Task: Write an article for a handbook for incoming freshmen in which you discuss techniques for effective speechwriting.

Guidelines:

Be sure to
- Tell your audience what they need to know about techniques for effective speechwriting
- Use specific, accurate, and relevant information from the speech to support your discussion
- Use a tone and level of language appropriate for an article for high school freshmen
- Organize your ideas in a logical and coherent manner
- Indicate any words taken directly from the speech by using quotation marks or referring to the speaker
- Follow the conventions of standard written English

Note: For this portion of the examination, the teacher will read a passage aloud. You will not actually see the passage reprinted below. Therefore, you are encouraged to have someone read the passage to you, in order to simulate the examination as closely as possible.

Listening Passage

... You see, I have a theory that giving a speech is a lot like giving a party. You, the audience, are the invited guests. As the speaker, I am the host—at least for the moment. The speech I am delivering to you is like a meal. I want it to be nourishing food for thought—full of substance, with interesting ideas for you to chew on. I want to present it in a way that's appealing, so you'll be eager to take in my ideas. And like a good meal, I want my speech to be appropriate for this particular occasion.

If you think of a speech that way, then where does the speechwriter fit in? Actually, I like to think of myself as a kind of verbal caterer. You call on professionals like me when you don't have the time or expertise to do the job yourself, or when you have a special occasion and you want that extra something that will really make your speech stand out....

So in my role as caterer, I'd like to take this opportunity to share my basic recipe for a successful presentation. Follow this easy three step recipe and you can't go wrong:
- Know who's coming to the party,
- Use only the best ingredients, and
- Focus on the main course.

First, know who's coming....

What do we need to know about audiences? Size, for one thing. This is important because smaller audiences pay closer attention. When a group is small, the speaker can easily maintain eye contact and hold people's attention. The larger the audience, the easier it is for listeners to feel anonymous and to drift off, so a speaker has to offer more entertainment value. With large convention-sized audiences of hundreds, or even thousands of people, this is essential: bring in audiovisual support whenever you can; add stories and humor. Keep it moving, and keep it short, or you'll lose them.

To the extent that it's possible, speechwriters also want to know the age range of the audience. Will it be a group of seniors, or young professionals, or students—or a mixed group? This affects the kinds of stories, humor, and other support material we will choose to make the speaker's points. Because so much of humor comes out of life experience, the jokes Grandma enjoys may fall completely flat with your teenage son. If your audience includes a wide range of ages, you need to find humor that has a very broad appeal.

This is also true for any examples from history. A number of years ago, a friend of mine was once asked to speak to a church youth group on the subject of war and whether or not it is ever justified. He started by telling about how he had felt, as a senior in college at the height of the Vietnam War, when his draft notice arrived in the mail. A young man in the group interrupted him to say, "Oh, yeah, Vietnam. We read about that in history last week."

My friend was barely 30 at the time, and he said he had never felt so old in all his life! But it was an important lesson for him as a speaker: never assume that your audience shares your experience or knowledge of history, and be sure to give your illustrations the historical context they need—especially if you are speaking to a younger audience.

Speechwriters also want to know what the gender mix of an audience will be. Will there be more men than women, or vice versa? Again, this information affects the kinds of illustrations we choose. One of my clients, a product sales manager at Citibank, recently gave a speech to pump up a group of brokers who were being asked to meet some new revenue goals. We used a story featuring the retired Notre Dame coach Lou Holtz. The story ends with a great one-liner about a quarterback who runs 85 yards to score a winning goal. The speaker delivered it beautifully, and he got a big laugh—the vast majority of his listeners were men. It was perfect for that group, but if the audience had been more mixed, I probably would have used something different.

For the speech I'm delivering to you, I actually had to think twice about my food image. At first I thought the comparison might be a little too domestic for an audience of professional women. But after giving it some thought, I decided that since so many of the world's great chefs are men, and since we all have to eat, this image can work for both male and female audiences. My point is that it was important for me to go through the process of thinking about the gender of this audience and how that could affect the way you receive my ideas....

So ... know who's coming to the party.

Second, use only the best ingredients. When I give a dinner party, I like to experiment with recipes that have an exotic twist—like a special ingredient I can't get down the street—maybe something I'll only find at Balducci's [gourmet food store] or the green market. The shopping is fun and interesting, and the new ingredient gives a special flavor to the whole meal.

The same is true with researching a speech. It's fun because I'm always learning something new. I have learned that it's worth going out of my way to find a little known fact or two that can help make the speech memorable. A National Geographic Society executive was once asked to accept an award on behalf of the Society from the Leukemia Society of America. In researching his remarks, I learned about a small periwinkle that grows in the tropical rainforest. This little flower is the source of the medication that saves the lives of 95 percent of the children who contract childhood leukemia. With that fact, the speaker was able to relate National Geographic's interest in saving the environment to the life-saving work of the Leukemia Society. The extra effort it took to find that little tidbit of information was really worth it.

Once you have the information you need for a speech, spice it up! A speech-writing guide called *American Speaker* points out that "Good quotes in a speech, like good seasoning in a stew, are meant to add zest without detracting from the essential nature of the dish and its basic ingredients." That's true not only of quotes, but of anecdotes and humor as well. These elements must add something to the speech, not detract from it. I think most audiences are impatient with speakers who start out with a belly laugh, then take off in an entirely different direction.

Not only is this annoying, but what a waste of a good story! The whole reason for telling stories in your speech is to help people pay closer attention and remember your ideas. So make sure your illustrations relate to your message, and make the connection clear for the audience....,

Your audience will enjoy the story, but more than that, they'll enjoy the way you use it to reinforce your message.

So ... know who's coming to the party, use only the best ingredients, and third, focus on the main course. Every great meal has a great main course, a piece de resistance. And every successful speech has a main focus, a central idea that listeners can take home. This is the concept that pulls the whole speech together and helps your audience remember your supporting points....

At the beginning of the speechwriting process, many speakers aren't sure how to focus their messages. At this stage, it's important to ask, "If your audience remembered only one thing, what would you want it to be?" The answer is often a range of choices....

Having a focus not only helps tie the speech together, it helps answer what I consider to be the most important question in speechwriting: "What should I leave out?" Usually the answer is, "Much—even most of the material I've found." If the idea or example doesn't support your main point in some way, drop it, no matter how fascinating it is. Save it for another speech.

This will help you keep the speech to 20 minutes or so. That's important, because most audiences begin losing concentration after that amount of time. If you're asked to speak for longer than that, find ways to break it up, perhaps with Q&A, slides, a video, or some kind of interactive exercise. Remember: a speech is like a meal. We can only eat so much at one sitting, and we can only hear so much at one sitting. Mark Twain said that few sinners are saved after the first 20 minutes of a sermon. That's true of just about any oral presentation. So keep it short.

Then you can think of the Q&A as a kind of dessert. Leave room for it, and time. You don't want your listeners to feel like that grand old lady who died during dinner. She was the sister of an 18th century French writer named Brillat-Savarin, and she expired at the table one night just before her 100th birthday. Her last words were, "Bring on the dessert. I think I'm about to die."

— excerpted from "Speeches That Satisfy"
Executive Speeches, June/July 1997

Notes

Multiple-Choice Questions

Directions (1–6): Use your notes to answer the following questions about the passage read to you. Select the best suggested answer and write its number in the space provided. The questions may help you think about ideas and information you might use in your writing. You may return to these questions anytime you wish.

1 According to the speaker, keeping listeners' attention is more difficult with a large audience than with a small audience because people in large groups

  (1) feel pressured by peers
  (2) feel unnoticed
  (3) cannot hear the speaker clearly
  (4) cannot see the speaker   1 _____

2 According to the speaker, knowing the age range of the audience would be helpful to a speechwriter in

  (1) selecting support materials
  (2) finding a topic
  (3) choosing a setting
  (4) predicting the number of participants   2 _____

3 The speaker expresses concern about the use of the "food image" to illustrate the importance of choosing stories according to an audience's

  (1) size   (3) gender
  (2) location   (4) age   3 _____

4 As an example of her advice to speechwriters to "use only the best ingredients," the speaker recommends that speeches include

  (1) sophisticated vocabulary
  (2) an unusual fact
  (3) foreign phrases
  (4) a generally accepted theory   4 _____

5 According to the speaker, the speechwriter's main purpose in using appealing quotations and stories is to

  (1) add historical accuracy
  (2) provide comic relief
  (3) improve the speaker's credibility
  (4) help the audience remember ideas   5 _____

6 By asking the question, "If your audience remembered only one thing, what would you want it to be?" a speechwriter can establish

  (1) an intriguing opening
  (2) a strong ending
  (3) a main idea
  (4) an organizing principle   6 _____

After you have finished these questions, review **The Situation** and read **Your Task** and the **Guidelines**. Use scrap paper to plan your response. Then write your response on separate sheets of paper. After you finish your response for Part A, complete Part B.

Part B

Directions: Read the text and study the graphic on the following pages, answer the multiple-choice questions, and write a response based on the situation described below. You may use the margins to take notes as you read and scrap paper to plan your response.

> **The Situation:** As part of a social studies unit on contemporary issues, your class is preparing a panel discussion on the topic "Forest fires: What are the best ways to deal with them?" In preparing for the panel discussion, your teacher has asked you to write an essay in which you discuss the practices that lead to forest fires and recommend ways to deal with forest fires.

Your Task: Using relevant information from *both* documents, write an essay in which you discuss the practices that lead to forest fires and recommend ways to deal with forest fires.

Guidelines:
Be sure to
- Tell your audience what they need to know about forest fires and the practices that lead to forest fires
- Recommend ways to deal with forest fires
- Use specific, accurate, and relevant information from the text *and* the graphic to support your discussion
- Use a tone and level of language appropriate for an essay for your social studies class
- Organize your ideas in a logical and coherent manner
- Indicate any words taken directly from the text by using quotation marks or referring to the author
- Follow the conventions of standard written English

Text

Ninety years ago today, in the choking heat of a summer without rain in the northern Rockies, the sun disappeared from the sky and a sound not unlike cannon fire began rattling throughout Montana and Idaho. The Big Burn, as the three-million-acre firestorm of 1910 was called, eventually consumed entire
(5)   towns, killed 87 people and burned a lesson into the fledgling United States Forest Service.

Thereafter, the service vowed, it would snuff out every fire, at one point swearing to do so by 10 a.m. on the day after the fire started. The best-known forester of that time, Gifford Pinchot, equated wildfire with slavery as a historic
(10) scourge of the nation. Another, Bernhard Fernow, blamed "bad habits and loose morals" for the fires.

Now, in the midst of the worst wildfire year in nearly half a century, a new round of finger-pointing is under way. Touring Montana last week, J. Dennis Hastert, the speaker of the House, blamed the Clinton administration for not
(15) logging the tinder-dry forests. Environmentalists pointed at the timber industry and development for altering forest ecology and creating an artificial landscape ripe for catastrophe.

But the Forest Service remains focused on its own primary culprit: the symbol of fire eradication, Smokey Bear.

(20) The era of prevention and suppression represented by Smokey and his shovel may have been good for safety, but it was not the best thing for forests. The agency had reached that conclusion even before the additional evidence foresters drew from the fires that tore through almost half of Yellowstone National Park in 1988.

(25) Fire is as much a part of nature as creeks and wildflowers. Most forests have a natural cycle, in which a purging burn comes through every 10, 20, 50 or 100 years. The cycle may be suppressed, foresters say, but only at the cost of more powerful fires when it re-emerges.

"We have a problem when people say these fires are destroying all these areas,"
(30) said Mr. Wiebe, the former Smokejumper. "It's just not correct to say a forest is destroyed by fire."

During the decades when fires were routinely suppressed, forests choked themselves with excess growth, creating better habitats for tree-killing insects. The dying trees became tinder.

(35)   "These forests are long overdue," said Mick Harrington, a research fire ecologist with the Forest Service in Montana, a state that has just been declared a disaster area. "They were just ready to go."

The fires that have already run through five million acres this year are hotter, faster-burning, more ferocious than any burns of modern times, the people *(40)* battling them say. And a number of reports say future fire seasons may be worse, identifying about 40 million acres of public land as being at risk of catastrophic fire.

Fire suppression is only part of the problem. In some forests, experts say, logging has removed the biggest and most fire-resistant trees. Their replacements *(45)* —some planted, some natural—are crowded stands of young and disease-prone trees, with 500 or more to the acre, where there used to be 50. Foresters also point to other elements—excessive grazing by cattle and sheep, diversion of rivers to newly developing areas—that have contributed to what some call ghost forests, spectral stands of diseased and dying timber now baking, if not yet *(50)* burning, in the August sun.

In addition, there are many new areas demanding fire protection. Homes and vacation cottages that have sprung up at the edge of national forest boundaries have become firefighters' front lines.

"We've become so good at putting out fires because that's what the public *(55)* wants," said Lindon Wiebe, a fire ecology specialist with the Forest Service in Washington, and a former Smokejumper, as the service's firefighters are called. "But what we can do is pretty small compared to what Mother Nature wants to do."

Just as people have gradually learned not to build homes in areas prone to *(60)* flooding, they need to understand the danger of erecting structures in fire zones, says Dr. Phil Omi, a professor of forest fire science at Colorado State University and director of the Western Forest Fire Research Center.

"Somebody has got to get the message to these people that they are putting themselves at risk, whether it's the insurance industry or the government," Dr. *(65)* Omi said. But he said he could not blame the Forest Service, or homeowners, for being slow to understand the nature of wild fire in the West. "Our understanding of forest fire ecology is relatively new," he said.

Those trying to address the future fire threat are focusing on two solutions: taking out more trees by logging or thinning, and deliberately setting fires.

(70)   Under Mr. Clinton, logging in national forests has declined by nearly 75 percent, and some critics blame this decline for the explosive fires. A number of Western senators back the idea of allowing the timber industry to remove more trees.

(75)   However, environmental groups point out that the biggest fires in Montana and Idaho are burning not in wilderness areas, but in land that has been developed or logged. Such areas also account for 90 percent of the acreage identified as most vulnerable to wildfire, the Forest Service says.

     "Commercial logging is not a prescription for forest health—it is one of the major causes of unhealthy forest conditions," said Thomas Powers, chairman of *(80)* the economics department at the University of Montana, whose specialty is natural resource issues.

     The other solution—planned fire—has become a public relations debacle. Last year, a record 1.4 million acres of Forest Service land was deliberately burned. Most prescribed burns go off without trouble. But it only takes one to stir *(85)* public ire. And this year, the one that got away, a 43,000-acre blaze set by the National Park Service near Los Alamos, N.M., destroyed more than 200 homes.

     And no matter how convinced the experts are that Los Alamos was an exception, the fires now raging in every state of the West look horrific on television, blackening national treasures like Mesa Verde National Park and *(90)* raining embers on popular campgrounds.

—Timothy Egan
"Why Foresters Prefer to Fight Fire with Fire"
The New York Times, August 20, 2000

Common Practices Contributing to Forest Fires

Hazardous Homes

Building a home in or near the edge of forest land brings the risk of fire, but many homeowners and builders fail to take simple precautions that could reduce damage.

Logging and Clear-Cutting

In many areas, logging removed the oldest, most fire-resistant trees. The smaller, denser tree stands that grew in their absence burn more easily. Logging can also leave behind debris that acts as kindling for wildfires.

Water Diversion

Diverting the natural waterways to serve growing communities can also change the ecology of surrounding forests, leaving them dry and undernourished. Also, rivers that once served as natural barriers to fast-moving wildfires have been narrowed, enabling flames to leap to neighboring groups of trees easily.

Fire Suppression

Development in general led to a consistent policy of stifling fires, but this inhibited the natural process of burning and allowed stands of fire-prone trees to grow.

Grazing

The growth of cattle raising throughout the 19th and 20th centuries reduced grasslands, which fuel natural forest fires and keep the flames low to the ground.

Sources: National Forest Service; Great Lakes Forest Fire Compact; and Tom Zeller and John Papasian / *The New York Times* (adapted and taken from a larger set of graphics that accompanied the article)

Roofing

Metal, tile and fiberglass are best; common materials like asphalt shingles and tar paper are more flammable.

Outer Walls

Although it seems natural to build a forest home of wood, the danger is obvious. Stone, brick and metal are best.

Air Pockets

An open foundation and raised decks can stoke flames as they pass through. Storing fuel tanks in these areas is particularly dangerous.

Building on Slopes

Although a hillside may offer the best views, slopes create a natural chimney for advancing flames.

Multiple-Choice Questions

Directions (7–16): Select the best suggested answer to each question and write its number in the space provided. The questions may help you think about ideas and information you might want to use in your writing. You may return to these questions anytime you wish.

7 According to the author, one result of the Big Burn in 1910 was that the Forest Service adopted a policy of

  (1) gradually removing dead trees from dry areas
  (2) quickly extinguishing all fires
  (3) routinely setting small, controlled fires
  (4) occasionally thinning out healthy trees   7 _____

8 As used in line 26, "purging" most nearly means

  (1) cleansing   (3) alarming
  (2) damaging   (4) frightening   8 _____

9 In saying that it is "not correct to say a forest is destroyed by fire" (lines 30 and 31), Mr. Wiebe implies that

  (1) most fires could be prevented
  (2) fire is less destructive than smoke
  (3) few forest animals are harmed by fire
  (4) some fires should be allowed to burn   9 _____

10 The author implies that one result of the practice of suppressing forest fires is that, eventually,

  (1) trees become more resistant to fire
  (2) the public loses interest in fire prevention
  (3) forest fires do more damage
  (4) more fires occur outside of forests   10 _____

11 Lindon Wiebe's comment that "what we can do is pretty small compared to what Mother Nature wants to do" (lines 57 and 58) emphasizes the capacity of nature to

(1) inspire   (3) confuse

(2) adapt   (4) destroy   11 _____

12 What question is at the center of the disagreement about logging?

(1) How can logging national forests be made less difficult?

(2) How can data about logging and forests be made more reliable?

(3) What is the effect of logging on the health of forests?

(4) Who should pay for the logging of the national forests?   12 _____

13 The author implies that the primary purpose of prescribed burns is to

(1) remove excess growth

(2) train firefighters

(3) educate the public

(4) research forest ecology   13 _____

14 The irrigation system shown at the right of the graphic is an illustration of what practice?

(1) removing the oldest trees

(2) diverting natural waterways

(3) stifling fires

(4) raising cattle   14 _____

15 According to the graphic, houses in forests can be made somewhat safer if builders

    (1) cover roofs with asphalt shingles
    (2) use small logs for outer walls
    (3) enclose areas under the houses
    (4) situate houses on slopes   15 _____

16 All of the practices on the graphic are closely related to

    (1) slowing economy
    (2) changing climate
    (3) decreasing population
    (4) increasing development   16 _____

After you have finished these questions, review **The Situation** and read **Your Task** and the **Guidelines**. Use scrap paper to plan your response. Then write your response to Part B on separate sheets of paper.

Session Two

Part A

Directions: Read the passages on the following pages (a poem and an essay). Write the number of the answer to each multiple-choice question in the space provided. Then write the essay on separate sheets of paper as described in **Your Task**. You may use the margins to take notes as you read and scrap paper to plan your response.

Your Task:

> After you have read the passages and answered the multiple-choice questions, write a unified essay about lessons from childhood as revealed in the passages. In your essay, use ideas from **both** passages to establish a controlling idea about lessons from childhood. Using evidence from **each** passage, develop your controlling idea and show how the author uses specific literary elements or techniques to convey that idea.

Guidelines:
Be sure to
- Use ideas from **both** passages to establish a controlling idea about lessons from childhood
- Use specific and relevant evidence from **each** passage to develop your controlling idea
- Show how each author uses specific literary elements (for example: theme, characterization, structure, point of view) or techniques (for example: symbolism, irony, figurative language) to convey the controlling idea
- Organize your ideas in a logical and coherent manner
- Use language that communicates ideas effectively
- Follow the conventions of standard written English

Passage I

The Thing You Must Remember

The thing you must remember is how, as a child,
you worked hours in the art room, the teacher's
hands over yours, molding the little clay dog.
You must remember, how nothing mattered
(5)   but the imagined dog's fur, the shape of his ears
and his paws. The gray clay felt dangerous,
your small hands were pressing what you couldn't
say with your limited words. When the dog's back
stiffened, then cracked to white shards
(10)   in the kiln, you learned how the beautiful
suffers from too much attention, how clumsy
a single vision can grow, and fragile
with trying too hard. The thing you must
remember is the art teacher's capable
(15)   hands: large, rough and grainy,
over yours, holding on.

— Maggie Anderson
from *Windfall*, 2000
University of Pittsburgh Press

Passage II

She was only about five feet tall and probably never weighed more than 110 pounds, but Miss Bessie was a towering presence in the classroom. She was the only woman tough enough to make me read *Beowulf* and think for a few foolish days that I liked it. From 1938 to 1942, when I attended Bernard High School in
(5) McMinnville, Tenn., she taught me English, history, civics—and a lot more than I realized.

I shall never forget the day she scolded me into reading *Beowulf*.

"But Miss Bessie," I complained, "I ain't much interested in it."

Her large brown eyes became daggerish slits. "Boy," she said, "how dare you
(10) say 'ain't' to me! I've taught you better than that."

"Miss Bessie," I pleaded, "I'm trying to make first-string end on the football team, and if I go around saying 'it isn't' and 'they aren't,' the guys are gonna laugh me off the squad."

"Boy," she responded, "you'll play football because you have guts. But do you
(15) know what *really* takes guts? Refusing to lower your standards to those of the crowd. It takes guts to say you've got to live and be somebody fifty years after all the football games are over."

I started saying "it isn't" and "they aren't," and I still made first-string end— and class valedictorian—without losing my buddies' respect.

(20) During her remarkable 44-year career, Mrs. Bessie Taylor Gwynn taught hundreds of economically deprived black youngsters—including my mother, my brother, my sisters and me. I remember her now with gratitude and affection— especially in this era when Americans are so wrought-up about a "rising tide of mediocrity" in public education and the problems of finding competent, caring
(25) teachers. Miss Bessie was an example of an informed, dedicated teacher, a blessing to children and an asset to the nation.

Born in 1895, in poverty, she grew up in Athens, Ala., where there was no public school for blacks. She attended Trinity School, a private institution for blacks run by the American Missionary Association, and in 1911 graduated from
(30) the Normal School (a "super" high school) at Fisk University in Nashville. Mrs. Gwynn, the essence of pride and privacy, never talked about her years in Athens; only in the months before her death did she reveal that she had never attended Fisk University itself because she could not afford the four-year course.

At Normal School she learned a lot about Shakespeare, but most of all about
(35) the profound importance of education—especially, for a people trying to move up
from slavery. "What you put in your head, boy," she once said, "can never be
pulled out by the Ku Klux Klan, the Congress or anybody."

Miss Bessie's bearing of dignity told anyone who met her that she was
"educated" in the best sense of the word. There was never a discipline problem
(40) in her classes. We didn't dare mess with a woman who knew about the Battle of
Hastings, the Magna Charta and the Bill of Rights—and who could also play the
piano.

This frail-looking woman could make sense of Shakespeare, Milton, Voltaire,
and bring to life Booker T. Washington and W. E. B. DuBois. Believing that it was
(45) important to know who the officials were that spent taxpayers' money and made
public policy, she made us memorize the names of everyone on the Supreme
Court and in the President's Cabinet. It could be embarrassing to be unprepared
when Miss Bessie said, "Get up and tell the class who Frances Perkins is and what
you think about her."

(50)   Miss Bessie knew that my family, like so many others during the Depression,
couldn't afford to subscribe to a newspaper. She knew we didn't even own a radio.
Still, she prodded me to "look out for your future and find some way to keep up
with what's going on in the world." So I became a delivery boy for the
Chattanooga *Times*. I rarely made a dollar a week, but I got to read a newspaper
(55) every day.

Miss Bessie noticed things that had nothing to do with schoolwork, but were
vital to a youngster's development. Once a few classmates made fun of my frayed,
hand-me-down overcoat, calling me "Strings." As I was leaving school, Miss
Bessie patted me on the back of that old overcoat and said, "Carl, never fret about
(60) what you *don't* have. Just make the most of what you *do* have—a brain."

Among the things that I did not have was electricity in the little frame house
that my father had built for $400 with his World War I bonus. But because of her
inspiration, I spent many hours squinting beside a kerosene lamp reading
Shakespeare and Thoreau, Samuel Pepys and William Cullen Bryant.

(65)   No one in my family had ever graduated from high school, so there was no
tradition of commitment to learning for me to lean on. Like millions of youngsters
in today's ghettos and barrios, I needed the push and stimulation of a teacher who
truly cared. Miss Bessie gave plenty of both, as she immersed me in a wonderful
world of similes, metaphors and even onomatopoeia. She led me to believe that I
(70) could write sonnets as well as Shakespeare, or iambic-pentameter verse to put
Alexander Pope to shame.

In those days the McMinnville school system was rigidly "Jim Crow," and poor black children had to struggle to put anything in their heads. Our high school was only slightly larger than the once-typical little red schoolhouse, and its library was (75) outrageously inadequate—so small, I like to say, that if two students were in it and one wanted to turn a page, the other one had to step outside.

Negroes, as we were called then, were not allowed in the town library, except to mop floors or dust tables. But through one of those secret Old South arrangements between whites of conscience and blacks of stature, Miss Bessie (80) kept getting books smuggled out of the white library. That is how she introduced me to the Brontës, Byron, Coleridge, Keats and Tennyson. "If you don't read, you can't write, and if you can't write, you might as well stop dreaming," Miss Bessie once told me.

So I read whatever Miss Bessie told me to, and tried to remember the things (85) she insisted that I store away. Forty-five years later, I can still recite her "truths to live by," such as Henry Wadsworth Longfellow's lines from "The Ladder of St. Augustine":

The heights by great men reached and kept
Were not attained by sudden flight,
(90)   But they, while their companions slept,
Were toiling upward in the night.

Years later, her inspiration, prodding, anger, cajoling and almost osmotic infusion of learning finally led to that lovely day when Miss Bessie dropped me a note saying, "I'm so proud to read your column in the Nashville *Tennessean*."

(95)   Miss Bessie was a spry 80 when I went back to McMinnville and visited her in a senior citizens' apartment building. Pointing out proudly that her building was racially integrated, she reached for two glasses and a pint of bourbon. I was momentarily shocked, because it would have been scandalous in the 1930s and '40s for word to get out that a teacher drank, and nobody had ever raised a rumor (100) that Miss Bessie did.

I felt a new sense of equality as she lifted her glass to mine. Then she revealed a softness and compassion that I had never known as a student.

"I've never forgotten that examination day," she said, "when Buster Martin held up seven fingers, obviously asking you for help with question number seven, (105) 'Name a common carrier.' I can still picture you looking at your exam paper and humming a few bars of 'Chattanooga Choo Choo.' I was so tickled, I couldn't punish either of you."

Miss Bessie was telling me, with bourbon-laced grace, that I never fooled her for a moment.

(110) When Miss Bessie died in 1980, at age 85, hundreds of her former students mourned. They knew the measure of a great teacher: love and motivation. Her wisdom and influence had rippled out across generations.

Some of her students who might normally have been doomed to poverty went on to become doctors, dentists and college professors. Many, guided by Miss *(115)* Bessie's example, became public-school teachers.

"The memory of Miss Bessie and how she conducted her classroom did more for me than anything I learned in college," recalls Gladys Wood of Knoxville, Tenn., a highly respected English teacher who spent 43 years in the state's school system. "So many times, when I faced a difficult classroom problem, I asked *(120)* myself, *How would Miss Bessie deal with this?* And I'd remember that she would handle it with laughter and love."

No child can get all the necessary support at home, and millions of poor children get *no* support at all. That is what makes a wise, educated, warm-hearted teacher like Miss Bessie so vital to the minds, hearts and souls of this country's *(125)* children.

—Carl T. Rowan
"Unforgettable Miss Bessie"
from *Readers Digest*, March 1985

Multiple-Choice Questions

Directions (1–10): Select the best suggested answer to each question and write its number in the space provided. The questions may help you think about the ideas and information you might want to use in your essay. You may return to these questions anytime you wish.

Passage I (the poem)—Questions 1–5 refer to Passage I.

1 In line 4, the words "how nothing mattered" help to emphasize the child's

(1) fear   (3) indifference

(2) memory   (4) concentration   1 _____

2 The description in lines 6 through 8 conveys the child's feeling of

(1) anxiety   (3) importance

(2) control   (4) resentment   2 _____

3 According to the poem, what is most likely the "thing you must remember"?

(1) the broken dog

(2) the hard work

(3) the teacher's support

(4) the clay's texture   3 _____

4 The tone of the poem is best described as

(1) bitter   (3) ironic

(2) reflective   (4) lively   4 _____

5 What aspect of the poet's craft suggests that the child and the speaker are the same person?

(1) the narrative point of view

(2) the simple words

(3) the blank verse

(4) the irregular line lengths   5 _____

Passage II (the essay)—Questions 6–10 refer to Passage II.

6 Miss Bessie's remarks about learning correct grammar
(lines 7 through 17) stress the importance of

(1) participating in sports
(2) avoiding peer pressure
(3) reading classical literature
(4) enforcing team spirit   6 _____

7 In lines 44 through 55, the author's references to
memorization and reading the newspaper serve to
emphasize Miss Bessie's desire that her students be

(1) financially independent
(2) socially adept
(3) emotionally stable
(4) politically aware   7 _____

8 The author's references to the world of poetry (lines
66 through 71) have the effect of stressing Miss
Bessie's power to

(1) instill confidence
(2) encourage dependence
(3) predict events
(4) discourage imitation   8 _____

9 Miss Bessie most likely recommended that her
students remember Longfellow's verse to illustrate
the value of

(1) spiritual discipline   (3) hard work
(2) regular rest   (4) heroic behavior   9 _____

10 The author most likely includes the quotation from
   Gladys Wood (lines 119 through 121) to emphasize
   the extent of

   (1) the author's grief
   (2) Miss Bessie's influence
   (3) the student's disobedience
   (4) Gladys Wood's success   10 _____

After you have finished these questions, review **Your
Task** and the **Guidelines**. Use scrap paper to plan
your response. Then write your response to Part A on
separate sheets of paper. After you finish your
response for Part A, complete Part B.

Part B

Your Task:

Write a critical essay in which you discuss *two* works of literature you have read from the particular perspective of the statement that is provided for you in the **Critical Lens**. In your essay, provide a valid interpretation of the statement, agree *or* disagree with the statement as you have interpreted it, and support your opinion using specific references to appropriate literary elements from the two works. You may use scrap paper to plan your response. Write your essay in Part B on separate sheets of paper.

Critical Lens:

> "Good people ... are good because they've come to wisdom through failure."
>
> —William Saroyan as quoted in
> "Room for Hate —and Hope"
> from *New York Journal-American*,
> August 23, 1961

Guidelines:

Be sure to

- Provide a valid interpretation of the critical lens that clearly establishes the criteria for analysis
- Indicate whether you agree *or* disagree with the statement as you have interpreted it
- Choose *two* works you have read that you believe best support your opinion
- Use the criteria suggested by the critical lens to analyze the works you have chosen
- Avoid plot summary. Instead, use specific references to appropriate literary elements (for example: theme, characterization, setting, point of view) to develop your analysis
- Organize your ideas in a unified and coherent manner
- Specify the titles and authors of the literature you choose
- Follow the conventions of standard written English

Regents Comprehensive Examination in English—June 2003
Chart for Determining the Final Examination Score (Use for June 2003 examination only.)

To determine the student's final examination score, locate the student's total essay score across the top of the chart and the student's total multiple-choice score down the side of the chart. The point where those two scores intersect is the student's final examination score. For example, a student receiving a total essay score of 19 and a total multiple-choice score of 23 would receive a final examination score of 87.

Total Multiple-Choice Score ↓ \ Total Essay Score →	0	1	2	3	4	5	6	7	8	9	10	11	12	13	14	15	16	17	18	19	20	21	22	23	24
0	0	1	2	3	4	6	8	10	12	15	18	21	24	27	31	34	38	41	45	48	52	56	60	63	67
1	1	2	3	4	5	7	9	11	14	16	19	22	25	29	32	36	39	43	47	50	54	58	61	65	69
2	1	3	3	4	6	8	10	12	15	18	21	24	27	31	34	38	41	45	48	52	56	60	63	67	70
3	2	3	4	5	7	9	11	14	16	19	22	25	29	32	36	39	43	47	50	54	58	61	65	69	72
4	2	3	4	6	8	10	12	15	18	21	24	27	31	34	38	41	45	48	52	56	60	63	67	70	74
5	3	4	5	7	9	11	14	16	19	22	25	29	32	36	39	43	47	50	54	58	61	65	69	72	75
6	3	4	6	8	10	12	15	18	21	24	27	31	34	38	41	45	48	52	56	60	63	67	70	74	77
7	4	5	7	9	11	14	16	19	22	25	29	32	36	39	43	47	50	54	58	61	65	69	72	75	79
8	4	6	8	10	12	15	18	21	24	27	31	34	38	41	45	48	52	56	60	63	67	70	74	77	80
9	5	7	9	11	14	16	19	22	25	29	32	36	39	43	47	50	54	58	61	65	69	72	75	79	82
10	6	8	10	12	15	18	21	24	27	31	34	38	41	45	48	52	56	60	63	67	70	74	77	80	83
11	7	9	11	14	16	19	22	25	29	32	36	39	43	47	50	54	58	61	65	69	72	75	79	82	85
12	8	10	12	15	18	21	24	27	31	34	38	41	45	48	52	56	60	63	67	70	74	77	80	83	86
13	9	11	14	16	19	22	25	29	32	36	39	43	47	50	54	58	61	65	69	72	75	79	82	85	87
14	11	13	15	18	21	24	27	31	34	38	41	45	48	52	56	60	63	67	70	74	77	80	83	86	89
15	12	14	16	19	22	25	29	32	36	39	43	47	50	54	58	61	65	69	72	75	79	82	85	87	90
16	14	16	18	21	24	27	31	34	38	41	45	48	52	56	60	63	67	70	74	77	80	83	86	89	91
17	16	18	19	22	25	29	32	36	39	43	47	50	54	58	61	65	69	72	75	79	82	85	87	90	92
18	18	19	21	24	27	31	34	38	41	45	48	52	56	60	63	67	70	74	77	80	83	86	89	91	93
19	19	21	22	25	29	32	36	39	43	47	50	54	58	61	65	69	72	75	79	82	85	87	90	92	94
20	21	22	24	27	31	34	38	41	45	48	52	56	60	63	67	70	74	77	80	83	86	89	91	93	95
21	22	24	25	29	32	36	39	43	47	50	54	58	61	65	69	72	75	79	82	85	87	90	92	94	96
22	24	25	27	31	34	38	41	45	48	52	56	60	63	67	70	74	77	80	83	86	89	91	93	95	97
23	25	27	29	32	36	39	43	47	50	54	58	61	65	69	72	75	79	82	85	87	90	92	94	96	98
24	27	29	31	34	38	41	45	48	52	56	60	63	67	70	74	77	80	83	86	89	91	93	95	97	99
25	29	31	32	36	39	43	47	50	54	58	61	65	69	72	75	79	82	85	87	90	92	94	96	98	99
26	31	32	34	38	41	45	48	52	56	60	63	67	70	74	77	80	83	86	89	91	93	95	97	99	100

Answers
June 2003
English

Answer Key

Session One, Part A	Session One, Part B	Session Two, Part A
1. 2	7. 2	1. 4
2. 1	8. 1	2. 1
3. 3	9. 4	3. 3
4. 2	10. 3	4. 2
5. 4	11. 4	5. 1
6. 3	12. 3	6. 2
	13. 1	7. 4
	14. 2	8. 1
	15. 3	9. 3
	16. 4	10. 2

Answers Explained

Session One

Part A   (1–6)

Note: Refer to Chapter 1 for review and strategy in responding to this part of the examination.

(1) **2** "feel unnoticed." One of the first examples of what the successful speechwriter needs to know is the size of the audience. She says, "The larger the audience, the easier it is for listeners to feel <u>anonymous</u> and to drift off. . . ." The key is in the term "anonymous," and the other choices are not offered as reasons for lack of audience interest.

(2) **1** "selecting support materials." The speaker explains that knowing the age range of the audience "affects the kinds of stories, humor, and other support material we will choose. . . ."

(3) **3** "gender." In explaining why she chose the image of food for this speech, the speaker says that "it was important for me to go through the process of thinking about the gender of this audience. . . ." She makes no reference to the other choices in this part of the speech.

(4) **2** "an unusual fact." In explaining why she enjoys researching a speech the speaker says that, "I have learned that . . . to find a little known fact or two . . . can help make the speech memorable. . . ."

(5) **4** "help the audience remember ideas." "The whole reason for telling stories in your speech is to help people pay closer attention and remember your ideas."

(6) **3** "a main idea." As she moves to the conclusion of her own speech, the speaker says, ". . . every successful speech has a main focus, a central idea that listeners can take home."

Part A   Sample Student Response Essay

Effective speechwriting involves several key points, or ingredients. A speech must be relevant, plausible, and memorable. To achieve this, a speech-writer must understand the audience and must have a central focus.

A speech becomes effective when your audience takes away key information and the ideas you have expressed in your speech. Jane Tully, a professional speechwriter, suggests three key pieces of information a speaker should have in order to write an effective speech. First, know who will be hearing your speech. This includes the audience's general age, gender, and size. For example, a smaller audience tends to pay more attention to the speaker because it does not feel anonymous or unnoticed. For large audiences, Tully suggests the need for entertainment elements, such as stories or audiovisuals. The age range of an audience will assist you in selecting support materials, especially stories, that will appeal to the audience directly. Your supporting materials should also be chosen in consideration of the gender of the audience. Telling a story that involves sports may not necessarily appeal to an audience of mostly women. Likewise, a story based on cooking may not normally appeal to men. Choose your content with age and gender in mind.

When considering a story that relates to the age and gender of your audience, also keep in mind that your story or anecdote is better received by the audience if it relates to your message. Find a story that is humorous and at the same time relevant. In many cases, a little known fact makes an entire speech memorable. The extra effort to find such materials can add zest to your speech and generate a positive response from the audience.

The third and final key suggestion that Jane Tully makes is to focus on your main idea, the one that you started out on. A successful speech maintains a consistent focus on your central idea or message. Unnecessary information can get in the way and cause the audience to lose interest. Aside from your anecdotes and illustrations, your main focus is what holds the speech together. Your goal is to have the audience take home your ideas. Keep this question in mind when you are preparing your speech: "If your audience remembered only one thing, what would you want it to be?" "Focusing on your main idea will help your audience remember that "one thing."

Tully suggests limiting a speech to about twenty minutes because most audiences begin to lose their concentration after that, and she suggests that you allow time for questions if possible. Tully concludes with advice that we can all appreciate: Keep it short.

Analysis

This writer has captured the key points of Tully's remarks and expressed them in a clear and well-organized essay. Tully's advice is well summarized, in language that is fluent and appropriate for the intended audience. The writer maintains his/her own focus, leading to an effective conclusion; the writer also demonstrates control of the conventions. Although the writer makes almost no use of Tully's analogy to giving a party and has misunderstood her comments on using the imagery of food, the essay would rate an overall high score for competence. (See pp. 31–35 for a detailed explanation of the rubric for this part of the examination.)

Part B   (7–16)

Note: Refer to Chapter 2 for review and strategy in responding to this part of the examination.

(7) **2** "quickly extinguishing all fires." The second paragraph of the text begins, "Thereafter, the service vowed, it would snuff out every fire. . . ."

(8) **1** "cleansing." In the section that begins with this paragraph (line 25), the article asserts that fires are part of a natural cycle to eliminate excess growth and underbrush. The examples that follow give context to the meaning of the term "purging," which is "cleansing," "eliminating," "purifying." This item is an example of how vocabulary is tested on the Regents exam.

(9) **4** "some fires should be allowed to burn." This and the previous paragraph stress the view that suppression of all fires creates conditions in which the fires that do ultimately occur are "hotter, faster-burning, [and] more ferocious. . . ."

(10) **3** "forest fires do more damage." See item 9 above.

(11) **4** "destroy." This passage concludes the development of the idea that fire is an essential, natural cycle. The illustrations also demonstrate that suppression of fires over time can lead to even more destructive ones when they occur.

(12) **3** "What is the effect of logging on the health of forests?" Beginning at line 70, arguments for and against more logging in national forests are presented. Some argue that the decline in logging has created conditions for more destructive fires, and others argue that the worst fires occur in areas that have been logged. Questions of difficulty, reliable data, and cost are not raised here.

(13) **1** "remove excess growth." One of the key points of the article is to show that excess growth is a major cause of destructive fires. At line 68, the author introduces discussion of two solutions to increased fire threat: thinning by logging and deliberately set fires, or "prescribed burns."

(14) **2** "diverting natural waterways." This part of the graphic is identified by the topic "Water Diversion," and the text develops that topic as well.

(15) **3** "enclose areas under the houses." The text enclosed in the circle at the bottom left of the graphic points out that asphalt shingles are more flammable, that stone or brick or metal are best as building materials, and that building on slopes creates a natural chimney for fires. Because open foundations and raised decks can "stoke flames," the reader should conclude that enclosing these areas can make these houses somewhat safer from fire.

(16) **4** "increasing development." There are no references to a slowing economy, to climate, nor to decreasing population in the graphic. The graphic offers examples of development in the building of houses, in logging, water diversion, and the growth of cattle raising.

Part B   Sample Student Response Essay

For those who grew up seeing posters of Smokey the Bear warning about the dangers of forest fires, the current controversies over how to deal with forest fires may be surprising. Nowadays, whenever a forest fire erupts, we see the devastation of land and homes on the evening television news. As a result, a majority of the American public still believes that forest fires should be suppressed whenever they erupt. This opinion, however, is uninformed. New knowledge about forest ecology has led to new and more complex views about forest fire prevention.

In 1910, fire destroyed three million acres of forest land in Montana and Idaho. Towns were destroyed and 87 people were killed. Shortly thereafter, the United States Forest Service vowed to extinguish any fire and to do so by 10 A.M. the following day. This new policy of immediate fire suppression became the American public's common conception of how to deal with forest fires. However, through experience, firefighters have come to realize that recent forest fires burn more intensely than others in the past. The Forest Service now understands that by suppressing all fires, they are also suppressing the natural, purging cycle of forest fires. Forests where natural fires are suppressed quickly rebound and create excess growth that chokes the forest. These conditions allow tree-killing insects to thrive, and those dead trees essentially become kindling for the next lightning strike. The resultant fire burns hotter and quicker than normal because of the earlier fire suppression in the area.

Another part of the problem of how to deal with forest fires involves logging. Some forest experts criticize logging companies for their practice of felling the strongest, most fire-resistant trees and replacing them with weak saplings, which are both disease- and fire-prone. Once again, these remaining trees become kindling for the next fire.

Other factors that contribute to more devastating forest fires are overgrazing and the diversion of rivers. The rapid growth of cattle raising during the 19th and 20th centuries reduced the natural grasslands; this loss of vegetation encouraged fires to burn high in the trees rather than low to the ground. The diversion of rivers to serve towns and agriculture also plays a part. Damming up of rivers can leave forests dry and sickly, making them prone to explosive fires that can also jump over dry riverbeds that once were natural fire breaks.

Increased development contributes to forest fires in other ways as well. People today may even build homes and cottages along the boundaries of national forests and parks, creating possible hazards and the expectation that fires must be fought to protect them.

We do not see universal agreement on the best ways to deal with forest fires. For some, limiting growth in previously wilderness areas is part of the solution; and it is felt that some fires should be permitted to burn as a natural cycle. The Forest Service uses controlled burns as a way to limit the destruction of greater fires, but if such a burn goes out of control and does great damage, the public then opposes the idea. Logging has also been touted as a way of thinning dangerous growth, but many conservationists see logging as a cause of fire and not as a means of prevention. As one prominent fire ecology specialist remarked, ". . . what we can do is pretty small compared to what Mother Nature wants to do."

Analysis

This is an exceptionally good response to the task. The essay reveals an in-depth analysis of the documents and is insightful in showing both the complexity of the problem and the unavoidable conclusion that increased development is a major cause of devastating forest fires. The writer makes excellent use of <u>both</u> documents (an important requirement in this section of the exam) and develops the ideas fully and clearly. The language is sophisticated as is the variety of sentence structure. Note too that the essay is well organized, with clear transitions and a very effective introduction; the concluding quote captures dramatically the key idea of the topic. This essay meets all the criteria for the highest score. (See pp. 48–53 for a detailed discussion of the rubric for this part of the examination.)

Session Two

Part A (1–10)

Note: See Chapter 3 for review and strategy in responding to this part of the examination.

(1) **4** "concentration." The image in this part of the poem is of the small child, working for hours, trying to shape the figure of a dog out of clay.

(2) **1** "anxiety." The key image here is that the "gray clay felt dangerous. . . ." The child is not confident that she can shape the clay as she wishes, and her words are limited. The poem does not suggest a sense of importance or resentment in the child.

(3) **3** "the teacher's support." The poem opens with the image of the "teacher's hands over yours"; the repetition of this image and the phrase "holding on" at the end emphasize the supporting presence of the teacher as what "you must remember."

(4) **2** "reflective." Reflective here means looking back with thought and understanding. That captures best the tone of the poem. The feeling of the poem is not "lively," and there is nothing to suggest bitterness or irony.

(5) **1** "the narrative point of view." The effect here is of the speaker addressing herself. The details are expressed with a vividness that comes from the speaker's own remembered experience; the poem captures what the speaker felt, not simply what she may have observed in another child.

(6) **2** "avoiding peer pressure." The key line in this passage is when Miss Bessie says that what "<u>really</u> takes guts" is "Refusing to lower your standards to those of the crowd."

(7) **4** "politically aware." Note that the examples of what Miss Bessie thought it important to know were the "officials . . . that spent taxpayers' money and made public policy." She expected her students to memorize the names of the members of the Supreme Court and the President's Cabinet. There is nothing to suggest that she felt it would make her students financially independent, socially aware, or more emotionally stable.

(8) **1** "instill confidence." Because Carl Rowan's family had no "tradition of commitment to learning," he needed the "push and stimulation of a teacher who truly cared." She also convinced him that he could write sonnets as well as Shakespeare!

(9) **3** "hard work." The image in the Longfellow verse is of great men who reach their heights by ". . . <u>toiling</u> upward in the night." Toil denotes constant effort and hard work.

(10) **2** "Miss Bessie's influence." Gladys Wood's comments reveal the extent to which she would think about how Miss Bessie would have responded to a difficult classroom situation. Wood also says that Miss Bessie's memory taught her more "than anything I learned in college."

Part A Sample Student Response Essay

Both the poem and the prose passage detail lessons learned in an academic setting, but neither is primarily about academic content. Both pieces reveal that the most valuable lessons from childhood are those that are still valued in maturity.

Written in poetic form but employing the language of everyday speech, "The Thing You Must Remember" recalls the experience of a young child in art class trying to shape a dog out of clay. The speaker reveals how, even for a child, the creation of art transcends language—"pressing what you couldn't say with your limited words." When the dog shatters in the heat of the kiln, the speaker "must remember" that the "beautiful suffers from too much attention" and that a single vision may grow clumsy "and fragile with trying too hard." What the poet most remembers is found in the opening and in the final image of the poem, the art teacher's "hands over yours." The most important lesson from the child's effort to make a clay dog was in feeling the guidance and reassurance of her teacher.

Passage II, in the form of personal narrative, recalls a teacher who had a profound influence on the experiences of a black youth in the preintegration

South. Though much of the passage details the academic expectations of the demanding "Miss Bessie," the passage reveals the more important life lessons she taught. Beginning with the initial vignette when Miss Bessie upbraids the reluctant scholar for using "ain't" and calling him "Boy," to the quote from Longfellow that represented her "truths to live by," we see how this "frail-looking woman" inspired and truly educated her students. Not only did Carl Rowan go on to become a nationally known journalist, but some of her other students who "might have been doomed to poverty" went on to professional careers of their own.

Miss Bessie taught Rowan to resist peer pressure and to be proud of his intelligence, especially when he feared it might keep him from being accepted as a football player. She also taught the importance of reading the newspaper and being an informed citizen by not only knowing who was on the Supreme Court and in the President's Cabinet, but also by cultivating opinions about those figures. Rowan's memoir reveals, however, that the most important things Miss Bessie taught came from her "inspiration, prodding . . . and infusion of learning" in a child whose family had no tradition of a commitment to learning.

In both the poem and the personal narrative, the writers are remembering teachers who gave them lessons that transcend skill, ordinary lessons, and tests. These teachers taught about confidence and gave inspiration.

Analysis

This response demonstrates insightful appreciation of the texts. The introduction establishes the controlling idea that "the most valuable lessons of childhood are those that are still valued in maturity." Relevant quotes from both passages support the development of ideas and give variety to the sentences. While the discussion of literary elements is not extensive, discussion of the poem in particular shows the writer's understanding of how imagery and point of view contribute to the common theme. The essay is also well organized, with the discussion leading in each section to the most important point or "lesson." The conclusion is effective because it reinforces the controlling idea and heightens our appreciation of what is common to the two passages. The language of the essay is appropriate and often very sophisticated. This essay meets the criteria for a high score. (See pp. 68–71 for a detailed discussion of the rubric for this part of the examination.)

Part B Sample Student Response Essay

Note: See Chapter 4 for review and strategy in responding to this part of the examination.

William Saroyan's assertion that "Good people . . . are good because they've come to wisdom through failure" may be interpreted to mean that a person who appears to be a failure but who gains knowledge of his own inadequacies, may redeem himself through a final act that leads to his being judged "good." Two such characters in literature are Willy Loman of Arthur Miller's Death of a Salesman *and Sydney Carton of Charles Dickens'* A Tale of Two Cities. *Both of these characters gain self-knowledge through a life of failure yet undertake what they hope will redeem their final acts to obtain "good ends."*

Willy Loman is truly a low man. However much he struggles to achieve his vision of success, he is a man barely making a living after a lifetime on the road as a salesman. As the play opens, we see a man who is exhausted by his life and no longer able to go on. Willy has always believed that personal magnetism, "being liked," is what makes a man successful, and he has taught this unfortunate lesson to his sons. Over the course of the play, Willy is forced to remember things from the past that reveal his failures in business and especially in the disappointing way his older son, Biff, turns out. In a gesture that he believes will redeem him, he kills himself by crashing his car, believing that the proceeds of his life insurance will finally give Biff the possibility of being "great." Willy's death is only sad and confusing for his family, but we can see it as a last effort to achieve something meaningful.

Sydney Carton is introduced early in A Tale of Two Cities *as a drunken lawyer who seems to have no interest in life and claims that he does not care about himself or others. Dickens allows us to see more into Carton when he saves Charles Darnay for the first time and as he discovers his feelings for Lucie Manette before she marries Darnay. Even though he still sees himself as unworthy, he does declare his love for Lucie and retains his admiration for her. Carton's redemption for an otherwise meaningless life comes at the end of the novel. In the violence of the French Revolution, Darnay has been imprisoned for trying to save his own servants and is going to be led to the guillotine. Carton has been introduced at the beginning of the novel as a man who looks very much like Charles Darnay, and in a brave and clever act, he manages to exchange places in the Bastille with Darnay. It is he who will be executed so that Lucie, Charles, and their family may live and be happy. In this act, Carton knows that this sacrifice is a "far better thing" than anything he has done in his life.*

The theme of self-knowledge achieved through a failure is evident in both works. Both Sydney Carton and Willy Loman die believing they have achieved something good at the end. Even though Willy's sacrifice may not have the result he wishes for, we understand his last desperate effort to be a good father. In Carton's sacrifice, we know that the "good end" he sought will be realized.

Analysis

Many students chose to disagree with the statement in the critical lens, but this essay is a very successful example of a controlling idea and discussion in support of Saroyan's assertion. The writer has chosen works in which the main character "sacrifices" his life to achieve good for others, and the essay offers an interpretation of the critical lens that is sophisticated and convincing. The discussion of each character is well developed; the language is precise and at an appropriately high level. The writer also demonstrates awareness of the audience in references to how each character is perceived by the reader as distinct from how he may see himself. The organization is clear, and the discussion remains focused on character, avoiding unnecessary plot summary. This writer demonstrates good control of the conventions and skill in varying sentences. This essay meets all the criteria for a high score. (See pp. 80–83 for a full discussion of the rubric for this part of the examination.)

Examination August 2003
English

Session One

Part A

Overview: For this part of the test, you will listen to an account about running a successful business, answer some multiple-choice questions, and write a response based on the situation described below. You will hear the account twice. You may take notes on the page allotted anytime you wish during the readings.

The Situation: You are in charge of fund-raising for your graduating class. As part of the planning process, you must write a proposal to your faculty class advisor explaining how you would use business strategies to plan a successful fund-raising campaign. In preparation for writing your proposal, listen to an account by businessman Sam Walton about running a successful business. Then use relevant information from the account to write your proposal.

Your Task: Write a proposal to your faculty class advisor in which you explain how Sam Walton's business strategies would contribute to a successful fund-raising campaign.

Guidelines:

Be sure to

- Tell your audience what they need to know about Sam Walton's business strategies and how they would contribute to a successful fund-raising campaign
- Use specific, accurate, and relevant information from the account to support your proposal
- Use a tone and level of language appropriate for a proposal to a faculty class advisor
- Organize your ideas in a logical and coherent manner
- Indicate any words taken directly from the account by using quotation marks or referring to the speaker
- Follow the conventions of standard written English

Note: For this portion of the examination, the teacher will read a passage aloud. You will not actually see the passage reprinted below. Therefore, you are encouraged to have someone read the passage to you, in order to simulate the examination as closely as possible.

Listening Passage

I think we've covered the story of how all my partners and associates and I over the years built Wal-Mart into what it is today. And in the telling, I think we've covered all the principles which resulted in the company's amazing success. A whole lot has changed about the retailing business in the forty-seven years we've been in it—including some of my theories. We've changed our minds about some significant things along the way and adopted some new principles—particularly about the concept of partnership in a corporation. But most of the values and the rules and the techniques we've relied on have stayed the same the whole way. Some of them are such simple common sense old favorites that they hardly seem worth mentioning.

This isn't the first time I've been asked to come up with a list of rules for success, but it *is* the first time I've actually sat down and done it. I'm glad I did because it's been a revealing exercise for me. The truth is [businessman] David Glass is right. I do seem to have a couple of dozen things that I've singled out at one time or another as the "key" to the whole thing. One I don't even have on my list is "work hard." If you don't know that already, or you're not willing to do it, you probably won't be going far enough to need my list anyway. And another I didn't include on the list is the idea of building a team. If you want to build an enterprise of any size at all, it almost goes without saying that you absolutely must create a team of people who work together and give real meaning to that overused word "teamwork." To me, that's more the goal of the whole thing, rather than some way to get there.

I believe in always having goals, and always setting them high. I can certainly tell you that the folks at Wal-Mart have always had goals in front of them. In fact, we have sometimes built real scoreboards on the stage at Saturday morning meetings.

One more thing. If you're really looking for my advice here, trying to get something serious out of this exercise I put myself through, remember: these rules are not in any way intended to be the Ten Commandments of Business. They are some rules that worked for me. But I always prided myself on breaking everybody else's rules, and I always favored the mavericks who challenged my rules. I may have fought them all the way, but I respected them, and, in the end, I listened to them a lot more closely than I did the pack who always agreed with everything I said. So pay special attention to Rule 10, and if you interpret it in the right spirit —as it applies to you—it could mean simply: Break All the Rules.

For what they're worth, here they are. Sam's Rules for Building a Business:

Rule 1: Commit to your business. Believe in it more than anybody else. I think I overcame every single one of my personal shortcomings by the sheer passion I brought to my work. I don't know if you're born with this kind of passion, or if you can learn it. But I do know you need it. If you love your work, you'll be out there every day trying to do it the best you possibly can, and pretty soon everybody around will catch the passion from you—like a fever.

Rule 2: Share your profits with all your associates, and treat them as partners. In turn, they will treat you as a partner, and together you will all perform beyond your wildest expectations. Remain a corporation and retain control if you like, but behave as a servant leader in a partnership. Encourage your associates to hold a stake in the company. Offer discounted stock, and grant them stock for their retirement. It's the single best thing we ever did.

Rule 3: Motivate your partners. Money and ownership alone aren't enough. Constantly, day by day, think of new and more interesting ways to motivate and challenge your partners. Set high goals, encourage competition, and then keep score. Make bets with outrageous payoffs. If things get stale, cross-pollinate; have managers switch jobs with one another to stay challenged. Keep everybody guessing as to what your next trick is going to be. Don't become too predictable.

Rule 4: Communicate everything you possibly can to your partners. The more they know, the more they'll understand. The more they understand, the more they'll care. Once they care, there's no stopping them. If you don't trust your associates to know what's going on, they'll know you don't really consider them partners. Information is power, and the gain you get from empowering your associates more than offsets the risks of informing your competitors.

Rule 5: Appreciate everything your associates do for the business. A paycheck and a stock option will buy one kind of loyalty. But all of us like to be told how much somebody appreciates what we do for them. We like to hear it often, and especially when we have done something we're really proud of. Nothing else can quite substitute for a few well-chosen, well-timed, sincere words of praise. They're absolutely free—and worth a fortune.

Rule 6: Celebrate your successes. Find some humor in your failures. Don't take yourself so seriously. Loosen up, and everybody around you will loosen up. Have fun. Show enthusiasm—always. When all else fails, put on a costume and sing a silly song. Then make everybody else sing with you. Don't do a hula on Wall Street. It's been done. Think up your own stunt. All of this is more important, and more fun, than you think, and it really fools the competition. "Why should we take those cornballs at Wal-Mart seriously?"

Rule 7: Listen to everyone in your company. And figure out ways to get them talking. The folks on the front lines—the ones who actually talk to the customer— are the only ones who really know what's going on out there. You'd better find out what they know. This really is what total quality is all about. To push responsibility down in your organization, and to force good ideas to bubble up within it, you *must* listen to what your associates are trying to tell you.

Rule 8: Exceed your customers' expectations. If you do, they'll come back over and over. Give them what they want—and a little more. Let them know you appreciate them. Make good on all your mistakes, and don't make excuses— apologize. Stand behind everything you do. The two most important words I ever wrote were on that first Wal-Mart sign: "Satisfaction Guaranteed." They're still up there, and they have made all the difference.

Rule 9: Control your expenses better than your competition. This is where you can always find the competitive advantage. For twenty-five years running— long before Wal-Mart was known as the nation's largest retailer—we ranked number one in our industry for the lowest ratio of expenses to sales. You can make a lot of different mistakes and still recover if you run an efficient operation. Or you can be brilliant and still go out of business if you're too inefficient.

Rule 10: Swim upstream. Go the other way. Ignore the conventional wisdom. If everybody else is doing it one way, there's a good chance you can find your niche by going in exactly the opposite direction. But be prepared for a lot of folks to wave you down and tell you you're headed the wrong way. I guess in all my years, what I heard more often than anything was: a town of less than 50,000 population cannot support a discount store for very long.

Those are some pretty ordinary rules, some would say even simplistic. The hard part, the real challenge, is to constantly figure out ways to execute them. You can't just keep doing what works one time, because everything around you is always changing. To succeed, you have to stay out in front of that change.

— Sam Walton with John Huey
from *Sam Walton, Made in America: My Story*, 1992

Notes

Multiple-Choice Questions

Directions (1 6): Use your notes to answer the following questions about the passage read to you. Select the best suggested answer and write its number in the space provided. The questions may help you think about ideas and information you might use in your writing. You may return to these questions anytime you wish.

1 The speaker implies that he values the opinions of people who challenge his rules because they tend to have

(1) efficient problem-solving strategies
(2) strong work ethics
(3) clear ideas for team building
(4) different points of view   1_____

2 The speaker implies that giving employees a stake in a company has the effect of

(1) assuring customer loyalty
(2) improving job performance
(3) removing legal restrictions
(4) reducing operating expenses   2_____

3 The speaker's use of the expression "satisfaction guaranteed" reflects his concern for his

(1) customers   (3) employees
(2) suppliers   (4) investors   3_____

4 According to the speaker, "the competitive advantage" results when a business has the

(1) smallest percentage of returns
(2) highest level of product safety
(3) greatest variety of inventory
(4) lowest ratio of expenses to sales   4_____

5 According to the speaker, what aspect of his rules
  has changed over time?

  (1) the methods for explaining them
  (2) the ways they are carried out
  (3) the degree to which they are accepted
  (4) the reasons for using them   5____

6 One intended effect of these rules on employees is
  to encourage them to

  (1) design new products
  (2) start a business
  (3) share a goal
  (4) solve personal problems   6____

After you have finished these questions, review **The
Situation** and read **Your Task** and the **Guidelines**.
Use scrap paper to plan your response. Then write
your response on separate sheets of paper. After you
finish your response for Part A, complete Part B.

Part B

Directions: Read the text and study the table on the following pages,
answer the multiple-choice questions, and write a response based
on the situation described below. You may use the margins to take
notes as you read and scrap paper to plan your response.

The Situation: Your community is planning to build
a new playground. As a member of the playground
planning committee, you must write a report for the
committee in which you recommend a design for the
playground which incorporates elements of safety and
satisfies the needs of potential users.

Your Task: Using relevant information from *both* documents, write a report for the playground planning committee in which you recommend a design for the playground which incorporates elements of safety and satisfies the needs of potential users.

Guidelines:
Be sure to
- Tell your audience what they need to know about your recommended design for the playground
- Explain how your design incorporates elements of safety and satisfies the needs of potential users
- Use specific, accurate, and relevant information from the text *and* the table to support your recommendations for a design
- Use a tone and level of language appropriate for a report for the playground planning committee
- Organize your ideas in a logical and coherent manner
- Indicate any words taken directly from the text by using quotation marks or referring to the author
- Follow the conventions of standard written English

Text

    . . . Over the years different types of playgrounds have been given unique names to help people identify their special design characteristics. We have seen adventure playgrounds, creative playgrounds, tot lots, mini parks, and theme parks. *Playscape* is a term which has been used in the past but is poorly defined.
(5)   The term was coined by merging the terms "play" and "landscape" in an effort to emphasize that the total environment can contribute to play value . . . .

    [T]he needs of children must be the foremost playscape design criteria. It is necessary that the definition of a playscape start with an acceptance of the standards imposed by parks for safety, maintenance, and budget but the
(10) definition can not stop there, the developmental needs of the children must also be included. If a playscape is to meet the needs of park departments, neighborhoods and children, the following elements must be included:

Active Play

The new modular [pipe and plastic] play structures are very successful at providing for the active play needs of children. This is a proven concept that *(15)* rightfully belongs in any park. The way these systems are configured, however, could be improved. We need to do a better job of including upper body building events, interesting climbers, and dynamic balance events.

Constructive and Manipulative Play

The essence of play is the freedom it provides children. A good playscape would empower children to create and change it. In the "old" days we believed in the *(20)* value of the "adventure playground" which children could build themselves. Concerns for liability, maintenance and aesthetics destroyed the few experiments that were tried in the U.S. In many other countries the idea is alive and well, and has evolved into a practical program easily included in many park settings.

Perhaps we can't go as far as the adventure playground, but we can and should *(25)* include, at a minimum, sand and water play. Note that the criteria is sand *and* water. Dry sand under an active play structure may provide a good fall surface, but it does not provide for constructive play. Sand must be moist if it is to be used in the building of sand castles. Just because it is difficult to design a low maintenance water feature doesn't mean that the function should be abandoned. *(30)* According to Kazuo Abby, of Royston, Hanamoto, Alley and Abby, "Water features within the total play environment are extremely important. The wet sand provides unlimited creativity and it's safe, simple, and fun."

The first "manipulative" piece of equipment was the steering wheel. Recently we have seen the development of a variety of game boards, like tic-tac-toe panels. *(35)* Some companies have been adding a variety of controls, levers, binoculars, etc., to their theme play equipment. This greatly expands the play value of what is essentially static equipment.

Social Play

To create social play areas only two basic criteria need to be met. First, there should be a "transaction interface." This is simply a window, counter, or storefront *(40)* that creates an "inside" and an "outside." Such an arrangement literally sets the stage for all sorts of dramatic play.

Second, a sense of enclosure is necessary. It is possible to provide small semi-enclosed spaces which offer a sense of intimacy but also allow for supervision. When properly scaled, such spaces are too small to provide cover for vagrants.

Uniqueness

(45)   Communities need and value unique features in their parks. Playgrounds with trains, ships, sculpture, and other special features create a sense of identity . . . While it was [once] thought that theme equipment would inhibit children's play, it is now known that such equipment can stimulate rich imaginative play. Children are not particularly troubled by playing "Star Wars" on an old fashioned looking ship . . . .

Accessibility and Integration

(50)   As many advocates have brought to our attention, integrating all citizens is not only ethically correct, it is also the law. There is every indication that the federal government is going to actively enforce the new Americans With Disabilities Act: this means playgrounds will have to be made accessible. While it is not easy, we can design play areas for those who have restricted mobility in order for them to

(55) be integrated with the general population. The problem is that there are few really satisfying design solutions to this problem. The manufacturers of equipment have generally offered only ramps. A few provide low horizontal ladders or ground level steering wheels.

Only a few manufacturers have addressed the problem of creating transfer

(60) stations so that children may play out of their wheelchairs.

Most advocates for accessibility say that ramps have a very small role in providing for the needs of people with various disabilities. Despite what most equipment manufacturers have concluded, wheelchair access is not the only issue to be addressed in creating an integrated environment. Putting a ramp to an active play structure on

(65) which there is nothing appropriate for the child who is physically disabled to do is insulting and can even be dangerous when used by skateboarders. On the other hand, providing access to wonderful places for social, constructive, and imaginative play, like the ship at Peacock Gap [a park in San Rafael, California], is right, and realistic . . . .

Multi-cultural

California has been a multi-cultural community since its founding. The golden

(70) age playgrounds reflected this diversity. The new playgrounds have a post-modern industrial appearance devoid[1] of any cultural connotations. Resistance to celebrating the cultural heritage of particular neighborhoods in park design stems from the political content which has been included in some of these efforts in the past. While a radical La Raza mural may have reflected the cultural identity of the

---

[1] devoid — without

(75)   barrio,[2] it also made a political statement which some members of other communities found offensive. A dragon play structure in the Chinese Community; a ship in the harbor park, or a Spanish-influenced site are all appropriate expressions in public facilities. The playscape concept needs to define what are the proper limitations for ethnic expression and the proper
(80)   venue[3] for particular political points of view.

Age Appropriate

While the modern multi-functional modular play systems are great for kids from six to nine years, they are less appropriate for other children who need more social and constructive play opportunities. Adolescents have been a particularly forgotten age group. While they do, of course, use the ball fields, they are also interested in
(85)   free play. One need only watch them on their skateboards to confirm this. They are also interested in just "hanging out" in small groups where boys and girls can "check each other out." Adults have concerns about such groups of teens; are they going to do something dangerous to themselves or others? The playscape concept can help reduce these concerns. A playscape, because of its rich array of unique attractions,
(90)   will be used by more concerned citizens over a longer part of the day. This high-use brings with it increased adult supervision which, in turn, will help reduce inappropriate behaviors. Welcoming in adolescents makes the playscape a place where they feel they belong and removes it as a target for vandalism.

Comfort

It seems obvious that a playground should be a comfortable place for people
(95)   to visit. But it is surprising how many parks are built without even a bench close to the play area. The issue of a clean, safe, and open bathroom is also central to the comfortable use of the playscape. Park benches can be selected which offer real comfort, but do not encourage people to sleep on them if this is a concern. Shade and shelter from wind should also be considered. . . .

— Jay Beckwith
excerpted from "No More Cookie Cutter Parks,"
www.bpfp.org

---

[2] barrio — Spanish-speaking neighborhood
[3] venue — place

Table

Properties of Playground Surface Materials

Material	Uncompressed Depth			Compressed Depth	Advantages	Disadvantages
	6 inches	9 inches	12 inches	9 inches		
	This depth of material provides protection from life-threatening head injury in a child who falls from a height of:					
Wood Chips	7 feet	10 feet	11 feet	10 feet	• Low initial cost • Ease of installation • Attractive appearance • Readily available	• Decomposes and compacts • Subject to microbial growth • Conceals sharp objects • Flammable
Double Shredded Bark Mulch	6 feet	10 feet	11 feet	7 feet		
Engineered Wood Fibers	6 feet	7 feet	greater than 12 feet	6 feet		
Fine Sand	5 feet	5 feet	9 feet	5 feet	• Low initial cost • Ease of installation • Does not pulverize • Low-microbial growth • Non-flammable	• Can blow or be thrown into eyes • Can be swallowed • Sand can be tracked out of area • Sand is abrasive • Wet sand is highly compactible
Coarse Sand	5 feet	5 feet	6 feet	4 feet		
Fine Gravel	6 feet	7 feet	10 feet	6 feet		
Medium Gravel	5 feet	5 feet	6 feet	5 feet		
Shredded Tires	10–12 feet	Data Not Available			• Non-abrasive • Does not compact easily • Low-microbial growth	• Flammable • May soil clothing • May be swallowed

Falls are the most common type of playground accident. The number and severity of injuries can be reduced by using softer surfaces under playground equipment.

Sources: (adapted) *Handbook for Public Playground Safety*.
United States Consumer Product Safety Commission, www.cpsc.gov
and "Playground Safety – A Guide to Playground Safety,"
American Academy of Orthopaedic Surgeons, www.aaos.org

Multiple-Choice Questions

Directions (7–16): Select the best suggested answer to each question and write its number in the space provided. The questions may help you think about ideas and information you might want to use in your writing. You may return to these questions anytime you wish.

7 The author's use of the word *"Playscape"* (line 4) suggests that playgrounds should be thought of as

  (1) places for children to escape to
  (2) toys used by everyone
  (3) fields where children observe nature
  (4) areas designed for recreation   7 _____

8 The article suggests that modular play structures are especially suitable for meeting children's developmental need for

  (1) physical exercise   (3) creative expression
  (2) social interaction   (4) mental stimulation   8 _____

9 The author's insistence on "sand *and* water" (lines 25 and 26) suggests the importance of providing children the opportunity to

  (1) swim   (3) fall
  (2) build   (4) share   9 _____

10 According to the author, play structures that create an "inside" and an "outside" are desirable because they provide

  (1) shelter from weather
  (2) encouragement to exercise
  (3) opportunities for playacting
  (4) spaces for unsupervised play   10 _____

11 The purpose of a transfer station (lines 59 and 60) is to permit a child who has a physical disability to

   (1) navigate a wheelchair around a playground
   (2) move from a wheelchair onto a structure
   (3) observe other children from a safe spot
   (4) avoid games that require a ramp   11 ____

12 The author implies that one way to make adolescents feel welcome in playgrounds is to provide opportunities for them to

   (1) assist younger children
   (2) report acts of vandalism
   (3) engage in social play
   (4) reduce adult supervision   12 ____

13 The author suggests that one area of concern when planning facilities for comfort is the possibility of

   (1) improper use
   (2) rising costs
   (3) diminishing interest
   (4) unsafe construction   13 ____

14 What element of playground design is the main focus of the table?

   (1) accessibility
   (2) safety
   (3) play value
   (4) comfort   14 ____

15 According to the table, 9 inches of engineered wood fibers, uncompressed, provides the same protection as

   (1) 9 inches of coarse sand, uncompressed
   (2) 9 inches of fine gravel, uncompressed
   (3) 12 inches of fine sand, uncompressed
   (4) 12 inches of medium gravel, uncompressed   15 ____

16 Compared to other surface materials in the table, shredded tires have the disadvantage of

(1) offering less protection
(2) compacting more readily
(3) being dirtier
(4) being heavier   16 _____

After you have finished these questions, review **The Situation** and read **Your Task** and the **Guidelines**. Use scrap paper to plan your response. Then write your response to Part B on separate sheets of paper.

Session Two

Part A

Directions: Read the passages on the following pages (an essay and a poem). Write the number of the answer to each multiple-choice question in the space provided. Then write the essay on separate sheets of paper as described in **Your Task**. You may use the margins to take notes as you read and scrap paper to plan your response.

Your Task:

After you have read the passages and answered the multiple-choice questions, write a unified essay about reaching beyond oneself as revealed in the passages. In your essay, use ideas from **both** passages to establish a controlling idea about reaching beyond oneself. Using evidence from **each** passage, develop your controlling idea and show how the author uses specific literary elements or techniques to convey that idea.

Guidelines:
Be sure to

- Use ideas from **both** passages to establish a controlling idea about reaching beyond oneself
- Use specific and relevant evidence from **each** passage to develop your controlling idea
- Show how each author uses specific literary elements (for example: theme, characterization, structure, point of view) or techniques (for example: symbolism, irony, figurative language) to convey the controlling idea
- Organize your ideas in a logical and coherent manner
- Use language that communicates ideas effectively
- Follow the conventions of standard written English

Passage I

A round, green cardboard sign hangs from a string proclaiming, "We built a proud new feeling," the slogan of a local supermarket. It is a souvenir from one of my brother's last jobs. In addition to being a bagger, he's worked at a fast-food restaurant, a gas station, a garage and a textile factory. Now, in the icy clutches of the

(5) Northeastern winter, he is unemployed. He will soon be a father. He is 19 years old.

In mid-December I was at Stanford, among the palm trees and weighty chores of academe. And all I wanted to do was get out. I joined the rest of the undergrads in a chorus of excitement, singing the praises of Christmas break. No classes, no midterms, no finals ... and no freshmen! (I'm a resident assistant.)

(10) Awesome! I was looking forward to escaping. I never gave a thought to what I was escaping to.

Once I got home to New Jersey, reality returned. My dreaded freshmen had been replaced by unemployed relatives; badgering professors had been replaced by hard-working single mothers, and cold classrooms by dilapidated bedrooms

(15) and kitchens. The room in which the "proud new feeling" sign hung contained the belongings of myself, my mom and my brother. But for these two weeks it was mine. They slept downstairs on couches.

Most students who travel between the universes of poverty and affluence during breaks experience similar conditions, as well as the guilt, the helplessness

(20) and, sometimes, the embarrassment associated with them. Our friends are willing

to listen, but most of them are unable to imagine the pain of the impoverished lives that we see every six months. Each time I return home I feel further away from the realities of poverty in America and more ashamed that they are allowed to persist. What frightens me most is not that the American socioeconomic
(25) system permits poverty to continue, but that by participating in that system I share some of the blame.

Last year I lived in an on-campus apartment, with a (relatively) modern bathroom, kitchen and two bedrooms. Using summer earnings, I added some expensive prints, a potted palm and some other plants, making the place look like
(30) the more-than-humble abode of a New York City Yuppie. I gave dinner parties, even a *soirée française.*[1]

For my roommate, a doctor's son, this kind of life was nothing extraordinary. But my mom was struggling to provide a life for herself and my brother. In addition to working 24-hour-a-day cases as a practical nurse, she was trying to
(35) ensure that my brother would graduate from high school and have a decent life. She knew that she had to compete for his attention with drugs and other potentially dangerous things that can look attractive to a young man when he sees no better future.

Living in my grandmother's house this Christmas break restored all the
(40) forgotten, and the never acknowledged, guilt. I had gone to boarding school on a full scholarship since the ninth grade, so being away from poverty was not new. But my own growing affluence has increased my distance. My friends say that I should not feel guilty: what could I do substantially for my family at this age, they ask. Even though I know that education is the right thing to do, I can't help but
(45) feel, sometimes, that I have it too good. There is no reason that I deserve security and warmth, while my brother has to cope with potential unemployment and prejudice. I, too, encounter prejudice, but it is softened by my status as a student in an affluent and intellectual community.

More than my sense of guilt, my sense of helplessness increases each time I
(50) return home. As my success leads me further away for longer periods of time, poverty becomes harder to conceptualize and feels that much more oppressive when I visit with it. The first night of break, I lay in our bedroom, on a couch that let out into a bed that took up the whole room, except for a space heater. It was a little hard to sleep because the springs from the couch stuck through at
(55) inconvenient spots. But it would have been impossible to sleep anyway because of the groans coming from my grandmother's room next door. Only in her early

---

[1] la soirée française — a French party

60s, she suffers from many chronic diseases and couldn't help but moan, then pray aloud, then moan, then pray aloud.

Not very festive: This wrenching of my heart was interrupted by the 3 a.m. (60) entry of a relative who had been allowed to stay at the house despite rowdy behavior and threats toward the family in the past. As he came into the house, he slammed the door, and his heavy steps shook the second floor as he stomped into my grandmother's room to take his place, at the foot of her bed. There he slept, without blankets on a bare mattress. This was the first night. Later in the vacation, (65) a Christmas turkey and a Christmas ham were stolen from my aunt's refrigerator on Christmas Eve. We think the thief was a relative. My mom and I decided not to exchange gifts that year because it just didn't seem festive.

A few days after New Year's I returned to California. The Northeast was soon hit by a blizzard. They were there, and I was here. That was the way it had to be, (70) for now. I haven't forgotten; the ache of knowing their suffering is always there. It has to be kept deep down, or I can't find the logic in studying and partying while people, my people, are being killed by poverty. Ironically, success drives me away from those I most want to help by getting an education.

Somewhere in the midst of all that misery, my family has built, within me, "a (75) proud feeling." As I travel between the two worlds it becomes harder to remember just how proud I should be — not just because of where I have come from and where I am going, but because of where they are. The fact that they survive in the world in which they live is something to be very proud of, indeed. It inspires within me a sense of tenacity and accomplishment that I hope every (80) college graduate will someday possess.

— Marcus Mabry
"Living in Two Worlds"
from *Newsweek on Campus,* April 1988

Passage II

Life for my child is simple, and is good.
He knows his wish. Yes, but that is not all.
Because I know mine too.
And we both want joy of undeep and unabiding[1] things,
(5) Like kicking over a chair or throwing blocks out of a window
Or tipping over an ice box pan
Or snatching down curtains or fingering an electric outlet
Or a journey or a friend or an illegal kiss.
No. There is more to it than that.
(10) It is that he has never been afraid.
Rather, he reaches out and lo the chair falls with a beautiful crash,
And the blocks fall, down on the people's heads,
And the water comes slooshing sloppily out across the floor.
And so forth.
(15) Not that success, for him, is sure, infallible.
But never has he been afraid to reach.
His lesions[2] are legion.[3]
But reaching is his rule.

— Gwendolyn Brooks
from *Annie Allen*, 1949
Harper & Brothers

_____

[1] unabiding — temporary
[2] lesions — injuries
[3] legion — numerous

Multiple-Choice Questions

Directions (1–10): Select the best suggested answer to each question and write its number in the space provided. The questions may help you think about the ideas and information you might want to use in your essay. You may return to these questions anytime you wish.

Passage I (the essay) — Questions 1–6 refer to Passage I.

1 One of the reasons that the sign in the bedroom is ironic is because the brother

   (1) collects souvenirs
   (2) has quit school
   (3) is unemployed
   (4) sleeps downstairs   1 _____

2 The statement "badgering professors had been replaced by hard-working single mothers" (lines 13 and 14) is one example of the author's use of

   (1) cause and effect
   (2) analogy
   (3) chronological order
   (4) comparison and contrast   2 _____

3 The author's description of his on-campus apartment at Stanford University as "like the more-than-humble abode of a New York City Yuppie" (lines 29 and 30) emphasizes his

   (1) distance from his family's situation
   (2) contempt for city residents
   (3) need for his family's approval
   (4) desire to live simply   3 _____

4 The author admires his mother primarily for her

   (1) cleverness   (3) knowledge
   (2) perseverance   (4) beauty   4 _____

5 The descriptions in lines 49 through 67 convey a sense of

(1) disorder and futility
(2) competitiveness and over-achievement
(3) comfort and security
(4) forgiveness and redemption   5____

6 The author's emotional conflict can best be described as

(1) anger versus joy
(2) guilt versus pride
(3) humility versus power
(4) fear versus security   6____

Passage II (the poem) — Questions 7–10 refer to Passage II.

7 The actions in lines 5 through 7 and 11 through 13 refer to

(1) parental wishes
(2) childhood pleasures
(3) unfulfilled dreams
(4) early failures   7____

8 As used in line 15, the word "infallible" most nearly means

(1) certain
(2) possible
(3) desirable
(4) understandable   8____

9 Line 16 indicates the child's willingness to

(1) show feelings   (3) take risks
(2) break rules   (4) make demands   9____

10 The sentence "His lesions are legion" (line 17) emphasizes the child's many

   (1) wishes and desires
   (2) cuts and bruises
   (3) fears and restraints
   (4) strengths and skills   10 _____

After you have finished these questions, review **Your Task** and the **Guidelines**. Use scrap paper to plan your response. Then write your response to Part A on separate sheets of paper. After you finish your response for Part A, complete Part B.

Part B

Your Task:

Write a critical essay in which you discuss *two* works of literature you have read from the particular perspective of the statement that is provided for you in the **Critical Lens**. In your essay, provide a valid interpretation of the statement, agree *or* disagree with the statement as you have interpreted it, and support your opinion using specific references to appropriate literary elements from the two works. You may use scrap paper to plan your response. Write your essay in Part B on separate sheets of paper.

Critical Lens:

> "We do not read novels* for improvement or instruction."
>
> —Oliver Wendell Holmes
> *The Occasional Speeches of*
> *Justice Oliver Wendell Holmes*, 1962

*For the purpose of writing your critical essay, you may interpret the word novels to include plays, short stories, poems, biographies, and books of true experience.

Guidelines:

Be sure to

• Provide a valid interpretation of the critical lens that clearly establishes the criteria for analysis
• Indicate whether you agree *or* disagree with the statement as you have interpreted it
• Choose *two* works you have read that you believe best support your opinion.(**Remember that you may use any genre of literature including novels, plays, short stories, poems, biographies, and books of true experience.**)
• Use the criteria suggested by the critical lens to analyze the works you have chosen

- Avoid plot summary. Instead, use specific references to appropriate literary elements (for example: theme, characterization, setting, point of view) to develop your analysis
- Organize your ideas in a unified and coherent manner
- Specify the titles and authors of the literature you choose
- Follow the conventions of standard written English

Regents Comprehensive Examination in English—August 2003

Chart for Determining the Final Examination Score (Use for August 2003 examination only.)

To determine the student's final examination score, locate the student's total essay score across the top of the chart and the student's total multiple-choice score down the side of the chart. The point where those two scores intersect is the student's final examination score. For example, a student receiving a total essay score of 20 and a total multiple-choice score of 22 would receive a final examination score of 87.

Total Essay Score →

Total Multiple-Choice Score ↓	0	1	2	3	4	5	6	7	8	9	10	11	12	13	14	15	16	17	18	19	20	21	22	23	24
0	0	2	3	5	7	10	12	15	17	20	23	26	28	31	35	38	41	44	47	51	54	57	60	63	67
1	1	2	4	6	9	11	13	16	18	21	24	27	30	33	36	39	42	46	49	52	55	59	62	65	68
2	2	3	5	7	10	12	15	17	20	23	26	28	31	35	38	41	44	47	51	54	57	60	63	67	70
3	3	4	6	9	11	13	16	18	21	24	27	30	33	36	39	42	46	49	52	55	59	62	65	68	71
4	4	5	7	10	12	15	17	20	23	26	28	31	35	38	41	44	47	51	54	57	60	63	67	70	73
5	5	6	9	11	13	16	18	21	24	27	30	33	36	39	42	46	49	52	55	59	62	65	68	71	74
6	6	7	10	12	15	17	20	23	26	28	31	35	38	41	44	47	51	54	57	60	63	67	70	73	76
7	7	9	11	13	16	18	21	24	27	30	33	36	39	42	46	49	52	55	59	62	65	68	71	74	77
8	8	10	12	15	17	20	23	26	28	31	35	38	41	44	47	51	54	57	60	63	67	70	73	76	79
9	9	11	13	16	18	21	24	27	30	33	36	39	42	46	49	52	55	59	62	65	68	71	74	77	80
10	10	12	15	17	20	23	26	28	31	35	38	41	44	47	51	54	57	60	63	67	70	73	76	79	81
11	11	13	16	18	21	24	27	30	33	36	39	42	46	49	52	55	59	62	65	68	71	74	77	80	83
12	12	15	17	20	23	26	28	31	35	38	41	44	47	51	54	57	60	63	67	70	73	76	79	81	84
13	13	16	18	21	24	27	30	33	36	39	42	46	49	52	55	59	62	65	68	71	74	77	80	83	85
14	15	17	20	23	26	28	31	35	38	41	44	47	51	54	57	60	63	67	70	73	76	79	81	84	87
15	16	18	21	24	27	30	33	36	39	42	46	49	52	55	59	62	65	68	71	74	77	80	83	85	88
16	17	20	23	26	28	31	35	38	41	44	47	51	54	57	60	63	67	70	73	76	79	81	84	87	89
17	18	21	24	27	30	33	36	39	42	46	49	52	55	59	62	65	68	71	74	77	80	83	85	88	91
18	20	23	26	28	31	35	38	41	44	47	51	54	57	60	63	67	70	73	76	79	81	84	87	89	92
19	21	24	27	30	33	36	39	42	46	49	52	55	59	62	65	68	71	74	77	80	83	85	88	91	93
20	23	26	28	31	35	38	41	44	47	51	54	57	60	63	67	70	73	76	79	81	84	87	89	92	94
21	24	27	30	33	36	39	42	46	49	52	55	59	62	65	68	71	74	77	80	83	85	88	91	93	95
22	26	28	31	35	38	41	44	47	51	54	57	60	63	67	70	73	76	79	81	84	87	89	92	94	96
23	27	30	33	36	39	42	46	49	52	55	59	62	65	68	71	74	77	80	83	85	88	91	93	95	97
24	28	31	35	38	41	44	47	51	54	57	60	63	67	70	73	76	79	81	84	87	89	92	94	96	98
25	30	33	36	39	42	46	49	52	55	59	62	65	68	71	74	77	80	83	85	88	91	93	95	97	99
26	31	35	38	41	44	47	51	54	57	60	63	67	70	73	76	79	81	84	87	89	92	94	96	98	100

Answers
August 2003
English

Answer Key

Session One, Part A	Session One, Part B	Session Two, Part A
1. 4	7. 4	1. 3
2. 2	8. 1	2. 4
3. 1	9. 2	3. 1
4. 4	10. 3	4. 2
5. 2	11. 2	5. 1
6. 3	12. 3	6. 2
	13. 1	7. 2
	14. 2	8. 1
	15. 2	9. 3
	16. 3	10. 2

Answers Explained

Session One

Part A   (1–6)

Note: Refer to Chapter 1 for review and strategy in responding to this part of the examination.

(1) **4** "different points of view." This answer is supported in several parts of the speech. First, Walton says that he always listened more closely to the people who challenged him than to those who always agreed. He also concludes the speech by saying that you must always be ready to change because "You can't just keep doing what works one time . . . ."

(2) **2** "improving job performance." At least five of Walton's rules emphasize the importance of giving employees a stake in the business. In Rule 2, he says, ". . . treat them as partners . . . and together you will all perform beyond your wildest expectations."

(3) **1** "customers." "Satisfaction guaranteed" is the key to Rule 8, which concerns meeting customers' expectations, giving them what they want, and standing "behind everything you do."

(4) **4** "lowest ratio of expenses to sales." Rule 9 is "Control your expenses better than your competition." Walton also asserts directly that, "[f]or twenty-five years . . . we ranked number one . . . for the lowest ratio of expenses to sales."

(5) **2** "the ways they are carried out." In the concluding statements of the speech, Walton says of his "Rules" that the "hard part . . . is to constantly figure out ways to execute them [carry them out] . . . everything around you is always changing . . . you have to stay out in front of that change."

(6) **3** "share a goal." All of the Rules concerning employees involve engaging them in the success of the business, through sharing profits, ideas, and information; that is, employee relations are meant to create a common goal in the success of Wal-Mart.

Part A   Sample Student Response Essay

As next year's head of fund-raising for the senior class, I am proposing some procedural changes that I hope you will consider. My goal is to increase student involvement, and I would like to open for discussion the whole question of what kind of fund-raising activities we should sponsor. To support my proposals, I have drawn on the business strategies of Sam Walton, of Wal-Mart fame. Is there any better authority on how to optimize profit, organize workers, create a team, and satisfy customers?

I know that any fund-raiser we undertake will require that the class work together as a team, and that we each give the team our best effort. According to Walton, what is also required, and what may have been missing from our previous fund-raising attempts, is commitment. If each of us believes in the goal, and in the class, that enthusiasm will spread, and we will be able to launch some high-energy projects.

The profits from new activities will be ours to share, and how we spend them should reflect the diversity of the interests of our class. There will, of course, be the senior prom and class trip, but we could also make a donation to a local charity or community project. Or perhaps we could sponsor a needy child or purchase some new equipment for the school. Everyone involved in the work should be part of the decision making.

Another recommended strategy of Walton's I'll be employing is good communication. The entire class needs to be kept informed, even in the earliest stages of planning. Fund-raising meetings will be well publicized and open to everyone. Students can be made aware periodically of fund-raising plans and progress via the morning announcements and the class e-mail network. In Walton's words, "The more they [employees] understand, the more they care." I also intend to ensure that all our "workers" feel appreciated. In fund-raising, some tasks are more visible than others, but all volunteers should be made to feel valued.

One of Sam Walton's most interesting strategies is to celebrate all successes. I am sure my classmates and I can propose ways to use some of our profits to recognize student achievement at the individual and class-wide levels. Perhaps we can give movie tickets to those who raise the most money, or have a pizza party for the most successful committees. Such rewards will also allow us to "loosen up" and "have fun," as Walton suggests.

Perhaps the most important of Walton's strategies is to listen to everyone. In every class, there seems to be an unspoken hierarchy, where an elite few make all the important decisions. If we were to seek the opinion of every classmate, I cannot imagine all the new ideas we might come up with— enough to make our fund-raisers genuinely original.

Finally, two of Walton's more practical strategies must be employed. We must do our best to satisfy our customers. In most fund-raisers, the emphasis is on collecting money. If we could offer a "product" or service that people really wanted, our profits would soar. We must also be careful to keep our expenses low. The less we spend, the more we have, and that, after all, is our goal.

Analysis

This essay represents an excellent response to the task, which requires applying the information presented in the speech to a new context and presenting proposals to a specific audience, a faculty sponsor. This writer reveals a thorough understanding and appreciation of Walton's remarks and makes skillful application of them to a fund-raising campaign for a graduating class. The rhetorical question at the end of the introduction is particularly effective.

Ideas are well developed here, and the organization is strengthened by the use of transitions and the way in which examples are ordered. The second paragraph declares the general purpose; the body of the essay applies Walton's "Rules" to a school setting. Language and varied sentence structure are sophisticated, and the tone is highly appropriate. This is a well-written and convincing response; it would merit a high score.

(See pp. 31–35 for a detailed explanation of the rubric for this part of the examination.)

Part B   (7–16)

Note: Refer to Chapter 2 for review and strategy in responding to this part of the examination.

(7) **4** "areas designed for recreation." In line 5, the term *"Playscape"* is defined as a "merging [of] the terms 'play' and 'landscape.'" While play may sometimes represent a form of "escape," that is not the idea developed here. The article emphasizes playscapes as areas for active and imaginative play and, more broadly, as areas of recreation for all ages.

(8) **1** "physical exercise." The third paragraph states that modular structures provide for "active play," or physical activity. Physical exercise is also emphasized in the need to expand the opportunities for "upper body building events . . . and dynamic balance events." Social interaction, creative expression, and mental stimulation are all implied functions of a well-designed playground, but they are not linked here to the modular play structures.

(9) **2** "build." In this paragraph, the text points out that "Sand must be moist if it is to be used in the building of sand castles." One designer of playgrounds also asserts that " . . . wet sand provides unlimited creativity . . . . "

(10) **3** "opportunities for playacting." In the section on Social Play, the article points out that an "inside" and an "outside" arrangement "literally sets the stage for all sorts of dramatic play."

(11) **2** "move from a wheelchair onto a structure." The following paragraph shows how the concept of accessibility means more than providing simple ramps and passive access to an area. The purpose of a transfer station is to allow children to "play out of their wheelchairs."

(12) **3** "engage in social play." The article reminds us that adolescents are also interested in "just hanging out" or in checking each other out. This is what the author might also call "social play." There is no suggestion here that adolescents should be expected to assist or supervise younger children.

(13) **1** "improper use." This is what is suggested in the comment that comfortable benches should be provided but should be designed so people are not encouraged to sleep on them. There is no reference to costs, diminishing interest, or construction in this section.

(14) **2** "safety." The purpose of the table is stated in the text at the bottom, which declares that "...injuries can be reduced by using softer surfaces under playground equipment." The source of the information is also cited as the *Handbook for Public Playground Safety*. The table compares the effectiveness of various materials in providing protection from "life-threatening head injury in a child . . . . "

(15) **2** "9 inches of fine gravel, uncompressed." To answer this question, you must find in the second column that 9 inches of engineered wood fibers provide protection for a child who falls from a height of 7 feet. Of the choices offered, only fine gravel also offers protection for falls from a height of 7 feet.

(16) **3** "being dirtier." In the column listing Disadvantages, it is noted that shredded tires "may soil clothing." The other disadvantages are not included among the choices.

Part B Sample Student Response Essay

In order for our planned new playground to successfully contribute to the community, it must be designed to incorporate elements of safety as well as to satisfy the needs of its potential users. In matters of safety, both the construction and the materials used in the playground play a central role; the design of the playground must also be stimulating and serve children's developmental needs. Finally, the playground should be available to people of varying ages and conditions to better serve the community as a whole.

One very important factor in providing for the safety of children on playgrounds is in the choice of surface material. Surface materials serve to break falls and prevent life-threatening head injuries. According to the U.S. Consumer Product Safety Commission, "[t]he number and severity of injuries can be reduced by using softer surfaces under playground equipment." My research indicates that shredded tires form the material that provides the greatest protection from injury in falls. Compared with 6 inches of uncompressed wood chips that provide protection for a fall from up to 7 feet, the same amount of shredded tires can provide protection for a fall from up to 10 or 12 feet. Other advantages to shredded tires include the fact that they form a nonabrasive surface that also has low microbial growth. While shredded tires may form a somewhat dirtier material than others, it does not compress easily and will not conceal sharp objects.

According to J. Beckwith, in a report on playground design, the structures chosen for the playground can play a vital role in a child's development. Children's physical strength is built up when playgrounds include the new pipe and plastic modular structures. Our playground should also include activities that serve to increase children's upper body strength and equipment to improve their climbing and balancing skills. A well-designed children's playground should also offer children freedom of activity and opportunities for creativity. For example, an area for wet sand should be available for building. As Kazuo Abby states, "The wet sand provides unlimited creativity and it's safe, simple, and fun."

Other theme equipment, such as steering wheels and fame boards would also contribute to a child's creativity. It is also important to create areas for what is called "transaction interface," areas with "indoor" and "outdoor" spaces. These set the stage for various role-playing activities. Low play structures and what are called "transfer stations" should also be provided for children with disabilities, especially those in wheelchairs. It is possible to design structures other than simple ramps to enable children to move from wheelchairs to play areas.

Our new playground, aside from providing for children, should be built with the entire community in mind. Because we live near the Hudson, we could include play areas that reflect life on the river; the rural nature of the area could be reflected in "play" tractors and farm animals. Our community's adolescents should also be included. The playground might simply encourage

*them to "hang out" in an area where there are also children and supervising
adults. Beckwith suggests this might actually discourage vandalism or other
destructive behavior. Furthermore, park benches and clean, public bathrooms
must be provided, especially for the adults who bring their children to play.
Seating areas can be designed to discourage people from sleeping on them,
but such amenities would enhance the playground's role as a social gathering
place in our community.*

*I propose that these material and structural recommendations be incor-
porated into our plan for a playground that will provide play and development for children and a place of recreation for the whole community.*

Analysis

The writer of this essay demonstrates an in-depth understanding of the documents and shows particular insight into
the task by proposing details that reflect the specific community: "life on the river," "tractors and farm animals." Note that
the task is to propose a design for a playground, not simply
summarize the information presented. The key ideas regarding surface materials and the need for stimulating play areas
are well developed and supported by relevant details from
<u>both</u> the text and the table. Transitions provide coherence,
and the organization follows the outline of ideas established in
the introduction. The writer uses language that is clear, precise, and appropriate for the intended audience; sentences are
varied, and there are no significant errors in the use of conventions. This essay meets all the criteria for a high score.
(See pp. 48–53 for a detailed discussion of the rubric for this
part of the examination.)

Session Two

Part A   (1–10)

Note: See Chapter 3 for review and strategy in responding to this part of the
examination.

(1) **3** "is unemployed." The opening paragraph "shows" us the sign
from the supermarket, followed by a list of the brother's other jobs. Our
expectation is that this reflects a positive direction in his brother's life;
instead, we are told that "he is unemployed."

(2) **4** "comparison and contrast." The third paragraph is developed as a series of sharply contrasting images to show the reality of the author's life in New Jersey, compared with his life at Stanford. The rhetorical elements of cause and effect, analogy, and chronology are not evident in this section.

(3) **1** "distance from his family's situation." The preceding paragraph develops the theme of distance between the "universes of poverty and affluence"; the author also comments on the fact that each time he returns home, he feels "further away" from the realities of poverty that persist in America.

(4) **2** "perseverance." In lines 33–34, the author speaks of his mother "struggling to provide" for herself and her son by working "24-hour-a-day cases." Her work and her determination to keep the younger boy in school and away from drugs and other dangers are strong images of perseverance. The author does not refer in this selection to his mother's beauty, knowledge, or cleverness.

(5) **1** "disorder and futility." The sense of futility or helplessness (line 49) is evident in the author's descriptions of relatives who come noisily into the house at late hours and of others who apparently steal food. Mabry also refers to his grandmother's chronic diseases.

(6) **2** "guilt versus pride." The paragraph that begins at line 39 develops in detail the author's feelings of guilt: He has been in privileged settings for his education since ninth grade even as the rest of his family struggle to survive. He concludes this article, however, by also pointing out that their survival is "something to be proud of" and gives him his sense of tenacity and accomplishment.

(7) **2** "childhood pleasures." The images are those of a toddler reaching to tip, throw, and snatch things and taking delight in the results. The poet introduces them as the "joy of undeep and unabiding things . . . ."

(8) **1** "certain." In this line, "infallible" is presented as another way of saying "sure," or certain.

(9) **3** "take risks." In this line "reach" is both literal and figurative. In reaching to touch or throw things the child is also testing what he can do: ". . . reaching is his rule."

(10) **2** "cuts and bruises." The vocabulary notes make it clear that the child has a number of injuries.

Part A   Sample Student Response Essay

In these two passages, the authors develop the theme of reaching beyond oneself. Both the essay and the poem dramatize the need to take risks in order to achieve one's objectives. The passages also convey the idea that reaching beyond oneself is an essential quality, worthwhile even if it has the potential to produce frustration, guilt, or even physical injury.

In the first passage, we encounter a troubled college student who is, in essence, compelled to reach beyond himself. He is a successful student at Stanford, a prestigious university, and experiencing life "among the palm trees and weighty chores of academe." His roommate is a wealthy doctor's son, and they live comfortably in an on-campus apartment that resembles the "abode of a New York City Yuppie." This young man, it would seem, should feel happy and proud. There is, however, a serious conflict in his life. His family lives in a dilapidated home in New Jersey, surrounded by poverty and inhabited by defeated or disruptive relatives. His return home for Christmas break will not be a joyful escape; rather, it will deliver him to his real universe —one in which he feels true helplessness and shame. The opening paragraph establishes the irony of his situation. The sign, "We built a proud new feeling," which hangs in his brother's room, is a reminder of one of the many jobs he no longer has. Even the harshness of the Northeastern winter looms in direct contrast to the sunny warmth of his idyllic California college.

Marcus Mabry's guilt is further compounded by the fact that he feels powerless to change the wretched home situation. The poverty will continue, the suffering will increase, and his feelings of hopelessness will endure. His "growing affluence" haunts him, and he feels guilty that he has such a privileged life in contrast to that of his family. He does, however, experience a revelation of sorts. He realizes that he must continue to bridge the two worlds of his universe. His family, particularly his hard-working mother, has instilled in him a "proud feeling"; she has inspired him to reach well beyond himself and their circumstances to survive and be proud of his accomplishments. He also knows that only by being educated will he be able to help his family and others like them. "Ironically, success drives me away from those I most want to help by getting an education."

Passage II, the poem, also presents us with the theme of one who is willing to reach beyond himself in order to succeed. The situation, however, is far different from that of the college student depicted in Passage I. The primary character in the poem is a young child, whose life is "simple" and "good." His mother, the poem's speaker, observes that he knows exactly what he wants and is fearless in his pursuit of it. He seeks only temporary things, such as "kicking over a chair" or perhaps "throwing blocks out of a window." Pulling down curtains or sticking a finger into an electric outlet would also be among the things that attract him. He loves the sounds of his success: the "beautiful crash" of a chair or the "slooshing" of spilled water cascading onto the floor. The child sometimes fails, but he is never afraid to try something. His injuries are numerous, but he will never cease, since "reaching is his rule."

The images of the young child suggest a person who may be destined to succeed in life. The experiences of his simple life may be valuable to him later. The child's willingness to reach beyond himself for toy blocks or for an ice box tray today suggest he will reach out and take risks for more complicated objectives in the future. He is fearless and accepts pain as part of the price for success.

The authors of both passages use narrative, direct language, and vivid images to depict characters who are willing to reach beyond themselves, to endure many hardships, including physical pain or guilt, to reach their objectives.

Analysis

This essay begins very well, by establishing a sophisticated controlling idea that reflects an insightful reading of the essay and the poem. The observation that the college student is "compelled" (by circumstance and guilt) to reach beyond himself is well stated; the writer fully appreciates the complexity of Mabry's feelings. The essay also goes beyond simply mentioning such literary elements as irony and imagery to show how those elements contribute to the meaning of the works. The discussion of the poem reveals the writer's appreciation of the child's "reaching" as a powerful metaphor and succeeds in linking the experience of the child to that of the student.

The development of the essay also reflects the narrative quality of the passages. Focus on the central idea of reaching beyond oneself is maintained throughout, and the writer's own language is rich, vivid, and appropriate. Sentences are varied, and elements such as parallel construction are used to good effect: "The poverty will continue, the suffering will increase, and his feelings of hopelessness will endure." This is an excellent essay and would merit a high score. (See pp. 68–71 for a detailed discussion of the rubric for this part of the examination.)

Part B   Sample Student Response Essay

Note: See Chapter 4 for review and strategy in responding to this part of the examination.

Although Oliver Wendell Holmes believes that "we do not read novels for improvement or instruction," not all readers will agree that literature is merely for enjoyment or entertainment. Many works offer a moral truth to be examined, or new knowledge or opinions to be gained, which challenge a reader's beliefs. While one may read literature to learn enjoyably, improvement and instruction are an inevitable part of the reading process. Two works that present a contradiction to Holmes' view are <u>Animal Farm</u>, by George Orwell and <u>The Tragedy of Othello</u>, by William Shakespeare. In each, it is vivid characterization that gives us our understanding.

    <u>Animal Farm</u> is an allegory, satirizing Communist Russia. Using animals to represent major figures in Russian history, Orwell dramatizes events from the Bolshevik Revolution to the corruption of the then Soviet Union. To demonstrate the flaws of the system, Orwell used the animals as symbols; sheep represented the masses, unable to think for themselves, mindlessly blearing the words of theirs leaders: "Four legs good, two legs bad." Boxer, a

cart horse, spends all of his effort working for the dream of equality, chanting, "I will work harder." Napoleon, a boar, represents the leaders of the Communist Party, who abuse their power and convince the gullible animals that all is well. When Boxer finally speaks out, noticing that the pigs are treated differently, he is killed.

Orwell's theme evolves throughout the story, showing that despite the goal of equality for all, the ideals of the revolution will be corrupted when leaders have unlimited power. The pigs will declare that "All animals are equal, but some are more equal than others." Animal Farm teaches that blindly following slogans and persuasive individuals will lead inevitably to corruption; when corrupt leaders prosper, it is at the expense of others.

In Othello, Shakespeare portrays the destructive power of jealousy. Iago, the antagonist, and Othello, the protagonist, are developed in parallel. Iago represents pure evil; jealous of other characters, he seeks to destroy them. Resentful that Othello has promoted another officer, Cassio, to a position Iago felt he deserved, Iago determines to destroy both men. He convinces Othello that Cassio is having an affair with Othello's beloved wife, Desdemona.

Othello, who is honorable and of pure intentions at the outset of the play, succumbs to his doubts and begins to believe Iago's vicious lies about his innocent wife. As Othello's jealous rage grows, Iago feeds it with clever deceptions. Iago's evil is evident in the way he uses his knowledge of human nature to destroy those around him. He is able to twist Othello's trusting nature and Desdemona's true goodness to the point that Othello will kill what he most loves. Iago even kills his own wife when she discovers the truth of what he has done.

In each of these works, readers are able to add the insights of the authors to their own. Observing the actions of characters in literature may give readers insights into their own motivations or into those within their society. Reading literature is certainly enjoyable, but it may also be instructive.

Analysis

This essay meets the first important guideline by offering a thoughtful interpretation of the critical lens and establishing criteria for analysis of the two works. The writer acknowledges Holmes' point but goes on to say that there is more to reading than simple pleasure or escape. The focus on character is insightful and the discussion that follows is persuasive, supported with relevant details from the novel and the play. The essay would be even stronger with more development of a shared theme that evil or corrupt characters achieve their ends by manipulating the innocence of others.

The organization follows a useful pattern of discussing the works separately, then linking them in the conclusion with an affirmation of the controlling idea. The writer demonstrates understanding of such literary elements as allegory, symbol, and characterization, and shows how they contribute to the meaning of these works. Language and sentence structure are sophisticated, and there are no significant errors in the use of conventions. This essay meets the criteria for a high score. (See pp. 80–83 for a detailed discussion of the rubric for this part of the examination.)

Examination June 2004
English

Session One

Part A

Overview: For this part of the test, you will listen to an account about running a successful business, answer some multiple-choice questions, and write a response based on the situation described below. You will hear the account twice. You may take notes on the page allotted anytime you wish during the readings.

> **The Situation:** Your speech class is studying oral traditions and plans to publish a series of articles in booklet form explaining these traditions. You have chosen to write an article in which you describe the griot tradition of West Africa and explain how that tradition is passed on. In preparation for writing your article, listen to an account by Ken Hawkinson. Then use relevant information from the account to write your article.

Your Task: Write an article for a booklet for your speech class in which you describe the griot tradition of West Africa and explain how that tradition is passed on.

Guidelines:

Be sure to

- Tell your audience what they need to know about the griot tradition of West Africa
- Explain how that tradition is passed on
- Use specific, accurate, and relevant information from the account to support your discussion
- Use a tone and level of language appropriate for an article for a high school speech class
- Organize your ideas in a logical and coherent manner
- Indicate any words taken directly from the account by using quotation marks or referring to the speaker
- Follow the conventions of standard written English

Note: For this portion of the examination, the teacher will read a passage aloud. You will not actually see the passage reprinted below. Therefore, you are encouraged to have someone read the passage to you, in order to simulate the examination as closely as possible.

Listening Passage

In West Africa, there is a saying: "Among the things existing in the world, speech is the only thing giving birth to its mother." What is meant here is that little discussions lead to bigger discussions through which all problems may be solved. It is believed that speech links people together and establishes order. Whenever a lesson is to be taught, a decision made, or a problem solved, the people in a traditional village will sit beneath a tree and engage in a discourse filled with images, metaphors, stories, and proverbs. Much of this discourse speaks to the importance of listening to the elders for it is they who hold within them the wisdom gained by previous generations. It is said, "An old person's mouth smells bad, but it utters good things," "When the mother cow is chewing the grass, the young calves watch its mouth," and finally, "Old cooking pots make better sauce." The traditional leader of this discourse, and he who has been called to educate and entertain the people of his village, is the griot.

While many children of West Africa are provided with the opportunity to attend a formal school, others still receive their education through traditional methods. Through the folklore, children may learn the values of their society, acquire a sense of place in the hierarchy of their group, and hear of the traditional practices and rituals that are a part of their daily life. While here in the West we use science to explain many of the secrets of our world, in traditional West Africa, mythology serves to explain the unexplainable and pass the collective knowledge of one generation on to the next. When I was in Mali, I had the opportunity to observe how a full eclipse of the moon was understood. The people around me chose to believe in the explanation provided by their oral tradition, that a black cat was covering the moon. Most of the night, the beating of drums could be heard while that cat was slowly driven away.

All people know and tell folktales in West Africa, but only the hereditary griots pass on the myths, epics, and history of their people. They also memorize the lineage of their clan and the noble family to whom they are attached, they sing songs of praise to the family's greatness and wisdom, they tell the stories that teach people to live productively and cohesively in society, they provide the music both to entertain the people and to support the many rituals and ceremonies, and they serve as living libraries for the traditional mythology that links people to their cultural heritage. These myths, epics, histories, tales, songs, and music have come to be known as the "old speech." The griots have been designated by their generation to be the depository of this collective knowledge and they spend their lives making themselves aware of it and developing the necessary skills needed to share it effectively with others.

To be a griot one must be born into the griot caste. Members of this caste live near noble families who are their benefactors. In return for keeping their family genealogy and history, and composing and singing songs of praise, nobles will help support the griot families. Since most villages have families of noble caste living within them, so too do most villages have griots. Those villages without nobles or griots are visited by traveling griots, much like the circuit preacher on the American frontier.

Everyone born into this caste carries the name "griot" but not all will become storytellers and musicians. Beginning at an early age, griot children attend storytelling events with their parents and are introduced to the stories and music. Only those who show particular promise are called to go into an apprenticeship with a master griot. Those not called take on the work of their tribe and become farmers, fishermen, or herders.

Each clan or extended family has a master griot who takes in these young apprentices and trains them throughout their youth and young adulthood. The apprentices begin by doing much of the cooking and cleaning in the compound while all the time listening, and observing the older students and master. Formal training begins with the apprentices learning to repair and build instruments. They receive instruction on how to play the instruments and gradually become proficient on the guitar, the kora, the drums, or balafone, and in time learn the tunes and rhythms that accompany all the stories in their masters' repertoires. As the years go by they learn and memorize the genealogy and history of the noble families, their praise songs, and the internal politics of the families so one day they may serve as effective arbitrators. They practice simple storytelling and are coached by their elders on how to enhance their use of voice, movement, gesture, and overall delivery style. Gradually, their memory and skill develops to the point where they can recite the great epics of their people, playing an instrument as they speak.

But to be a griot involves far more than the training. Africans believe that to be a griot one must be born a griot, one must be anointed with the "old speech" which is acquired from one's mother and refers to the special knowledge embedded in one at birth. It is believed that the ensuing years of training are simply to release that which is already within. This belief also applies to the griots' ability to play the instruments: they were born with the ability to sing and play, and the years of practice and training merely allow that ability to appear. It generally takes fifty years before a griot realizes his full potential ....

In the presence of the structured form of European education in West Africa, there is a question about what is to become of griots and the "old speech" in the future. While perhaps necessary if one is to exist in the "modern" world, this type of education with its tilt toward a discursive world view may undermine the African's ability to understand the "old speech." There are also the problems resulting from television, which is pulling people away from the performances and messages of the traditional griots. Perhaps the most macabre experience I had in my three years in Africa occurred on a Sunday night, while visiting friends in a desert village. The chief brought out his generator and television, and along with the entire village, I sat in the sand and watched an episode of Dynasty dubbed into French. Many in Africa now prefer such television shows to the traditional stories told by griots ....

Though the future may look bleak, most Africans say that the "old speech" can never die. They say that the worst that can happen is that it will fall dormant for a time. Then, some day, when the knowledge and wisdom of ancient tradition is called for again, it will reemerge in the songs of a new generation of griots.

— from "Old Speech,"
Parabola, Spring 1994

Notes

Multiple-Choice Questions

Directions (1–6): Use your notes to answer the following questions about the passage read to you. Select the best suggested answer and write its number in the space provided. The questions may help you think about ideas and information you might use in your writing. You may return to these questions anytime you wish.

1 According to the speaker, decisions in West African villages are made through discussions led by

  (1) wise historians
  (2) elected representatives
  (3) heroic nobles
  (4) appointed chiefs   1_____

2 The speaker uses the anecdote about an eclipse of the moon to illustrate the importance the people of Mali attach to

  (1) science
  (2) history
  (3) genealogy
  (4) mythology   2_____

3 The term "old speech" refers to

  (1) the earliest known examples of writing
  (2) the quality of an elder's voice
  (3) a collection of tales and songs
  (4) an ancient African language   3_____

4 In stating that "to be a griot one must be born into the griot caste" the speaker indicates that griot apprenticeship is available only to those people who

  (1) receive a university education
  (2) belong to a certain social class
  (3) have a particular physical appearance
  (4) give away all their possessions   4_____

5 Nobles help support griots because the griots

 (1) preserve the nobles' past
 (2) care for the nobles' children
 (3) write the nobles' messages
 (4) protect the nobles' property   5 ____

6 According to the speaker, the purpose of an apprentice's extensive training is to

 (1) change poor habits
 (2) develop social networks
 (3) enhance formal schooling
 (4) release natural abilities   6 ____

After you have finished these questions, review **The Situation** and read **Your Task** and the **Guidelines**. Use scrap paper to plan your response. Then write your response on separate sheets of paper. After you finish your response for Part A, complete Part B.

Part B

Directions: Read the text and study the map on the following pages, answer the multiple-choice questions, and write a response based on the situation described below. You may use the margins to take notes as you read and scrap paper to plan your response.

The Situation: Your Earth Science class has been studying changing weather patterns. In order to increase public awareness, you have decided to write a letter to the local newspaper discussing global warming and explaining how global warming may affect humans.

Your Task: Using relevant information from *both* documents, write a letter to your local newspaper in which you discuss global warming and explain how global warming may affect humans. *Write only the body of the letter.*

Guidelines:
Be sure to
• Tell your audience what they need to know about global warming
• Explain how global warming may affect humans
• Use specific, accurate, and relevant information from the text *and* the map to develop your letter
• Use a tone and level of language appropriate for a letter to your local newspaper
• Organize your ideas in a logical and coherent manner
• Indicate any words taken directly from the text by using quotation marks or referring to the author
• Follow the conventions of standard written English

Life in the Greenhouse

. . . A decade ago, the idea that the planet was warming up as a result of human activity was largely theoretical. We knew that since the Industrial Revolution began in the 18th century, factories and power plants and automobiles and farms have been loading the atmosphere with heat-trapping gases, including carbon
(5)   dioxide and methane. But evidence that the climate was actually getting hotter was still murky.

Not anymore. As an authoritative report issued a few weeks ago [in 2001] by the U.N.-sponsored Intergovernmental Panel on Climate Change makes plain, the trend toward a warmer world has unquestionably begun. Worldwide
(10)   temperatures have climbed more than 1°F over the past century, and the 1990s were the hottest decade on record. After analyzing data going back at least two decades on everything from air and ocean temperatures to the spread and retreat of wildlife, the IPCC asserts that this slow but steady warming has had an impact on no fewer than 420 physical processes and animal and plant species on all
(15)   continents.

Glaciers, including the legendary snows of Kilimanjaro, are disappearing from mountaintops around the globe. Coral reefs are dying off as the seas get too warm for comfort. Drought is the norm in parts of Asia and Africa. El Niño events, which trigger devastating weather in the eastern Pacific, are more
(20)   frequent. The Arctic permafrost is starting to melt. Lakes and rivers in colder climates are freezing later and thawing earlier each year. Plants and animals are shifting their ranges poleward and to higher altitudes, and migration patterns for animals as diverse as polar bears, butterflies and beluga whales are being disrupted.

(25)   Faced with these hard facts, scientists no longer doubt that global warming is happening, and almost nobody questions the fact that humans are at least partly responsible. Nor are the changes over. Already, humans have increased the concentration of carbon dioxide, the most abundant heat-trapping gas in the atmosphere, to 30% above pre-industrial levels—and each year the rate of
(30)   increase gets faster. The obvious conclusion: temperatures will keep going up.

Unfortunately, they may be rising faster and heading higher than anyone expected. By 2100, says the IPCC, average temperatures will increase between 2.5°F and 10.4°F—more than 50% higher than predictions of just a half-decade ago. That may not seem like much, but consider that it took only a 9°F shift to end
(35)   the last ice age. Even at the low end, the changes could be problematic enough, with storms getting more frequent and intense, droughts more pronounced, coastal areas ever more severely eroded by rising seas, rainfall scarcer on agricultural land and ecosystems thrown out of balance.

But if the rise is significantly larger, the result could be disastrous. With seas
(40)   rising as much as 3 ft., enormous areas of densely populated land—coastal Florida, much of Louisiana, the Nile Delta, the Maldives, Bangladesh—would become uninhabitable. Entire climatic zones might shift dramatically, making central Canada look more like central Illinois, Georgia more like Guatemala. Agriculture would be thrown into turmoil. Hundreds of millions of people would
(45)   have to migrate out of unlivable regions.

Public health could suffer. Rising seas would contaminate water supplies with salt. Higher levels of urban ozone, the result of stronger sunlight and warmer temperatures, could worsen respiratory illnesses. More frequent hot spells could lead to a rise in heat-related deaths. Warmer temperatures could widen the range
(50)   of disease-carrying rodents and bugs, such as mosquitoes and ticks, increasing the incidence of dengue fever, malaria, encephalitis, Lyme disease and other afflictions. Worst of all, this increase in temperatures is happening at a pace that outstrips anything the earth has seen in the past 100 million years. Humans will

have a hard enough time adjusting, especially in poorer countries, but for wildlife,
(55) the changes could be devastating.

Like any other area of science, the case for human-induced global warming
has uncertainties—and like many pro-business lobbyists, President Bush has
proclaimed those uncertainties a reason to study the problem further rather than
act. But while the evidence is circumstantial, it is powerful, thanks to the IPCC's
(60) painstaking research. The U.N.-sponsored group was organized in the late 1980s.
Its mission: to sift through climate-related studies from a dozen different fields
and integrate them into a coherent picture. "It isn't just the work of a few green
people," says Sir John Houghton, one of the early leaders who at the time ran the
British Meteorological Office. "The IPCC scientists come from a wide range of
(65) backgrounds and countries."

Measuring the warming that has already taken place is relatively simple; the
trick is unraveling the causes and projecting what will happen over the next
century. To do that, IPCC scientists fed a wide range of scenarios involving
varying estimates of population and economic growth, changes in technology and
(70) other factors into computers. That process gave them about 35 estimates, ranging
from 6 billion to 35 billion tons, of how much excess carbon dioxide will enter the
atmosphere.

Then they loaded those estimates into the even larger, more powerful
computer programs that attempt to model the planet's climate. Because no one
(75) climate model is considered definitive, they used seven different versions, which
yielded 235 independent predictions of global temperature increase. That's
where the range of 2.5°F to 10.4°F (1.4°C to 5.8°C) comes from....

The models still aren't perfect. One major flaw, agree critics and champions
alike, is that they don't adequately account for clouds. In a warmer world, more
(80) water will evaporate from the oceans and presumably form more clouds. If they
are billowy cumulus clouds, they will tend to shade the planet and slow down
warming; if they are high, feathery cirrus clouds, they will trap even more heat....

It won't take the greatest extremes of warming to make life uncomfortable for
large numbers of people. Even slightly higher temperatures in regions that are
(85) already drought- or flood-prone would exacerbate those conditions. In temperate
zones, warmth and increased CO_2 would make some crops flourish—at first. But
beyond 3° of warming, says Bill Easterling, a professor of geography and
agronomy at Penn State and a lead author of the IPCC report, "there would be a
dramatic turning point. U.S. crop yields would start to decline rapidly." In the
(90) tropics, where crops are already at the limit of their temperature range, the
decrease would start right away.

Even if temperatures rise only moderately, some scientists fear, the climate would reach a "tipping point"—a point at which even a tiny additional increase would throw the system into violent change. If peat bogs and Arctic permafrost (95) warm enough to start releasing the methane stored within them, for example, that potent greenhouse gas would suddenly accelerate the heat-trapping process.

By contrast, if melting ice caps dilute the salt content of the sea, major ocean currents like the Gulf Stream could slow or even stop, and so would their warming effects on northern regions. More snowfall reflecting more sunlight (100) back into space could actually cause a net cooling. Global warming could, paradoxically, throw the planet into another ice age.

Even if such a tipping point doesn't materialize, the more drastic effects of global warming might be only postponed rather than avoided The IPCC'S calculations end with the year 2100, but the warming won't. World Bank chief (105) scientist, Robert Watson, currently serving as IPCC chair, points out that the CO_2 entering the atmosphere today will be there for a century. Says Watson: "If we stabilize [CO_2 emissions] now, the concentration will continue to go up for hundreds of years. Temperatures will rise over that time."

That could be truly catastrophic. The ongoing disruption of ecosystems and (110) weather patterns would be bad enough. But if temperatures reach the IPCC'S worst-case levels and stay there for as long as 1,000 years, says Michael Oppenheimer, chief scientist at Environmental Defense, vast ice sheets in Greenland and Antarctica could melt, raising sea level more than 30 ft. Florida would be history, and every city on the U.S. Eastern seaboard would be (115) inundated.

In the short run, there's not much chance of halting global warming, not even if every nation in the world ratifies the Kyoto Protocol tomorrow. The treaty doesn't require reductions in carbon dioxide emissions until 2008. By that time, a great deal of damage will already have been done. But we can slow things down. (120) If action today can keep the climate from eventually reaching an unstable tipping point or can finally begin to reverse the warming trend a century from now, the effort would hardly be futile. Humanity embarked unknowingly on the dangerous experiment of tinkering with the climate of our planet. Now that we know what we're doing, it would be utterly foolish to continue.

— Michael D. Lemonick
excerpted from "Life in the Greenhouse"
Time, April 9, 2001

MAP
Consequences of Global Warming

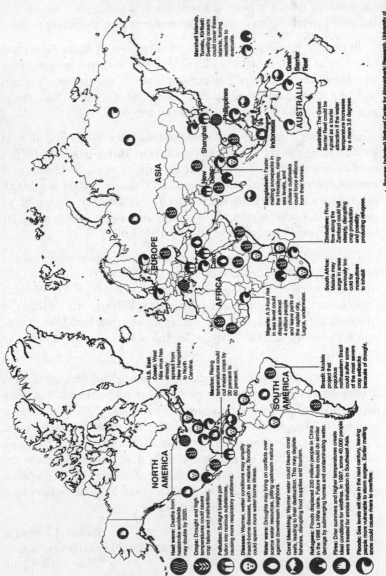

Marshall Islands, Tuvalu, Kiribati: Swelling oceans could cover these islands, forcing residents to evacuate.

Great Barrier Reef

Australia: The Great Barrier Reef could be ruined as a tourist attraction if the water temperature increases by a mere 3.6 degrees.

Bangladesh: Faster melting snowpacks in the Himalayas, rising sea levels, and cholera outbreaks could force millions from their homes.

Zimbabwe: River flow along the Zambezi could fall steeply, cutting crop production and possibly producing refugees.

South Africa: Malaria may surge in areas previously too cold for mosquitoes to inhabit.

Nigeria: A 3-foot rise in sea level could displace almost 4 million people and leave parts of the capital city, Lagos, underwater.

U.S. East Coast: West Nile virus has already spread from New Hampshire to North Carolina.

Mexico: Rising temperatures could cut maize crops by 20 percent to 60 percent.

Brazil: Models project that populous northeastern Brazil could suffer some of the most severe consequences of drought.

Sources: (adapted) National Center for Atmospheric Research, University of Virginia, Worldwatch Institute, National Climatic Data Center, World Meteorological Organization, and staff reports; and Rod Dale, Rob Cady, and Stephen Rountree / U.S. News and World Report, February 5, 2001.

Heat wave: Deaths from heatstroke worldwide may double by 2020.

Crops: Drought and high temperatures could cause crop failure and malnutrition.

Pollution: Sunlight breaks pollution into various substances, causing more respiratory problems.

Disease: Warmer, wetter conditions may amplify insect-borne diseases, such as malaria; flooding could spawn more water-borne illness.

Water waves: Droughts may bring on conflicts over scarce water resources, pitting upstream nations against downstream neighbors.

Coral bleaching: Warmer water could bleach coral reefs, leading to their destruction. This may deplete fisheries, disrupting food supplies and tourism.

Refugees: Floods displaced 230 million people in China in the 1998 La Niña rains. Future floods could do similar damage by submerging homes and contaminating water.

Fires: Drier summers and higher temperatures create ideal conditions for wildfires. In 1997, some 40,000 people were treated for smoke inhalation in Southeast Asia.

Floods: Sea levels will rise in the next century, leaving people more vulnerable to storm surges. Earlier melting snow could cause rivers to overflow.

Multiple-Choice Questions

Directions (7–16): Select the best suggested answer to each question and write its number in the space provided. The questions may help you think about ideas and information you might want to use in your writing. You may return to these questions anytime you wish.

7 According to the article, the IPCC confirmed the effects of global warming by

  (1) surveying scientists in several countries
  (2) experimenting with specific plants
  (3) studying data collected over time
  (4) establishing standard units for measuring temperature   7 _____

8 Lines 16 through 24 present a list of

  (1) possible methods of preventing global warming
  (2) controversial theories about global warming
  (3) probable causes of global warming
  (4) observable evidence of global warming   8 _____

9 The article cites "coastal Florida, much of Louisiana, the Nile Delta, the Maldives, Bangladesh" (lines 40 and 41) as areas that could become uninhabitable due to

  (1) flooding   (3) storms
  (2) drought   (4) earthquakes   9 _____

10 According to the article, what is one way people will be affected by rising sea levels?

  (1) Sea plants will be harder to harvest.
  (2) The number of water-related accidents will increase.
  (3) Current ocean maps will become unreliable.
  (4) Drinking water will be less plentiful.   10 _____

11 According to the article, global warming may result
in more cases of malaria because

    (1) humans' immune systems will be weakened
    (2) habitats favorable to some insects will increase
    (3) most rodents cannot survive in hot climates
    (4) people will tend to move to cooler regions   11____

12 According to the article, how might agriculture in
temperate zones be affected by slightly higher temperatures?

    (1) Farmers would use less fuel.
    (2) Green plants would be more nutritious.
    (3) Crop yields would increase temporarily.
    (4) Farm animals would require less food.   12____

13 The article implies that a "greenhouse gas" (line 96)
is a gas that

    (1) produces both heat and light
    (2) stimulates plants to give off heat
    (3) absorbs heat from the earth's surface
    (4) prevents heat from leaving the atmosphere   13____

14 The map indicates an increased danger of death
from heat stroke in

    (1) North America   (3) Africa
    (2) South America   (4) Australia   14____

15 According to the map, one effect of global warming
on countries in the southern half of Africa will be

    (1) depleted water supplies for downstream nations
    (2) depleted fishing from coral bleaching
    (3) increased rates of insect-borne disease
    (4) increased incidents of wildfires   15____

16 According to the map, global warming would lead
   to increased respiratory problems in which country?

   (1) United States   (3) Brazil

   (2) Mexico   (4) Nigeria   16 _____

After you have finished these questions, review **The
Situation** and read **Your Task** and the **Guidelines**.
Use scrap paper to plan your response. Then write
your response to Part B on separate sheets of paper.

Session Two

Part A

Directions: Read the passages on the following pages (a short story
excerpt and an autobiographical excerpt). Write the number of the
answer to each multiple-choice question in the space provided.
Then write the essay on separate sheets of paper as described in
Your Task. You may use the margins to take notes as you read and
scrap paper to plan your response.

Your Task:

After you have read the passages and answered the
multiple-choice questions, write a unified essay about
the things mothers do for their children as revealed in
the passages. In your essay, use ideas from **both** passages to establish a controlling idea about the things
mothers do for their children. Using evidence from
each passage, develop your controlling idea and show
how the author uses specific literary elements or techniques to convey that idea.

Guidelines:
Be sure to
- Use ideas from *both* passages to establish a controlling idea about the things mothers do for their children
- Use specific and relevant evidence from *each* passage to develop your controlling idea
- Show how each author uses specific literary elements (for example: theme, characterization, structure, point of view) or techniques (for example: symbolism, irony, figurative language) to convey the controlling idea
- Organize your ideas in a logical and coherent manner
- Use language that communicates ideas effectively
- Follow the conventions of standard written English

Passage I

. . . "Well, Mary." Aunt Elvera heaved herself up the porch steps and drew off her gauntlet gloves. "I can see you are having a busy day." Mama's hands were fire red from strawberry juice and the heat of the stove. Mine were scratched all over from picking every ripe berry in the patch.

(5) "One day's like another on the farm," Mama remarked.

"Then I will not mince words," Aunt Elvera said, overlooking me. "I'd have rung you up if you were connected to the telephone system."

"What about, Elvera?" She and Mama weren't sisters. They were sisters-in-law.

"Why, the Fair, of course!" Aunt Elvera bristled in an important way. "What
(10) else? The Louisiana Purchase Exposition in St. Louis. The world will be there. It puts St. Louis at the hub of the universe." Aunt Elvera's mouth worked wordlessly.

"Well, I do know about it," Mama said. "I take it you'll be going?"

Aunt Elvera waved her away. "My stars, yes. You know how Schumate can be. Tight as a new boot. But I put my foot down. Mary, this is the opportunity of a
(15) lifetime. We will not see such wonders again during our span."

"Ah," Mama said, and my mind wandered— took a giant leap and landed in St. Louis. We knew about the Fair. The calendar the peddler gave us at Christmas featured a different pictorial view of the Fair for every month. There were white palaces in gardens with gondolas in waterways, everything electric-lit. Castles from
(20) Europe and paper houses from Japan. For the month of May the calendar featured the great floral clock on the fairgrounds.

"Send us a postal," Mama said.

"The thing is ..." Aunt Elvera's eyes slid toward Dorothy. "We thought we'd invite Geneva to go with us."

(25) My heart liked to lurch out of my apron. Me? They wanted to take me to the Fair?

"She'll be company for Dorothy."

Then I saw how it was. Dorothy was dim, but she could set her heels like a mule. She wanted somebody with her at the Fair so she wouldn't have to trail after
(30) her mother every minute. We were about the same age. We were in the same grade, but she was a year older, having repeated fourth grade. She could read, but her lips moved. And we were cousins, not friends.

"It will be educational for them both," Aunt Elvera said. "All the progress of civilization as we know it will be on display. They say a visit to the Fair is tantamount
(35) to a year of high school."

"Mercy," Mama said.

"We will take the Wabash Railroad directly to the gates of the Exposition," Aunt Elvera explained, "and we will be staying on the grounds themselves at the Inside Inn." She leaned nearer Mama, and her voice fell. "I'm sorry to say that there will
(40) be stimulants for sale on the fairgrounds. You know how St. Louis is in the hands of the breweries." Aunt Elvera was sergeant-at-arms of the Women's Christian Temperance Union, and to her, strong drink was a mocker. "But we will keep the girls away from that sort of thing." Her voice fell to a whisper. "And we naturally won't set foot on the Pike."

(45) We knew what the Pike was. It was the midway of the Fair, like a giant carnival with all sorts of goings-on.

"Well, many thanks, but I don't think so," Mama said.

My heart didn't exactly sink. It never dawned on me that I'd see the Fair. I was only a little cast down because I might never get another glimpse of the world.

(50)   "Now, you're not to think of the money," Aunt Elvera said. "Dismiss that from your mind. Schumate and I will be glad to cover all Geneva's expenses. She can sleep in the bed with Dorothy, and we are carrying a good deal of our eats. I know these aren't flush times for farmers, Mary, but do not let your pride stand in Geneva's way."

(55)   "Oh, no," Mama said mildly. "Pride cometh before a fall. But we may be running down to the Fair ourselves."

Aunt Elvera's eyes narrowed, and I didn't believe Mama, either. It was just her way of fending off my aunt. Kept me from being in the same bed with Dorothy, too. . . .

(60)   I could tell you very little about the rest of that day. My mind was miles off. I know Mama wrung the neck off a fryer, and we had baking-powder biscuits to go with the warm jam. After supper my brothers hitched up Fanny to the trap and went into town. I took a bottle brush to the lamp chimneys and trimmed the wicks. After that I was back out on the porch swing while there was some daylight left. The
(65)   lightning bugs were coming out, so that reminded me of how the Fair was lit up at night with electricity, brighter than day.

Then Mama came out and settled in the swing beside me, which was unusual, since she never sat out until the nights got hotter than this. We swung together awhile. Then she said in a quiet voice, "I meant it. I want you to see the Fair."

(70)   Everything stopped then. I still didn't believe it, but my heart turned over.

"I spoke to your dad about it. He can't get away, and he can't spare the boys. But I want us to go to the Fair."

Oh, she was brave to say it, she who hadn't been anywhere in her life. Brave even to think it. "I've got some egg money put back," she said. We didn't keep
(75)   enough chickens to sell the eggs, but anything you managed to save was called egg money.

"That's for a rainy day," I said, being practical.

"I know it," she said. "But I'd like to see that floral clock."

Mama was famous for her garden flowers. When her glads were up, every color,
(80)   people drove by to see them. And there was nobody to touch her for zinnias.

Oh, Mama, I thought, *is this just a game we're playing?* "What'll we wear?" I asked, to test her.

"They'll be dressy down at the Fair, won't they?" She said. "You know those artificial cornflowers I've got. I thought I'd trim my hat with them. And you're
(85) getting to be a big girl. Time you had a corset."

So then I knew she meant business. . . .

— Richard Peck
"The Electric Summer"
from *Time Capsule*, 1999
Delacorte Press

Passage II

I began working in journalism when I was eight years old. It was my mother's idea. She wanted me to "make something" of myself and, after a levelheaded appraisal of my strengths, decided I had better start young if I was to have any chance of keeping up with the competition....

(5)   With my load of magazines I headed toward Belleville Avenue. That's where the people were. There were two filling stations at the intersection with Union Avenue, as well as an A&P, a fruit stand, a bakery, a barber shop, Zuccarelli's drugstore, and a diner shaped like a railroad car. For several hours I made myself highly visible, shifting position now and then from corner to corner, from shop

(10)   window to shop window, to make sure everyone could see the heavy black lettering on the canvas bag that said THE SATURDAY EVENING POST. When the angle of the light indicated it was suppertime, I walked back to the house.

"How many did you sell, Buddy?" my mother asked.

"None."

(15)   "Where did you go?"

"The corner of Belleville and Union Avenues."

"What did you do?"

"Stood on the corner waiting for somebody to buy a *Saturday Evening Post.*"

"You just stood there?"

(20)   "Didn't sell a single one."

"For God's sake, Russell!"

Uncle Allen intervened. "I've been thinking about it for some time," he said, "and I've about decided to take the *Post* regularly. Put me down as a regular customer." I handed him a magazine and he paid me a nickel. It was the first

(25)   nickel I earned.

Afterwards my mother instructed me in salesmanship. I would have to ring doorbells, address adults with charming self-confidence, and break down resistance with a sales talk pointing out that no one, no matter how poor, could afford to be without the *Saturday Evening Post* in the home.

(30)   I told my mother I'd changed my mind about wanting to succeed in the magazine business.

"If you think I'm going to raise a good-for-nothing," she replied, "you've got another think coming." She told me to hit the streets with the canvas bag and start ringing doorbells the instant school was out next day. When I objected that I *(35)* didn't feel any aptitude for salesmanship, she asked how I'd like to lend her my leather belt so she could whack some sense into me. I bowed to superior will and entered journalism with a heavy heart.

My mother and I had fought this battle almost as long as I could remember. It probably started even before memory began, when I was a country child in *(40)* northern Virginia and my mother, dissatisfied with my father's plain workman's life, determined that I would not grow up like him and his people, with calluses on their hands, overalls on their backs, and fourth-grade educations in their heads. She had fancier ideas of life's possibilities. Introducing me to the *Saturday Evening Post*, she was trying to wean me as early as possible from my father's *(45)* world where men left with their lunch pails at sunup, worked with their hands until the grime ate into the pores, and died with a few sticks of mail-order furniture as their legacy. In my mother's vision of the better life there were desks and white collars, well-pressed suits, evenings of reading and lively talk, and perhaps—if a man were very, very lucky and hit the jackpot, really made *(50)* something important of himself—perhaps there might be a fantastic salary of $5,000 a year to support a big house and a Buick with a rumble seat and a vacation in Atlantic City....

—Russell Baker
from *Growing Up*, 1982
Congdon & Weed

Multiple-Choice Questions

Directions (1–10): Select the best suggested answer to each question and write its number in the space provided. The questions may help you think about the ideas and information you might want to use in your essay. You may return to these questions anytime you wish.

Passage I (the short story excerpt) — Questions 1–6 refer to Passage I.

1 Mama's statement, "One day's like another on the farm," (line 5) indicates that Mama felt

  (1) homesick   (3) jealous

  (2) resigned   (4) curious   1 _____

2 The narrator concludes that she is being invited to the Fair primarily because

  (1) Aunt Elvera pities her

  (2) Dorothy admires her

  (3) Aunt Elvera values education

  (4) Dorothy wants a companion   2 _____

3 In line 74 "egg money" refers to money set aside for

  (1) investment   (3) emergencies

  (2) supplies   (4) food   3 _____

4 The narrator thinks that Mama is brave to talk about going to the Fair because Mama

  (1) has never traveled before

  (2) dislikes being in a crowded place

  (3) fears Geneva would be embarrassed

  (4) is worried about her husband and sons   4 _____

5 The narrator implies that Mama's true reason for
  visiting the Fair is to

  (1) sell the eggs and chickens
  (2) find a husband for Geneva
  (3) show off her new clothes
  (4) give Geneva an unusual experience   5____

6 The sentence, "So then I knew she meant business,"
  (line 86) suggests that Mama's talk about the Fair is
  becoming a

  (1) plan   (3) fantasy
  (2) burden   (4) disaster   6____

Passage II (the autobiographical excerpt) — Questions 7–10 refer
to Passage II.

7 The list of details in lines 6 through 8 establishes
  the setting as

  (1) an elegant residential area
  (2) a busy shopping area
  (3) an empty railway station
  (4) a quiet office building   7____

8 The dialogue in lines 13 through 21 reveals the
  mother's sense of

  (1) fear   (3) dismay
  (2) greed   (4) remorse   8____

9 Uncle Allen probably decided to buy the *Post*
  because he

  (1) preferred the *Post* to other magazines
  (2) hoped to impress Russell's mother
  (3) wanted a career in journalism
  (4) felt sorry for Russell   9____

10 The narrator suggests that his battle with his mother was the result of her

   (1) appreciation of journalism
   (2) desire to get him out of the house
   (3) ideas about success
   (4) admiration for her husband's work   10 _____

After you have finished these questions, review **Your Task** and the **Guidelines**. Use scrap paper to plan your response. Then write your response to Part A on separate sheets of paper. After you finish your response for Part A, complete Part B.

Part B

Your Task:

Write a critical essay in which you discuss *two* works of literature you have read from the particular perspective of the statement that is provided for you in the **Critical Lens**. In your essay, provide a valid interpretation of the statement, agree *or* disagree with the statement as you have interpreted it, and support your opinion using specific references to appropriate literary elements from the two works. You may use scrap paper to plan your response. Write your essay in Part B on separate sheets of paper.

Critical Lens:

> "In a dark time, the eye begins to see,..."
> — Theodore Roethke
> *The Collected Poems of Theodore Roethke*, 1966

Guidelines:

Be sure to

- Provide a valid interpretation of the critical lens that clearly establishes the criteria for analysis
- Indicate whether you agree *or* disagree with the statement as you have interpreted it
- Choose *two* works you have read that you believe best support your opinion
- Use the criteria suggested by the critical lens to analyze the works you have chosen
- Avoid plot summary. Instead, use specific references to appropriate literary elements (for example: theme, characterization, setting, point of view) to develop your analysis
- Organize your ideas in a unified and coherent manner
- Specify the titles and authors of the literature you choose
- Follow the conventions of standard written English

Regents Comprehensive Examination in English—June 2004
Chart for Determining the Final Examination Score (Use for June 2004 examination only.)

To determine the student's final examination score, locate the student's total essay score across the top of the chart and the student's total multiple-choice score down the side of the chart. The point where those two scores intersect is the student's final examination score. For example, a student receiving a total essay score of 17 and a total multiple-choice score of 20 would receive a final examination score of 77.

Total Multiple-Choice Score \ Total Essay Score	0	1	2	3	4	5	6	7	8	9	10	11	12	13	14	15	16	17	18	19	20	21	22	23	24
0	0	1	2	3	4	5	7	9	11	14	17	20	23	26	30	33	37	40	44	48	52	56	59	63	67
1	1	2	3	4	5	6	8	10	13	15	18	21	24	28	31	35	39	42	46	50	54	58	61	65	69
2	1	3	4	4	5	7	8	11	14	17	20	23	26	30	33	37	40	44	48	52	56	59	63	67	70
3	2	3	5	6	6	8	10	13	15	18	21	24	28	31	35	39	42	46	50	54	58	61	65	69	72
4	2	4	5	6	7	9	11	14	17	20	23	26	30	33	37	40	44	48	52	56	59	63	67	70	74
5	3	4	6	7	8	10	13	15	18	21	24	28	31	35	39	42	46	50	54	58	61	65	69	72	76
6	3	5	6	8	9	11	14	17	20	23	26	30	33	37	40	44	48	52	56	59	63	67	70	74	77
7	4	5	7	9	10	13	15	18	21	24	28	31	35	39	42	46	50	54	58	61	65	69	72	76	79
8	4	6	8	9	11	14	17	20	23	26	30	33	37	40	44	48	52	56	59	63	67	70	74	77	80
9	5	6	9	10	13	15	18	21	24	28	31	35	39	42	46	50	54	58	61	65	69	72	76	79	82
10	5	7	9	11	14	17	20	23	26	30	33	37	40	44	48	52	56	59	63	67	70	74	77	80	84
11	6	8	10	13	15	18	21	24	28	31	35	39	42	46	50	54	58	61	65	69	72	76	79	82	85
12	7	9	11	14	17	20	23	26	30	33	37	40	44	48	52	56	59	63	67	70	74	77	80	84	86
13	8	10	13	15	18	21	24	28	31	35	39	42	46	50	54	58	61	65	69	72	76	79	82	85	88
14	9	11	14	17	20	23	26	30	33	37	40	44	48	52	56	59	63	67	70	74	77	80	84	86	89
15	10	13	15	18	21	24	28	31	35	39	42	46	50	54	58	61	65	69	72	76	79	82	85	88	90
16	11	14	17	20	23	26	30	33	37	40	44	48	52	56	59	63	67	70	74	77	80	84	86	89	92
17	13	15	18	21	24	28	31	35	39	42	46	50	54	58	61	65	69	72	76	79	82	85	88	90	93
18	14	17	20	23	26	30	33	37	40	44	48	52	56	59	63	67	70	74	77	80	84	86	89	92	94
19	15	18	21	24	28	31	35	39	42	46	50	54	58	61	65	69	72	76	79	82	85	88	90	93	95
20	17	20	23	26	30	33	37	40	44	48	52	56	59	63	67	70	74	77	80	84	86	89	92	94	96
21	18	21	24	28	31	35	39	42	46	50	54	58	61	65	69	72	76	79	82	85	88	90	93	95	97
22	20	23	26	30	33	37	40	44	48	52	56	59	63	67	70	74	77	80	84	86	89	92	94	96	97
23	21	24	28	31	35	39	42	46	50	54	58	61	65	69	72	76	79	82	85	88	90	93	95	97	98
24	23	26	30	33	37	40	44	48	52	56	59	63	67	70	74	77	80	84	86	89	92	94	96	97	99
25	24	28	31	35	39	42	46	50	54	58	61	65	69	72	76	79	82	85	88	90	93	95	97	98	99
26	26	30	33	37	40	44	48	52	56	59	63	67	70	74	77	80	84	86	89	92	94	96	97	99	100

Answers
June 2004
English

Answer Key

Session One, Part A	Session One, Part B	Session Two, Part A
1. 1	7. 3	1. 2
2. 4	8. 4	2. 4
3. 3	9. 1	3. 3
4. 2	10. 4	4. 1
5. 1	11. 2	5. 4
6. 4	12. 3	6. 1
	13. 4	7. 2
	14. 1	8. 3
	15. 3	9. 4
	16. 2	10. 3

Answers Explained

Session One

Part A   (1–6)

Note: Refer to Chapter 1 for review and strategy in responding to this part of the examination.

(1) **1** "wise historians." At the beginning of the passage, the speaker points out the importance in West African villages of ". . . listening to the elders for it is they who hold within them the wisdom gained by previous generations."

(2) **4** "mythology." The anecdote about the eclipse of the moon illustrates the speaker's assertion that, ". . . in traditional West Africa, mythology serves to explain the unexplainable . . . ."

(3) **3** "a collection of tales and songs." The speaker reports that, "These myths, epics . . . tales, songs . . . have come to be known as the 'old speech.'"

(4) **2** "belong to a certain social class." The term "caste" means social class or rank. (This is an example of how knowledge of vocabulary is tested in context.)

(5) **1** "preserve the nobles' past." The speaker tells us that, "In return for keeping their family genealogy and history . . . and singing songs of praise, nobles will help support the griot famlies."

(6) **4** "release natural abilities." Toward the end of the passage, the speaker reports that the years of training of griots ". . . are simply to release that which is already within."

Part A   Sample Student Response Essay

In ancient times, culture was preserved through an oral tradition of epic storytelling. However, in most societies today, modern media have undermined this function of speech.

In West Africa, though, there is a saying that persists even today: "Among the things existing in the world, speech is the only thing giving birth to its mother." In West Africa, members of the griot caste are responsible for maintaining and passing on the history, myths, and traditions that are the cultural fabric of their people.

A griot performs many functions in West African village life. In addition to maintaining the folklore, history, and mythology of his people, he is responsible for passing on the accumulated wisdom of previous generations. Lessons are often taught or problems solved in village meetings, where the *griots tell their people meaningful stories and often sing songs in praise of the noble families that support them. The West Africans refer to this repository of collective knowledge as "old speech."*

Filling such an important role in community life requires a long apprenticeship and formal training. It is the tradition that to be a griot one must be born into the griot caste and that griots have the special knowledge in them at birth. The many years of training "release that which is already within." However, only those children who reveal unusual talent are chosen to apprentice with a master griot. Apprentices begin formal training by doing menial tasks such as cooking and cleaning, but they are also observing and listening to a master griot. The apprentice must first memorize the folklore, history, and mythology of his people. In addition to gaining the skills needed for effective storytelling, the students become skilled in design, repair, and playing of musical instruments. Eventually they will memorize all the elements of the "old speech" and be able to dramatically recite their people's epics accompanied by music. A griot may need as many as fifty years to reach proficiency.

The speaker indicates that the griot tradition is threatened by modern education and, of course, by such things as television. But he also points out that many believe that it might only become dormant and reemerge with a new generation of griots.

Analysis

This essay is successful in meeting the requirements of the task: to describe the griot tradition and explain how the tradition is passed on. The writer reveals a thorough understanding of the text by outlining the importance of the griot tradition and showing in detail the development of an apprentice griot. The writer has included several important details, which support development of the essay.

The organization is clear in the way the writer moves from the importance of oral tradition to the role of the griot in West African village life, to the process by which the griot develops his skills, to a conclusion about the place of the griot in a modern world. Sentence structure is varied and ideas are expressed in language that is rich and appropriate: ". . . *myths, and traditions that are the cultural fabric of their people;*" "*this repository of collective knowledge. . . .*" The writer also demonstrates control of the conventions. This essay meets the criteria for a high score.

(See pp. 31–35 for a detailed explanation of the rubric for this part of the examination.)

Part B   (7–16)

Note: Refer to Chapter 2 for review and strategy in responding to this part of the examination.

(7) **3** "studying data collected over time." At lines 11–12, the article reports that the IPPC analyzed "data going back at least two decades. . ." to confirm the effects of global warming.

(8) **4** "observable evidence of global warming." The paragraph cites as evidence of global warming the disappearance of glaciers, death of coral reefs, drought, and the shift in habitat of many plants and animals. This paragraph makes no reference to prevention, theories, or probable causes.

(9) **1** "flooding." This paragraph reports on the possibility of seas "rising as much as 3 ft.," which would make these areas uninhabitable.

(10) **4** "Drinking water will be less plentiful." At lines 46–47, the article asserts that "Rising seas would contaminate water supplies with salt."

(11) **2** "habitats favorable to some insects will increase." At lines 49–51, the article points out that, "Warmer temperatures could widen the range of disease-carrying . . . bugs, such as mosquitoes . . ., increasing the incidence of dengue fever, malaria, . . ."etc.

(12) **3** "Crop yields would increase temporarily." In the paragraph that begins at line 83, Lemonick points out that even slightly higher temperatures "would make some crops flourish—at first."

(13) **4** "prevents heat from leaving the atmosphere." The paragraph ends with the assertion that with a large release of methane, "that potent greenhouse gas would suddenly accelerate the <u>heat-trapping process</u>."

(14) **1** "North America." Of the four choices, North America is the only area on the map to show the symbol for heat wave.

(15) **3** "increased rates of insect-borne disease." The skull symbol, denoting incidence of malaria and other insect-borne disease, appears in three different regions of the southern half of Africa.

(16) **2** "Mexico." Of the four countries offered as choices, the map shows only Mexico with the symbol for pollution, which denotes increased risk of respiratory problems.

Part B   Sample Student Response Essay

Global warming is a significant problem that threatens all the inhabitants of the earth. Humans, animals, even plants will be the victims of the detrimental effects of global warming. The seeds of global warming were planted in the 1700s, with the advent of the Industrial Revolution. Since then, greenhouse gases (gases that prevent heat from leaving the atmosphere) have built up, causing an average worldwide temperature increase of more than 1° F over the past century. Although 1° may seem an insignificant increase, it has already begun to affect the global climate.

According to a study by the Intergovernmental Panel on Climate Change, this degree of warming has already caused glaciers to melt, coral reefs to die, and droughts to become prevalent in Asia and Africa. Migration patterns of some animals are also changing. The effects of these changes are not yet very pronounced, but they could eventually become disastrous. Melting glaciers could cause sea levels to rise, flooding many coastal areas such as Louisiana, Florida, and Bangladesh. Rising seawater will also contaminate our supplies of fresh water. Writing in an article for Time magazine in 2001, Michael D. Lemonick also points out that rising temperatures could "widen the range of disease-carrying rodents and bugs," leading to higher rates of diseases such as malaria.

The environmental changes caused by global warming could have other devastating effects on humans around the world. In North America and south-eastern Europe, for example, rising temperatures could double the number of deaths from heatstroke in just the next 17 years. And in Europe and Asia, respiratory illnesses could increase as a result of increased pollution. A scarcity of drinking water could lead to conflict in areas within Africa, and many regions of the globe will be subject to devastating fires. The effects of global warming on our world are serious and they cannot be ignored. In addition to the effects on human life, we may see changes in the habitat of many species of plants and animals, or we may see their disappearance altogether.

Global warming is not necessarily a naturally occurring phenomenon; it has been brought on by the actions of humans. Since we are responsible for causing it, we must be responsible for the consequences. We cannot undo the damage that has already been inflicted upon the environment nor can we prevent global warming that is underway. As Lemonick points out in his article, however, we can slow the process. This is of vital importance to avoid reaching what scientists call the "tipping point," the point at which "even a tiny additional increase would throw the system into violent change." If we are unable to prevent the climate from warming to this point, the world will suffer many or all of the catastrophic effects scientists and disaster movies predict.

Analysis

This essay meets the requirements of the task very well. The writer has summarized key points from the article, which is long and dense with information, and shown how serious the consequences of unchecked global warming could be. The organization of the essay follows the guidelines by first explaining what global warming is and then outlining some of its most serious consequences. The writer maintains a serious and thoughtful tone, keeping in mind that the purpose of the essay is to "increase public awareness."

This writer demonstrates a thorough understanding of the article and develops the ideas with information from both the article and the map. The first two paragraphs are based primarily on information from the article, and the third paragraph synthesizes information from the map. The discussion throughout remains focused on the serious threat posed by global warming, and the concluding reference to scientific predictions and disaster movies is very effective. The language is precise and sentences are often stylistically sophisticated: *"The seeds of global warming were planted in the 1700s"; "we may see changes in the habitat of many species of plants and animals, or we may see their disappearance altogether"; Since we are responsible for causing it, we must be responsible for the consequences."* The writer also demonstrates control of the conventions. This essay meets all the criteria for a high score.

(See pp. 48–53 for a detailed discussion of the rubric for this part of the examination.)

Session Two

Part A   (1–10)

Note: See Chapter 3 for review and strategy in responding to this part of the examination.

(1) **2** "resigned." To be resigned to something is to be uncomplaining, accepting. This best expresses the tone in Mama's remark.

(2) **4** "Dorothy wants a companion." At line 28, the narrator says, "Then I saw how it was. . . . She wanted somebody with her at the Fair so she wouldn't have to trail after her mother every minute." Aunt Elvera certainly values education, but Geneva understands that this was probably Dorothy's idea.

(3) **3** "emergencies." The narrator reminds her mother, "That's for a rainy day." This expression usually signifies setting something aside for emergencies or the unexpected.

(4) **1** "[Mama] has never traveled before." In line 73, Geneva remarks on how brave her mother was, ". . . she who hadn't been anywhere in her life."

(5) **4** "give Geneva an unusual experience." The passage suggests that Geneva's mother sees this as an opportunity for her daughter to have new experiences. She probably also sensed Geneva's desire to go in her reactions to Aunt Elvera's offer. When Mama comes out to sit on the swing she says, "I meant it. I want you to see the Fair."

(6) **1** "a plan." Geneva's mother is thinking about how to dress for the trip and has already decided how to trim her hat. She is also thinking about what Geneva will need, now that she is ". . . getting to be a big girl."

(7) **2** "a busy shopping area." The description here includes two filling stations, a grocery store and a fruitstand, a bakery, etc. There is nothing to suggest a residential area, office building, or railway station.

(8) **3** "dismay." Russell's mother is expressing her shock and exasperation at Russell's complete lack of effort to sell anything. She seems dumbfounded by his behavior.

(9) **4** "felt sorry for Russell." Russell says here that his uncle "intervened." That is, he stepped in to rescue Russell from greater anger in his mother.

(10) **3** "ideas about success." The final paragraph of the passage explains that Russell's mother was dissatisfied with her husband's plain workman's life and had "fancier ideas of life's possibilities." For her, success means white collars, suits, and a man's making "something important of himself. . . ." Baker says that from even before he could remember, his mother was battling to get him to aspire to something "better" for himself.

Part A   Sample Student Response Essay

In these two passages, a single incident offers a brief portrait of a mother who is determined that her child has a fuller or "better" life than her own. In each, the story is told from the point of view of the child as he or she remembers the experience. The setting of each suggests a time early in the twentieth century and families struggling to earn a living.

Mary, the mother in the first passage, sees an opportunity to give her daughter (and herself) some knowledge and experience beyond that of life on the farm. This opportunity arises when Aunt Elvera, Mary's sister-in-law, offers to take her daughter Geneva to the Louisiana Purchase Exposition in St. Louis as a companion for her own daughter. Geneva's narration exposes Aunt Elvera as somewhat condescending when she points out that the family is not "connected to the telephone system," and suggests that Mary and her family may not even know about the Fair and how important it is. Geneva also knows that Dorothy is not as bright as she is but perceives right away that Dorothy "wanted somebody with her . . . so she wouldn't have to trail after her mother every minute." Seeing Aunt Elvera and Dorothy through Geneva's eyes helps the reader understand why Geneva's mother would reject the offer. Nonetheless, the reader can't help but share Geneva's surprise when Mary says, mildly, that ". . . we may be running down to the Fair ourselves."

The bond between mother and daughter is a unifying theme introduced in the opening images of Geneva and her mother making jam. Geneva also knows her mother is trying to fend off her aunt and does not think she really means to go to the Fair. Geneva's understanding of her mother is also revealed in Geneva's recognition of her mother's "bravery" and willingness to spend the "egg money." The image of the two of them sitting in the swing talking about what clothes would be needed makes Mary's determination to offer her daughter a special experience vivid and convincing.

In the second passage, from Russell Baker's memoir, we see a mother who is determined that her son "make something of himself," whether he wants to or not. The passage reveals his mother's battle to "wean [him]" from his father's plain workman's life. The tone of the passage is ironic from the beginning, when Baker says that he "began working in journalism when I was eight years old." His mother, of course, wants him to develop ambition and salesmanship. In a few brief lines of dialogue, we hear an account of his first day selling and his mother's exasperation with him. Although Russell Baker is writing this many years later, he allows us to see him in the way his mother did and then accounts for her determination by explaining how dissatisfied she was with her husband's life.

In both passages, narrated from the child's perspective, we have a portrait of a mother who wants a better or fuller life for her child and who selects experiences she believes will support that goal. Through dialogue and narrative of a single incident, the author offers insight into the relationship of the mother and child.

Analysis

This essay has many strengths. The introduction establishes a controlling idea in the "portrait of a mother" and indicates which literary elements will be the focus of the essay: incident and point of view. These points are elaborated to show how dialogue in particular is effective in revealing character.

Development is especially good in the discussion of the first passage. The writer shows how "Geneva's narration exposes" the character of Aunt Elvera and later reveals her appreciation of what her mother has decided to do for her. The discussion is also enhanced by the writer's reference to images that support the theme of a bond between mother and daughter. The observation that "the reader can't help but share Geneva's surprise" is also insightful and well expressed.

The discussion of the Russell Baker passage is somewhat less focused, but the writer recognizes the irony in the tone and makes an excellent observation about point of view: ". . . he allows us to see him in the way his mother did." The emphasis on narration of a single incident also links the two passages and gives the essay coherence. Sentence structure is varied and quotes are well integrated. The writer also shows good control of the conventions. This essay meets all the criteria for a high score.

(See pp. 68–71 for a detailed discussion of the rubric for this part of the examination.)

Session Two

Note: See Chapter 4 for review and strategy in responding to this part of the examination.

Part B   Sample Student Response Essay

"In a dark time, the eyes begin to see . . . ." In this statement, Theodore Roethke expresses the belief that during hard, dark, and cruel times, your eyes are opened; you may discover new truths about yourself or about those around you. In both The Crucible, *by Arthur Miller, and* Macbeth, *by William Shakespeare, characters discover harsh truths in "dark times."*

In the Puritan colonies in 1692 the echoing cry of "witch" could be heard, especially in Salem, Massachusetts. John Proctor, characterized as a rugged and independent farmer, sees his wife accused of witchcraft by a young woman, Abigail Williams, with whom Proctor had once betrayed his wife. While in jail Goody Proctor faced hardships, but during the awful period she came to forgive her husband for his adultery and to understand his fundamental goodness. Had she not had this dark period to endure, she may never have "seen" her forgiveness and love for her husband. In his struggle to free his innocent wife, Proctor also tries to reveal Abby as a symbol of the jealousy and revenge in Salem's citizens.

The people of Salem represent some of the darkest qualities in the Puritans: they are closed-minded and ready to see evil or the devil in anyone who does not conform. The citizens of Salem had an aversion to the forest, which was a symbol of Satan and darkness. When several Puritan girls are discovered dancing in the forest, they save themselves from punishment by claiming to be the victims of witchcraft practiced by innocent women of the town. For Abigail, it also becomes an opportunity to condemn Proctor's wife.

Ironically, Abby appeared to the townsfolk of Salem as a "saint," bringing the witches of Salem to trial when actually, she and the other girls were making false accusations to protect themselves. It was also ironic that the only way those falsely accused could save themselves from hanging would be to "confess" to witchcraft; those who refused to commit the sin of lying were condemned. Proctor himself is condemned after trying to expose the fraud of the girls, but he refuses to save himself by confessing to something he has not done. His wife assures him that he is right not to "give them my name" and confirms her love for him. History tells us that the people of Salem later came to "see" the horror of what they had done.

The characters of Banquo and MacDuff in Macbeth were also able to see in a dark time. When Macbeth's future was foretold by the three witches, Banquo became suspicious of Macbeth's reaction to "thou shalt be king hereafter." After King Duncan is murdered in Macbeth's castle, the kingdom is plunged into darkness and fear. Because he fears Banquo may "see" what he has done, Macbeth has Banquo murdered.

It is the character of MacDuff who is the first to see that there is something unnatural in the circumstances of Duncan's death, and he refuses to attend Macbeth's coronation. After the murder of Banquo, MacDuff's suspicions grow stronger and he joins forces with Duncan's son to reclaim the throne.

It is also ironic that Lady Macbeth, who was stronger than her husband in planning the murder of Duncan, goes mad and is tormented by nightmares in which she "sees" the horror of what they have done. Even Macbeth will see what he has become and see that he has made his life a "tale told by an idiot . . . signifying nothing."

Analysis

This writer offers a brief but effective analysis of the critical lens and establishes a controlling idea in the metaphor of seeing as discovering "new truths about yourself or about those around you." The choice of works is especially appropriate to the image of "a dark time." The essay is developed with emphasis on characterization and with sufficient details from the plot to support the controlling idea. The discussion of irony links the two works and gives the essay coherence: ". . . the people of Salem later came to 'see' the horror of what they had done"; and in her madness, "Lady Macbeth . . . [must] 'see' the horror of what they have done."

The essay is logical in its organization as well. The writer briefly recalls the setting of each work to establish the "dark time," then shows how the characters discover truths about the evil around them and ultimately about themselves. The language is well chosen and reflects the works: "fundamental goodness," "a symbol of Satan and darkness," "an opportunity to condemn," "plunged into darkness and fear," "tormented by nightmares."

Composition is excellent as the writer is able to express complex ideas in appropriate sentence structures: "Ironically, Abby appeared to the townsfolk of Salem as a 'saint,' bringing the witches of Salem to trial, when in fact she and the other girls were making false accusations to protect themselves." "Because he fears Banquo may 'see' what he has done, Macbeth has Banquo murdered." Finally, this writer shows good control of the conventions and shows skill in the use of quotation. Although the essay has no formal conclusion, the insightful development of the controlling idea and the quality of the writing meet the criteria for a high score. (See pp. 80–83 for a full discussion of the rubric for this part of the examination.)

Examination August 2004

English

Session One

Part A

Overview: For this part of the test, you will listen to an account about sculptor Casimer Michalczyk, answer some multiple-choice questions, and write a response based on the situation described below. You will hear the account twice. You may take notes on the page alloted anytime you wish during the readings.

The Situation: As a member of your school's art club, you have been asked to write a feature article about an artist you admire for your club's newsletter. You have decided to write about sculptor Casimer Michalczyk and to describe his admirable qualities. In preparation for writing your feature article, listen to an account by writer Edie Clark about sculptor Casimer Michalczyk. Then use relevant information from the account to write your feature article.

Your Task: Write a feature article for your school's art club newsletter in which you describe the admirable qualities of sculptor Casimer Michalczyk.

Guidelines:
Be sure to

- Tell your audience what they need to know about Casimer Michalczyk and his admirable qualities
- Use specific, accurate, and relevant information from the account to support your discussion
- Use a tone and level of language appropriate for a feature article for an art club newsletter
- Organize your ideas in a logical and coherent manner
- Indicate any words taken directly from the account by using quotation marks or referring to the speaker
- Follow the conventions of standard written English

Note: For this portion of the examination, the teacher will read a passage aloud. You will not actually see the passage reprinted below. Therefore, you are encouraged to have someone read the passage to you, in order to simulate the examination as closely as possible.

Listening Passage

When Casimer Michalczyk graduated from Rhode Island School of Design (RISD) in 1938, he set forth to be a sculptor. But a sculptor is nothing without tools. As a student during the Depression, Casimer knew how to save money, and as a man of creative talent, he knew how to turn something that isn't into something that is. "I originally bought tools like everyone else, but they were expensive, and I found I could make my own and save money."

Over the course of his more-than-60-year career, carving everything from wind-tunnel models for experimental aircraft at Pratt & Whitney to the Justice statue that adorns the Old State House in Hartford to gravestones from slate, Casimer has amassed a fortune in tools — nearly 3,000 chisels, spatulas, brushes, knives, scrapers, saws, scribes, loops, pounders, gouges, and picks, the vast majority of them of his own devising. The homemade standard was not always about salvage. He found that what started out as a matter of thrift ended up as its own kind of art. "There's a reward in making your own tools. There were things I wanted to do that commercial tools could not do. Sculptors search for the best tool to bring a concept into being. A lot of times what I was looking for was a piece with an interesting shape or a different curve that could give the effect I was looking for in my work." He kept his eyes open wherever he went — scrap heaps, yard sales, and his own backyard.

Casimer, who has worked his entire career in dual studios in Glastonbury, Connecticut, and on Martha's Vineyard, used whatever he could find that was made of good hard steel, bronze, or brass: umbrella wire, threaded rod, bicycle-tire rims, motorcycle-chain links, old saw blades, C-clamps, lawn-mower blades, old dental tools, brass plumbing fixtures. For the handles, he turned to bamboo and steel tubing, which he especially liked for their hollow nature, shrub stalks, wooden dowels, tree branches, pencils. Old bones and animal horns worked well, as did, of course, discarded knife handles.

He calls these tools his "findings," but they are much more than that. Using a high-speed abrasive wheel, Casimer shaped the tools to his needs. "It's still the human hand that's the finest tool," he says. Long ago, Casimer trained himself to work ambidextrously so that when one hand gets tired, he can switch to the other. In his career, he has crafted markers for some 150 graves, not just stone markers but exquisite works of art.

Casimer is now 85 and looking at retirement. Over the past couple of years, he began to take apart his collection of tools. He brought them down from their shelves, where they have been set like paintbrushes in extra-large coffee cans and rinsed-out number-ten tomato cans. He selected 900 tools, many of them embedded with the dust of the slate stones he has carved, and donated them to the sculpture department at RISD. "I hope these will be useful to the students learning to work in three dimensions," he wrote in his letter informing the school of his decision. Michael Beresford, head of RISD's sculpture department, pronounced Casimer's unusual endowment "a wonderful opportunity."

By the year 2000, Casimer had hoped to endow his other alma mater, the Yale School of Art, with a similar gift. However, the school declined his offer, explaining that it no longer instructs its students in the art of carving in three dimensions. Rather, its sculpture department teaches only "assembly."

"I was astounded," Casimer says, clearly unhappy about this turn of events in the art world. He turned then to the Lyme Academy of Fine Arts in Old Lyme, Connecticut. Another 500 of his tools will go to that relatively new school, which he is delighted to know teaches the traditional art of sculpture.

In spite of all this generosity, Casimer has not left himself barren of tools. He continues to carve. He recently finished two new gravestones, one of them for the mother of Mary Travers (of Peter, Paul, and Mary fame). "I'm not working on a stone right now, but I'm thinking about one for myself," he says. "Just thinking."

—"Casimer's Gift"
from *Yankee*, December 1999

Notes

Multiple-Choice Questions

Directions (1–6): Use your notes to answer the following questions about the passage read to you. Select the best suggested answer and write its number in the space provided. The questions may help you think about ideas and information you might use in your writing. You may return to these questions anytime you wish.

1 The body of work produced by Casimer Michalczyk can best be described as being

   (1) difficult to understand
   (2) satirical and witty
   (3) varied in form and purpose
   (4) ahead of its time   1 _____

2 Later in his career Casimer Michalczyk suggested that his "reward" for making his own tools was an increase in his

   (1) creativity
   (2) fame
   (3) profit
   (4) security   2 _____

3 What quality in Michalczyk is suggested by his continuous use of discarded items in making tools?

   (1) kindness
   (2) playfulness
   (3) shyness
   (4) resourcefulness   3 _____

4 Casimer Michalczyk indicates that a sculptor's best tool is the

   (1) chisel
   (2) hand
   (3) saw
   (4) mind   4 _____

5 The fact that Casimer Michalczyk "trained himself to work ambidextrously" suggests that he possesses

  (1) competitiveness
  (2) honesty
  (3) dedication
  (4) sophistication   5 _____

6 What action did Casimer Michalczyk take to show his concern for the future of carving in three dimensions?

  (1) established a scholarship to the Yale School of Arts
  (2) founded his own art school
  (3) taught at the Rhode Island School of Design
  (4) presented a gift to the Lyme Academy of Fine Arts   6 _____

After you have finished these questions, review **The Situation** and read **Your Task** and the **Guidelines**. Use scrap paper to plan your response. Then write your response on separate sheets of paper. After you finish your response for Part A, complete Part B.

Part B

Directions: Read the text and study the map on the following pages, answer the multiple-choice questions, and write a response based on the situation described below. You may use the margins to take notes as you read and scrap paper to plan your response.

> **The Situation:** Your science class has just completed a unit on energy and your teacher has asked each student to write a position paper about one type of energy. You have chosen to write a position paper about wind power as an energy source and whether or not it could be useful in New York State.

Your Task: Using relevant information from **both** documents, write a position paper for your science class in which you explain how wind power is used as an energy source and whether you agree **or** disagree that wind power could be useful in New York State.

Guidelines:
Be sure to
- Tell your audience what they need to know about how wind power is used as an energy source
- Indicate whether you agree **or** disagree that wind power could be useful in New York State
- Use specific, accurate, and relevant information from the text **and** the map to support your opinion
- Use a tone and level of language appropriate for a position paper for your science class
- Organize your ideas in a logical and coherent manner
- Indicate any words taken directly from the text by using quotation marks or referring to the author
- Follow the conventions of standard written English

Quick Facts about Wind Energy

What is wind energy? The terms "wind energy" or "wind power" describe the process by which the wind is used to generate mechanical power or electricity. Wind turbines convert the kinetic energy in the wind into mechanical power. This mechanical power can be used for specific tasks (such as grinding
(5)   grain or pumping water) or a generator can convert this mechanical power into electricity to power homes, businesses, schools, and the like.

What causes the wind to blow? Wind is a form of solar energy. Winds are caused by the uneven heating of the atmosphere by the sun, the irregularities of the earth's surface, and the rotation of the earth. Wind flow patterns are modified
(10) by the earth's terrain, bodies of water, and vegetative cover. This wind flow, or motion energy, when "harvested" by modern wind turbines can be used to generate electricity.

When was wind energy first used? Since earliest recorded history, wind power has been used to move ships, grind grain and pump water. There is
(15) evidence that wind energy was used to propel boats along the Nile River as early as 5000 B.C. Within several centuries before Christ, simple windmills were used in China to pump water.

In the United States, millions of windmills were erected as the American West was developed during the late 19th century. Most of them were used to
(20) pump water for farms and ranches. By 1900, small electric wind systems were developed to generate direct current, but most of these units fell into disuse as inexpensive grid power was extended to rural areas during the 1930s. By 1910, wind turbine generators were producing electricity in many European countries.

How is the energy in the wind captured? Wind turbines, like aircraft
(25) propeller blades, turn in the moving air and power an electric generator which supplies an electric current. Modern wind turbines fall into two basic groups; the horizontal-axis variety, like the traditional farm windmills used for pumping water; and the vertical-axis design, like the eggbeater-style Darrieus model, named after its French inventor. Modern wind technology takes advantage of
(30) advances in materials, engineering, electronics, and aerodynamics. Wind turbines are often grouped together into a single wind power plant, also known as a wind farm, and generate bulk electrical power. Electricity from these turbines is fed into the local utility grid and distributed to customers just as it is with conventional power plants.

(35)   **How big are wind turbines?** Wind turbines are available in a variety of sizes, and therefore power ratings. The largest machine, such as the one built in Hawaii, has propellers that span more than the length of a football field and stands 20 building stories high, and produces enough electricity to power 1400 homes. A small home-sized wind machine has rotors between 8 and 25 feet in
(40)   diameter and stands upwards of 30 feet and can supply the power needs of an all-electric home or small business.

What are wind turbines made of? All electric-generating wind turbines, no matter what size, are comprised of a few basic components: the rotor (the part that actually rotates in the wind), the electrical generator, a speed control system,
(45)   and a tower. Some wind machines have fail-safe shutdown systems so that if part of the machine fails, the shutdown systems turn the blades out of the wind or put on brakes.

Are there good wind resources in the United States? Wind energy is very abundant in many parts of the United States. Wind resources are
(50)   characterized by wind-power density classes, ranging from class 1 (the lowest) to class 7 (the highest). Good wind resources (class 3 and above) which have an average annual wind speed of at least 13 miles per hour, are found along the east coast, the Appalachian Mountain chain, the Great Plains, the Pacific Northwest, and some other locations. North Dakota, alone, has enough energy from class 4
(55)   and higher winds to supply 36% of the electricity of the lower 48 states. Of course, it would be impractical to move electricity everywhere from North Dakota. Wind speed is a critical feature of wind resources, because the energy in wind is proportional to the cube of the wind speed. In other words, a stronger wind means a lot more power.

(60)   **What are the advantages of wind-generated electricity?** Numerous public opinion surveys have consistently shown that the public prefers wind and other renewable energy forms over conventional sources of generation. Wind energy is a free, renewable resource, so no matter how much is used today, there will still be the same supply in the future. Wind energy is also a source of clean,
(65)   non-polluting electricity. Unlike conventional power plants, wind plants emit no air pollutants or greenhouse gases. In 1990, California's wind power plants offset the emission of more than 2.5 billion pounds of carbon dioxide, and 15 million pounds of other pollutants that would have otherwise been produced. It would take a forest of 90 million to 175 million trees to provide the same air quality.

(70)   **What are the economic obstacles to greater wind power usage?** Even though the cost of wind power has decreased dramatically in the past 10 years,

the technology requires a higher initial investment than fossil-fueled generators[1]. Roughly 80% of the cost is the machinery, with the balance being the site preparation and installation. If wind generating systems are compared with fossil-
(75) fueled systems on a "life-cycle" cost basis (counting fuel and operating expenses for the life of the generator), however, wind costs are much more competitive with other generating technologies because there is no fuel to purchase and minimal operating expenses.

     Are there environmental problems facing wind power? Although wind
(80) power plants have relatively little impact on the environment compared to other conventional power plants, there is some concern over the noise produced by the rotor blades, aesthetic (visual) impacts, and sometimes birds have been killed by flying into the rotors. Most of these problems have been resolved or greatly reduced through technological development or by properly siting wind plants.
(85) Avian mortality[2] remains an issue to be better understood and resolved.

     Are there other drawbacks to the use of wind energy? The major challenge to using wind as a source of power is that it is intermittent and it does not always blow when electricity is needed. Wind cannot be stored (unless batteries are used); and not all winds can be harnessed to meet the timing of
(90) electricity demands. Further, good wind sites are often located in remote locations far from areas of electric power demand (such as cities). Finally, wind resource development may compete with other uses for the land and those alternative uses may be more highly valued than electricity generation. However, wind turbines can be located on land that is also used for grazing or even farming.

(95) **Is wind energy good for the economy?** Wind energy avoids the external or societal costs associated with conventional resources, namely, the trade deficit from importing foreign oil and other fuels, the health and environmental costs of pollution, and the cost of depleted resources. Wind energy is a domestic, reliable resource that provides more jobs per dollar invested than any other energy
(100) technology—more than five times that from coal or nuclear power. In 1994, wind turbine and component manufacturers contributed directly to the economies of 44 states, creating thousands of jobs for Americans....

     Wind industry ... today The wind energy industry has grown steadily over the last 10 years and American companies are now competing aggressively in
(105) energy markets across the nation and around the world. The industry, in partnership with the U.S. Department of Energy, continues to expand and

---

[1]fossil-fueled generators — generators using coal or oil
[2]avian mortality — bird death

develop a full range of highly reliable, efficient wind turbines. These new-generation turbines, when installed, perform at 98 percent reliability in the field, representing remarkable progress since the technology was first introduced in the
(110) early 1980s.

Wind power ... tomorrow Wind power has an expansive future according to experts. Wind energy has been the fastest growing source of electricity generation in the world in the 1990s. However, the majority of this growth has been in Europe, where government policies and high conventional energy costs
(115) favor the use of wind energy. The U.S. Department of Energy recently announced the Wind Powering America initiative with goals to power at least 5% of the nation's electricity with wind by 2020, increase the number of states with more than 20 megawatts of wind to 16 by 2005 and 24 by 2010, and increase federal use of wind energy to 5% by 2010....

— U.S. Department of Energy
excerpted from "Quick Facts about Wind Energy"
www.eren.doe.gov

MAP

New York Annual Average Wind Power

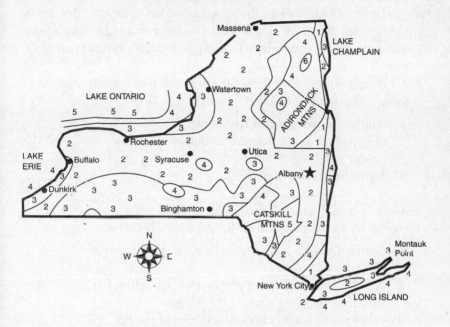

Wind resource is given in terms of wind power classes, ranging
from class 1 (the lowest) to class 7 (the highest). Areas designated
class 3 or greater are suitable for most wind turbine applications, whereas
class 2 areas are marginal. Class 1 areas are generally not suitable.

Source: (adapted) Wind Energy Resource Atlas of the United States, 1986
rredc.nrel.gov

Multiple-Choice Questions

Directions (7–16): Select the best suggested answer to each question and write its number in the space provided. The questions may help you think about ideas and information you might want to use in your writing. You may return to these questions anytime you wish.

7 According to the text, a decline in the use of windmills occurred in the 1930s because

(1) windmills broke down frequently
(2) affordable energy became available
(3) power needs decreased
(4) farms were abandoned   7_____

8 According to the text, North Dakota could *not* supply electricity to the rest of the United States because

(1) North Dakota has too little wind to generate electricity
(2) North Dakota's terrain is not suitable for installing wind turbines
(3) other states have sufficient sources of energy
(4) transporting electricity over great distances is inefficient   8_____

9 The author of the passage implies that wind power is desirable because

(1) windmills can be used everywhere
(2) wind travels at a constant speed
(3) wind energy is "clean" energy
(4) windmills are visually pleasing   9_____

10 According to the text, one environmental objection to wind turbines is that they

(1) spoil the scenery
(2) disturb wind patterns
(3) pollute the air
(4) create traffic problems   10 _____

11 As used in line 87, the word "intermittent" most nearly means

(1) cool
(2) occasional
(3) expensive
(4) impure   11 _____

12 The text implies that in 1994 most of the new jobs created by the wind power industry involved

(1) locating productive sites for wind power plants
(2) converting conventional power plants to wind power
(3) producing machine parts for wind power plants
(4) informing the public about wind power   12 _____

13 The text implies that one reason why the use of wind power has grown faster in Europe than in the United States is because, compared to the United States, Europe

(1) has more room for wind turbines
(2) has a windier climate
(3) pays more for fossil fuels
(4) provides better training for technicians   13 _____

14 According to the map, the location where the highest level of wind power in New York State occurs is

    (1) in the Catskill Mountains
    (2) in the Adirondack Mountains
    (3) around Syracuse
    (4) around Buffalo   14_____

15 The curved lines on the map are used to

    (1) define areas of similar wind power
    (2) indicate sites of conventional power plants
    (3) indicate the direction of prevailing winds
    (4) designate areas of power shortages   15_____

16 Wind power is *least* likely in the area that is immediately

    (1) east of Binghamton
    (2) south of Massena
    (3) west of Watertown
    (4) north of New York City   16_____

After you have finished these questions, review **The Situation** and read **Your Task** and the **Guidelines**. Use scrap paper to plan your response. Then write your response to Part B on separate sheets of paper.

Session Two

Part A

Directions: Read the passages on the following pages (an excerpt from a nonfiction work and a poem). Write the number of the answer to each multiple-choice question in the space provided. Then write the essay on separate sheets of paper as described in **Your Task.** You may use the margins to take notes as you read and scrap paper to plan your response.

Your Task:

> After you have read the passages and answered the multiple-choice questions, write a unified essay about the natural environment as revealed in the passages. In your essay, use ideas from **both** passages to establish a controlling idea about the natural environment. Using evidence from **each** passage, develop your controlling idea and show how the author uses specific literary elements or techniques to convey that idea.

Guidelines:
Be sure to

- Use ideas from **both** passages to establish a controlling idea about the natural environment
- Use specific and relevant evidence from **each** passage to develop your controlling idea
- Show how each author uses specific literary elements (for example: theme, characterization, structure, point of view) or techniques (for example: symbolism, irony, figurative language) to convey the controlling idea
- Organize your ideas in a logical and coherent manner
- Use language that communicates ideas effectively
- Follow the conventions of standard written English

Passage I

... With the dusk a strange bird came to the island from its nesting grounds on the outer banks. Its wings were pure black, and from tip to tip their spread was more than the length of a man's arm. It flew steadily and without haste across the sound, its progress as measured and as meaningful as that of the shadows
(5) which little by little were dulling the bright water path. The bird was called Rynchops, the black skimmer....

About sunset the tide had been out. Now it was rising, covering the afternoon resting places of the skimmers, moving through the inlet, and flowing up into the marshes. Through most of the night the skimmers would feed, gliding
(10) on slender wings above the water in search of the small fishes that had moved in with the tide to the shelter of grassy shallows. Because they fed on the rising tide, the skimmers were called flood gulls.

On the south beach of the island, where water no deeper than a man's hand ran over gently ribbed bottom, Rynchops began to wheel and quarter over the
(15) shallows. He flew with a curious, lilting motion, lifting his wings high after the downstroke. His head was bent sharply so that the long lower bill, shaped like a scissor blade, might cut the water.

The blade or cutwater plowed a miniature furrow over the placid sheet of the sound, setting up wavelets of its own and sending vibrations thudding down
(20) through the water to rebound from the sandy bottom. The wave messages were received by the blennies and killifish that were roving the shallows on the alert for food. In the fish world many things are told by sound waves. Sometimes the vibrations tell of food animals like small shrimps or oar-footed crustaceans moving in swarms overhead. And so at the passing of the skimmer the small
(25) fishes came nosing at the surface, curious and hungry. Rynchops, wheeling about, returned along the way he had come and snapped up three of the fishes by the rapid opening and closing of his short upper bill....

In the waters bordering the island many creatures besides the skimmers were abroad that night, foraging in the shallows. As the darkness grew and the
(30) incoming tide lapped higher and higher among the marsh grasses, two diamondback terrapins slipped into the water to join the moving forms of others of their kind. These were females, who had just finished laying their eggs above the high-tide line. They had dug nests in the soft sand, working with hind feet until they scooped out jug-shaped holes not quite so deep as their own bodies
(35) were long. Then they had deposited their eggs, one five, the other eight. These they had carefully covered with sand, crawling back and forth to conceal the location of the nest. There were other nests in the sand, but none more than two

weeks old, for May is the beginning of the nesting season among the diamondbacks.

(40)   As Rynchops followed the killifish in toward the shelter of the marsh he saw the terrapins swimming in the shallow water where the tide was moving swiftly. The terrapins nibbled at the marsh grasses and picked off small coiled snails that had crept up the flat blades. Sometimes they swam down to take crabs off the bottom. One of the two terrapins passed between two slender uprights *(45)* like stakes thrust into the sand. They were the legs of the solitary great blue heron who flew every night from his rookery three miles away to fish from the island.

The heron stood motionless, his neck curved back on his shoulders, his bill poised to spear fish as they darted past his legs. As the terrapin moved out into deeper water she startled a young mullet and sent it racing toward the beach in *(50)* confusion and panic. The sharp-eyed heron saw the movement and with a quick dart seized the fish crosswise in his bill. He tossed it into the air, caught it head first, and swallowed it. It was the first fish other than small fry that he had caught that night....

There were many fish moving in through the deep water of the channel *(55)* that night. They were full-bellied fish, soft-finned and covered with large silvery scales. It was a run of spawning shad, fresh from the sea. For days the shad had lain outside the line of breakers beyond the inlet. Tonight with the rising tide they had moved in past the clanging buoy that guided fishermen returning from the outer grounds, had passed through the inlet, and were crossing the sound by way *(60)* of the channel....

The fisherman who lived on the island had gone out about nightfall to set the gill nets that he owned with another fisherman from the town. They had anchored a large net almost at right angles to the west shore of the river and extending well out into the stream. All the local fishermen knew from their *(65)* fathers, who had it from their fathers, that shad coming in from the channel of the sound usually struck in toward the west bank of the river when they entered the shallow estuary, where no channel was kept open. For this reason the west bank was crowded with fixed fishing gear, like pound nets, and the fishermen who operated movable gear competed bitterly for the few remaining places to set their *(70)* nets....

About midnight, as the tide neared the full, the cork line bobbed as the first of the migrating shad struck the gill net. The line vibrated and several of the cork floats disappeared under the water. The shad, a four-pound roe, had thrust her head through one of the meshes of the net and was struggling to free herself. The *(75)* taut circle of twine that had slipped under the gill covers cut deeper into the delicate gill filaments as the fish lunged against the net; lunged again to free herself from something that was like a burning, choking collar; something that held her in an invisible vise and would neither let her go on upstream nor turn and seek sanctuary in the sea she had left....

(80)   By the time the first half-dozen shad had been caught in the net, the eels that lived in the estuary had become aware that a feast was in the offing. Since dusk they had glided with sinuating motion along the banks, thrusting their snouts into crabholes and seizing whatever they could catch in the way of small water creatures. The eels lived partly by their own industry but were also robbers
(85)   who plundered the fishermen's gill nets when they could....

As the eels poked their heads out of the holes under the roots of the marsh grasses and swayed gently back and forth, savoring eagerly the water that they drew into their mouths, their keen senses caught the taste of fish blood which was diffusing slowly through the water as the gilled shad struggled to escape. One by
(90)   one they slipped out of their holes and followed the taste trail through the water to the net.

The eels feasted royally that night, since most of the fish caught by the net were roe shad. The eels bit into the abdomens with sharp teeth and ate out the roe. Sometimes they ate out all the flesh as well, so that nothing remained but a
(95)   bag of skin, with an eel or two inside. The marauders could not catch a live shad free in the river, so their only chance for such a meal was to rob the gill nets....

Although there was as yet no light in the east, the blackness of water and air was perceptibly lessening, as though the darkness that remained were something less solid and impenetrable than that of midnight. A freshening air
(100)   moved across the sound from the east and, blowing across the receding water, sent little wavelets splashing on the beach....

The next time Rynchops flew up the estuary he met the fishermen coming downstream on the ebbing tide, net piled in the boat over some half-dozen shad. All the others had been gutted or reduced to skeletons by the eels. Already gulls
(105)   were gathering on the water where the gill net had been set, screaming their pleasure over the refuse which the fishermen had thrown overboard.

The tide was ebbing fast, surging through the gutter and running out to sea. As the sun's rays broke through the clouds in the east and sped across the sound, Rynchops turned to follow the racing water seaward.

— Rachel L. Carson
from *Under the Sea-Wind*, 1941
Simon and Schuster

Passage II

In Trackless Woods

In trackless woods, it puzzled me to find
Four great rock maples seemingly aligned,
As if they had been set out in a row
Before some house a century ago,
(5)   To edge the property and lend some shade.
I looked to see if ancient wheels had made
Old ruts to which these trees ran parallel,
But there were none, so far as I could tell—
There'd been no roadway. Nor could I find the square
(10)   Depression of a cellar anywhere,
And so I tramped on further, to survey
Amazing patterns in a hornbeam[1] spray
Or spirals in a pinecone, under trees
Not subject to our stiff geometries.

—— Richard Wilbur
from *The New Yorker*,
March 31, 2003

---

[1]hornbeam — tree of the birch family

Multiple-Choice Questions

Directions (1–10): Select the best suggested answer to each question and write its number in the space provided. The questions may help you think about the ideas and information you might want to use in your essay. You may return to these questions anytime you wish.

Passage I (the excerpt from a nonfiction work)—Questions 1–5 refer to Passage I.

1   According to the narrator, black skimmers' feeding habits are connected to the movement of

   (1) migrating birds
   (2) incoming tides
   (3) passing storms
   (4) fishing boats   1 _____

2   The action of Rynchops' bill (lines 16 through 20) is illustrated through

   (1) comparisons
   (2) measurements
   (3) historical references
   (4) numerous examples   2 _____

3   According to the narrator, black skimmers create vibrations in order to

   (1) assess water depth
   (2) signal danger
   (3) find their young
   (4) attract prey   3 _____

4 The phrase "foraging in the shallows" in line 29 suggests that the creatures are

   (1) finding shelter
   (2) seeking food
   (3) digging nests
   (4) looking for mates   4____

5 A key idea implied in this passage is that connections exist between

   (1) scientists and artists
   (2) the planets and the tides
   (3) one animal species and another
   (4) pollution and climate   5____

Passage II (the poem)—Questions 6–10 refer to Passage II.

6 The poem uses the word "trackless" (line 1) to introduce a

   (1) rhyme
   (2) contrast
   (3) simile
   (4) hyperbole   6____

7 The narrator is "puzzled" by the four maples because they are

   (1) at least 100 years old
   (2) near a large clearing
   (3) beside an old road
   (4) in a straight line   7____

8 Lines 6 through 10 tell us of the search for evidence of

   (1) man's altering of nature
   (2) time's passing in nature
   (3) nature's effect on man
   (4) nature's display of mathematics   8____

9 In lines 11 through 14 the narrator decides to look for

(1) additional varieties of trees
(2) further evidence of past dwellers
(3) other arrangements in nature
(4) another path out of the woods

9 _____

10 The author prepares the reader for the final line by using frequent references to

(1) effects of light
(2) types of trees
(3) surveying
(4) mathematics

10 _____

After you have finished these questions, review **Your Task** and the **Guidelines**. Use scrap paper to plan your response. Then write your response to Part A on separate sheets of paper. After you finish your response for Part A, complete Part B.

Part B

Your Task:

Write a critical essay in which you discuss *two* works of literature you have read from the particular perspective of the statement that is provided for you in the **Critical Lens**. In your essay, provide a valid interpretation of the statement, agree *or* disagree with the statement as you have interpreted it, and support your opinion using specific references to appropriate literary elements from the two works. You may use scrap paper to plan your response. Write your essay in Part B on separate sheets of paper.

Critical Lens:

> "A person is a person through other persons..."
>
> — Archbishop Desmond Tutu
> (The Right Reverend Desmond Mpilo Tutu)
> *Hope and Suffering: Sermons and Speeches*, 1983

Guidelines:

Be sure to

- Provide a valid interpretation of the critical lens that clearly establishes the criteria for analysis
- Indicate whether you agree *or* disagree with the statement as you have interpreted it
- Choose *two* works you have read that you believe best support your opinion
- Use the criteria suggested by the critical lens to analyze the works you have chosen
- Avoid plot summary. Instead, use specific references to appropriate literary elements (for example: theme, characterization, setting, point of view) to develop your analysis
- Organize your ideas in a unified and coherent manner
- Specify the titles and authors of the literature you choose
- Follow the conventions of standard written English

Regents Comprehensive Examination in English—August 2004
Chart for Determining the Final Examination Score (Use for August 2004 examination only.)

To determine the student's final examination score, locate the student's total essay score across the top of the chart and the student's total multiple-choice score down the side of the chart. The point where those two scores intersect is the student's final examination score. For example, a student receiving a total essay score of 17 and a total multiple-choice score of 20 would receive a final examination score of 77.

Total Multiple-Choice Score ↓ \ Total Essay Score →	0	1	2	3	4	5	6	7	8	9	10	11	12	13	14	15	16	17	18	19	20	21	22	23	24
0	0	1	2	3	4	5	7	9	11	14	17	20	23	26	30	33	37	40	44	48	52	56	59	63	67
1	1	2	3	4	5	6	8	10	13	15	18	21	24	28	31	35	39	42	46	50	54	58	61	65	69
2	1	2	3	4	5	7	9	11	14	17	20	23	26	30	33	37	40	44	48	52	56	59	63	67	70
3	2	3	4	5	6	8	10	13	15	18	21	24	28	31	35	39	42	46	50	54	58	61	65	69	72
4	2	3	5	5	7	9	11	14	17	20	23	26	30	33	37	40	44	48	52	56	59	63	67	70	74
5	3	4	5	6	8	10	13	15	18	21	24	28	31	35	39	42	46	50	54	58	61	65	69	72	76
6	3	4	6	7	9	11	13	16	19	22	25	28	31	35	39	42	46	50	54	58	61	65	67	72	76
7	4	5	6	8	10	13	15	18	20	23	26	30	33	37	40	44	48	52	56	59	63	67	70	74	77
8	4	6	7	9	11	14	17	20	23	26	28	31	35	39	42	46	50	54	58	61	65	69	72	76	79
9	5	7	8	10	13	16	18	21	24	28	30	33	37	40	44	48	52	56	59	63	67	70	74	77	80
10	5	8	9	11	14	17	20	23	26	28	31	35	37	40	44	48	50	54	58	61	65	69	72	76	82
11	6	9	11	13	17	20	23	26	28	31	35	37	40	44	48	52	56	59	63	67	70	74	77	80	84
12	7	9	11	14	17	20	23	26	30	33	37	40	44	48	52	56	59	63	67	70	74	77	80	84	85
13	8	10	13	15	18	22	25	28	31	35	39	42	46	50	54	58	61	65	69	72	76	79	82	85	86
14	9	11	14	17	20	23	26	30	33	37	40	44	48	52	56	59	63	67	70	74	77	80	84	86	88
15	10	13	15	18	21	25	28	32	35	39	42	46	50	54	58	61	65	69	72	76	79	82	85	88	89
16	11	14	17	20	23	26	30	33	37	40	44	48	52	56	59	63	67	70	74	77	80	84	86	89	90
17	13	16	18	21	24	28	32	35	39	42	46	50	54	58	61	65	69	72	76	79	82	85	88	90	92
18	14	17	20	23	26	30	33	37	40	44	48	52	56	59	63	67	70	74	77	80	84	86	89	92	93
19	16	18	22	25	28	32	35	39	42	46	50	54	58	61	65	69	72	76	79	82	85	88	90	93	94
20	17	20	23	26	30	33	37	40	44	48	52	56	59	63	67	70	74	77	80	84	86	89	92	94	95
21	18	21	24	28	31	35	39	42	46	50	54	58	61	65	69	72	76	79	82	85	88	90	93	95	96
22	20	23	26	30	33	37	40	44	48	52	56	59	63	67	70	74	77	80	84	86	89	92	94	96	97
23	21	24	28	31	35	39	42	46	50	54	58	61	65	69	72	76	79	82	85	88	90	93	95	96	98
24	23	26	30	33	37	40	44	48	52	56	59	63	67	70	74	77	80	84	86	89	92	94	96	97	99
25	24	28	31	35	39	42	46	50	54	58	61	65	69	72	76	79	82	85	88	90	93	95	96	98	99
26	26	30	33	37	40	44	48	52	56	59	63	67	70	74	77	80	84	86	89	92	94	96	97	99	100

Answers
August 2004
English

Answer Key

Session One, Part A	Session One, Part B	Session Two, Part A
1. **3**	7. **2**	1. **2**
2. **1**	8. **4**	2. **1**
3. **4**	9. **3**	3. **4**
4. **2**	10. **1**	4. **2**
5. **3**	11. **2**	5. **3**
6. **4**	12. **3**	6. **2**
	13. **3**	7. **4**
	14. **2**	8. **1**
	15. **1**	9. **3**
	16. **4**	10. **4**

Answers Explained

Session One

Part A   (1–6)

Note: Refer to Chapter 1 for review and strategy in responding to this part of the examination

    (1) **3** "varied in form and purpose." In introducing the section on Michalczyk's wide array of tools, the speaker points out that the sculptor has carved "everything from wind-tunnel models for experimental aircraft . . . to the Justice statue . . . in Hartford to gravestones in slate. . . ."

    (2) **1** "creativity." Michalczyk is quoted as saying that "There were things I wanted to do that commercial tools could not do." He indicates that in creating his own tools he was also looking for shapes or curves "that could give the effect I was looking for in my work." The passage offers no indication that his fame, profit, or security were directly rewarded by his making his own tools.

    (3) **4** "resourcefulness." To be "resourceful" means to be inventive, clever, and imaginative. It also denotes the ability to make good use of things as they are available. These qualities are evident in the description of how Michalczyk made use of "whatever he could find that was made of good hard steel, bronze, or brass. . . ."

    (4) **2** "hand." The sculptor is quoted directly as saying, "It's still the human hand that's the finest tool."

    (5) **3** "dedication." Like question 3 above, this is an example of how vocabulary is assessed on the Regents exam. The passage points out that Michalczyk trained himself to work "ambidextrously," that is, equally well with either hand. This ability allowed him to keep working even as one hand became tired. It suggests a devotion and commitment to working best described as "dedication."

    (6) **4** "presented a gift to the Lyme Academy of Fine Arts." The passage recounts that Michalczyk had planned to donate some of his tools to the Yale School of Art and was astounded to learn that Yale no longer taught "the art of carving in three dimensions." Instead, therefore, he gave his tools to the Lyme Academy, "which he is delighted to know teaches the traditional art of sculpture."

Part A Sample Student Response Essay

Casimer Michalczyk is a well-known sculptor and a man of many admirable qualities. He is known for the great variety in his work, which includes structures to test aircraft as well as statues and gravestones. He is also admirable for his resourcefulness, dedication, and generosity.

As a student at the Rhode Island School of Design during the Great Depression, Michalczyk learned early on the value of resourcefulness. In order to save money during those difficult times, he found ways to make many of his own tools. His creative nature allowed him to turn "a matter of thrift" into another form of his art. Describing his work, Michalczyk says, "There's a reward in making our own tools." The variety of tools he devised enabled him to create new effects in his sculpture; the tools he made for himself allowed him to do things he could not do with commercial tools. Michalczyk "kept his eyes open" and found materials in junk heaps, yard sales and backyards. He used anything he could find that was made of good steel or other metals. Michalczyk made tools out of saw blades, bicycle chains, old wire, and discarded plumbing fixtures; the handles were made from bamboo or steel tubing, or from tree branches, pencils, and old knife handles. He called these his "findings," and his collection includes over 3,000 chisels, knives, scrapers and other implements.

Casimer Michalczyk is also characterized by his dedication. Among the things he is best known for are grave markers. He has done more than 150 of those, and they are considered works of art. As a young man, he trained himself to be ambidextrous. He explains that he did this so that if one hand became tired, he could continue working with the other. His story suggests a man who loves his work, and at 85 he is only beginning to think of retiring.

Michalczyk's devotion to sculpture and his generosity are seen in the donations he has made to schools that teach the "art of carving in three dimensions." In the past few years, he took many of his tools from the large tomato cans where he stores them and made a gift of over 900 to his old school, the Rhode Island School of Design. Michael Burrisford [sic], head of the sculpture department was delighted to have the donation and saw it as a wonderful opportunity for the students. Michalczyk wanted to make a similar donation to Yale's art school and was astounded when they turned it down because Yale no longer teaches carving in three dimensions. Instead, he was delighted to make a large donation of tools to the Lyme Academy of Fine Arts in Connecticut, where traditional sculpture is still taught.

This resourceful, dedicated, and generous man is not completely without tools, and he continues to work on new gravestones. Is he working on one for himself? No, he is "just thinking."

Analysis

This writer shows how to restate the key term of the task into a controlling idea, which will guide the development of the rest of the essay. In the third sentence of the introduction, the concept of "admirable" is reiterated and the order of details for discussion is established: "his resourcefulness, dedication, and generosity."

The discussion reveals a thorough understanding and appreciation of the text. Ideas are well developed, with rich details from the passage. This suggests that the writer not only listened well but also took useful notes, including material for quotes. The organization is clear and follows the outline established in the introduction; the transition at the beginning of the third paragraph is simple, but effective: "Casimer Michalczyk is also characterized by his dedication." And the first sentence of the following paragraph links the sculptor's dedication to his generosity, the final point to be developed.

The essay maintains the focus on the controlling idea, and the language is precise and vivid. Sentences are varied and express complex ideas clearly; the use of a question and answer in the conclusion is also very effective. This writer demonstrates control of the conventions, including use of the semicolon and quotation. This essay meets all the criteria for a high score. (See pp. 31–35 for a detailed explanation of the rubric for this part of the examination.)

Part B (7–16)

Note: Refer to Chapter 2 for review and strategy in responding to this part of the examination.

(7) **2** "affordable energy became available." In the third section of the text (line 22) the article reports that "inexpensive grid power was extended to rural areas during the 1930s."

(8) **4** "transporting electricity over great distances is inefficient." At line 55, in discussion of the wind resources in North Dakota, the text also points out that ". . . it would be impractical to move electricity everywhere. . . ." The other choices are contradicted by information in the text.

(9) **3** "wind energy is 'clean' energy." The passage reports that public opinion strongly supports renewable sources of energy over conventional ones (line 61) and thus implies that cleaner sources of energy are also more

desirable. Beginning at line 64, the text asserts that "wind energy is also a source of clean, non-polluting energy . . . ," and offers details on the amount of pollution that "would otherwise have been produced."

(10) **1** "spoil the scenery." At line 82, the text cites "aesthetic (visual) impacts" among the environmental problems faced by wind power plants. None of the other choices is supported by the text.

(11) **2** "occasional." This is an example of a question about vocabulary in context. The text points out that wind "does not always blow when electricity is needed." Wind is not a constant or reliable source of power.

(12) **3** "producing machine parts for wind power plants." At line 100, the text reports that, "In 1994, wind turbine and component manufacturers . . . [created] thousands of jobs for Americans. . . ." Here the term "component" (basic part) is meant to be understood in context.

(13) **3** "pays more for fossil fuels." In the last paragraph, the text reports that the majority of growth in the development of wind energy has been in Europe, ". . . where high conventional [fossil fuel] energy costs favor the use of wind energy." None of the other choices is suggested by the text.

(14) **2** "in the Adirondack Mountains." The text accompanying the map explains that wind power classes range from 1 (lowest) to 7 (highest). The northern section of the Adirondack Mountains includes an area of level 6, the highest shown for the entire state.

(15) **1** "define areas of similar wind power." The areas within curved lines contain a single number, to show wind power classes. The text for the map refers only to areas of wind power classes; there is no reference to conventional power plants, prevailing winds, or power shortages.

(16) **4** "north of New York City." On the map, the area surrounding New York City to the north is identified as a class 1, defined as an area "generally not suitable" for wind power. Each of the other choices designates an area with a higher number or wind power class.

Part B   Sample Student Response Essay

As the nation grows and changes, and the population swells to even larger numbers, the need for energy increases. A source of cheap and effective energy is needed as we continue to deplete the limited fossil fuel resources. Wind power is a source of energy with tremendous potential: not only is it free, it is also clean and renewable. Harnessing wind energy would be a wise approach to adding sources of power for New York State.

The process of harnessing and using wind energy is a relatively simple one. Blades on a windmill structure or turbine rotate as the wind blows; this rotation powers an electric generator, and the generator supplies electric current. The idea behind the windmill itself is also a simple one. The kinetic energy, the energy of motion from the wind is turned into "mechanical" energy, which can be used to power things or can be further converted to electrical energy. Wind power plants, also known as "wind farms," can be used to create bulk electrical energy that can be sent into the local power grids and used as any other form of electricity would be.

The fact that wind energy is easily converted to power is not, by far, the only reason it should be used as a power source for New York State. The state is well suited because it has adequate wind resource levels, 3 or higher, in many regions. The eastern part of the state and the Adirondack Mountain range are especially suitable. Another important reason to support development of wind energy is that wind is free and the source of electricity is nonpolluting. Although the "technology requires a higher initial investment than fossil-fueled generators," in the long run, wind farms are much more cost effective "because there is no fuel to purchase." Another important reason to support development of wind energy is that it contributes directly to our economy. The U.S. Department of Energy reports that, "in 1994, wind turbine and component manufacturers contributed directly to the economies of 44 states, creating thousands of jobs for Americans. . . ."

Are there objections to the development of wind energy? There are some environmental concerns about wind power—some feel that the windmills are ugly and spoil the landscape, and they can also be noisy. Another serious concern is that birds are killed if they fly into the rotors. Supporters of wind energy point out that these problems can be reduced and people are trying to resolve the problem of "avian mortality."

On balance, I believe the use of wind energy as a power source for New York State is a good idea. The benefits far outweigh the disadvantages. Wind energy is free, clean, unpolluting and constantly renewable. If the state converts even partially to wind energy, by the time our fossil fuel resources run out, New York will already have alternate power sources in place. Development of wind energy makes good economic and environmental sense.

Analysis

The introduction reveals the writer's understanding of the task, to write a position paper about wind power as a source of energy for New York State. The paragraph summarizes a number of positive features of wind power, and the final sentence makes the writer's position clear: "Harnessing wind energy would be a wise approach. . . ."

Ideas are well developed here, with extensive use of detail and language from the text. The writer also makes good use of quotations. The organization is clear and supports the writer's position in favor of developing wind power as a source of energy. Use of the rhetorical question, "Are there objections . . .?" is a very effective way to introduce the paragraph that acknowledges the problems associated with wind power. The writer then responds to the opposition with a conclusion that begins, "On balance. . . ." These phrases are good transitions and good markers of the development of the writer's position.

Sentences are varied, and complex ideas are well explained. The essay has no significant errors in the conventions and meets all the criteria for a high score. (See pp. 48–53 for a detailed discussion of the rubric for this part of the examination.)

Session Two

Part A (1–10)

Note: See Chapter 3 for review and strategy in responding to this part of the examination.

(1) **2** "incoming tides." In line 11, the passage indicates that the skimmers "fed on the rising tide. . . ." This introduction to the description of the Rynchops or black skimmer makes no reference to migration, passing storms, or fishing boats.

(2) **1** "comparisons." In this passage Carson says of the Rynchops, ". . . the long lower bill, shaped like a scissor blade . . . or cutwater plowed a miniature furrow. . . ." These comparisons to a scissor blade and a plow offer vivid images of how the bird skims the water and cuts the surface with its beak.

(3) **4** "attract prey." Beginning at line 24, the passage notes that small fishes respond to the vibrations of the skimming bird by coming to the surface, where the skimmer then returns to snap them up.

(4) **2** "seeking food." *To forage* means to search or hunt for food. Note how the context leads to the meaning of the word. The sentence follows the paragraph describing how the skimmer hunts its food, and says, ". . . many creatures beside the skimmers were . . . foraging in the shallows."

(5) **3** "one animal species and another." This passage offers a detailed and lyrical description of the relationship of birds and sea life in a food chain, which also includes the human species as fishermen.

(6) **2** "contrast." The "trackless woods," meaning woods in which there is no evidence of a path or a road, are the setting for the narrator's experience of discovering that "amazing patterns" occur in nature, in contrast to the lines and squares of "our [human] stiff geometries." This contrast is the central theme of the poem. Although the third line might suggest a simile, it does not refer to "trackless."

(7) **4** "in a straight line." The four rock maple trees are "aligned/As if they had been set out in a row. . . ." The narrator even looks for evidence of a road or property line to account for the ordered arrangement (*alignment*) of the trees.

(8) **1** "man's altering of nature." The narrator describes his search for ruts left by a road or evidence that a cellar had been dug. Digging for a road or for a cellar would be examples of man's altering of a natural landscape.

(9) **3** "other arrangements in nature." The narrator says he "tramps on . . . to survey," that is, study or examine, "amazing patterns" in the branches of a birch tree and in the "spirals in a pinecone. . . ."

(10) **4** "mathematics." In reading the poem, we might not think specifically of mathematics, but the cumulative effect of the images in "aligned," "edge," "parallel," and "square" prepares us for Wilbur's use of "stiff geometries" to represent the ordinary patterns in roads, cellars, and property lines.

Part A   Sample Student Response Essay

Nature is often taken for granted and the beauty and complexity of its creatures are often overlooked. Humans sometimes need to open their eyes and appreciate the wonder of the natural surroundings, which they have <u>not</u> created. In these two passages, by author Rachel Carson and poet Richard Wilbur, the narrator discovers some of the wonders of the natural world. The effect of each passage is achieved through imagery, narrative, and figurative language.

Passage I is presented by an omniscient narrator, who observes the activity of birds and sea life around an island. The narration begins at dusk and ends the following morning, revealing the search for food by the Rynchops skimmer and other creatures; it also shows how the terrapins lay their eggs in the sandy beach, and how fishermen set out their nets at night. The author uses intricate details to describe the appearance and movements of the wildlife: the Rynchops' "wings were pure black," the terrapin females "scooped out jug-shaped holes" for nests, and "The heron stood motionless . . . his bill poised to spear fish as they darted past his legs." The action of the skimmer is expressed in a simile of cutting the surface of the water with its "long, lower bill, shaped like a scissor blade." There is also a sense of personification in the image of the shad in the gill net, struggling to "free herself from something that was like a burning, choking collar." Even the predator eels are described as feasting "royally" as though they were lords enjoying a banquet. Rachel Carson shows the wonder and even the horror in an ecosystem that most of us do not observe.

The poem "In Trackless Woods" tells of the narrator's unexpected discovery of "amazing patterns" in nature. Walking in the woods, the narrator comes across a line of four trees as though set deliberately in a row and then sees that no man created this formation. Realizing that this was a natural pattern, the narrator "tramped on further" to seek out other patterns in the branches of trees and in "the spirals" in a pinecone.

The theme of contrast between human and natural patterns is expressed in an extended metaphor. There are many references to mathematics and strict human order such as, "seemingly aligned," "trees ran parallel," "nor could I find the square." Finally, the most important part of the metaphor is at the end of the poem in the image of the "trees/Not subject to our stiff geometries." The narrator has come to appreciate how wonderful nature can be, and has come to see it through different eyes. He no longer looks for strict human order but instead, seeks out nature's own varieties of order.

Although both passages describe views of nature that most might normally overlook, they are also different. Passage I describes an intricate, natural world to show a beauty most would not discover. Passage II, the poem, portrays the poet's personal experience of discovering that nature has its own patterns apart from man's. Both passages are intended to lead the reader to a greater appreciation of the natural world we hurry past every day

---

Analysis

The introduction reveals that this writer has an excellent understanding of the two passages, and the discussion of narrative structure and extended metaphor is particularly insightful. The introduction establishes a controlling idea in "seeing" or discovering what might be overlooked in the natural world, and the final sentence skillfully restates the controlling idea as the theme of the two passages.

The essay offers specific details, often in the form of well-chosen quotes, to support the argument. Ideas are briefly but clearly developed, and this writer is especially skillful in discussing the use of various literary elements without sounding clumsy or artificial: *"Passage I is presented by an omniscient narrator, who observes . . . ." "Passage II, the poem, portrays the poet's personal experience . . . ." "The action of the skimmer is expressed in a simile . . . . There is also a sense of personification in the image of the shad."* Language and sentence structure are sophisticated, and there are essentially no errors in the conventions. This essay meets the criteria for a high score. (See pp. 68–71 for a detailed discussion of the rubric for this part of the examination.)

Session Two

Note: See Chapter 4 for review and strategy in responding to this part of the examination.

Part B   Sample Student Response Essay

"*A person is a person through other persons . . . .*" By this, Bishop Desmond Tutu may have meant that someone's personality, someone's character, can develop only when exposed to the views and experiences of other people. In history and in literature, we can see how a person may develop in positive or negative ways, depending on the kind of influence other people have. This influence may come from individuals or from society. Two works of literature that show how an individual's character is influenced by those around him are Fahrenheit 451, by Ray Bradbury, and Adventures of Huckleberry Finn, by Mark Twain. These works are also satires of the societies in which these characters live.

In Fahrenheit 451, the character of Guy Montag is first seen as a model citizen of the futuristic society he lives in. He conforms to the view that owning or reading books is illegal, and as a fireman, his job is to find people who secretly have books and to burn down their houses. His friendship with a neighbor, Clarisse, leads him to question whether he is happy in his life and in his marriage, where his wife spends most of her time watching television and taking tranquilizers. Out of curiosity, Montag secretly begins to take books from the houses he is sent to burn, and later he encounters a woman who refuses to leave her house and remains to be destroyed with her books. When the books he has hidden are discovered, Montag must burn down his own house. After these experiences, Montag kills his chief and becomes a fugitive. With the help of Faber, a former professor who has encouraged Montag to read and to think for himself, Montag escapes and joins a group of people who were once writers and teachers. When the city Montag has fled is destroyed, this group will seek to establish a society based on books and freedom of thought.

Adventures of Huckleberry Finn is set in towns along the Mississippi River, in the period before the Civil War. When the novel begins, the boy Huck is living with the Widow Douglas because his father is the town drunk and because the Widow and others in the town are eager to "civilize" Huck, who has been growing up free and on his own. In the Widow's house, Huck must develop acceptable behavior, wear clean clothes, and learn table manners. He is also forced to go to school and church and is lectured on his language. Huck has also grown up to believe like everyone else that slaves are property, and that they are superstitious and easily made fun of. After Huck escapes from the Widow and his abusive father by staging his own "murder," he discovers the runaway slave Jim hiding on an island in the river. The rest of the novel is about the adventures Huck and Jim have as they journey by raft down the Mississippi.

Throughout the story, we see that Huck accepts what his friend Tom Sawyer and all the adults around him say is correct behavior. When he first finds Jim, Huck is shocked that he has run away; Huck even believes that he is wrong to help Jim escape since Jim is the property of Miss Watson, who had always tried to be nice to him. The irony in the novel is that when Huckleberry does the "right" thing by helping Jim escape, he is sure that he is doing something terribly wrong and should be punished for it. Because he believes Jim is ignorant and just doesn't know any better, Huck constantly struggles with his conscience when he saves Jim several times from bounty hunters. Even though Huck never really understands that what he has been told by others is wrong, he acts out of his heart and his loyalty to Jim.

Bradbury's satire attacks a society that seeks to control its citizens by making independent thought and books illegal. In the character of Montag, he shows how the desire to think for oneself can be encouraged by others, even in a totalitarian world. In Adventures of Huckleberry Finn, *Twain's satire shows a society that is morally corrupt through the eyes of an ignorant and good-hearted boy, who does what is right but believes that he is wrong and uncivilized.*

Analysis

This writer provides an especially thoughtful interpretation of the critical lens, one that is faithful to the prompt yet complex enough to apply to a variety of literary works, in this case, two well-known works of satire. The controlling idea is developed through thoughtful discussion of character, plot, and irony. This essay also offers a good example of how to use plot summary to illustrate theme and character in a novel.

Ideas are sufficiently well developed and there are relevant details from each work. Focus is maintained on the central character and on how others have influenced the moral development of that character, both positively and negatively. The writer uses language that is sophisticated and demonstrates mastery of complex sentence structures to express ideas. There are no significant errors in usage or punctuation. This essay meets all the criteria for a high score. (See pp. 80–83 for a detailed discussion of the rubric for this part of the examination.)

Examination June 2005
English

Session One

Part A

Overview: For this part of the test, you will listen to an excerpt from a documentary about Nellie Bly, answer some multiple-choice questions, and write a response based on the situation described below. You will hear the excerpt from the documentary twice. You may take notes on the page alloted anytime you wish during the readings.

> **The Situation:** For women's history month, your local public library is sponsoring a forum on women who possess the qualities of an American hero. You have chosen to make a presentation on Nellie Bly. In preparation for your presentation, listen to an excerpt from a documentary broadcast on PBS about Nellie Bly. Then use relevant information from the excerpt of the documentary to write your presentation.

Your Task: Write a presentation for your local library forum in which you explain the qualities that make Nellie Bly an American hero.

Guidelines:
Be sure to
- Tell your audience what they need to know about the qualities that make Nellie Bly an American hero
- Use specific, accurate, and relevant information from the excerpt from the documentary to support your presentation
- Use a tone and level of language appropriate for a presentation for a library forum
- Organize your ideas in a logical and coherent manner
- Indicate any words taken directly from the excerpt from the documentary by using quotation marks or referring to the speaker
- Follow the conventions of standard written English

Note: For this portion of the examination, the teacher will read a passage aloud. You will not actually see the passage reprinted below. Therefore, you are encouraged to have someone read the passage to you, in order to simulate the examination as closely as possible.

Listening Passage

As Nellie Bly tells the story, it was on a Sunday in the fall of 1888 that the idea came to her. Feeling restless, she had the urge to go elsewhere and travel the globe like the fictional Phileas Fogg, the protagonist of Jules Verne's well-read "Around the World in Eighty Days."

It was then that the inspiration came to Bly: Why not have the "New York World," the newspaper she worked for, send her on a race around the globe to beat the 80-day trek of the fictional Fogg? Like so many other Bly story ideas, this was a winner that would capture the public's interest—and once again put the young female journalist on center stage.

On Monday morning, she proposed the idea to managing editor John A. Cockerill. For a year, Cockerill and the other men at the newspaper put off Bly. Much of the senior staff's reluctance had to do with Bly's gender. "[New York] World" business manager George W. Turner preferred a man for the project. A man did not need a chaperone, Turner argued. Besides, he said, a man could leave behind the "dozen trunks" that a woman would also need for such a trip.

Bly was far from convinced. She replied that she would travel light—and that she did not need a chaperone. After a year of rebukes, Bly heard rumors that the editors had selected a man. Her direct and feisty response was classic Bly. "Very well," she threatened. "Start the man and I'll start the same day for some other newspaper and beat him."

Cockerill acquiesced. The decision was made to send her on a Monday, and on Thursday she sailed off in an attempt to better the 80 days of the fictional Fogg. Bly carried only one piece of hand luggage for the journey and it was just 16 inches wide and seven inches high. Into it she squeezed two traveling caps, three veils, a pair of slippers, toilet articles, an ink stand, pens, pencils, paper, pins, needles, thread, a dressing gown, a tennis blazer, a small flask, a drinking cup, a few changes of underwear, handkerchiefs and a jar of cold cream. Many suggested she take along a revolver. She left it behind. . . .

On the morning of November 14, 1889, Bly set sail from Hoboken Pier on a liner named the Augusta Victoria. The "[New York] World," once reluctant to send her, now put its full resources behind the voyage. "The 'World' today undertakes the task of turning a dream into reality..." read the newspaper's page-one story. "Nellie Bly, so well known to millions who have read of her doings, as told by her captivating pen, will set out as a female Phileas Fogg. . . ."

In a little over six days, Bly arrived in England. The "World"'s London correspondent, Tracy Greaves, met her and told her that Jules Verne wanted to meet her. Assured the side trip would not ruin her tight schedule, Bly traveled day and night to Amiens, France.

Verne asked her where Bly would stop. She had her itinerary memorized: New York to London, then Calais, Brindisi, Port Said, Ismailia, Suez, Aden, Colombo, Penang, Singapore, Hong Kong, Yokohama, San Francisco, and then, if all went as planned, a triumphant return to New York City. If Bly could be said to be riding on Verne's literary success, she repaid the favor by bringing fresh publicity to his novel. "Around the World in 80 Days" was re-issued in over 10 new editions.

Since Bly's reports took a long time to arrive back in New York, the "[New York] World" had to fabricate news during the time she was gone. One ploy was to launch a sweepstakes that asked readers to guess exactly how long Bly's trip would take. By the end of the solo circumnavigation, the newspaper would receive over half a million guesses.

Everywhere Bly went, she brought her feminist and progressive perspective on the world. In Port Said, Bly saw that, to keep the beggars at bay, the male boat passengers took to the streets with canes and the women with parasols. Bly refused to take the casual weapons with her, saying that "a stick beats more ugliness into a person than it ever beats out." On shore in Singapore, Bly visited a

Hindu temple, but a holy man prevented her from entering. Bly's response was true to form:

> "Why?" I demanded, curious to know why my sex in heathen lands should exclude me from a temple, as in America it confines me to the side entrances of hotels and other strange and incommodious things. . . .

Bly observed the world around her carefully, but also kept a worried watch on the pace of her trip. After a required overnight in Singapore that threatened her next connection in Hong Kong, she later wrote, "What agony of suspense and impatience I suffered that night!" Caught in a brutal storm on her way to Japan that again threatened the success she said, "I'd rather go back to New York dead than not a winner."

When she arrived in San Francisco, it became apparent that her fears were for naught: she would best Fogg's fictional record. She described the transcontinental run that followed as a "maze of happy greetings, happy wishes, congratulating telegrams, fruit, flowers, loud cheers, wild hurrahs, rapid hand-shaking and a beautiful car filled with fragrant flowers attached to a swift engine that was tearing like mad through flower-dotted valleys and over snow-tipped mountains."

Bly described her journey as a queen's ride. Everywhere she went she met cheering crowds. Bly wrote that she "rejoiced with them that it was an American girl who had done it." At the tender age of 25, Bly was the most famous woman on earth. Nellie Bly songs were sung in music halls. A Nellie Bly housecoat was advertised. The "[New York] World," not afraid to cash in on its star reporter, even marketed a parlor game called "Round the World with Nellie Bly."

When a reporter from "The San Francisco Chronicle" remarked that her mad dash around the world was something quite remarkable, Bly responded: "Oh, I don't know. It's not so very much for a woman to do who has the pluck, energy and independence which characterize many women in this day of push and get-there." Bly was suggesting that she was more than just a lone and feisty reporter. Her bold trip was a symbol of the newly politicized and independent women of her age who fought for new possibilities that now included a trip around the world—without a chaperone.

—excerpted from "A Trip Around the World,"
PBS Online 1999–2000

Notes

Multiple-Choice Questions

Directions (1–6): Use your notes to answer the following questions about the passage read to you. Select the best suggested answer and write its number in the space provided. The questions may help you think about ideas and information you might use in your writing. You may return to these questions anytime you wish.

1 Who was Phileas Fogg, the inspiration for Bly's 80-day trip around the world?

  (1) a character from literature
  (2) the owner of a newspaper
  (3) a well-known author
  (4) an editor of a magazine　　　　　　　　1 _____

2 What was Nellie Bly's job at *The New York World*?

  (1) literary critic
  (2) travel editor
  (3) salesperson
  (4) reporter　　　　　　　　　　　　　　2 _____

3 According to the speaker, the idea for Bly's trip around the world grew out of her desire for

  (1) wealth
  (2) adventure
  (3) companionship
  (4) relaxation　　　　　　　　　　　　　3 _____

4 According to the speaker, Bly's response to rumors that a man would be sent on the journey in her place shows her

  (1) diplomacy
  (2) generosity
  (3) competitiveness
  (4) forgiveness　　　　　　　　　　　　4 _____

5 In using the sentence "Cockerill acquiesced," the speaker suggests that Cockerill

   (1) accepted reluctantly
   (2) decided quickly
   (3) profited immensely
   (4) complained frequently   5 _____

6 Nellie Bly dismissed the reporter's comment that her trip was "something quite remarkable" because she believed

   (1) her editor deserved the credit
   (2) other men had previously completed the journey
   (3) her idea was not original
   (4) women of her time were similarly capable   6 _____

After you have finished these questions, review **The Situation** and read **Your Task** and the **Guidelines**. Use scrap paper to plan your response. Then write your response on separate sheets of paper. After you finish your response for Part A, complete Part B.

Part B

Directions: Read the text and study the chart on the following pages, answer the multiple-choice questions, and write a response based on the situation described below. You may use the margins to take notes as you read and scrap paper to plan your response.

The Situation: The students in your social studies class are going to design a model community. To prepare the class for this design project, your teacher has asked each student to write a report identifying a problem facing communities and suggesting ways a community might solve that problem. You have decided to write your report on the problem of pedestrian safety.

Your Task: Using relevant information from *both* documents, write a report for your social studies class in which you explain the problem of pedestrian safety and suggest ways a community might solve that problem.

Guidelines:
Be sure to
- Tell your audience what they need to know about the problem of pedestrian safety
- Suggest ways a community might solve that problem
- Use specific, accurate, and relevant information from the text *and* the chart to support your explanation
- Use a tone and level of language appropriate for a report for your social studies class
- Organize your ideas in a logical and coherent manner
- Indicate any words taken directly from the text by using quotation marks or referring to the author
- Follow the conventions of standard written English

Text

. . . About thirteen percent of all the people who died in traffic accidents during 1997-1998 were pedestrians. But this only begins to describe the scope of the problem. Pedestrians also pay a heavy toll in injuries. Data from the National Highway Traffic Safety Administration (NHTSA) reveal that in 1997 and 1998,
(5) for every pedestrian killed by a car, approximately fourteen more were injured. Government estimates show that in 1998 alone, 69,000 pedestrians were hit by cars and injured. However, this number may be low because of under-reporting. . . .

Who Is at Risk?

Children deserve particular attention when considering pedestrian safety,
(10) because they rely more heavily than adults on walking to get where they need to go. In 1997–1998, sixteen percent of pedestrian deaths were people under 18 years old. Challenging street crossings that involve high speeds and many lanes of traffic can be particularly hard for young children. . . .

In addition, elderly people face a higher risk of death as pedestrians. Twenty-
(15) two percent of all pedestrians killed were over 65, even though only 13 percent of the population is elderly. Many pedestrian facilities, particularly walk signals, are timed for use by young adults in good health, and don't give elderly people enough time to cross in safety.

Some ethnic groups may also be at higher risk. While national statistics are
(20) not available, several local studies point to a problem. An STPP study of California pedestrian safety found that a high proportion of pedestrian deaths and injuries in those under 20 years old were young Latinos or African Americans. In 1996, Latino children represented 38.5 percent of the total population of children in California, but they were involved in 47.9 percent of all child
(25) pedestrian incidents (fatalities and injuries). In 1996, African American children comprised 7.8 percent of the total population of children in California, but were involved in 14.2 percent of all child-related pedestrian incidents. The Latino Issues Forum attributed the discrepancy to the higher level of walking among Latinos, even though they often live and go to school in areas where walking is
(30) difficult and dangerous. The Centers for Disease Control reported recently that in Atlanta, Latinos had pedestrian fatality rates six times that of whites. Latino groups in Atlanta are pushing for better pedestrian facilities along a major seven-lane road where many pedestrians have died. A survey in suburban Washington, DC also found that Latinos were disproportionately represented in pedestrian
(35) deaths. . . .

The Decline in Walking

Americans are walking much less than they used to. The number of trips people take on foot has dropped by 42 percent in the last 20 years. The Nationwide Personal Transportation Survey, conducted by the U.S. Department of Transportation, documents the decline in the amount Americans walk. *(40)* Walking dropped from 9.3 percent of all trips in 1977 to just 5.4 percent in 1995. Yet more than one-quarter of all trips are still one mile or less, and by one calculation at least 123 million car trips made each day in the United States were short enough to have been made on foot.

Much of the decline in walking can be attributed to the increase in *(45)* neighborhoods designed so that it is not safe or convenient to travel by foot. Residential areas with no sidewalks and wide streets have been built with high-speed car travel in mind. The nearest store, school, or workplace is often far beyond the quarter- to half-mile radius that is most convenient for foot travel. Workplaces are often located in office parks accessible only by car, and isolated *(50)* from any other services.

There is ample evidence from dozens of studies that compact communities that mix housing, workplaces, and shopping are places where people take more trips on foot. But such "traditional" neighborhoods are often in the older part of town, and newer developments tend to be more automobile oriented. One recent *(55)* study of Seattle neighborhoods found that the newer the development, the less likely it is that residents will walk, bicycle, or take transit. . . .

The influence of community design on the decision of whether or not to walk is made clear by looking at the trend in the number of children who walk to school. Schools are increasingly isolated from the communities they serve. New *(60)* schools may be placed on the edge of communities, and wide, busy thoroughfares prevent children from biking or walking to school. Even schools that back up on subdivisions are often inaccessible by foot because there is no path to them: the only link is a circuitous street network. Many communities experience traffic jams around schools as parents deliver children to the door. Increasingly, mothers (and *(65)* some fathers) are becoming the bus drivers of the new millennium. Women with school-aged children now make more car trips each day than any other population group, and on average spend more than an hour a day in the car. . . .

Walking Less: A Threat to Health

. . . The American Medical Association (AMA) recently declared obesity an epidemic and a major public health concern. The AMA blames the epidemic on *(70)* people eating more, and on the fact that "opportunities in daily life to burn energy have diminished." In an editorial in its journal, the AMA noted that car trips have replaced trips that used to be made on foot or by bicycle, and says helping people get back to walking or bicycling should be a first target in combating the obesity epidemic. But it also noted, "Reliance on physical activity (75) as an alternative to car use is less likely to occur in many cities and towns unless they are designed or retro-fitted to permit walking or bicycling."

Obesity is just one of the health problems associated with a sedentary lifestyle. The Centers for Disease Control estimates that 300,000 Americans die each year from diseases associated with physical inactivity. Even modest physical (80) activity, such as walking, can decrease the risk of coronary heart disease, high blood pressure, colon cancer, diabetes, and even depression. . . .

Retrofitting Streets: More than Crosswalks

Since so many of our streets have been designed exclusively with automobiles in mind, it takes more than a crosswalk and a walk signal to make them safe and inviting for pedestrians. Many communities across the country are making streets (85) safer with traffic calming techniques. Traffic calming redesigns streets to reduce vehicle speeds and give more space and priority to cyclists and pedestrians. Traffic calming includes a variety of changes that slow or divert vehicle traffic, separate pedestrian pathways from vehicle traffic, and make the road corridor more pleasant. Common traffic calming measures include landscaped traffic (90) circles, medians or extended sidewalks that narrow the roadway, and partial closures to divert through traffic. Many communities are slowing traffic with speed humps, but the most successful projects integrate a variety of techniques that make the street more attractive and inviting for people on foot and bicycle. The Institute of Traffic Engineers has published a manual on traffic calming; to (95) see it visit http://www.ite.org/traffic/index.html. . . .

Designing for Pedestrians

Traffic calming is but one part of a broader attempt to fundamentally refocus the design of both streets and communities so that walking is safe and convenient.

Encouraging pedestrian travel means designing communities so that people have somewhere to walk to. That means developing neighborhoods where (100) residents are within a reasonable walking distance of shops, offices, schools, libraries, and transit stops. According to the American Planning Association's *Best Development Practices*, the best neighborhoods for walking are developed in small clusters, with well-defined centers and edges, and compact commercial centers. The street network in these neighborhoods should include multiple (105) connections and direct routes that allow pedestrians to choose the shortest distance to a destination. Schools should also be placed so children can walk and bicycle without having to cross high-speed streets. . . .

Investing In Pedestrian Safety

Making pedestrian safety a priority means investing transportation funds in pedestrian facilities and safer streets. Each state should attempt to align (110) pedestrian safety funding to pedestrian safety needs, as indicated by rates of fatalities and injuries: if 25 percent of a state's traffic deaths are pedestrians, it should consider allocating a similar share of safety funding to making walking safer. State Departments of Transportation should target such funding by using a systematic approach for identifying problem areas for pedestrians, similar to the (115) systems now used to identify high accident areas for vehicles. When it comes to funding, dangerous pedestrian areas should be considered on an equal footing with dangerous locations for motor vehicles. . . .

— Barbara McCann and Bianca DeLille
excerpted from "Mean Streets 2000"
www.transact.org

CHART
Some Traffic Calming Techniques

Technique	Description	Advantages	Disadvantages
Speed bumps, humps, and table	Raise pavement three to four inches. Bumps are narrow and abrupt. Humps and speed tables are more gradual, often 22 feet long, usually with a flat top.	• Make drivers think about the roadway • Effective in cutting down speed • Self-enforcing • Relatively inexpensive	• Noisy • Annoying to drivers • Slows down emergency vehicles
Chicanes, bends, and deviations	Roadway designs that make motorists drive around fixed objects, usually curbs extending alternately from opposite sides to form a serpentine pathway.	• Visually pleasing • Satisfactory for emergency vehicles	• Expensive
Neckdowns, chokers, and bulbs	Various forms of narrowing the road at midroad or intersections, usually by protruding sidewalks into the street from one or more sides.	• Can be visually pleasing • Helps pedestrians cross	• Can present problems for bicyclists, snow removal
Narrow roads	Use sidewalks, landscaping, or striping to narrow lanes to about 10 feet.	• Drivers slow instinctively • Pedestrian-friendly • Creates neighborly scene	• Can present problems for bicyclists • Eliminates on-street parking
Raised intersections and changes in road texture	Use grooved asphalt, colored paving stones, brick, or cobblestones.	• Gets drivers' attention • Good for pedestrians	• Noisy for neighbors • Can be bumpy for bicyclists
Direction changes	Accomplished by "diverters" that diagonally bisect an intersection or barriers that force cars to turn one direction.	• Effective in stopping short-cut and cut-through traffic	• Can be costly • Confusing to strangers • Adds to commutes and emergency response times

Source: (adapted) "Slow down, you're going too fast!" Public Technology, Inc., 2001

Multiple-Choice Questions

Directions (7–16): Select the best suggested answer to each question and write its number in the space provided. The questions may help you think about ideas and information you might want to use in your writing. You may return to these questions anytime you wish.

7 The authors indicate that elderly pedestrians are at greater risk than younger adults because the elderly tend to

(1) underestimate the speed of the traffic
(2) walk slowly when crossing streets
(3) ignore signals at crosswalks
(4) walk with friends or pets   7 _____

8 According to the text, Americans walk less than they used to because

(1) neighborhoods often lack sidewalks
(2) cars have become more affordable
(3) bicycle riding has replaced walking
(4) offices are located in residential areas   8 _____

9 The authors indicate that older neighborhoods are better for walking because, in those neighborhoods,

(1) speed limits are strictly enforced
(2) cars are parked in driveways
(3) homes and stores are close together
(4) children and elderly people are supervised   9 _____

10 The authors imply that the decision of whether or not a child walks to school is based largely on the

(1) age of the child
(2) starting time of the school day
(3) income level of the parents
(4) location of the school   10 _____

11 According to the text, the main purpose of traffic calming is to

   (1) conserve energy
   (2) save money
   (3) slow automobiles
   (4) reduce crime   11 _____

12 The text implies that community designers can best encourage walking by providing pedestrians with

   (1) shelters
   (2) destinations
   (3) rules
   (4) vehicles   12 _____

13 According to the text, the amount of money a state spends on pedestrian safety needs should be based on the number of

   (1) pedestrian accidents
   (2) traffic lights
   (3) automobiles
   (4) crosswalks   13 _____

14 According to the chart, in the description of the pathway formed by chicanes, bends, or deviations, the word "serpentine" most nearly means

   (1) wide
   (2) bumpy
   (3) winding
   (4) slippery   14 _____

15 Which technique in the chart is cited as presenting a difficulty for maintaining the roadway in winter?

   (1) speed bumps, humps, and tables
   (2) neckdowns, chokers, and bulbs
   (3) narrow roads
   (4) raised intersections and changes in road texture 15 _____

16 From the information in the chart, what conclusion may be drawn regarding the use of traffic calming techniques in community design?

(1) Most techniques are too expensive to be used often.

(2) Few techniques are appropriate for commercial areas.

(3) The least expensive techniques are also the least effective.

(4) No single technique is correct for all situations.   16 _____

After you have finished these questions, review **The Situation** and read **Your Task** and the **Guidelines**. Use scrap paper to plan your response. Then write your response to Part B on separate sheets of paper.

Session Two

Part A

Directions: Read the passages on the following pages (an excerpt from a short story and a poem). Write the number of the answer to each multiple-choice question in the space provided. Then write the essay on separate sheets of paper as described in **Your Task**. You may use the margins to take notes as you read and scrap paper to plan your response.

Your Task:

> After you have read the passages and answered the multiple-choice questions, write a unified essay about parental expectations as revealed in the passages. In your essay, use ideas from **both** passages to establish a controlling idea about parental expectations. Using evidence from **each** passage, develop your controlling idea and show how the author uses specific literary elements or techniques to convey that idea.

Guidelines:
Be sure to
- Use ideas from **both** passages to establish a controlling idea about parental expectations
- Use specific and relevant evidence from **each** passage to develop your controlling idea
- Show how each author uses specific literary elements (for example: theme, characterization, structure, point of view) or techniques (for example: symbolism, irony, figurative language) to convey the controlling idea
- Organize your ideas in a logical and coherent manner
- Use language that communicates ideas effectively
- Follow the conventions of standard written English

Passage I

"Mobiles¹?" Fegley echoed over the telephone, with a sinking feeling. He
was an internationally known junk sculptor whose annual income ran well into six
figures, but in his mind he was still an unpopular and ill-coordinated adolescent
walking out to a rural mailbox in Missouri to place in it a brown envelope
(5)   containing cartoons and addressed to *Collier's*, or else to discover there a brown
envelope returned from the same magazine with a rejection slip. Partch, Hoff,
Rea—he imitated them all, and yet everything came back. Once, he tried to sell
the nearest city's only newspaper a comic strip and then took the same cartoons
to the local department store, as the possible basis for an advertising scheme. His
(10) mother went with him into the city that day, since he was too young to drive, and
a street photographer snapped a picture of them walking together, she clutching
her purse, he holding his portfolio under a skinny arm, both of them looking
distracted and tired. His mother had sponsored his "creativity," indulged it.
Almost his first memory of her was of a young woman sitting on the threadbare
(15) carpet with him, crayoning solid a space at the top of a page of the coloring book
on the floor before him; it seemed marvellous to the child that she, sitting
opposite him, could color upside down, as well as with such even, gentle strokes,
which never strayed outside the printed outlines. Fegley's father, who
supplemented the income from the farm by working as a non-union carpenter,
(20) wrung his hands to think of his son's wasting his life on hopeless ambitions.
"Learn a trade," he begged the boy. "Get a solid trade, and then you can fool
around with this artsy-craftsy stuff." One night in bed, Fegley, shortly before
going off to a New York art school, overheard his father confide to his mother
downstairs, "They'll just break his heart."

(25)   Overhearing this, the boy had inwardly scoffed. And eventually, moving from
cartooning, by way of imitating the playful sculpture of Picasso and Ipoustéguy,
into a world of galleries and spacious duplexes and expectant museum spaces that
his father had never dreamed existed, he proved the old man wrong. Yet the older
that Fegley himself grew, the more it seemed his father had been essentially
(30) right.

In the pattern of his generation he had married young, had four children, and
eventually got a divorce. His first wife, met at the art school, had been herself
artistic: Sarah painted delicate impressionistic still-lifes and landscapes that were
often abandoned before the corners were filled. There was usually something
(35) wrong with the perspective, though the colors were remarkably true. He

---

¹ mobile—a construction or sculpture ... with parts that can be set in motion by air currents

sometimes blamed himself, in their years together, for not encouraging her more; but in truth all "this artsy-craftsy stuff" depressed him, and he hoped that his children would become scientists. He plied the two boys, especially, with telescopes and microscopes, chemistry sets and books of mathematical puzzles;

(40)   they squinted at Saturn's rings for an evening and at magnified salt granules for an afternoon, and then the expensive tubes of brass and chrome drifted toward the closets already full of deflated footballs and gadgets whose batteries had given out. Fegley's two daughters, as they grew into women, with the distances and silences of women, took watercolor brushes and pads on their sunbathing

(45)   expeditions, and at home solemnly inscribed haiku on pebble board with crow-quill pens. Their mother encouraged all this, having set the example by her own dabbling, which fitfully continued into her middle age; the house was strewn with Sarah's half-completed canvases. Fegley did his powerful, successful sculpture—most famously, the series of giant burnished insects fabricated from discarded

(50)   engine blocks and transmission systems—in an old machine shop he rented two miles from the house, down low along the Hudson. He did not encourage his children to visit him there, and even had his subscription to *Artnews* directed to that address. He was like a man who, having miraculously survived a shipwreck, wants to warn all others back at the edge of the sea. As the two boys grew older,

(55)   he congratulated himself that they seemed more concerned with putting their feet to leather balls and car accelerators than with setting implements to paper. Unlike his youthful self, they were popular and well-coordinated, and expert at sports. The older went off to college determined to make the football varsity, having been a spectacularly shifty tight end for his boarding school, but

(60)   somewhere under the cloud of his parents' divorce proceedings he dropped out of athletics and into film studies; he took courses (college courses! for credit!) that analyzed the cutting rhythm in old Laurel and Hardy comedies and the advance of camera mobility in musical comedies of the Forties. Now he was living in a squalid Manhattan loft with several other aspirants to the world of film, lost

(65)   young souls stoned on media, pounding the sidewalks and virtually (who knows?—maybe actually) selling their bodies for the whisper of a promise of becoming an assistant grip's assistant in a public-television documentary on the African killer bee. Fegley's daughters had also faded into the limbo of artistic endeavor; one was in northern California making "pinch pots" out of her lover's

(70)   back-yard clay, and the other was editing a journal of genealogy in Cincinnati while working on a highly ambitious feminist novel called *Ever Since Eve*. This left uncontaminated by creativity only the younger son, Warren. Warren was a broad-shouldered brown-eyed nineteen-year-old who had once collected butterflies and rock specimens and who was clever with his hands; he had even

(75)   given signs of becoming a carpenter, working alongside his grandfather for a few

summers, before the old man died. Here at last, Fegley had thought, was my practical, down-to-earth child.

So it was with a sinking feeling that Fegley heard that the boy was making mobiles this summer. "But what about his job?" he asked.

(80) "I don't think he ever called that number Clara gave him," Sarah said.

Clara, Fegley's present wife, was a civil engineer with a firm in White Plains and had given her stepson a lead on a summer job with a road-repair crew.

"What do you mean exactly, mobiles?" Fegley asked.

"They're lovely," the distant voice answered. "They really must be seen to be
(85) believed. You should come look." Her voice was fading; one of her annoying habits, which he had not been much aware of as long as they lived together, was that of dropping the telephone mouthpiece to her chin as she talked.

"All right, damn it: I'll be right over," Fegley said. "I want to *talk* to Warren. Clara went to a lot of trouble to find a contractor who had filled his minority
(90) quota." He left his new studio, an abandoned gas station in Port Chester, with its friendly mounds of junk and pleasant, unifying stench of the acetylene torch, and swung his Porsche up onto the battered road, into the overtrafficked grid interconnecting Westchester County's hidden green hives of plenty. . . .

—John Updike
excerpted from "Learn a Trade"
Trust Me, 1987
Alfred A. Knopf

Passage II

To My Father's Business

Leo bends over his desk
Gazing at a memorandum
While Stuart stands beside him
With a smile, saying,
(5)   "Leo, the order for those desks
Came in today
From Youngstown Needle and Thread!"
C. Loth Inc., there you are
Like Balboa the conqueror
(10) Of those who want to buy office furniture
Or bar fixtures
In nineteen forty in Cincinnati, Ohio!
Secretaries pound out
Invoices on antique typewriters—
(15) Dactyllographs[1]
And fingernail biters.
I am sitting on a desk
Looking at my daddy
Who is proud of but feels unsure about
(20) Some aspects of his little laddie.[2]
I will go on to explore
Deep and/or nonsensical themes
While my father's on the dark hardwood floor
Hit by a couple of Ohio sunbeams.
(25) Kenny, he says, some day you'll work in the store.
But I felt "never more" or "never ever"
Harvard was far away
World War Two was distant
Psychoanalysis was extremely expensive
(30) All of these saved me from you.
C. Loth you made my father happy
I saw his face shining
He laughed a lot, working in you
He said to Miss Ritter
(35) His secretary

---

[1] dactyllographs (dactylographs) — fingerprints
[2] laddie — young boy

"Ritt, this is my boy, Kenny!"
"Hello there Kenny," she said
My heart in an uproar
I loved you but couldn't think
(40) Of staying with you
I can see the virtues now
That could come from being in you
A sense of balance
Compromise and acceptance—
(45) Not isolated moments of brilliance
Like a girl without a shoe,
But someone that you
Care for every day—
Need for customers and the economy
(50) Don't go away.
There were little pamphlets
Distributed in you
About success in business
Each about eight to twelve pages long
(55) One whole series of them
All ended with the words
"P.S. He got the job"
One a story about a boy who said,
"I swept up the street, Sir,
(60) Before you got up." Or
"There were five hundred extra catalogues
So I took them to people in the city who have a dog"—
P.S. He got the job.
I didn't get the job
(65) I didn't think that I could do the job
I thought I might go crazy in the job
Staying in you
You whom I could love
But not be part of
(70) The secretaries clicked
Their Smith Coronas[3] closed at five p.m.
And took the streetcars to Kentucky then
And I left too.

— Kenneth Koch
from *Poetry*, January 2000

---

[3] Smith Coronas — brand of typewriters

Multiple-Choice Questions

Directions (1–10): Select the best suggested answer to each question and write its number in the space provided. The questions may help you think about the ideas and information you might want to use in your essay. You may return to these questions anytime you wish.

Passage I (the short story excerpt)—Questions 1–4 refer to Passage I.

1 Lines 18 through 24 imply that Fegley's father wanted his son to develop

  (1) artistic talent
  (2) realistic expectations
  (3) personal goals
  (4) serious relationships   1 _____

2 Fegley tried to influence his sons' career choices by

  (1) bribing them to study
  (2) giving them art lessons
  (3) sending them to school
  (4) providing hobby equipment   2 _____

3 Fegley's attitude toward his children's becoming artists is ironic because he

  (1) is a successful artist
  (2) wants them to make money
  (3) is married to an artist
  (4) recognizes their talent   3 _____

4 The passage is a flashback framed by Fegley's conversation concerning his

  (1) younger daughter
  (2) older daughter
  (3) younger son
  (4) older son   4 _____

Passage II (the poem)—Questions 5–9 refer to Passage II.

5 The interaction between Leo and Stuart (lines 1 through 7) is used to establish and illustrate a

(1) plot
(2) setting
(3) point of view
(4) stanza

5 _____

6 In the poem the father brings Kenny to work because he hopes that Kenny will

(1) get a job
(2) follow in his footsteps
(3) stop his rebellion
(4) take on responsibility

6 _____

7 The narrator's references of "Harvard," "World War Two," and "Psychoanalysis"(lines 27 through 29) are used to convey the fact that the narrator

(1) is now an adult
(2) respects education
(3) is wealthy
(4) likes to travel

7 _____

8 Lines 41 through 50 indicate that the narrator's attitude toward his father's workplace is one of

(1) blame   (3) joy
(2) anger   (4) appreciation

8 _____

9 It may be inferred from the poem that the narrator did *not* get a job in his father's workplace because he

(1) did not want it
(2) developed a mental disorder
(3) had to go to war
(4) did not have the necessary skills

9 _____

Question 10 refers to both passages.

10 Fegley and the narrator of the poem are similar in
that they may be described as

   (1) unreliable
   (2) greedy
   (3) concerned
   (4) dishonest   10 _____

After you have finished these questions, review **Your
Task** and the **Guidelines**. Use scrap paper to plan
your response. Then write your response to Part A on
separate sheets of paper. After you finish your
response for Part A, complete Part B.

Part B

Your Task:
Write a critical essay in which you discuss *two* works of literature you have read from the particular perspective of the statement that is provided for you in the **Critical Lens**. In your essay, provide a valid interpretation of the statement, agree *or* disagree with the statement as you have interpreted it, and support your opinion using specific references to appropriate literary elements from the two works. You may use scrap paper to plan your response. Write your essay in Part B on separate sheets of paper.

Critical Lens:

> "In this world goodness is destined to be defeated."
>
>   — Walker Percy
>   *The Moviegoer*, 1962

Guidelines:
Be sure to
- Provide a valid interpretation of the critical lens that clearly establishes the criteria for analysis
- Indicate whether you agree *or* disagree with the statement as you have interpreted it
- Choose *two* works you have read that you believe best support your opinion
- Use the criteria suggested by the critical lens to analyze the works you have chosen
- Avoid plot summary. Instead, use specific references to appropriate literary elements (for example: theme, characterization, setting, point of view) to develop your analysis
- Organize your ideas in a unified and coherent manner
- Specify the titles and authors of the literature you choose
- Follow the conventions of standard written English

Regents Comprehensive Examination in English—June 2005
Chart for Determining the Final Examination Score (Use for June 2005 examination only.)

To determine the student's final examination score, locate the student's total essay score across the top of the chart and the student's total multiple-choice score down the side of the chart. The point where those two scores intersect is the student's final examination score. For example, a student receiving a total essay score of 19 and a total multiple-choice score of 16 would receive a final examination score of 77.

Total Essay Score →

Total Multiple-Choice Score	0	1	2	3	4	5	6	7	8	9	10	11	12	13	14	15	16	17	18	19	20	21	22	23	24
0	0	1	2	2	3	4	6	8	10	13	15	18	21	24	28	32	36	39	43	47	51	55	58	62	66
1	1	1	2	3	4	5	7	9	11	14	17	20	23	26	30	34	38	41	45	49	53	57	60	64	68
2	1	2	2	3	4	6	8	10	13	15	18	21	24	28	32	36	39	43	47	51	55	58	62	66	70
3	1	2	3	4	5	7	9	11	14	17	20	23	26	30	34	38	41	45	49	53	57	60	64	68	71
4	2	2	3	4	6	8	10	13	15	18	21	24	28	32	36	39	43	47	51	55	58	62	66	70	73
5	2	3	4	5	7	9	11	14	17	20	23	26	30	34	38	41	45	49	53	57	60	64	68	71	75
6	2	3	4	6	8	10	13	15	18	21	24	28	32	36	39	43	47	51	55	58	62	66	70	73	77
7	3	4	5	7	9	11	14	17	20	23	26	30	34	38	41	45	49	53	57	60	64	68	71	75	78
8	3	4	6	8	10	13	15	18	21	24	28	32	36	39	43	47	51	55	58	62	66	70	73	77	80
9	4	5	7	9	11	14	17	20	23	26	30	34	38	41	45	49	53	57	60	64	68	71	75	78	81
10	4	6	8	10	13	15	18	21	24	28	32	36	39	43	47	51	55	58	62	66	70	73	77	80	83
11	5	7	9	11	14	17	20	23	26	30	34	38	41	45	49	53	57	60	64	68	71	75	78	81	85
12	6	8	10	13	15	18	21	24	28	32	36	39	43	47	51	55	58	62	66	70	73	77	80	83	86
13	7	9	11	14	17	20	23	26	30	34	38	41	45	49	53	57	60	64	68	71	75	78	81	85	87
14	8	10	13	15	18	21	24	28	32	36	39	43	47	51	55	58	62	66	70	73	77	80	83	86	89
15	9	11	14	17	20	23	26	30	34	38	41	45	49	53	57	60	64	68	71	75	78	81	85	87	90
16	10	13	15	18	21	24	28	32	36	39	43	47	51	55	58	62	66	70	73	77	80	83	86	89	91
17	11	14	17	20	23	26	30	34	38	41	45	49	53	57	60	64	68	71	75	78	81	85	87	90	93
18	13	15	18	21	24	28	32	36	39	43	47	51	55	58	62	66	70	73	77	80	83	86	89	91	94
19	14	17	20	23	26	30	34	38	41	45	49	53	57	60	64	68	71	75	78	81	85	87	90	93	95
20	15	18	21	24	28	32	36	39	43	47	51	55	58	62	66	70	73	77	80	83	86	89	91	94	96
21	17	20	23	26	30	34	38	41	45	49	53	57	60	64	68	71	75	78	81	85	87	90	93	95	97
22	18	21	24	28	32	36	39	43	47	51	55	58	62	66	70	73	77	80	83	86	89	91	94	96	98
23	20	23	26	30	34	38	41	45	49	53	57	60	64	68	71	75	78	81	85	87	90	93	95	97	99
24	21	24	28	32	36	39	43	47	51	55	58	62	66	70	73	77	80	83	86	89	91	94	96	98	99
25	23	26	30	34	38	41	45	49	53	57	60	64	68	71	75	78	81	85	87	90	93	95	97	99	99
26	24	28	32	36	39	43	47	51	55	58	62	66	70	73	77	80	83	86	89	91	94	96	98	99	100

Answers
June 2005
English

Answer Key

Session One, Part A	Session One, Part B	Session Two, Part A
1. 1	7. 2	1. 2
2. 4	8. 1	2. 4
3. 2	9. 3	3. 1
4. 3	10. 4	4. 3
5. 1	11. 3	5. 2
6. 4	12. 2	6. 2
	13. 1	7. 1
	14. 3	8. 4
	15. 2	9. 1
	16. 4	10. 3

Answers Explained

Session One

Part A   (1–6)

Note: Refer to Chapter 1 for review and strategy in responding to this part of the examination.

(1) **1** "a character from literature." The opening sentences of the passage reveal that Nellie Bly got the idea for her trip after reading Jules Verne's *Around the World in Eighty Days*. The opening also refers to the "fictional Phileas Fogg" as the protagonist of Verne's well-read book.

(2) **4** "reporter." In the beginning of the passage, Nellie Bly is referred to only as "a journalist," but at the end of the passage there are several references to her as the *New York World's* "star reporter" and "feisty reporter."

(3) **2** "adventure." In the opening of the passage, we are told that Bly was "feeling restless" and that "she had the urge to go elsewhere and travel the globe . . . ." None of the other choices is supported by the passage.

(4) **3** "competitiveness." This answer is supported by Nellie Bly's response when she says, "Start the man and I'll start the same day for some other newspaper and beat him." There is no sense of diplomacy, generosity, or forgiveness in her threat.

(5) **1** "accepted reluctantly." The definition of acquiescence is to "agree or go along with," often with a sense of giving in without necessarily supporting what is at issue. Though the passage might suggest that the editor decided quickly, the overall context makes it clear that Nellie Bly pressed her case for over a year and finally threatened to work for a competing newspaper, thus forcing her editor to accept her proposal.

(6) **4** "women of her time were similarly capable." The closing section of the passage quotes Nellie Bly as saying, "It's not so very much for a woman to do who has the pluck, energy and independence which characterize many women in this day of push and get-there." The speaker concludes the passage by saying that Bly's trip was "a symbol of the newly politicized and independent women of her age . . . ."

Part A   Sample Student Response Essay

American heroes come in many different guises. American heroes are as diverse as the Founding Fathers who wrote the Constitution, the cowboys who tamed the frontier, and the astronauts who explore worlds beyond our own. They may seem to have little in common; however, they all have a similar longing for independence, adventure, and knowledge that is intrinsic to the American psyche. Unfortunately, many American heroes get overlooked. Those who are not loud, gun-toting men tend to be forgotten or brushed aside. Nellie Bly is one of those heroes.

One day in 1888, Nellie Bly had an idea that would allow her to fulfill a desire for adventure. She wanted to travel around the world in fewer than 80 days and beat the "record" of the fictional Phileas Fogg. Nellie Bly was at the time a successful reporter for the <u>New York World</u>, and she also believed that this trip would be the next best step for her career. Her editors argued that a man should take the journey instead, but Nellie would not relent. To arguments saying that a man would cost less because he wouldn't need a chaperone, she argued that she wouldn't take one; to arguments about luggage, she stated that she would pack light. When she heard rumors that a man had been chosen to take the trip, Nellie responded with a challenge. She threatened to get another to sponsor her, start out on the same day as the man, and beat him back to New York. Her superiors, seeing that she, in the best American tradition, would not let go of her dream, finally agreed to let her go.

Nellie Bly packed one small piece of luggage and set off alone, on November 14, 1889, asserting that women could travel just fine with no chaperones. Her independence inspired many, and her adventure produced a flood of publicity. The <u>New York World</u> hailed her as a "female Phileas Fogg" who was "turning a dream into reality." Wherever she went, people were excited to see her. When Nellie Bly arrived in London she was persuaded to take a side trip to France to meet Jules Verne, whose novel <u>Around the World in Eighty Days</u> was republished due to interest in her mission.

In her travels, she displayed heroic traits in her desire for knowledge and her demonstration of bravery. Everywhere she went, she expressed her feminist and progressive views. When denied entrance to a Hindu temple because of her sex, she, with classic American defiance, demanded to know why she should be excluded. In Port Said, where she saw rich travelers keeping beggars at bay with canes and parasols, she refused to join in, believing violence more harmful than corrective. Toward the end of her journey, during a violent storm off Japan, she said, "I'd rather go back to New York dead than not a winner."

Nellie Bly was even an American hero in the realm of economics. "Around the world" merchandise offered Nellie Bly housecoats, board games, and music. When she returned to America, her transcontinental journey showed her just how much Americans idolized her. She was showered with gifts and flowers, praise and cheers. She was an inspiration to American women who still did not have the right to vote, but were beginning to realize and make others understand how ridiculous that inequality was. If a woman could travel around the world in fewer than 80 days, unchaperoned, women might have thought, "What can't we do?"

When a reporter praised her journey as extraordinary, Nellie replied, "It's not so much for a woman to do if she has pluck and energy." Her successful quest for independence, adventure, and knowledge make her an American hero for all time.

Analysis

This is a very strong response to the task. The writer demonstrates not only thorough understanding of the passage but also genuine interest in the subject. The introduction establishes a clever and vivid definition of an American hero, by linking the founding fathers, "gun-toting" cowboys, and astronauts to qualities of independence, adventure, and a quest for knowledge. The essay is then developed with specific examples of how Nellie Bly exemplified them, making her an American hero.

The chronological account of Bly's journey offers a clear and natural organization, and the discussion is developed with well-chosen examples of her bravery and independent character. As noted above, the language is appropriate for the intended audience and is often vivid and original. Sentence structure is varied, and the use of parallel construction is especially effective in the second paragraph: "To arguments . . . she argued . . . to arguments . . . she stated . . . ." This writer also demonstrates excellent control of the conventions. This essay meets all the criteria for a high score.

(See pp. 31–35 for a detailed explanation of the rubric for this part of the examination.)

Part B   (7–16)

Note: Refer to Chapter 2 for review and strategy in responding to this part of the examination.

(7) **2** "walk slowly when crossing streets." At line 17, the text asserts that many walk signals are timed for young, healthy adults and ". . . don't give elderly people enough time to cross in safety."

(8) **1** "neighborhoods often lack sidewalks." Beginning at line 44, the text points out that newer neighborhoods have been designed "with no sidewalks" and residential areas have "streets . . . built with high-speed car travel in mind."

(9) **3** "homes and stores are close together." In the paragraph beginning at line 51, the text contrasts newer with "traditional" neighborhoods, which mixed "housing, workplaces and shopping," and made it more likely people would move about on foot. None of the other choices is supported by the text.

(10) **4** "location of the school." Beginning at line 59, the text points out that "Schools are increasingly isolated from the communities they serve . . . [and] may be placed on the edge of communities [where] wide, busy thoroughfares prevent children from biking or walking to school."

(11) **3** "slow automobiles." Beginning at line 85, the text points out that "Traffic calming redesigns streets to reduce vehicle speeds . . . ."

(12) **2** "destinations." At line 98, the text asserts that "Encouraging pedestrian travel means designing communities so that people have somewhere to walk to." That is, shops and public services such as transit stops, libraries, and schools, should be within walking distance of the neighborhoods they serve.

(13) **1** "pedestrian accidents." The text concludes with the authors' position that funding for pedestrian safety should be "aligned" with actual needs, "as indicated by rates of fatalities and injuries." Just as high accident areas for vehicles may be identified, ". . . dangerous pedestrian areas should be considered on an equal footing . . . ." and safety funds should be allocated accordingly.

(14) **3** "winding." The description of roadway designs that make motorists move from side to side and around various curbs suggests the winding or twisting form of a serpent; that is, the roadway bends and curves like a snake in motion. The description in this section of the chart does not suggest anything wide, bumpy, or slippery in its design.

(15) **2** "neckdowns, chokers, and bulbs." In the column listing disadvantages of the various traffic calming techniques, only this one includes a specific reference to winter by citing problems for snow removal.

(16) **4** "no single technique is correct for all situations." Because the chart details clear advantages and disadvantages for each of the techniques described, this is the most appropriate conclusion to be drawn. It should also be noted that there is not enough information in this chart to support any of the other choices.

Part B Sample Student Response Essay

In many communities, pedestrian safety is proving to be a difficult problem. The lack of any clear-cut solutions is making this problem even harder to solve. Communities are also suffering a decline in people choosing to walk or to ride bikes for transportation. By implementing new and different techniques, hopefully communities will be able to cut down on pedestrian casualties and make it safe for those who choose to walk.

In traffic accidents, many people who are injured or killed are pedestrians. The two groups who are most at risk are children and the elderly. Children are at risk when they cannot rely on adults because it is difficult for them to deal with challenging street crossings and automobile speeds. The elderly are at a huge risk and suffer even more fatalities than children. The elderly tend to move more slowly and can have trouble crossing a street within the time available. Most walk signals are timed for the young and healthy and not with the elderly in mind.

There are a number ways to remedy problems of pedestrian safety, and many communities use what are called traffic calming techniques. These are techniques designed to slow traffic down and may include speed bumps, bends, and deviations, or techniques that narrow points in a road, all of which force drivers to go more slowly. Nearly all these techniques have both positive and negative aspects. Some are very expensive, others are noisy, and many create problems for snowplows or for emergency vehicles.

Over the last couple of decades, there has been a substantial decline in the number of people walking on a regular basis. This can be credited in part to the design of newer neighborhoods, which are often built with wide streets and no sidewalks, in order to accommodate vehicular traffic. In these areas, destinations such as schools and shopping areas are often isolated or located on busy highways, making them inaccessible on foot.

The decline in walking is also a threat to public health and well-being. The lack of regular walking or biking as exercise may contribute to increased risk of heart disease, high blood pressure, and other health problems. In order to encourage walking, communities need to redesign streets to provide a safe walking environment and locate at least some destinations within a reasonable walking distance.

Pedestrian safety is a problem that needs to be addressed. Walking needs to be made safer and more convenient, and roads should be safe for all. In designing a community, the priority should be the people and not the automobile.

Analysis

Here the task is to prepare a report on a specific issue, and this essay meets that task well. The introduction reveals thorough understanding of the documents by recognizing both the need to reduce pedestrian casualties and to encourage people to walk more. These themes are developed with relevant and specific information from the article and from the chart.

The organization is clear and effective: the second paragraph outlines the fundamental safety issues, and the third offers examples of how traffic may be slowed. The fourth paragraph introduces examples of how the design of newer communities may contribute to problems of pedestrian safety, and the next paragraph explains why the decline in walking is also a public health issue, offering a brief summary of how communities might be better designed to encourage walking. The conclusion is brief, but the final assertion keeps it from being simply mechanical. Though not extensive, the development of each section is adequate. The language and sentence structure reflect the material in the documents and are appropriate for a report. This essay would receive a high score for the task.

(See pp. 48–53 for a detailed discussion of the rubric for this part of the examination.)

Session Two

Part A   (1–10)

Note: See Chapter 3 for review and strategy in responding to this part of the examination.

(1) **2** "realistic expectations." This passage stresses the father's fear that his son's artistic ambitions are hopeless and that in art school, "They'll just break his heart." Fegley's father "begs" him to "get a solid trade," not because he disapproves of art but because he fears a future of failure and disappointment for his son.

(2) **4** "providing hobby equipment." Beginning at line 37, the passage reveals that Fegley "hoped that his children would become scientists." The passage goes on to enumerate all the hobbies, toys, and instructional activities that he provided his sons in order to encourage them. There is no reference to giving them art lessons, bribing them to study, or sending them to school.

(3) **1** "is a successful artist." While the other choices are true or likely, the most ironic is in the fact that Fegley himself is not only successful but seems to have fulfilled his own ambitions as an artist. It is incongruous and unexpected (ironic) that he would not want to encourage artistic talent in his own children.

(4) **3** "younger son." At line 72, in the long passage summarizing the creative lives of Fegley's three other children, he gets to Warren, the younger son, and the only one "left uncontaminated by creativity . . . ." At line 78, the narrative returns to the phone conversation that opens the passage, and we realize that the conversation is about Warren, who is spending his summer making mobiles instead of working at a practical job in construction as Fegley had expected.

(5) **2** "setting." This is the best choice here, for these lines create the image of two men at work in a business establishment, which in turn becomes the setting for the poet's rendering of his father's work life and for the story of how the boy will grow up to reject his father's expectations. There are no separate stanzas in this poem, and the plot and point of view of the poem are established only after these introductory lines.

(6) **2** "follow in his footsteps." This expectation is evident throughout the poem, first suggested at line 19 and made explicit at line 25: ". . . some day you'll work in the store." The other choices are not evident in the poem.

(7) **1** "is now an adult." As with most poems, the meaning of this one becomes clear only with more than one reading. Careful reading reveals that the poem is about the narrator's love and respect for his father but also about his own need to be saved from his father's expectations. The shifts in time that occur at lines 21 and 27 signal that the poem is a series of recollected scenes from childhood at the father's workplace and the reflection of an adult on why he could not become what his father was.

(8) **4** "appreciation." This section begins with the narrator saying, "I can see the virtues now . . . ." and goes on to list those virtues of balance, compromise, acceptance, and "Need for customers and the economy . . . ." There is no sense of blame or anger here, nor is there the intensity of joy. Clearly, however, the narrator can respect and admire what his father values.

(9) **1** "did not want it." We are prepared for the final line, "And I left too," at several points in the poem: "But I felt 'never more,' or 'never ever,'" "I loved you but couldn't think/Of staying with you," "I didn't think I could do the job . . . Staying in you/You whom I could love/But not be a part of."

(10) **3** "concerned." The narrators in both passages express genuine interest and care, Fegley for the future of his children and the poet for the expectations of his father. Fegley's concern about his children's creativity is ironic but not dishonest, and in the poem the narrator's struggle is in loving his father and remaining true to himself. Neither passage suggests that the narrator is unreliable or greedy.

Part A   Sample Student Response Essay

Often in life, the expectations that parents have for their children are overcome by circumstance or they conflict with the children's own dreams. In these two passages, we see how a father's concern for his children's future conflicts with their own dreams and ambitions. In passage I, a successful artist tries to discourage his children's creative interests. In passage II, a father who is deeply satisfied with his work in business hopes that his son will follow in his footsteps.

Through flashback, passage I relates the early and present life of a famous artist. When Fegley was a boy, his father urged him to "get a solid trade," fearing that art school in New York would only "break his heart." Fegley, however, is determined and proves his father's concern wrong. Though very successful as an adult, Fegley has become "depressed by artsy-craftsy stuff" and tries to guide his own children toward careers in science. In the line, "He was like a man who...wants to warn all others back at the edge of the sea," Updike suggests that Fegley may have the same fears his own father had, that pursuing life as an artist is difficult and may lead to disappointment. Ironically, we learn that each child has grown up to pursue a career in art, writing, or film, and the passage ends with Fegley determined to talk his younger son, the only one "left uncontaminated by creativity," out of giving up a job in construction in order to make mobiles.

The poem, by Kenneth Koch, has a similar theme to the first passage, but a contrast emerges. Here the father hopes that his son will follow in his footsteps. He has a business that has been his life, and he encourages his son to have the same passion. The poem is developed as a series of vivid scenes in an office, with secretaries and typewriters, followed by the narrator's reflections on why he could not become what his father desired. The store represents a fear felt by the young boy that he may remain forever within the prison walls of an office. As a grown man, the narrator is looking back on the emotional tug-of-war he experienced: "My heart in an uproar/I loved you but couldn't think/of staying with you," and C. Loth Inc. is personified when the narrator says, "I can see the virtues now/That could come from being in you."

In each passage, we see how a father genuinely concerned about a child's future may have expectations that cannot satisfy the child's desires or ambitions. In the Updike story we see how a father's expectations seem to contradict his own life; in the poem, we see how a young man must reject what his father loves and values in order to become what he truly desires. Both passages depict the emotional depth of such conflicts.

Analysis

This essay has many strengths and reveals good understanding and appreciation of both texts. The introduction establishes a controlling idea in summarizing the common theme in each passage, reserving the most insightful observation for the conclusion.

The organization is simple and clear, with a brief discussion of each passage to illustrate the theme. The choice of relevant details is excellent as are the references to flashback, irony, and personification. Development is adequate, but the passages and the writer's own insights merit even further elaboration. The discussion is well written, with good command of language, sentence structure, and the conventions. Overall, this response would rate a high score.

(See pp. 68–71 for a detailed discussion of the rubric for this part of the examination.)

Session Two

Note: See Chapter 4 for review and strategy in responding to this part of the examination.

Part B   Sample Student Response Essay

According to Walker Percy, "In this world, goodness is destined to be defeated." Percy suggests that all goodness will inevitably be conquered and the remaining evil will reign. Percy's statement, unfortunately, is accurate. Through William Golding's <u>Lord of the Flies</u> and Elie Wiesel's <u>Night</u>, the defeat of goodness and the dominant control of evil is apparent.

<u>Lord of the Flies</u> demonstrates a classic example of good versus evil. Struggles are revealed within characters, between characters, and thematically through resolution of the plot. In all three struggles, evil triumphs. The setting, an isolated island, represents a miniature world. The characters are boys from a British private school, who have been stranded on the island as a result of enemy hostility during war. The plane on which they were being sent to safety is shot down. In this opening with a savage attack on children, evil achieves its first victory.

As the story progresses, tension on the island intensifies between protagonists Ralph, Piggy, and Simon, and antagonist Jack. Jack represents crude evil through his sadistic and savage behavior. Ralph, Piggy, and Simon exhibit qualities of goodness and civilized behavior. Ralph, the originally elected leader, loses his influence to Jack and evil begins to triumph over goodness among the boys. Jack and his band of hunters become more and more savage once they have experienced the thrill of killing a pig and will later kill the intellectual Piggy. In one central episode, nearly all the boys will attack and kill Simon, thinking he is the "Beast." In the killing of Simon, Golding dramatizes the view that savagery and evil may be inherent in everyone. By the end of the novel, Ralph is fleeing for his life as Jack and his band are hunting him down. The story is resolved when a naval ship arrives to rescue the boys, but on the island evil has already fully triumphed over goodness.

Elie Wiesel's <u>Night</u> takes place during the Holocaust, a time of hate and evil dictatorship in Hitler's Germany. This work is based on Wiesel's own experiences as a child in the concentration camps, but it employs many of the techniques of a novel. In the various characters and the story itself, or plot, Wiesel shows how "goodness is destined to be defeated." Wiesel's story is especially powerful because it is told in the first person.

Eliezer, a young and observant Jewish boy, tells of life in the camp, where he and his father have been sent, separated from the rest of their family. In the camp, he experiences the suffering and death of this father, witnesses the execution of other prisoners, and sees how men may abandon their own families for survival. As the evil overwhelms him he questions his faith and the existence of God. Wiesel's story shows how feeling itself has been destroyed, in the young Elie and in those around him. Elie survives, and when he is finally freed, he looks in a mirror and sees only a skeleton. Although Eliezer survived, his body lacked the spirituality and feeling that compose life. The triumph of evil has dehumanized him as it had those who carried out the Holocaust. Wiesel's purpose is to show the human capacity for evil and to remind us of events that occurred not very long ago.

In both these literary works, characters, narrative, and theme demonstrate the power of evil to destroy human goodness.

Analysis

As many responses to a critical lens do, this one relies primarily on a discussion of plot to show why the writer agrees with Walker Percy's statement. The introduction is brief but clear in establishing an interpretation that is essentially a restatement of the critical lens, and the novels are especially well chosen to support the topic. This writer also shows how theme and development of characters in these two works support the interpretation.

The essay is clearly organized and maintains focus on the topic. The discussion of each work is well developed with relevant details, which outline the ultimate destruction of goodness by evil. This "outline" or progression of details also gives the essay coherence. The choice of language is appropriate and sophisticated, and there is excellent variety in sentence structure. Note too how several paragraphs are concluded with especially insightful observations: *"In this opening with a savage attack on children, evil achieves its first victory on the island." ". . . evil has already fully triumphed over goodness." "Wiesel's story is especially powerful because it is told in the first person."* This is a thoughtful and well-written essay, with no significant errors in the conventions. It would merit a high score. (See pp. 80–83 for a detailed discussion of the rubric for this part of the examination.)

Examination
August 2005
English

Session One

Part A

Overview: For this part of the test, you will listen to an account about United States currency, answer some multiple-choice questions, and write a response based on the situation described below. You will hear the account twice. You may take notes on the page alloted anytime you wish during the readings.

> **The Situation:** Your social studies class is studying the international monetary system. You have been assigned to report on the evolution of the United States dollar. In preparation for writing your report, listen to an account by Daniel Gross. Then use relevant information from the account to write your report.

Your Task: Write a report for your social studies class in which you discuss the evolution of the United States dollar.

Guidelines:
Be sure to

- Tell your audience what they need to know about the evolution of the United States dollar
- Use specific, accurate, and relevant information from the account to support your discussion
- Use a tone and level of language appropriate for a report for a social studies class
- Organize your ideas in a logical and coherent manner
- Indicate any words taken directly from the account by using quotation marks or referring to the speaker
- Follow the conventions of standard written English

Listening Passage

The Swedish krona and Bolivian boliviano aren't merely answers to crossword puzzle clues, they're meaningful national and historical symbols. Indeed, a nation's self-image and identity is inextricably linked with its currency. But currencies come and go. Wars and revolutions cause new regimes to replace outmoded systems. More recently, the advent of the ecumenical Euro has dispatched 12 once-proud monetary systems to the pages of history.

Given this, a currency that lasts for 200 years—say, the U.S. dollar, which has been legal tender since 1791—is a marvel. And it's especially noteworthy that this nation, which self-consciously engages in constant reinvention, has stuck so fiercely to its ancient money. Of course, when you consider that the dollar is one of America's greatest brands, this stubborn attachment to the greenback makes more sense.

The U.S. system of representative democracy and free markets may not be universally accepted. But the U.S. dollar sure is. It's more graciously received around the globe than American Express and Visa combined. Ecuador uses the American dollar as its own currency, and local currencies from Hong Kong to Jamaica are pegged to the U.S. dollar. All of which shows a remarkable faith in what is really more an idea than a hard currency. "Money is a belief that has to be shared with other people," notes Justin Goodwin, in his entertaining and discursive book, *Greenback*.

As Goodwin shows, the mighty dollar has humble origins. In the sixteenth century, coins made in Joachimstal, which lies in a valley (a *thal*, in German) in what is now the Czech Republic, were widely used. That coin, and others like it, came to be known as the *thaler*—in English, the *dollar*. (Despite intrepid investigations, the origin of the $ symbol remains obscure.)

When the English settled the New World, colonists used as currency things they had or found: corn, peas, rum, nails, and strings of beads and shells (what the Massachusetts Indians called wampum). The rare silver dollars that found their way into circulation were ineffective for small transactions, and frugal traders would knock them into eight pieces. (Which is why, to this day, people refer to a quarter as "two bits.")

Of course, paying for 20 acres of land with several barrels of rum didn't prove an effective means of commerce. So the colonists turned to paper money. In 1691, Massachusetts became, in Goodwin's words, "the first state since medieval China to issue its own paper currency." And the question of how to establish a colonial paper currency occupied the leading minds of the colonies. Benjamin Franklin made his debut as a pamphleteer in 1729 with a piece titled "A Modest Enquiry into the Nature and Necessity of a Paper-Currency." (His agitation for paper money was a little self-serving, because Franklin owned a chain of print shops in New England.)

It wasn't until 1775 that the newly established Continental Congress printed its own paper bills, calling them Continentals. These first dollars bore several features—the Great Seal, with the eagle, the pyramid with the disembodied eye on top, and the term *E Pluribus Unum*—variations of which survive to this day. But since these first bucks were backed only by the credit of the struggling colonial government, the bills depreciated rapidly.

For much of the nineteenth century, printing money was generally the province of banks that obtained charters from states. By 1813, 208 banks were literally making money, from the Delaware City Bank to the Bank of Saint Nicholas in New York, whose bills featured Santa Claus. But not all dollars were created equal. In theory, every bill could be taken to the bank from which it was issued and redeemed for gold or silver. But due to significant distances and skepticism surrounding unfamiliar bills, a dollar bank note from a Massachusetts bank might be worth only 93 cents in Ohio, and even less in Indiana. The closest thing the young nation had to a national currency were the notes issued by the Philadelphia-based Bank of the United States, which had a 29-city branch network. But as the bank rose as a central power, President Andrew Jackson took it on in an epic political battle. The bank went out of business in 1841.

The Civil War established the federal government as a force in currency. Faced with bare coffers—at the start of the war, the United States had just $200,000—

and a need to pay the growing Union Army, the government in 1862 first issued notes on the credit of what remained of the United States. Black on the front and green on the back, they came to be known as "greenbacks." But these war bucks quickly lost value as negative battlefield reports came in. The federal ten-cent bills were dubbed "shinplaster," in part because they resembled the sort of paper one might use to plaster a sore leg, and in part because that was pretty much all they were good for. Nonetheless, the National Bank Act of 1863 gave the federal government the exclusive right to issue money.

The dollar would remain a poor stepsister to European currencies until the world's financial center of gravity shifted after World War I across the Atlantic. With the Old World's power in decline and the New World's might in ascendance, shrewd European observers recognized a tectonic shift. "If the English pound is not to be the standard which everyone knows and can trust, the business not only of the British Empire but of Europe as well might have to be transacted in dollars instead of pounds sterling," Winston Churchill declared in 1925. Even then, the dollar stood for something more than 100 cents. By the 1920s, Goodwin notes, it was "a brand like the other brands already beginning to conquer and even define aspects of the nation."

In fact, like Coca-Cola, Disney, McDonald's, and Starbucks, the dollar has been one of the great global brands of the past century. People the world over seek it out and use it, not just because it meets a need, but because it conjures up a positive image in consumers' minds, and because it stands for something that its competitors don't.

In many ways, Americans regard the dollar the way they do other consumer brands. Just as some long-time patrons rejected New Coke and didn't swallow all the innovations in the traditional McDonald's menu, so have Americans proved reluctant to accept changes to the dollar. Neither the $2 bill nor the Susan B. Anthony caught on. And the design tweaks introduced in the 1990s—intended to foil counterfeiters—were met with less than universal approval.

For a forward-looking nation like the United States, our attitude toward the dollar may seem overly nostalgic. But with currencies, as is generally the rule in business, why mess with success?

—from "Eight Bits"
Attaché, April 2003

Notes

Multiple-Choice Questions

Directions (1–6): Use your notes to answer the following questions about the passage read to you. Select the best suggested answer and write its number in the space provided. The questions may help you think about ideas and information you might use in your writing. You may return to these questions anytime you wish.

1 The speaker refers to the United States dollar as "ancient" in order to stress the dollar's

   (1) symbolic value
   (2) frequent changes
   (3) universal acceptance
   (4) long life   1 _____

2 What did early settlers of the New World use as currency?

   (1) quarters
   (2) common items
   (3) paper money
   (4) land   2 _____

3 A problem with the currencies printed by banks during the nineteenth century was that these dollars were

   (1) unequally valued
   (2) redeemable for gold
   (3) rapidly devalued
   (4) replaced by coins   3 _____

4 The federal government gained the exclusive right to print money during

   (1) the Revolutionary War
   (2) the Civil War
   (3) World War I
   (4) World War II   4 _____

5 The two-dollar bill and the Susan B. Anthony coin are noted in order to stress the dollar's

(1) positive image
(2) difficulty to counterfeit
(3) green and black color
(4) resistance to change

5 _____

6 The predominant organizational pattern of the account is

(1) cause and effect
(2) order of importance
(3) chronological order
(4) spatial order

6 _____

After you have finished these questions, review **The Situation** and read **Your Task** and the **Guidelines**. Use scrap paper to plan your response. Then write your response on separate sheets of paper. After you finish your response for Part A, complete Part B.

Part B

Directions: Read the text and study the graph on the following pages, answer the multiple-choice questions, and write a response based on the situation described below. You may use the margins to take notes as you read and scrap paper to plan your response.

The Situation: The student council in your school is organizing a volunteer program, matching student volunteers with individuals and community organizations in need of assistance. You have been asked to write an article for your school newspaper encouraging students to volunteer by describing the trend toward student volunteerism and the benefits of such programs for both recipients and volunteers.

Your Task: Using relevant information from *both* documents, write an article for your school newspaper in which you encourage students to volunteer by describing the trend toward teen volunteerism and the benefits of such programs for both recipients and volunteers.

Guidelines:
Be sure to
- Tell your audience what they need to know about the trend toward teen volunteerism and the benefits of such programs for both recipients and volunteers
- Use specific, accurate, and relevant information from the text *and* the graph to support your discussion
- Use a tone and level of language appropriate for an article for your school newspaper
- Organize your ideas in a logical and coherent manner
- Indicate any words taken directly from the text by using quotation marks or referring to the author
- Follow the conventions of standard written English

Volunteerism's new face

. . . Volunteering has become a significant part of teen culture. Fifty-nine percent of 12- to 17-year-olds said they'd volunteered in the past year, according to a 1996 study by the Independent Sector, the most recent national study on teen volunteering habits available. In a fall 1999 teen-age marketing and lifestyles
(5)   study done by the marketing firm Teenage Research Unlimited, six in 10 teens said that volunteering was "in."

"A lot of people think we're this big community of bad kids, and half [of] us aren't like that at all," says Clara, a freshman at Grant High School. "This is one way to prove that."
(10)   It is, for many teens, the new norm, a given, reinforced by the community service requirements that many schools now require to graduate, and the increase of service learning — which combines classroom lessons with volunteer projects — in many school curricula.

Teen music reflects and celebrates the trend: The Backstreet Boys lend the
(15)   name of their song "Larger than Life," and free concert tickets, to a contest promoting public service. Rage Against the Machine's album "The Battle of Los Angeles," full of calls to action and celebrations of activism, debuts at the top of the billboard charts, selling 430,000 copies in one week. The album's CD-liner notes explain how to contact or get involved with groups such as Rock for Choice
(20)   and Women Alive. Hip-hop artist Lauryn Hill tucks information about her nonprofit, The Refugee Project, in the liner notes of her album "The Miseducation of Lauryn Hill."

"It's part of the culture now," says Clayton Miller, 16, a junior at Lincoln High School who, along with his twin brother, Greg, has traveled to Mexico to help
(25)   build homes for the needy and helped shop for groceries for Portland-area people who couldn't get to the store.

"It's kind of like learning how to read," Greg says. "When you are taught how to help others, it begins to come naturally after a while."

Teens say they are far from being passive drones, just going through the
(30)   motions of required service. They acknowledge without judgment that there are a fair number of résumé padders and kids just serving their time who make up the volunteer numbers. But young people and those who work with them say what's interesting about teens right now is how many are choosing to do community service work beyond what is required of them, driving the trend and
(35)   changing the way teen volunteers are viewed.

A couple of years ago, volunteers from the AmeriCorps program going into Portland-area high schools and middle schools to help coordinate service learning projects began noticing something: A lot of kids were approaching them after

class, wanting to learn more about volunteering. The kids wanted to find out what
(40) they could do outside of school, where they could go for more information. . . .

More than a decade ago, some foretold the increase in teen volunteerism. In
their 1991 book "Generations," William Strauss and Neil Howe predicted that
this generation of teens would be civic-oriented. "Teen peer leaders will express
a growing interest in community affairs and a growing enthusiasm for collective
(45) action," they wrote.

In the four years following that prediction, the number of volunteers grew by
7 percent, from 12.4 million teens to 13.3 million, according to the 1996
Independent Sector study.

The number of schools involving students in community service has increased
(50) dramatically in the last decade, according to a 1999 U.S. Department of
Education survey.

In 1984, 27 percent of high schools said they had students participating in
community service. In 1999, 83 percent said they did, according to the study.
Nearly half of the schools surveyed in 1999 said service learning was part of their
(55) curriculum.

And students are taking volunteering beyond the classroom in increasing
numbers if you look at the service organizations teens choose. Membership in
Key Club, an after-school service club for high-schoolers sponsored by the
Kiwanis Club, has increased steadily for the past three years. Two years ago, there
(60) were 196,000 members. Now there are 205,000, according to the national
organization.

At Grant High School the Octagon Club, a community service club sponsored
by the Optimist Society of Lloyd Center, has grown from four members six years
ago to more than 50 members this year. It's now one of the largest Octagon Clubs
(65) in the country. For one of its projects, students feed the homeless two times a
month at Grace Memorial Episcopal Church. So many students were showing up
that they had more help than they could use, says adviser John Mears.

A lot of teens are interested in doing volunteer work that is different from
projects many teens may have done in the past, says Megan Buscho, a 15-year-old
(70) sophomore who helped set up the Youth Involvement Center at Cleveland High
school and helps other students find volunteer opportunities that fit their interests.

"A lot of kids aren't interested in the usual kinds of volunteer opportunities
like serving people in a soup kitchen," she says. "They're more interested in doing
things that get to the root of the problem, like finding out what gets people in the
(75) soup kitchen in the first place and preventing that."

Some of what's behind this is teens' realization that they may not be able to
vote, says Buscho. "But we can affect change before then. By getting out there
and volunteering, adults can see what we are thinking about, what we care about,

and we can influence how adults think about young people."

(80)   While teens such as Clara Ard are aware that volunteering is one way to mend the negative stereotypes adults may harbor about their generation, what's drawing them out to rainy riverbanks on the weekends or moving them to set a table for seniors goes beyond that, teens say.

Some perceive volunteering as a way to give back to their community. "The
(85)   seniors at our church pray for our youth group regularly," Ard says, "and I think it's important to thank them."

It is a chance for teens to exercise their values — whether it's their religious convictions, political motivations or sense of social justice. Volunteering is a way for them to be connected to something larger.

(90)   "Helping others makes me feel so good," says Josi Henderson, 18, a senior at Grant. "I really feel like my day isn't complete without practicing some act of kindness." She credits her volunteer experiences in high school with helping her decide what she wants to do with her life. She wants to major in speech pathology in college and, afterward, join the Peace Corps. "I really want to devote my life
(95)   to helping others," she says.

"I think our generation is changing the definition of what it means to be a good citizen," Buscho says. "It used to be that being a good citizen was about patriotism and being true to your country. Now the definition is: Know what's going on in your country, be involved, and then you can change things. Through
(100) volunteering, we can start doing things about the issues that affect us."

— Inara Verzemnieks
excerpted from "Volunteerism's new face"
The Oregonian, December 25, 1999

GRAPH

Importance of benefits gained from teen Volunteering – 1996 and 1992

Benefits Gained *

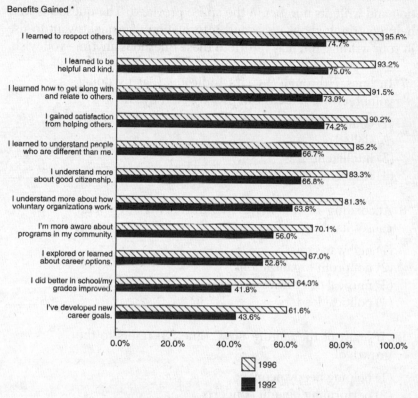

* Based on the percentage of respondents who
stated that a specific benefit was "Very
important" or "Somewhat important."

Source: (adapted) Independent Sector, 2000

Multiple-Choice Questions

Directions (7–16): Select the best suggested answer to each question and write its number in the space provided. The questions may help you think about ideas and information you might want to use in your writing. You may return to these questions anytime you wish.

7 In lines 7 through 9 Clara indicates that by doing volunteer work, teens can prove that they are

(1) competitive
(2) skilled
(3) intelligent
(4) respectable   7____

8 According to the writer, volunteering for social causes has been promoted by

(1) highway signs
(2) nonprofit organizations
(3) musical celebrities
(4) political leaders   8____

9 "It's part of the culture now" (line 23) refers to the growth of

(1) helping needy people
(2) performing benefit concerts
(3) mentoring young artists
(4) traveling to Mexico   9____

10 As used in line 29, "passive drones" most nearly means people who

(1) eliminate resistance
(2) avoid work
(3) use caution
(4) accept challenge   10____

11 The prediction of an increase in the civic orientation of teens (line 41) is supported by

(1) personal interviews
(2) expert testimonials
(3) studies and surveys
(4) questions and answers   11____

12 As used in line 74, getting to "the root of the problem" most nearly means discovering the problem's

(1) origin
(2) effects
(3) solution
(4) frequency   12____

13 Students who are too young to vote see volunteering as a way to demonstrate their

(1) independence
(2) talents
(3) beliefs
(4) education   13____

14 The experience of Josi Henderson (lines 90 through
95) is most likely included to demonstrate that student volunteer work may lead to

(1) finding hobbies
(2) discovering a vocation
(3) building a résumé
(4) developing friendships   14____

15 According to the graph, the greatest increase in
benefit between 1992 and 1996 was in

(1) getting along with and relating to others
(2) understanding about good citizenship
(3) exploring or learning about career options
(4) improving academically   15____

16 According to the graph, for 1996 which benefit was
most important to teen volunteers?

(1) respecting others
(2) gaining satisfaction from helping
(3) understanding differences
(4) being aware of community   16 _____

After you have finished these questions, review **The
Situation** and read **Your Task** and the **Guidelines**.
Use scrap paper to plan your response. Then write
your response to Part B on separate sheets of paper.

Session Two

Part A

Directions: Read the passages on the following pages (an excerpt from a short story and a poem). Write the number of the answer to each multiple-choice question in the space provided. Then write the essay on separate sheets of paper as described in **Your Task**. You may use the margins to take notes as you read and scrap paper to plan your response.

Your Task:

After you have read the passages and answered the multiple-choice questions, write a unified essay about opportunities for learning as revealed in the passages. In your essay, use ideas from **both** passages to establish a controlling idea about opportunities for learning. Using evidence from **each** passage, develop your controlling idea and show how the author uses specific literary elements or techniques to convey that idea.

Guidelines:
Be sure to
- Use ideas from **both** passages to establish a controlling idea about opportunities for learning
- Use specific and relevant evidence from **each** passage to develop your controlling idea
- Show how each author uses specific literary elements (for example: theme, characterization, structure, point of view) or techniques (for example: symbolism, irony, figurative language) to convey the controlling idea
- Organize your ideas in a logical and coherent manner
- Use language that communicates ideas effectively
- Follow the conventions of standard written English

Passage I

I was very late for school that morning, and I was terribly afraid of being scolded, especially as Monsieur Hamel had told us that he should examine us on participles, and I did not know the first thing about them. For a moment I thought of staying away from school and wandering about the fields. It was such
(5) a warm, lovely day. I could hear the blackbirds whistling on the edge of the wood, and in the Rippert field, behind the sawmill, the Prussians going through their drill. All that was much more tempting to me than the rules concerning participles; but I had the strength to resist, and I ran as fast as I could to school.

As I passed the mayor's office, I saw that there were people gathered about
(10) the little board on which notices were posted. For two years all our bad news had come from that board—battles lost, conscriptions, orders from headquarters; and I thought without stopping:

"What can it be now?"

Then, as I ran across the square, Wachter the blacksmith, who stood there
(15) with his apprentice, reading the placard, called out to me:

"Don't hurry so, my boy; you'll get to your school soon enough!"

I thought that he was making fun of me, and I ran into Monsieur Hamel's little yard all out of breath.

Usually, at the beginning of school, there was a great uproar which could be
(20) heard in the street, desks opening and closing, lessons repeated aloud in unison, with our ears stuffed in order to learn quicker, and the teacher's stout ruler beating on the desk:

"A little more quiet!"

I counted on all this noise to reach my bench unnoticed; but as it happened,
(25) that day everything was quiet, like a Sunday morning. Through the open window I saw my comrades already in their places, and Monsieur Hamel walking back and forth with the terrible iron ruler under his arm. I had to open the door and enter, in the midst of that perfect silence. You can imagine whether I blushed and whether I was afraid!

(30) But no! Monsieur Hamel looked at me with no sign of anger and said very gently:

"Go at once to your seat, my little Frantz; we were going to begin without you."

I stepped over the bench and sat down at once at my desk. Not until then,
(35) when I partly recovered from my fright, did I notice that our teacher had on his handsome blue coat, his plaited ruff, and the black silk embroidered breeches, which he wore only on days of inspection or of distribution of prizes. Moreover, there was something extraordinary, something solemn about the whole class. But

(40) what surprised me most was to see at the back of the room, on the benches which were usually empty, some people from the village sitting, as silent as we were: old Hauser with his three-cornered hat, the ex-mayor, the ex-postman, and others besides. They all seemed depressed; and Hauser had brought an old spelling-book with gnawed edges, which he held wide-open on his knee, with his great spectacles askew.

(45) While I was wondering at all this, Monsieur Hamel had mounted his platform, and in the same gentle and serious voice with which he had welcomed me, he said to us:

"My children, this is the last time that I shall teach you. Orders have come from Berlin to teach nothing but German in the schools of Alsace and Lorraine. *(50)* The new teacher arrives to-morrow. This is the last class in French, so I beg you to be very attentive."

Those few words overwhelmed me. Ah! the villains! that was what they had posted at the mayor's office.

My last class in French!

(55) And I barely knew how to write! So I should never learn! I must stop short where I was! How angry I was with myself because of the time I had wasted, the lessons I had missed, running about after nests, or sliding on the Saar! My books, which only a moment before I thought so tiresome, so heavy to carry—my grammar, my sacred history—seemed to me now like old friends, from whom I *(60)* should be terribly grieved to part. And it was the same about Monsieur Hamel. The thought that he was going away, that I should never see him again, made me forget the punishments, the blows with the ruler.

Poor man! It was in honour of that last lesson that he had put on his fine Sunday clothes; and I understood now why those old fellows from the village *(65)* were sitting at the end of the room. It seemed to mean that they regretted not having come oftener to the school. It was also a way of thanking our teacher for his forty years of faithful service, and of paying their respects to the fatherland which was vanishing ....

—Alphonse Daudet
from "The Last Class — The Story of a Little Alsatian"
from *Little French Masterpieces*, 1903
C. P. Putnam's Sons

Passage II

MORNING GLORY

The faces of the teachers
know we have failed and failed
yet they focus beyond, on the windowsill
the names of distant galaxies
(5)   and trees.

We have come in dragging.
If someone would give us
a needle and thread, or send us
on a mission to collect something
(10)   at a store, we could walk for twenty years
sorting it out. How do we open,
when we are so full?

The teachers have more faith than we do.
They have organized into units.
(15)   We would appreciate units
if we gave them a chance.
Nothing will ever again be so clear.

The teachers look at our papers
when they would rather be looking at
(20)   a fine scallop of bark
or their fathers and mothers thin as lace,
their own teachers remaining in front
of a class at the back of their minds.
So many seasons of rain, sun, wind
(25)   have crystallized their teachers.
They shine like something on a beach.
But we don't see that yet.

We're fat with binders and forgetting.
We're shaping the name of a new love
(30) on the underside of our thumb.
We're diagnosing rumor and trouble
and fear. We hear the teachers
as if they were far off, speaking
down a tube. Sometimes
(35) a whole sentence gets through.

But the teachers don't give up.
They rise, dress, appear before us
crisp and hopeful. They have a plan.
If cranes can fly 1,000 miles
(40) or that hummingbird return from Mexico
to find, curled on its crooked fence, a new vine,
surely. We may dip into the sweet
together, if we hover long enough.

—Naomi Shihab Nye
from *Fuel,* 1998
Boa Editions, Ltd.

Multiple-Choice Questions

Directions (1–10): Select the best suggested answer to each question and write its number in the space provided. The questions may help you think about the ideas and information you might want to use in your essay. You may return to these questions anytime you wish.

Passage I (the short story excerpt)—Questions 1–4 refer to Passage I.

1 When Frantz is introduced in the first paragraph, his most prominent characteristic is his

  (1) ability in athletics
  (2) love of learning
  (3) fear of punishment
  (4) knowledge about nature   1 _____

2 When he gets to school, Frantz *first* realizes that something is different when he is

  (1) made to stand alone
  (2) greeted with silence
  (3) praised by Monsieur Hamel
  (4) escorted to his desk   2 _____

3 Monsieur Hamel's attire and the presence of the people in the back of the classroom reinforce the

  (1) significance of the day
  (2) content of the lesson
  (3) need of attention
  (4) atmosphere of celebration   3 _____

4 What does Frantz conclude from the news that Monsieur Hamel is leaving?

  (1) Frantz will no longer be punished.
  (2) Frantz has used too much time studying.
  (3) Frantz will not be allowed back in school.
  (4) Frantz has a new perspective on school.   4 _____

Passage II (the poem)—Questions 5–10 refer to Passage II.

5 According to the poet, a characteristic displayed by teachers is

(1) happiness
(2) pessimism
(3) determination
(4) inattention

5 _____

6 The word "dragging" (line 6) suggests that the students are

(1) reluctant
(2) afraid
(3) angry
(4) disgusted

6 _____

7 The poet uses the word "open" (line 11) to indicate becoming

(1) eligible
(2) receptive
(3) employable
(4) satisfied

7 _____

8 According to the poet, teachers in the classroom model their educational practices on

(1) recent studies
(2) their best students
(3) their former teachers
(4) scientific theories

8 _____

9 Lines 28 through 32 are used to present examples of things that

(1) are a basis for lessons
(2) keep students in school
(3) cause sibling rivalry
(4) distract students from learning

9 _____

10 The poet mentions the experience of cranes (line 39) and the hummingbird (line 40) to reinforce the theme that

(1) persistence will produce results
(2) travel will enhance learning
(3) sweetness will improve the environment
(4) friendship will promote love

10 _____

After you have finished these questions, review **Your Task** and the **Guidelines**. Use scrap paper to plan your response. Then write your response to Part A on separate sheets of paper. After you finish your response for Part A, complete Part B.

Part B

Your Task:

Write a critical essay in which you discuss **two** works of literature you have read from the particular perspective of the statement that is provided for you in the **Critical Lens**. In your essay, provide a valid interpretation of the statement, agree **or** disagree with the statement as you have interpreted it, and support your opinion using specific references to appropriate literary elements from the two works. You may use scrap paper to plan your response. Write your essay in Part B on separate sheets of paper.

Critical Lens:

> "I like flawed characters because somewhere in them I see more of the truth."
>
> — Nicolas Cage, as quoted in "His Truth is Out There" from *Los Angeles Times,* November 12, 2000

Guidelines:

Be sure to

- Provide a valid interpretation of the critical lens that clearly establishes the criteria for analysis
- Indicate whether you agree **or** disagree with the statement as you have interpreted it
- Choose **two** works you have read that you believe best support your opinion
- Use the criteria suggested by the critical lens to analyze the works you have chosen
- Avoid plot summary. Instead, use specific references to appropriate literary elements (for example: theme, characterization, setting, point of view) to develop your analysis
- Organize your ideas in a unified and coherent manner
- Specify the titles and authors of the literature you choose
- Follow the conventions of standard written English

Regents Comprehensive Examination in English—August 2005
Chart for Determining the Final Examination Score (Use for August 2005 examination only.)

To determine the student's final examination score, locate the student's total essay score across the top of the chart and the student's total multiple-choice score down the side of the chart. The point where those two scores intersect is the student's final examination score. For example, a student receiving a total essay score of 19 and a total multiple-choice score of 16 would receive a final examination score of 77.

Total Multiple-Choice Score \ Total Essay Score →	0	1	2	3	4	5	6	7	8	9	10	11	12	13	14	15	16	17	18	19	20	21	22	23	24
0	0	1	2	3	3	4	6	8	10	13	16	19	22	25	29	32	36	40	43	47	51	55	59	62	67
1	1	1	2	3	3	5	7	9	12	14	18	21	24	27	31	34	38	41	45	49	53	57	61	65	69
2	1	2	2	3	5	6	8	10	13	16	19	22	25	29	32	36	40	43	47	51	55	59	62	67	70
3	1	2	3	3	5	7	9	12	14	18	21	24	27	31	34	38	41	45	49	53	57	61	65	69	72
4	2	3	3	5	6	8	10	13	16	19	22	25	29	32	36	40	43	47	51	55	59	62	67	70	74
5	2	3	5	6	7	9	12	14	18	21	24	27	31	34	38	41	45	49	53	57	61	65	69	72	76
6	3	4	6	6	8	10	13	16	19	22	25	29	32	36	40	43	47	51	55	59	62	67	70	74	77
7	3	5	6	7	9	12	14	18	21	24	27	31	34	38	41	45	49	53	57	61	65	69	72	76	79
8	3	6	7	8	10	13	16	19	22	25	29	32	36	40	43	47	51	55	59	62	67	70	74	77	80
9	3	6	8	9	12	14	18	21	24	27	31	34	38	41	45	49	53	57	59	65	69	72	76	79	82
10	4	6	9	10	13	16	19	22	25	29	32	36	40	43	47	51	55	57	61	67	70	74	77	80	84
11	5	7	9	12	14	18	21	25	29	32	36	40	43	47	49	53	57	61	65	69	72	76	79	82	85
12	6	8	10	13	16	19	22	25	29	32	36	40	43	47	51	55	59	62	67	70	74	77	80	84	86
13	7	9	12	14	18	21	24	27	31	34	38	41	45	49	53	57	61	65	69	72	76	79	82	85	88
14	8	10	13	16	19	22	25	29	32	36	40	43	47	51	55	59	62	67	70	74	77	80	84	86	88
15	9	12	14	18	21	24	27	31	34	38	41	45	49	53	57	61	65	69	72	76	79	82	85	88	89
16	10	13	16	19	22	25	29	32	36	40	43	47	51	55	59	62	67	70	74	77	80	84	86	89	90
17	12	14	18	21	24	27	31	34	38	41	45	49	53	57	61	65	69	72	76	79	82	85	88	90	92
18	13	16	19	22	25	29	32	36	40	43	47	51	55	59	62	67	70	74	77	80	84	86	89	92	93
19	14	18	21	24	27	31	34	38	41	45	49	53	57	61	65	69	72	76	79	82	85	88	90	93	94
20	16	19	22	25	29	32	36	40	43	47	51	55	59	62	67	70	74	77	80	84	86	89	92	94	95
21	18	21	24	27	31	34	38	41	45	49	53	57	61	65	69	72	76	79	82	85	88	90	93	95	96
22	19	22	25	29	32	36	40	43	47	51	55	59	62	67	70	74	77	80	84	86	89	92	94	96	97
23	21	24	27	31	34	38	41	45	49	53	57	61	65	69	72	76	79	82	85	88	90	93	95	97	98
24	22	25	29	32	36	40	43	47	51	55	59	62	67	70	74	77	80	84	86	89	92	94	96	97	99
25	24	27	31	34	38	41	45	49	53	57	61	65	69	72	76	79	82	85	88	90	93	95	96	98	99
26	25	29	32	36	40	43	47	51	55	59	62	67	70	74	77	80	84	86	89	92	94	96	97	99	100

Answers
August 2005
English

Answer Key

Session One, Part A	Session One, Part B	Session Two, Part A
1. 4	7. 4	1. 3
2. 2	8. 3	2. 2
3. 1	9. 1	3. 1
4. 2	10. 2	4. 4
5. 4	11. 3	5. 3
6. 3	12. 1	6. 1
	13. 3	7. 2
	14. 2	8. 3
	15. 4	9. 4
	16. 1	10. 1

Answers Explained

Session One

Part A   (1–6)

Note: Refer to Chapter 1 for review and strategy in responding to this part of the examination.

(1) **4** "long life." Though use of the term "ancient" here is an exaggeration, it stresses the speaker's point that the United States has stuck to the dollar, which has been legal tender since 1791. The speaker calls it "one of America's greatest brands . . . ." Each of the other choices is expressed in the text but is not supported by the notion of "ancient."

(2) **2** "common items." The speaker points out that the early colonists "used as currency things they had or found: corn, peas, rum, nails . . . strings of beads and shells . . . ."

(3) **1** "unequally valued." In outlining the proliferation of banks in different states "literally making money," the speaker reports that, " . . . not all dollars were created equal." A dollar in one state might be worth only 93 cents in another. None of the other choices is cited as a *problem* with currencies printed by banks.

(4) **2** "the Civil War." The speaker tells us that the "Civil War established the federal government as a force in currency," and that "the National Bank Act of 1863 gave the federal government the exclusive right to issue money."

(5) **4** "resistance to change." The speaker concludes his account with examples of efforts to bring innovation to our popular culture, including currency, and the fact that they were "met with less than universal approval."

(6) **3** "chronological order." Following an introduction that emphasizes the link between a nation's currency and its self-identity and describes the importance of the U.S. dollar in world commerce, most of the discussion is a historical account of the dollar's origins and development over 200 years. Some details represent cause and effect, but the *predominant* organization is chronological.

Part A   Sample Student Response Essay

Currency offers more than a way to buy goods. It is a part of a country's national identity, and the United States dollar is one of the best-known examples. But where did this time-honored piece of American culture come from? A recent report by Daniel Gross tells some of the history of currency and of the American dollar.

The early colonists used common items like corn, nails, shawls, and beads for trade. The Indians called this wampum. Some silver dollars were available but were not useful for trading small items. Some traders broke these coins into eight pieces, and even today some people call a quarter "two bits," going back to this early practice. For larger transactions, such as buying land, the colonists needed something more efficient.

In 1691 the Massachusetts Colony was the first state since medieval China to print paper money. Daniel Gross reports that questions about how to establish a paper money became important to many of the best thinkers of the time. In 1729 Benjamin Franklin wrote one of his first pamphlets in order to advocate use of paper money. Gross also reminds us that Franklin was the owner of a chain of print shops in New England.

When the Continental Congress was formed, it printed a federal paper dollar in 1775. These bills were called "Continentals" and bore many of the marks the world still recognizes as American symbols. The bills had the Great Seal with the eagle, the pyramid with a single eye on top, and the saying E Pluribus Unum. The Continentals were printed in 29 cities that contained branches of the federal bank, but the money depressed rapidly with only the struggling new government to back it. The states continued to print their own money, and by 1813, 208 banks had received charters to print money. The value of each bill varied from place to place, and it was inconvenient to trade or buy with them, especially when traveling from one state to another.

The Civil War established the federal government as the leading force in American currency. With only $200,000 dollars at the beginning of the war and the need to pay the Union Army, the federal government began to issue notes known as "greenbacks." These bills were printed with black on the front and green on the back. As reports of losses on the battlefield came in, these too lost their value and came to be called "shin plaster" because they weren't worth much more than bandages. In 1863, however, the federal government passed a law that gave it the exclusive right to issue currency.

American money did not take the world stage until after World War I, when European power, especially British power, began to decline. Winston Churchill recognized in 1925 that the dollar would take the place of the British pound in European trade and commerce. Since then, the American dollar has dominated not only European, but also world markets.

Today, the U.S. dollar is a brand like Disney or Coca-Cola that is easily recognizable all over the world. This 200-year-old currency, first made legal tender in 1791, is now a world currency. Ecuador uses the dollar as its own and many countries base the value of their currency on the value of the dollar.

One writer claims that U.S. currency is more accepted around the world than American Express and Visa combined. The dollar has overcome its humble origins to become a worldwide symbol.

Analysis

This essay meets the requirements of the task, to compose a report, very well. The writer conveys a thorough understanding of the text and has noted accurately many of the relevant details. The organization is chronological, following the organization of the original passage and is especially appropriate for the subject, the evolution of the U.S. dollar. This organization and the selection of details for development also serve to maintain the focus.

The language is factual, clear, and suited to the subject, and some passages are effective in dramatizing the history of the dollar: *Currency offers more than a way to buy goods. It is a part of a country's national identity . . . American money did not take the world stage until after World War I.* The response demonstrates the writer's ability to vary sentence structures effectively, and there are no significant errors in the conventions. This essay would merit a high score. (See pp. 31–35 for a detailed explanation of the rubric for this part of the examination.)

Part B   (7–16)

Note: Refer to Chapter 2 for review and strategy in responding to this part of the examination.

(7) **4** "respectable." This is the best choice to counter what Clara says might be a community's impression of kids as "bad."

(8) **3** "musical celebrities." Beginning at line 14, this paragraph offers several examples of bands and artists who celebrate and promote the trend toward volunteering among teens. Political leaders and nonprofit organizations, even highway signs, may also promote this trend, but they are not cited by this writer.

(9) **1** "helping needy people." The examples that complete this paragraph are specific illustrations of young people helping others in need.

(10) **2** "avoid work." This is the best of the choices to describe students who only "go through the motions" and participate without genuine interest or commitment.

(11) **3** "studies and surveys." This is the best answer because the four brief paragraphs that follow cite a 1996 Independent Sector study, U.S. Department of Education surveys, and a report from the Kiwanis Club. Personal interviews and testimonials do appear in the article, but this section on the increase in civic orientation of teens is supported by the studies.

(12) **1** "origin." In the paragraph that begins at line 72, one student says that "[teens] are more interested . . . in finding out what gets people in the soup kitchen in the first place and preventing that." They want to address the root problems, not simply address effects.

(13) **3** "beliefs." Beginning at line 77, this same student says that in volunteering, people can "see what we are thinking about, what we care about . . . ."

(14) **2** "discovering a vocation." Josi Henderson reports that her volunteer work helped her decide what her college major would be and what kind of work she would want to do.

(15) **4** "improving academically." This answer is found by first looking at each pair of lines to find the greatest difference between the figures for 1992 and 1996, then doing an arithmetic estimate or calculation of the difference to confirm the answer.

(16) **1** "respecting others." This is evident both in the order of benefits as they are presented on the graph—learning to respect others is first—and in the figure of 95.6%

Part B   Sample Student Response Essay

One of the most important projects for the student council this year is to organize a new volunteer program. The goal is to match student volunteers with people and organizations in our community that are seeking assistance. We believe that students in our school, like many teens, will be eager to participate. According to recent studies, volunteering "has become a significant part of teen culture."

Over the past decade, student volunteer programs have grown in schools across the country. By getting actively involved in the community, students have discovered opportunities to learn and to express their beliefs as they help others. Because there are so many different people and organizations that might seek help from volunteers, students can choose opportunities that fit their interests. Some teens even discover a future vocation as a result of their volunteer activities.

In a recent article in The Oregonian, *Inara Verzemnieks quotes several students about their experiences in volunteering. Josi Henderson, a senior at Grant High School, said, "I really feel like my day isn't complete without practicing some act of kindness." In deciding to major in speech pathology in college, Henderson further explained, "I really want to devote my life to helping others." Another student remarked, "When you are taught how to help others, it begins to come naturally after a while."*

Verzemnieks reports another important benefit of teen volunteerism: It gives teens a chance to counter negative stereotypes. When teens become involved in their communities and are seen as eager to help others, adults can see them in a positive way. One student said, "Adults can see what we are thinking about, what we care about, and we can influence how adults think about young people."

Students also say they enjoy volunteering because friends can often work together, and they also get to know new people. Learning how to cooperate and work in groups is an experience many teens consider an important benefit of volunteering. Statistics from a teen volunteering poll in 1996 show that 91.5 percent considered learning how to get along with others an important benefit. That same poll showed that teens considered learning to respect others the most important benefit they received. Nearly 65 percent indicate that volunteering helped improve their grades in school.

Doing volunteer work does not have to be difficult, or even boring. There are so many varieties of volunteer activities that students can usually find an activity they really enjoy. Some serve food in soup kitchens or visit hospitals; others may offer to shop for the elderly or even become involved in improving housing. For some students, volunteer work is a way of being a good citizen. Verzemnieks quotes one student, who said "Through volunteering, we can start doing things about the issues that affect us."

Teen volunteerism has become a significant trend over the last decade, in part because many schools have a service requirement for graduation. But reports also show that teens have genuine interest in these activities and consider them more than a boring duty. The 1996 poll indicated that the majority of teens today consider volunteering "in." The ways in which one can become involved are endless and the benefits are numerous. The student council urges everyone in our school to help make a difference in our community.

Analysis

This response demonstrates a thorough understanding of the documents and offers a well-developed discussion of current trends in teen volunteerism and its benefits. The tone of the article, especially in the introduction and conclusion, also satisfies the requirements of the task: to write an article encouraging students to participate in volunteer programs. The essay is organized clearly, moving from general assertions about trends in volunteerism to specifics about activities and benefits that will appeal to the intended audience.

There is a great deal of information in the two documents, and this writer has made excellent choices of details to support the topic; sentences are varied and the writer incorporates quotes fluently: *In deciding to major in speech pathology in college, Henderson further explained, "I really want to devote my life to helping others."* Transitions between sections

> are brief and effective: *Over the past decade . . . In a recent article . . . Verzemnieks reports another important benefit . . . Students also say.*
>
> The writing demonstrates good control of the conventions and meets all the criteria for a high score. (See pp. 48–53 for a detailed discussion of the rubric for this part of the examination.)

Session Two

Part A   (1–10)

Note: See Chapter 3 for review and strategy in responding to this part of the examination.

(1) **3** "fear of punishment." In the very first sentence, Frantz reveals that he "was terribly afraid of being scolded . . . ," especially because there was to be a test on participles that day and he was quite unprepared for it.

(2) **2** "greeted with silence." In the paragraph beginning at line 24 Frantz says he counted on all the noise and uproar at the beginning of school to get to his bench unnoticed. Instead, ". . . that day everything was quiet, like a Sunday morning."

(3) **1** "significance of the day." This becomes more evident as the story continues from line 34. Note at line 37, Frantz tells us that his teacher was wearing the formal clothing he normally wore only on days of inspection or distribution of prizes, that is, on days of particular significance in school. The presence of others from the village also indicates that there was something "extraordinary . . . and solemn" about the class.

(4) **4** "Frantz has a new perspective on school." Upon the news that this will be his last class in French, Frantz says, "Those few words overwhelmed me." He goes on to reveal how angry he was with himself because of "the time I had wasted, the lessons I had missed . . . ."

(5) **3** "determination." This quality in the teachers is evident throughout the poem and is most clearly expressed in the last stanza: "But the teachers don't give up . . . ."

(6) **1** "reluctant." The image recalls other expressions of reluctance, such as "dragging one's feet" to suggest that the children are hesitant and unenthusiastic. There is little in the poem to suggest that the children are angry, afraid, or disgusted.

(7) **2** "receptive." To be receptive is to be interested and open to something new.

(8) **3** "their former teachers." In the fourth stanza, the teachers hold the image of their teachers "at the back of their minds." "So many seasons of rain, sun, wind/have crystallized their teachers./They shine like something on a beach."

(9) **4** "distract students from learning." The images in this stanza are of things students often think about instead of concentrating on a lesson: "a new love," rumors, things that may cause trouble or fear.

(10) **1** "persistence will produce results." The images of the cranes that "can fly 1,000 miles" or the hummingbirds that migrate from Mexico dramatize the fact that the teachers "don't give up." With patience and persistence from the teachers, the students may yet "dip into the sweet [knowledge] together . . . ."

Part A   Sample Student Response Essay

Numerous and invaluable opportunities for learning exist for children who truly desire them. Some students, however, do not appreciate the opportunities, which are regularly presented to them, or they become aware of them only when these chances are suddenly swept away. Two vivid passages, one from a short story and the other a poem, dramatize the devotion of teachers to students who may not appreciate them or what they have to offer. The authors use characterization, figurative language, and point of view to tell these stories of regret over lost opportunities to learn.

Passage I, an excerpt from a French story by Alphonse Daudet, is told by a young boy whose appreciation of school changes dramatically when he suddenly discovers that his teacher will be forced to leave the village school. The boy, Frantz, is presented as a fairly typical student, who tells us that he was "very late for school that morning" in part because he was not prepared for a test and because it was such a lovely day for "wandering about the fields." His teacher, Monsieur Hamel, is portrayed in the beginning as a very strict disciplinarian "with the terrible iron ruler under his arm," and Frantz fears he will be scolded severely.

When Frantz does arrive at school, he realizes that there is something different and very solemn about the day. The image of the town elders seated in the back of the room and Monsieur Hamel in his most formal clothes also tells Frantz that there is something extraordinary about class. Monsieur Hamel does not scold Frantz but seems to welcome him; then he informs the class that a new government decree will replace the French language and history with German, and that a new teacher will replace him. Frantz's entire perception of school changes; he becomes angry with himself because of the time he has wasted. In a simile to convey this sudden change in attitude, he tells us that the books he had "only a moment before thought so tiresome, so heavy to carry . . . seemed to me now like old friends, from whom I should be terribly grieved to part." The passage closes with Frantz's understanding that the "old fellows" in the back of the room probably also regretted not coming "oftener to the school," and had come to pay their respects to a teacher and to a language they were about to lose.

The poem "Morning Glory" trumpets loudly the sheer determination of teachers to give their students the opportunity to learn. The poet skillfully uses characterization and figurative language to convey the theme that teach-ers are resourceful, persevering people who never give up. They appear before their students daily, shining "like something on a beach," determined to provide an education to the reluctant students who "come in dragging." The students are so full of their own thoughts and distractions, like a new love or rumors, that they "hear the teachers as if they were far off, speaking down a tube." The teachers' voices are like a faraway noise forming a background to the students' own realities. The description of the teachers throughout the poem conveys the theme of persistence. The teachers "have a plan . . . they have organized into units . . . [they] appear before us crisp and hopeful." The voice of the poem is "we," representing the students who "know we have failed and failed," and the tone is almost remorseful. The speaker, however, appreciates what the teachers are trying to achieve and suggests in the final image of the cranes and the hummingbirds that return every year that the students may one day "hover long enough" to taste the sweetness of learning.

Analysis

This is a very good response to the task because it clearly reveals the writer's understanding of a common theme and sev-eral of the literary elements evident in the two passages. The introduction is clear in its statement of a controlling idea—regret over lost opportunities to learn—and the choice of char-acterization, figurative language, and point of view for develop-ment represents insightful reading. The controlling idea is also well developed with relevant quotes from the passages.

The essay is simply but clearly organized and offers many examples of fluent and appropriate language: "[they] *had come to pay their respects to a teacher and to a language they were about to lose." "The poem "Morning Glory" trumpets loudly . . . ." "The voice of the poem is 'we' . . . and the tone is almost remorseful."* This writer also demonstrates skill in using a variety of sentence structures and in control of the conventions. Although the essay lacks a formal conclusion, the strength of the ideas and the writing would merit a high score. (See pp. 68–71 for a detailed discussion of the rubric for this part of the examination.)

Session Two

Note: See Chapter 4 for review and strategy in responding to this part of the examination.

Part B   Sample Student Response Essay

Nicolas Cage once stated, "I like flawed characters because somewhere in them I see more of the truth." In other words, when a character seems to deviate from what is expected, or fails in some way, that's where the truth of the person is evident. I agree with Cage's view that their flaws are what make characters more real and human. Catcher in the Rye by J. D. Salinger is not your typical story of a teenage boy; rather, it is a story of a young man fighting his own inner battles. In Death of a Salesman by Arthur Miller, Willy Loman is so caught up trying to achieve an illusion of the American Dream that his own mind eventually fails him. In showing these characters' mistakes and flaws, the authors show how human they truly are.

The title of Catcher in the Rye is symbolic itself. At one point in the story, Holden Caulfield, a teenage boy, explains to his younger sister Phoebe how he wants to be the "catcher" in the rye, the one who hides in the rye fields near the edge of a cliff and protects any child playing in the fields from falling off. Phoebe laughs at him and points out how he has misquoted the words to the song, and that there is no catcher in the rye. Holden's desire to be a catcher who saves children is actually a reflection of his own struggle between adulthood and childhood.

Most of Holden's actions in the course of the novel are a result of his flawed view and his own confused character. After he is thrown out of the prep school he attends, he spends a few days in a New York City hotel before going home to tell his parents what has happened. Holden is able to buy drinks in a bar, pick up older women, and even engage a prostitute. Through most of these experiences, what he really wants to do is just talk to someone genuine. While trying to maintain his adult persona, inside Holden is still just a child at heart and he becomes very emotional over simple things. After experiencing what he considers to be the phoniness and ugliness of adult life, Holden is determined to protect every little kid, especially his sister, from those experiences. While his goal is genuine, it is also impossible to achieve—he cannot prevent children from growing up.

In Death of a Salesman, Willy Loman is a man at the end of his life, who is forced to see that he has struggled and failed in a life he was not suited for. Willy is skilled at working with his hands and building things, yet he persists in trying to make a living as a salesman. In the course of the play, we see that Willy has become so confused that he lives more in the past than in the present, and he is no longer able to earn even a small commission. He has been borrowing money from a neighbor every week, convincing himself he will pay it all back.

Willy is also forced to see that the values he raised his sons to share have led to their own failure. Willy Loman believed that being well liked and having a good personality was all his son Biff needed to become successful in business. In the course of the play, we see why Biff resents his father and why he has never amounted to anything. Because Willy cannot accept both his own failure and the idea that he may have been responsible for Biff's failure, he kills himself in the delusion that his life insurance will give Biff the start he needs to succeed. Even though Willy Loman had dreams he could not fulfill and made mistakes that nearly destroyed his family, we see how human he is in his devotion to his sons and to his own dream.

Although their emotional struggles are extreme, the characters of Holden Caulfield and Willy Loman have flaws that most readers can relate to in their own lives. I believe this is what Nicolas Cage means when he says that he "sees more of the truth" in flawed characters.

Analysis

This response is effective because it articulates clearly the writer's interpretation of the critical lens, both in the introduction and in the conclusion: "In other words . . . ." "I agree with . . . ." "I believe this is what Nicolas Cage means . . . ." Although students are often urged to avoid using the first person in literary essays, these phrases are appropriate in responding to this task. This essay is developed as a discussion of the two characters and the choice of relevant details is good; the writer also maintains the focus with examples of characters' flaws. The discussion of specific literary elements is weaker in response to the task because the use of characterization and plot is explored more implicitly than explicitly.

The organization of the essay is clear and straightforward—the introduction offers an interpretation of the critical lens and asserts the controlling idea in the last sentence. Strong final sentences in the two paragraphs about Holden provide coherence, and the idea of what Willy Loman is "forced to accept" provides an effective transition between the two paragraphs about *Death of a Salesman*. The conclusion is brief but effective in reiterating the relevance of these works to the writer's interpretation of the critical lens.

This writer uses language that is appropriate and occasionally sophisticated: Holden is *"trying to maintain his adult persona . . . ;" "Willy kills himself in the delusion . . ." "their emotional struggles are extreme . . . ."* The writer also demonstrates control of the conventions and in using varied sentence structures to express the conflict within the characters: *"While his goal is genuine, it is also impossible to achieve—he cannot prevent children from growing up." "Willy is skilled at working with his hands and building things, yet he persists in trying to make a living as a salesman."*

This is a thoughtful and well-written essay that meets the criteria for a high score. (See pp. 80–83 for a detailed discussion of the rubric for this part of the examination.)

Examination June 2006
English

Session One

Part A

Overview: For this part of the test, you will listen to an account by Christopher Reeve, answer some multiple-choice questions, and write a response based on the situation described below. You will hear the account twice. You may take notes on the page allotted anytime you wish during the readings.

The Situation: Your school is celebrating Diversity Day. As a member of the publicity committee, you have been asked to write a letter to the editor of your local newspaper promoting the accomplishments of individuals with disabilities. In preparation for writing your letter, listen to an account by actor and director Christopher Reeve. Then use relevant information from the account to write your letter.

Your Task: Write a letter to the editor of your local newspaper for Diversity Day discussing actor and director Christopher Reeve's accomplishments. ***Write only the body of the letter.***

Guidelines:
Be sure to
- Tell your audience what they need to know about Christopher Reeve's accomplishments
- Use specific, accurate, and relevant information from the account to support your discussion
- Use a tone and level of language appropriate for a letter to the editor of a local newspaper
- Organize your ideas in a logical and coherent manner
- Indicate any words taken directly from the account by using quotation marks or referring to the speaker
- Follow the conventions of standard written English

Note: For this portion of the examination, the teacher will read a passage aloud. You will not actually see the passage reprinted below. Therefore, you are encouraged to have someone read the passage to you, in order to simulate the examination as closely as possible.

Listening Passage

. . . I consider myself extremely fortunate because my schedule is so varied. Many patients have no choice but to become stuck in a routine, which of course makes it hard for them to be optimistic about the future. But I'm able to travel, to visit scientists in their laboratories and hear about progress in research months before the results are published in scientific journals. Thanks to the generosity of groups that hire me for speaking engagements, I've appeared all over the country, sharing my experiences and creating more awareness about the disabled. Often I speak at rehab centers and talk about what I've learned with other spinal cord patients. I had the opportunity to direct a film, which gave me great creative satisfaction and kept me from thinking so much about myself.

I spend much of my time planning events to raise money for the Christopher Reeve Foundation. In our first year of operation we raised more than $750,000; 70 percent of it went to the APA [American Paralysis Association] and the rest to groups dedicated to quality of life issues of the disabled. I was also involved in the creation of a paid commercial called *Circle of Friends* to benefit the APA. I approved the script and called friends like Paul Newman, Mel Gibson, and Meryl Streep as well as a number of scientists to ask for their participation. . . .

People often ask me what it's like to have sustained a spinal cord injury and be confined to a wheelchair. Apart from all the medical complications, I would say the worst part of it is leaving the physical world—having had to make the transition from participant to observer long before I would have expected. I think most of us are prepared to give up cherished physical activities gradually as we age. I certainly wouldn't be competing in combined training events in my sixties or skiing nearly as fast as I used to. If I went sailing in my later years I wouldn't go single-handed. Stronger arms and more agile bodies would be needed to raise and trim the sails or steer in a heavy sea. . . .

When the first Superman movie came out, I gave dozens of interviews to promote it. The most frequently asked question was: "What is a hero?" I remember how easily I'd talk about it, the glib response I repeated so many times. My answer was that a hero is someone who commits a courageous action without considering the consequences. A soldier who crawls out of a foxhole to drag an injured buddy back to safety, the prisoners of war who never stop trying to escape even though they know they may be executed if they're caught. And I also meant individuals who are slightly larger than life: Houdini and Lindbergh of course, John Wayne and JFK, and even sports figures who have taken on mythical proportions, such as Babe Ruth or Joe DiMaggio.

Now my definition is completely different. I think a hero is an ordinary individual who finds the strength to persevere and endure in spite of overwhelming obstacles. The fifteen-year-old boy down the hall at Kessler [Rehabilitation Hospital] who had landed on his head while wrestling with his brother, leaving him paralyzed and barely able to swallow or speak. Travis Roy, paralyzed in the first eleven seconds of a hockey game in his freshman year at college. Henry Steifel, paralyzed from the chest down in a car accident at seventeen, completing his education and working on Wall Street at age thirty-two, but having missed so much of what life has to offer. These are real heroes, and so are the families and friends who have stood by them.

At UVA [The University of Virginia Health Sciences Center] and at Kessler, I always kept the picture of the Pyramid of Quetzalcoatl in front of me. I would look at the hundreds of steps leading up to the clouds and imagine myself climbing slowly but surely to the top. That desire sustained me in the early days after my injury, but during the next couple of years I had to learn to face the reality: you manage to climb one or two steps, but then something happens and you fall back three. The worst of it is the unpredictability. Several times I've made a commitment to appear at a function or give a speech, but the night before, or even that morning, a skin tear, or dysreflexia, or a lung infection suddenly developed and I had to go to the hospital instead.

Climbing up the steps, I've appeared at the Oscars, spoken at the Democratic Convention, directed a film, written this book, worked on political issues, and traveled more extensively than most high-level quadriplegics. But, falling backwards, I've been hospitalized eleven times for dysreflexia, pneumonia, a collapsed lung, a broken arm, two blood clots, a possible hip fracture, and the infection in my left ankle that nearly resulted in the partial amputation of my leg. . . .

The sensory deprivation hurts the most: I haven't been able to give [my son] Will a hug since he was two years old, and now he's five and a half. This is the reason [my wife] Dana and I decided not to have another child; it would be too painful not to be able to hold and embrace this little creature the way I did with the others. The physical world is still very meaningful to me; I have not been able to detach myself from it and live entirely in my mind. While I believe it's true that we are not our bodies, that our bodies are like houses we live in while we're here on earth, that concept is more of an intellectual construct than a philosophy I can live by on a daily basis. I'm jealous when someone talks about a recent skiing vacation, when friends embrace each other, or even when Will plays hockey in the driveway with someone else.

If someone were to ask me what is the most difficult lesson I've learned from all this, I'm very clear about it: I know I have to give when sometimes I really want to take. I've realized instinctively that it's part of my job as a father now not to cause Will to worry about me. If I were to give in to self-pity or express my anger in front of him, it would place an unfair burden on this carefree five-year-old. If I were to turn inward and spend my time mourning the past, I couldn't be as close to [my children] Matthew and Alexandra, two teenagers who naturally need to turn to me for advice. And what kind of life would it be for Dana if I let myself go and became just a depressed hulk in a wheelchair? All of this takes effort on my part, because it's still very difficult to accept the turn my life has taken, simply because of one unlucky moment. . . .

excerpted from *Still Me*, 1998
Random House

Notes

Multiple-Choice Questions

Directions (1–6): Use your notes to answer the following questions about the passage read to you. Select the best suggested answer and write its number in the space provided. The questions may help you think about ideas and information you might use in your writing. You may return to these questions anytime you wish.

1 Reeve's sense of selflessness is reflected through his

    (1) book writing
    (2) film directing
    (3) fundraising efforts
    (4) therapy sessions   1____

2 Since his injury, Reeve has revised his definition of hero from someone who performs a courageous act regardless of consequences to someone who

    (1) persists through adversity
    (2) has worldwide respect
    (3) puts others first
    (4) defends the powerless   2____

3 The hardest psychological adjustment for Reeve was from

    (1) actor to lecturer
    (2) protagonist to antagonist
    (3) laborer to employer
    (4) doer to watcher   3____

4 Reeve uses the steps of the Pyramid at Quetzalcoatl to explain his changed attitude toward

    (1) seeking adventure
    (2) measuring progress
    (3) accepting help
    (4) judging others   4____

5 Reeve uses the term "falling backward" to refer to his

  (1) disabling accident
  (2) social engagements
  (3) lost time
  (4) medical setbacks   5____

6 An example of Reeve's "sensory deprivation" is his inability to

  (1) embrace physically
  (2) think logically
  (3) communicate clearly
  (4) travel extensively   6____

After you have finished these questions, review **The Situation** and read **Your Task** and the **Guidelines**. Use scrap paper to plan your response. Then write your response on separate sheets of paper. After you finish your response for Part A, complete Part B.

Part B

Directions: Read the text and study the graph on the following pages, answer the multiple-choice questions, and write a response based on the situation described below. You may use the margins to take notes as you read and scrap paper to plan your response.

The Situation: Your environmental science class has been researching environmental issues. You have chosen to write a presentation for your class discussing the impact of acid rain on North America and suggesting what can be done to reduce the problem.

Your Task: Using relevant information from *both* documents, write a presentation for your environmental science class in which you discuss the impact of acid rain on North America and suggest what can be done to reduce the problem.

Guidelines:
Be sure to
• Tell your audience what they need to know about acid rain, its impact on North America, and what can be done to reduce the problem
• Use specific, accurate, and relevant information from the text *and* the graph to support your discussion
• Use a tone and level of language appropriate for a presentation to your environmental science class
• Organize your ideas in a logical and coherent manner
• Indicate any words taken directly from the text by using quotation marks or referring to the author
• Follow the conventions of standard written English

Acid Rain

What is Acid Rain and What Causes It?

"Acid rain" is a broad term used to describe several ways that acids fall out of the atmosphere. A more precise term is acid deposition, which has two parts: wet and dry.

(5) Wet deposition refers to acidic rain, fog, and snow. As this acidic water flows over and through the ground, it affects a variety of plants and animals. The strength of the effects depend on many factors, including how acidic the water is, the chemistry and buffering capacity of the soils involved, and the types of fish, trees, and other living things that rely on the water.

(10) Dry deposition refers to acidic gases and particles. About half of the acidity in the atmosphere falls back to earth through dry deposition. The wind blows these acidic particles and gases onto buildings, cars, homes, and trees. Dry deposited gases and particles can also be washed from trees and other surfaces by rainstorms. When that happens, the runoff water adds those acids to the acid rain, making the combination more acidic than the falling rain alone.

(15) Prevailing winds blow the compounds that cause both wet and dry acid deposition across state and national borders, and sometimes over hundreds of miles.

Scientists discovered, and have confirmed, that sulfur dioxide (SO_2) and nitrogen oxides (NO_x) are the primary causes of acid rain. In the US, about $2/3$ of *(20)* all SO_2 and $1/4$ of all NO_x comes from electric power generation that relies on burning fossil fuels like coal.

Acid rain occurs when these gases react in the atmosphere with water, oxygen, and other chemicals to form various acidic compounds. Sunlight increases the rate of most of these reactions. The result is a mild solution of sulfuric acid and nitric *(25)* acid.

How Do We Measure Acid Rain?

Acid rain is measured using a scale called "pH." The lower a substance's pH, the more acidic it is.

Pure water has a pH of 7.0. Normal rain is slightly acidic because carbon dioxide dissolves into it, so it has a pH of about 5.5. As of the year 2000, the most *(30)* acidic rain falling in the US has a pH of about 4.3.

Acid rain's pH, and the chemicals that cause acid rain, are monitored by two networks, both supported by EPA [Environmental Protection Agency]. The National Atmospheric Deposition Program measures wet deposition, and its Web site features maps of rainfall pH and other important precipitation chemistry *(35)* measurements.

The Clean Air Status and Trends Network (CASTNET) measures dry deposition. Its Web site features information about the data it collects, the measuring sites, and the kinds of equipment it uses.

What Are Acid Rain's Effects?

Acid deposition has a variety of effects, including damage to forests and soils,
(40) fish and other living things, materials, and human health. Acid rain also reduces how far and how clearly we can see through the air, an effect called visibility reduction. . . .

Effects of Acid Rain: Lakes and Streams

The ecological effects of acid rain are most clearly seen in the aquatic, or water, environments, such as streams, lakes, and marshes. Acid rain flows to streams,
(45) lakes, and marshes after falling on forests, fields, buildings, and roads. Acid rain also falls directly on aquatic habitats. Most lakes and streams have a pH between 6 and 8, although some lakes are naturally acidic even without the effects of acid rain. Acid rain primarily affects sensitive bodies of water, which are located in watersheds[1] whose soils have a limited ability to neutralize acidic compounds
(50) (called "buffering capacity"). Lakes and streams become acidic (pH value goes down) when the water itself and its surrounding soil cannot buffer the acid rain enough to neutralize it. In areas where buffering capacity is low, acid rain also releases aluminum from soils into lakes and streams; aluminum is highly toxic to many species of aquatic organisms. . . .

Where Does Acid Rain Affect Lakes and Streams?

(55)   Many lakes and streams examined in a National Surface Water Survey (NSWS) suffer from chronic acidity, a condition in which water has a constant low pH level. The survey investigated the effects of acidic deposition in over 1,000 lakes larger than 10 acres and in thousands of miles of streams believed to be sensitive to acidification. Of the lakes and streams surveyed, acid rain caused acidity in 75
(60) percent of the acidic lakes and about 50 percent of the acidic streams. Several regions in the U.S. were identified as containing many of the surface waters sensitive to acidification. They include the Adirondacks and Catskill Mountains in New York state, the mid-Appalachian highlands along the east coast, the upper Midwest, and mountainous areas of the Western United States. In areas like the
(65) Northeastern United States, where soil buffering capacity is poor, some lakes now have a pH value of less than 5. One of the most acidic lakes reported is Little Echo Pond in Franklin, New York. Little Echo Pond has a pH of 4.2. . . .

---

[1] watersheds—regions draining to particular bodies of water

(70) Emissions from U.S. sources also contribute to acidic deposition in eastern Canada, where the soil is very similar to the soil of the Adirondack Mountains, and the lakes are consequently extremely vulnerable to chronic acidification problems. The Canadian government has estimated that 14,000 lakes in eastern Canada are acidic.

How Does Acid Rain Affect Fish and Other Aquatic Organisms?

(75) Acid rain causes a cascade of effects that harm or kill individual fish, reduce fish population numbers, completely eliminate fish species from a waterbody, and decrease biodiversity. As acid rain flows through soils in a watershed, aluminum is released from soils into the lakes and streams located in that watershed. So, as pH in a lake or stream decreases, aluminum levels increase. Both low pH and increased aluminum levels are directly toxic to fish. In addition, low pH and increased aluminum levels cause chronic stress that may not kill individual fish, but leads to

(80) lower body weight and smaller size and makes fish less able to compete for food and habitat.

Some types of plants and animals are able to tolerate acidic waters. Others, however, are acid-sensitive and will be lost as the pH declines. Generally, the young of most species are more sensitive to environmental conditions than adults. At pH

(85) 5, most fish eggs cannot hatch. At lower pH levels, some adult fish die. Some acid lakes have no fish. . . .

How Does Acid Rain Affect Ecosystems?

Together, biological organisms and the environment in which they live are called an ecosystem. The plants and animals living within an ecosystem are highly interdependent. For example, frogs may tolerate relatively high levels of acidity, but

(90) if they eat insects like the mayfly, they may be affected because part of their food supply may disappear. Because of the connections between the many fish, plants, and other organisms living in an aquatic ecosystem, changes in pH or aluminum levels affect biodiversity as well. Thus, as lakes and streams become more acidic, the numbers and types of fish and other aquatic plants and animals that live in these

(95) waters decrease. . . .

What Society Can Do About Acid Deposition

There are several ways to reduce acid rain, more properly called acid deposition, ranging from societal changes to individual action ....

Clean Up Smokestacks and Exhaust Pipes

Almost all of the electricity that powers modern life comes from burning fossil fuels like coal, natural gas, and oil. Acid deposition is caused by two pollutants that

(100) are released into the atmosphere, or emitted, when these fuels are burned: sulfur dioxide (SO_2) and nitrogen oxides (NO_x). . . .

Use Alternative Energy Sources

There are other sources of electricity besides fossil fuels. They include: nuclear power, hydropower, wind energy, geothermal energy, and solar energy. Of these, nuclear and hydropower are used most widely; wind, solar, and geothermal energy
(105) have not yet been harnessed on a large scale in this country.

There are also alternative energies available to power automobiles, including natural gas powered vehicles, battery-powered cars, fuel cells, and combinations of alternative and gasoline powered vehicles.

All sources of energy have environmental costs as well as benefits. Some types
(110) of energy are more expensive to produce than others, which means that not all Americans can afford all types of energy. Nuclear power, hydropower, and coal are the cheapest forms today, but changes in technologies and environmental regulations may shift that in the future. All of these factors must be weighed when deciding which energy source to use today and which to invest in for tomorrow. . . .

Take Action as Individuals

(115)   It may seem like there is not much that one individual can do to stop acid deposition. However, like many environmental problems, acid deposition is caused by the cumulative actions of millions of individual people. Therefore, each individual can also reduce their contribution to the problem and become part of the solution. One of the first steps is to understand the problem and its solutions.

(120)   Individuals can contribute directly by conserving energy, since energy production causes the largest portion of the acid deposition problem. For example, you can:
   • Turn off lights, computers, and other appliances when you're not using them.
   • Use energy efficient appliances: lighting, air conditioners, heaters, refrigerators, washing machines, etc.
(125)   • Only use electric appliances when you need them.
   • Keep your thermostat at 68 F in the winter and 72 F in the summer. You can turn it even lower in the winter and higher in the summer when you are away from home.
   • Insulate your home as best you can.
(130)   • Carpool, use public transportation, or better yet, walk or bicycle whenever possible.
   • Buy vehicles with low NO_x emissions, and maintain all vehicles well.
   • Be well-informed.

—U.S. Environmental Protection Agency
adapted and excerpted from "Clean Air Markets—Environmental Issues"
www.epa.gov

GRAPH

**Emission Sources of Sulfur Dioxide (SO₂)
and Nitrogen Oxide (NOₓ) from Canada
and the United States (1998)**

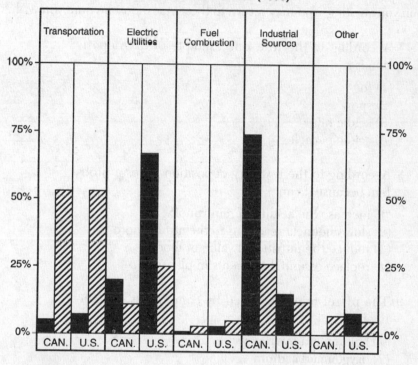

SO₂ Emissions

NOₓ Emissions

Source: (adapted) "Acid rain and the facts"
www.ec.gc.ca

Multiple-Choice Questions

Directions (7–16): Select the best suggested answer to each question and write its number in the space provided. The questions may help you think about ideas and information you might want to use in your writing. You may return to these questions anytime you wish.

7 According to the text, one example of dry deposition is

(1) fog
(2) snow
(3) acidic rain
(4) acidic particles   7____

8 According to the text, dry deposition poses a problem because it can

(1) increase the acidity of rain runoff
(2) slow chemical reactions in the atmosphere
(3) reduce the nutritional value of foods
(4) replace essential nutrients in plants   8____

9 The pH of rain is affected by compounds containing both

(1) helium and hydrogen
(2) oxygen and sodium
(3) aluminum and potassium
(4) sulfur and nitrogen   9____

10 According to the text, acid rain is characterized by a

(1) high overall density
(2) low pH value
(3) pleasant smell
(4) reddish color   10____

11 As used in the text, the term "chronic acidity" (line 56), most nearly means that the level of acidity

(1) fluctuates
(2) remains unchanged
(3) decreases steadily
(4) disappears   11____

12 The last section of the text is designed primarily to present

(1) personal reactions
(2) scientific data
(3) historical perspectives
(4) practical suggestions   12____

13 According to the graph, the largest source of nitrogen oxide (NO_x) emissions in both Canada and the United States is

(1) transportation
(2) electric utilities
(3) fuel combustion
(4) industrial sources   13____

14 According to the graph, what sources of nitrogen oxide (NO_x) in the United States produce identical emission percentages?

(1) fuel combustion and "other"
(2) transportation and industrial
(3) electric utilities and transportation
(4) fuel combustion and transportation   14____

15 According to the graph, the largest producer of sulfur dioxide emissions in the United States is

(1) transportation
(2) industrial sources
(3) fuel combustion
(4) electric utilities

15 _____

16 According to the graph, the United States and Canada have their lowest amount of sulfur dioxide (SO_2) in emissions caused by

(1) transportation   (3) fuel combustion
(2) electric utilities   (4) industrial sources

16 _____

After you have finished these questions, review **The Situation** and read **Your Task** and the **Guidelines**. Use scrap paper to plan your response. Then write your response to Part B on separate sheets of paper.

Session Two

Part A

Directions: Read the passages on the following pages (a poem and an excerpt from a short story). Write the number of the answer to each multiple-choice question in the space provided. Then write the essay on separate sheets of paper as described in **Your Task**. You may use the margins to take notes as you read and scrap paper to plan your response.

Your Task:

> After you have read the passages and answered the multiple-choice questions, write a unified essay about the power of reading as revealed in the passages. In your essay, use ideas from **both** passages to establish a controlling idea about the power of reading. Using evidence from **each** passage, develop your controlling idea and show how the author uses specific literary elements or techniques to convey that idea.

Guidelines:

Be sure to

- Use ideas from **both** passages to establish a controlling idea about the power of reading
- Use specific and relevant evidence from **each** passage to develop your controlling idea
- Show how each author uses specific literary elements (for example: theme, characterization, structure, point of view) or techniques (for example: symbolism, irony, figurative language) to convey the controlling idea
- Organize your ideas in a logical and coherent manner
- Use language that communicates ideas effectively
- Follow the conventions of standard written English

Passage I

The Reader

She is going back, these days, to the great stories
That charmed her younger mind. A shaded light
Shines on the nape half-shadowed by her curls,
And a page turns now with a scuffing sound.
(5)   Onward they come again, the orphans reaching
For a first handhold in a stony world,
The young provincials who at last look down
On the city's maze, and will descend into it,
The serious girl, once more, who would live nobly,
(10)   The sly one who aspires to marry so,
The young man bent on glory, and that other
Who seeks a burden. Knowing as she does
What will become of them in bloody field
Or Tuscan garden, it may be that at times
(15)   She sees their first and final selves at once,
As a god might to whom all time is now.
Or, having lived so much herself, perhaps
She meets them this time with a wiser eye,
Noting that Julien's calculating head
(20)   Is from the first too severed from his heart.
But the true wonder of it is that she,
For all that she may know of consequences,
Still turns enchanted to the next bright page
Like some Natasha in the ballroom door—
(25)   Caught in the flow of things wherever bound,
The blind delight of being, ready still
To enter life on life and see them through.

—Richard Wilbur
from *The New Yorker*
October 1, 2001

Passage II

One day, in the illustrious nation of Panduria, a suspicion crept into the minds of top officials: that books contained opinions hostile to military prestige. In fact trials and enquiries had revealed that the tendency, now so widespread, of thinking of generals as people actually capable of making mistakes and causing
(5)   catastrophes, and of wars as things that did not always amount to splendid cavalry charges towards a glorious destiny, was shared by a large number of books, ancient and modern, foreign and Pandurese.

Panduria's General Staff met together to assess the situation. But they didn't know where to begin, because none of them was particularly well-versed in
(10)   matters bibliographical. A commission of enquiry was set up under General Fedina, a severe and scrupulous official. The commission was to examine all the books in the biggest library in Panduria. . . .

The military took over the library one rainy morning in November. The general climbed off his horse, squat, stiff, his thick neck shaven, his eyebrows
(15)   frowning over pince-nez[1]; four lanky lieutenants, chins held high and eyelids lowered, got out of a car, each with a briefcase in his hand. Then came a squadron of soldiers who set up camp in the old courtyard, with mules, bales of hay, tents, cooking equipment, camp radio, and signalling flags. . . .

Of the library staff, only one little old man, Signor Crispino, was kept so that
(20)   he could explain to the officers how the books were arranged. He was a shortish fellow, with a bald, eggish pate and eyes like pinheads behind his spectacles. . . .

Then duties were assigned. Each lieutenant was allotted a particular branch of knowledge, a particular century of history. The general was to oversee the sorting of the volumes and the application of an appropriate rubber stamp
(25)   depending on whether a book had been judged suitable for officers, NCOs[2], common soldiers, or should be reported to the Military Court.

And the commission began its appointed task. Every evening the camp radio transmitted General Fedina's report to HQ. 'So many books examined. So many seized as suspect. So many declared suitable for officers and soldiers.' Only rarely
(30)   were these cold figures accompanied by something out of the ordinary: a request for a pair of glasses to correct short-sightedness for an officer who had broken his, the news that a mule had eaten a rare manuscript edition of Cicero left unattended.

But developments of far greater import were under way, about which the
(35)   camp radio transmitted no news at all. Rather than thinning out, the forest of books seemed to grow ever more tangled and insidious. The officers would have

---

[1] pince-nez—eyeglasses clipped to the nose by a spring
[2] NCOs—noncommissioned officers

lost their way had it not been for the help of Signor Crispino. Lieutenant Abrogati, for example, would jump to his feet and throw the book he was reading down on the table: 'But this is outrageous! A book about the Punic Wars that

(40) speaks well of the Carthaginians and criticizes the Romans! This must be reported at once!' (It should be said here that, rightly or wrongly, the Pandurians considered themselves descendants of the Romans.) Moving silently in soft slippers, the old librarian came up to him. 'That's nothing,' he would say, 'read what it says here, about the Romans again, you can put this in your report too,

(45) and this and this,' and he presented him with a pile of books. The lieutenant leafed nervously through them, then, getting interested, he began to read, to take notes. And he would scratch his head and mutter: 'For heaven's sake! The things you learn! Who would ever have thought!' Signor Crispino went over to Lieutenant Lucchetti who was closing a tome[3] in rage, declaring: 'Nice stuff this

(50) is! These people have the audacity to entertain doubts as to the purity of the ideals that inspired the Crusades! Yessir, the Crusades!' And Signor Crispino said with a smile: 'Oh, but look, if you have to make a report on that subject, may I suggest a few other books that will offer more details,' and he pulled down half a shelf-full. Lieutenant Lucchetti leaned forward and got stuck in, and for a week you could

(55) hear him flicking through the pages and muttering: 'These Crusades though, very nice I must say!'

In the commission's evening report, the number of books examined got bigger and bigger, but they no longer provided figures relative to positive and negative verdicts. General Fedina's rubber stamps lay idle. If, trying to check up on the

(60) work of one of the lieutenants, he asked, 'But why did you pass this novel? The soldiers come off better than the officers! This author has no respect for hierarchy!', the lieutenant would answer by quoting other authors and getting all muddled up in matters historical, philosophical and economic. This led to open discussions that went on for hours and hours. Moving silently in his slippers,

(65) almost invisible in his grey shirt, Signor Crispino would always join in at the right moment, offering some book which he felt contained interesting information on the subject under consideration, and which always had the effect of radically undermining General Fedina's convictions. . . .

Not much is known about the progress of the commission's work: what

(70) happened in the library through the long winter weeks was not reported. All we know is that General Fedina's radio reports to General Staff headquarters became ever more infrequent until finally they stopped altogether. The Chief of Staff was alarmed; he transmitted the order to wind up the enquiry as quickly as possible and present a full and detailed report.

---

[3] tome—large book

(75)   In the library, the order found the minds of Fedina and his men prey to conflicting sentiments: on the one hand they were constantly discovering new interests to satisfy and were enjoying their reading and studies more than they would ever have imagined; on the other hand they couldn't wait to be back in the world again, to take up life again, a world and a life that seemed so much more
(80)   complex now, as though renewed before their very eyes; and on yet another hand, the fact that the day was fast approaching when they would have to leave the library filled them with apprehension, for they would have to give an account of their mission, and with all the ideas that were bubbling up in their heads they had no idea how to get out of what had become a very tight corner indeed. . . .

(85)   One bright morning the commission finally left the library and went to report to the Chief of Staff; and Fedina illustrated the results of the enquiry before an assembly of the General Staff. His speech was a kind of compendium[4] of human history from its origins down to the present day, a compendium in which all those ideas considered beyond discussion by the right-minded folk of Panduria were
(90)   attacked, in which the ruling classes were declared responsible for the nation's misfortunes, and the people exalted as the heroic victims of mistaken policies and unnecessary wars. It was a somewhat confused presentation including, as can happen with those who have only recently embraced new ideas, declarations that were often simplistic and contradictory. But as to the overall meaning there could
(95)   be no doubt. The assembly of generals was stunned, their eyes opened wide, then they found their voices and began to shout. General Fedina was not even allowed to finish. There was talk of a court-martial, of his being reduced to the ranks. Then, afraid there might be a more serious scandal, the general and the four lieutenants were each pensioned off for health reasons, as a result of 'a serious
(100)   nervous breakdown suffered in the course of duty'. Dressed in civilian clothes, with heavy coats and thick sweaters so as not to freeze, they were often to be seen going into the old library where Signor Crispino would be waiting for them with his books.

—Italo Calvino
excerpted from "A General in the Library"
Numbers in the Dark and Other Stories, 1995
Jonathan Cape Ltd.

---

[4] compendium—summary

Multiple-Choice Questions

Directions (1–10): Select the best suggested answer to each question and write its number in the space provided. The questions may help you think about the ideas and information you might want to use in your essay. You may return to these questions anytime you wish.

Passage I (the poem)—Questions 1–5 refer to Passage I.

1 "She is going back, these days" (line 1) indicates that the reader is

   (1) looking at old photographs
   (2) rearranging a library
   (3) rereading old books
   (4) searching for new books   1 ____

2 Who are the people described in lines 5 through 12?

   (1) friends from childhood
   (2) characters from literature
   (3) famous actors
   (4) noted authors   2 ____

3 The "bloody field" (line 13) and the "Tuscan garden" (line 14) suggest the reader's interest in the

   (1) setting
   (2) plot
   (3) character
   (4) point of view   3 ____

4 The paradox in line 15 indicates that the reader

   (1) guesses her future
   (2) regrets her childhood
   (3) invents the characters
   (4) knows the endings   4 ____

5 In line 18, "a wiser eye" implies that the reader
now has

(1) superior goals
(2) better eyesight
(3) greater insight
(4) stronger opinions   5 ____

Passage II (the excerpt from a short story)—Questions 6–10 refer to
Passage II.

6 What is the commission's "appointed task" (line 27)?

(1) taking an inventory
(2) censoring books
(3) writing regulations
(4) protecting the library   6 ____

7 The statement, "General Fedina's rubber stamps
lay idle," (line 59) emphasizes that the men were
unable to

(1) comprehend complex material
(2) consider original sources
(3) reconfigure the library's contents
(4) perform their assigned task   7 ____

8 The word "undermining," as used in line 68, most
nearly means

(1) harvesting
(2) studying
(3) contradicting
(4) repeating   8 ____

9 General Fedina and his lieutenants avoided a court-martial because the assembly of generals wished to

(1) prevent a scandal
(2) close the library
(3) cure nervous breakdowns
(4) publish the results   9 _____

10 An ironic result of the mission was that the soldiers

(1) left Panduria for good
(2) returned to active duty
(3) received promotion in rank
(4) returned to the library   10 _____

After you have finished these questions, review **Your Task** and the **Guidelines.** Use scrap paper to plan your response. Then write your response to Part A, on separate sheets of paper. After you finish your response for Part A, complete Part B.

Part B

Your Task:
Write a critical essay in which you discuss **two** works of literature you have read from the particular perspective of the statement that is provided for you in the **Critical Lens**. In your essay, provide a valid interpretation of the statement, agree **or** disagree with the statement as you have interpreted it, and support your opinion using specific references to appropriate literary elements from the two works. You may use scrap paper to plan your response. Write your essay in Part B on separate sheets of paper.

Critical Lens:

> "The ultimate measure of a man is not where he stands in moments of comfort and convenience, but where he stands at times of challenge and controversy."
>
> — Martin Luther King, Jr.
> *Strength to Love*, 1963

Guidelines:
Be sure to
- Provide a valid interpretation of the critical lens that clearly establishes the criteria for analysis
- Indicate whether you agree **or** disagree with the statement as you have interpreted it
- Choose **two** works you have read that you believe best support your opinion
- Use the criteria suggested by the critical lens to analyze the works you have chosen
- Avoid plot summary. Instead, use specific references to appropriate literary elements (for example: theme, characterization, setting, point of view) to develop your analysis
- Organize your ideas in a unified and coherent manner
- Specify the titles and authors of the literature you choose
- Follow the conventions of standard written English

Regents Comprehensive Examination in English—June 2006
Chart for Determining the Final Examination Score (Use for June 2006 examination only.)

To determine the student's final examination score, locate the student's total essay score across the top of the chart and the student's total multiple-choice score down the side of the chart. The point where those two scores intersect is the student's final examination score. For example, a student receiving a total essay score of 16 and a total multiple-choice score of 19 would receive a final examination score of 72.

Total Multiple-Choice Score ↓ / Total Essay Score →	0	1	2	3	4	5	6	7	8	9	10	11	12	13	14	15	16	17	18	19	20	21	22	23	24
0	0	1	2	3	4	5	6	8	10	13	16	19	22	25	29	32	36	40	43	47	51	55	59	63	67
1	1	1	2	3	4	6	7	9	12	14	17	20	24	27	31	34	38	41	45	49	53	57	61	65	69
2	1	2	2	3	5	6	8	10	13	16	19	22	25	29	32	36	40	43	47	51	55	59	63	67	70
3	1	2	3	4	6	7	10	12	14	17	20	24	27	31	34	38	41	45	49	53	57	61	65	69	72
4	2	2	4	5	6	8	11	13	16	19	22	25	29	32	36	40	43	47	51	55	59	63	67	70	74
5	2	3	5	6	7	9	12	14	17	20	24	27	31	34	38	41	43	47	51	55	59	63	67	72	76
6	2	4	6	7	8	10	13	16	19	22	25	29	32	36	40	43	45	49	53	57	61	65	69	74	77
7	3	5	6	8	9	12	14	17	20	24	27	31	34	38	41	45	47	51	55	57	61	67	70	76	79
8	3	6	7	9	10	13	16	19	22	25	29	32	36	40	43	47	49	53	57	59	65	69	72	77	80
9	4	6	8	10	12	14	17	20	24	27	31	34	38	41	45	49	51	55	59	63	67	72	76	79	82
10	5	7	9	11	13	16	19	22	25	29	32	36	40	43	47	51	53	57	61	65	69	74	76	80	84
11	6	8	10	12	14	17	20	24	27	31	34	38	41	45	49	53	55	59	63	67	72	76	79	82	85
12	6	9	12	13	16	19	22	25	29	32	36	40	43	47	51	55	57	61	65	69	74	77	80	84	86
13	7	10	13	16	19	22	25	29	31	36	38	41	45	49	53	57	59	63	67	70	76	79	82	85	88
14	8	12	14	17	20	24	27	31	34	38	41	45	49	53	55	59	63	67	70	72	77	80	84	86	89
15	9	14	16	19	22	25	29	32	36	40	43	47	51	55	57	61	65	69	72	76	79	82	85	88	90
16	10	15	17	20	24	27	31	34	38	41	45	49	53	57	59	63	67	70	74	77	82	84	86	89	92
17	12	16	19	22	25	29	32	36	40	43	47	51	55	59	61	65	69	72	76	79	84	85	88	90	93
18	13	17	20	24	27	31	34	38	41	45	49	53	57	61	63	67	70	74	77	80	84	86	89	92	94
19	15	19	22	25	29	32	36	40	43	47	51	55	59	63	65	69	72	76	79	82	85	88	90	93	95
20	16	20	24	27	31	34	38	41	45	49	53	57	61	65	67	72	76	79	82	85	88	90	93	95	96
21	17	22	25	29	32	36	40	43	47	51	55	59	63	67	69	74	77	80	84	86	89	92	94	96	97
22	19	24	27	31	34	38	41	45	49	53	57	61	65	69	72	76	79	82	85	88	90	93	95	96	97
23	20	25	29	32	36	40	43	47	51	55	59	63	67	70	74	77	80	84	86	89	92	94	96	97	98
24	22	27	31	34	38	41	45	49	53	57	61	65	69	72	76	79	82	85	88	90	93	95	96	98	99
25	24	29	32	36	40	43	47	51	55	59	63	67	70	74	77	80	84	86	89	92	94	96	97	98	99
26	25	32	36	40	43	47	51	55	59	63	67	70	74	77	80	84	86	89	92	94	96	97	98	99	100

Answers
June 2006
English

Answer Key

Session One, Part A	Session One, Part B	Session Two, Part A
1. 3	7. 4	1. 3
2. 1	8. 1	2. 2
3. 4	9. 4	3. 1
4. 2	10. 2	4. 4
5. 4	11. 2	5. 3
6. 1	12. 4	6. 2
	13. 1	7. 4
	14. 1	8. 3
	15. 4	9. 1
	16. 3	10. 4

Answers Explained

Session One

Part A   (1–6)

Note: Refer to Chapter 1 for review and strategy in responding to this part of the examination.

(1) **3** "fundraising efforts." Reeve remarks in his introduction that he engages in speaking activities to keep ". . . from thinking so much about myself." He then lists several events and foundations he works with to raise money for groups "dedicated to quality of life issues of the disabled."

(2) **1** "persists through adversity." In explaining his new definition of a hero, Reeve says that "a hero is an ordinary individual who finds the strength to persevere and endure in spite of overwhelming obstacles."

(3) **4** "doer to watcher." Reeve says that "the worst part [of his situation] . . . is leaving the physical world . . . the transition from participant to observer." In this question and the one just above, the correct answer is a phrase expressed in synonyms or definitions of the key terms. Participant = doer, observer = watcher; in the item above, persists = has strength to persevere and endure, adversity = overwhelming obstacles.

(4) **2** "measuring progress." Reeve tells us that while he was in the hospital or in rehabilitation, he looked at the picture of the pyramid with ". . . hundreds of steps leading up to the clouds" and imagined himself ". . . climbing slowly but surely to the top." He develops that image in describing the reality of his progress: "You manage to climb one or two steps, but then something happens and you fall back three."

(5) **4** "medical setbacks." This item continues the ideas developed in the previous question. When Reeve is "climbing up the steps . . . " he is able to travel and make appearances, but in falling backward, he is hospitalized for a number of serious medical conditions, including pneumonia and fractures.

(6) **1** "embrace physically." Toward the end of his remarks, Reeve says that "the sensory deprivation hurts the most: I haven't been able to give [my son] Will a hug since he was two years old." He goes on to say that he is even jealous when he sees others able to embrace.

Part A   Sample Student Response Essay

As part of our school's Diversity Day celebration, I would like to make our community aware that disabled people are capable of many extraordinary accomplishments. One such individual is the actor Christopher Reeve.

Some of us may remember Christopher Reeve when he portrayed Superman in a movie about that comic book hero. After becoming paralyzed from the neck down after a riding accident, Reeve developed a very different idea of what a hero is. In an account of his life after that accident, Reeve says that a hero is someone who persists "in spite of overwhelming obstacles." Although he does not call himself a hero, Reeve's efforts to recover, remain devoted to his family, and to work to help others who have been disabled are a model what such a hero is. Christopher Reeve is also an example of what someone who is severely disabled may contribute to the world.

Christopher Reeve does not make his life sound only positive and without failures. He tells us that he often feels sadness and frustration, and he is sometimes jealous of those who remain active participants. Living with nearly total paralysis, Reeve is living in a world with no meaningful physical contact. No longer can he give his children a hug or embrace them lovingly. Reeve also tells us that living with his condition often means setbacks in his recovery. He can never know for sure that he will be able to travel or attend a special event; instead, he may find himself in the hospital again with a serious medical problem. He admits that it would be easy to retreat into himself and think only of his own difficulties.

Christopher Reeve, however, considers himself fortunate: he travels widely and speaks to many organizations to support scientific research. He also raises money for a foundation he created to raise awareness of quality of life issues for the disabled. Reeve even tries to help others by speaking to patients with conditions like his, to help them be optimistic about their lives and the possibilities for future cures for spinal cord injury. He has raised over $750,000 for the Reeve Foundation and has also made contributions to the American Paralysis Association. Along with raising money, he has also willingly appeared in commercials for the APA.

Reeve has admitted that it is hard to give and give when sometimes he really wants to take. He also admits that it can be difficult to keep his emotions about his condition to himself. He does this though for the sake of his family; he does not want to be an unfair emotional burden on his young son or his wife. Reeve also believes that family and friends who support the disabled should be considered heroes.

Despite overwhelming obstacles, Christopher Reeve has accomplished many extraordinary things, including maintaining a career as an actor and director, planning and organizing events to benefit causes for the disabled, and being a loving father and husband. Christopher Reeve's example can be a reminder for all of us that disabled people may also be capable of heroic accomplishments.

Analysis

This essay meets the guidelines of the task very well. The brief introduction is effective in declaring the specific audience and purpose of the essay and in giving focus to the discussion that follows. The essay conveys the writer's sound understanding of the text, and the development of ideas is built on relevant details from the passage and on key ideas and language in the multiple-choice questions.

The organization is clear and is faithful to the text in mirroring the balance between Reeve's extraordinary accomplishments and his own admission of the difficulties and frustrations he feels. The language and sentence structure are fluent, appropriate, and occasionally sophisticated: "Living with nearly total paralysis, Reeve is living in a world with no meaningful physical contact. No longer can he give his children a hug or embrace them lovingly." Finally, this essay demonstrates the writer's control of the conventions; it would rate a high score.

(See pp. 31–35 for a detailed explanation of the rubric for this part of the examination.)

Part B (7–16)

Note: Refer to Chapter 2 for review and strategy in responding to this part of the examination.

(7) **4** "acidic particles." The third paragraph of the article, in which dry deposition is explained, offers several examples of how acidic particles are spread. Fog, snow, and rain are examples of what is called wet deposition.

(8) **1** "increase the acidity of rain runoff." The third paragraph concludes with the point that, "the runoff water [containing dry deposition] adds . . . acids to the acid rain, making the combination more acidic . . . . "

(9) **4** "sulfur and nitrogen." Lines 18–25 elaborate on sulfur dioxide and nitrogen dioxide as the primary causes of acid rain. When these gases react in the atmosphere, they form "various acidic compounds." The pH scale measures the degree to which bodies of water or rain contain these acidic compounds.

(10) **2** "low pH value." The text states that "The lower a substance's pH, the more acidic it is" (lines 27–28). Acid rain, therefore, is characterized by a low pH value.

(11) **2** "remains unchanged." Chronic (meaning "long-term, always present") acidity is defined in the clause that follows: "a condition in which water has a *constant* low pH level." This is an example of how the Regents Exam assesses knowledge of vocabulary in context.

(12) **4** "practical suggestions." This section offers several examples of specific things individuals can do to conserve energy.

(13) **1** "transportation." The bars with crosshatches are highest for both countries in the first column, Transportation.

(14) **1** "fuel combustion and 'other'." This answer is determined by comparing visually the respective height of the crosshatched bars across all five columns.

(15) **4** "electric utilities." In comparing the height of the solid bars, the chart shows that it is highest for the United States in the Electric Utilities column. It is in Canada that industrial sources are the largest producer of sulfur dioxide emissions.

(16) **3** "fuel combustion." This answer is determined by simple observation: the vertical bars in the Fuel Combustion column are significantly lower than in any other group.

Part B   Sample Student Response Essay

Acid rain is becoming one of the most serious threats to the environment in the world today. Around the globe, acid rain is damaging our ecosystem and affecting the natural cycle of life for many species. The only way the nations of the world can battle this threat is if they become informed about acid rain, its impacts, and ways to prevent it from occurring. Recent research on acid rain in North America offers useful information on what acid rain really is and on ways to prevent its damaging effects.

First, it is important to know what acid rain really is. A recent article published by the U.S. Environmental Protection Agency or EPA points out that a more "precise term is acid deposition," which can be wet or dry. Wet deposition comes in the form of rain, fog, or snow that is highly acidic. Dry deposition "refers to acidic gases and particles" spread by the wind. The article points out that scientists have determined that the primary causes of acid rain are large amounts of sulfur dioxide and nitrogen dioxide in the atmosphere. Most of the SO_2 and NO_2 comes from using fossil fuels for transportation and to generate electric power. Other sources include fuel combustion and industrial activity.

What we call acid rain has many damaging effects on forests, our lakes and rivers, and on many materials. Acid rain can be damaging, even fatal, to fish and other living things, and is harmful to human health. The EPA tells us that acid rain even affects "how clearly we can see through the air!"

If we know what acid rain is and what causes it, are there things that governments, communities, or even individuals can do to help solve the problem? There are many ways we can reduce acid rain, and reverse some of the damage it has already caused. However, it will require society to become more aware of the problem and to be willing to take actions to solve it. Since we know that generating electricity with fossil fuels is one major source of acid rain, we can develop alternative energy sources. The article from the EPA points out that nuclear power and hydropower are already in wide use, *but other sources such as wind and solar energy can be more fully used. Not all sources of energy are equally efficient or safe, but we must explore all possibilities in order to save our environment.*

Nearly everyone agrees that conserving energy has many benefits and can help reduce the effects of acid rain. As individuals we can do many things: turn off computers, appliances, and lights when they are not being used; purchase efficient appliances and do whatever we can to have good insulation in our homes. The use of fossil fuels for automobiles is a major source of harmful emissions; citizens are urged to use public transportation if possible, and even consider biking or walking more. That can also be good for your health. These days, there is more and more interest in hybrid cars, which may one day be a factor in reducing pollution that leads to acid rain.

The problems caused by acid rain must be dealt with before the damage it has already caused becomes worse and spirals out of control. Societies and governments must make changes to adapt to the threat posed by acid rain. Individuals must be well informed and willing to consider what they can do to help solve this very serious environmental problem.

Analysis

This essay reveals the writer's thorough understanding of the texts and of the task. The introduction states the issue and outlines the discussion to follow. Development is clear and based on relevant ideas, though it is spare in use of the many details provided in the article. The organization is also effective because the transitions between paragraphs are lively and varied: "First, it is important to know what acid rain really is . . ."; "What we call acid rain has many damaging effects . . ."; "If we know what acid rain is and what causes it . . . ." These transitions also demonstrate excellent awareness of audience and purpose.

The writer is fluent in language to convey technical concepts with clarity and in appropriately varied sentence structure. There are no significant errors in the conventions. This essay would merit a high score.

(See pp. 48–53 for a detailed discussion of the rubric for this part of the examination.)

Session Two

Part A　(1–10)

Note: See Chapter 3 for review and strategy in responding to this part of the examination.

(1) **3** "rereading old books." This first line of the poem ends with the phrase "to the great stories . . . ," and is followed by the image of a reader turning pages.

(2) **2** "characters from literature." In these lines we see a sequence of references to popular literary types, "orphans . . . young provincials . . . the serious girl . . . the young man bent on glory . . . ." One would not refer to friends from childhood in such a way, and there is nothing to suggest famous actors or authors.

(3) **1** "setting." These are both images of places in which stories might take place.

(4) **4** "knows the endings." Because the reader in the poem is "going back . . . to the great stories/ That charmed her younger mind," we can trust that she knows how these stories end. There is no suggestion of her own future or childhood because she refers to *their* "first and final selves . . . "; nor is there any suggestion that she has invented these characters.

(5) **3** "greater insight." The phrase "a wiser eye" suggests greater knowledge and understanding of human affairs, that is, insight. None of the other choices suggests wisdom.

(6) **2** "censoring books." The opening paragraphs of the story reveal concern on the part of the generals and their establishment of a commission of enquiry into the content of books, suggesting that censorship may follow. The paragraph outlining the duties of the commission reveals explicitly that their task is to determine "whether a book had been judged suitable . . . ." (line 25)

(7) **4** "perform their assigned task." In the passage noted above, we are told that rubber stamps are used to designate which books are suitable, and for whom. The fact that the stamps now lay idle reveals that the men are no longer able to carry out their duty to censor.

(8) **3** "contradicting." This paragraph in the story reveals the inability of the men to censor books that challenge the General's convictions—firm beliefs—about military hierarchy and even reveals that there are now "discussions that [go] on for hours and hours." While Signor Crispino appears only to be helpful in offering more books on a subject, he is covertly working to undermine or weaken support for the General's beliefs.

(9) **1** "prevent a scandal." At line 98 the passage reveals that the assembly of generals was "afraid there might be a more serious scandal" over the failure of the commission if they punished Fedina and his lieutenants.

(10) **4** "returned to the library." This is a fitting conclusion to a story in which the tone is ironic, even satiric, from the beginning. Note also that the other three choices are factually inaccurate.

Part A   Sample Student Response Essay

These two passages, a poem and a short story, offer vivid examples of the power of reading to enrich and even profoundly change the lives of readers. These works show how reading has a strange and seductive power, which keeps the reader coming back for more. They also show how reading opens the mind to new and challenging ideas. In developing the theme of the power of reading, the authors use imagery, characterization, irony, and paradox.

The poem "The Reader" opens with the image of a woman deeply involved in reading; she is returning to the books "that charmed her . . . " when she was young. "Onward they come again"—images of the many different kinds of characters in the novels she reads and whose stories she already knows: the orphan, the young girl, the young man "bent on glory." The woman already knows the endings of these stories, yet she is still enthralled and "still turns enchanted to the next bright page . . . ." Reading these works with knowledge of both their "first and final selves," the reader is like a god who can know all time at once. Knowing the stories as she does, the reader's appreciation of the characters is richer and wiser. Paradoxically, however, she remains like the characters, on the threshold of new experience, "caught in the flow of things . . . and ready still to enter life . . . ."

The Calvino short story also develops the theme of the power of reading, but dramatizes the power of reading to overcome censorship and thought control. The story is set in an imaginary place called Panduria, where top officials become concerned that the people might be reading books "that contained opinions hostile to military prestige."

The ironic tone of the story is established from the beginning when the narrator, who reports without comment or judgment, explains that the generals did not know where to begin their task of reviewing the suitability of books in the library because "none of them was particularly well-versed in matters bibliographical." The image of a squadron setting up a military camp in the courtyard of the library and the use of a "rubber stamp" to show which books were suitable for officers or common soldiers add to the reader's sense of the story as a satire.

The story develops to show how, in carrying out their task of reviewing books for dangerous ideas, the soldiers had to read them. However, as they began to form an opinion on a particular topic, the librarian would "helpfully" offer more books on the same idea, leading the soldiers to remark: "For heaven's sake! The things you learn! Who would ever have thought!" As the soldiers encountered new ideas, they began to ask for more and more to read. What the soldiers knew and what they thought was so greatly expanded that it was impossible to agree on one judgment, and as the number of ideas and books piled up, reports to the General Staff stopped. When the general in charge of the commission was finally asked to present his report, his speech was "somewhat confused . . . as can happen with those who have only recently embraced new ideas . . . ."

Fearing scandal, the assembly of generals decides not to punish General Fedina and his men but rather allows them to quietly retire. In the final irony of the story, we are told that these men could later be seen "going into the old library where Signor Crispino would be waiting for them with his books." The theme that books contain ideas that may be "dangerous" to an established order is one that readers who know Orwell's 1984 *or Ray Bradbury's* Fahrenheit 451 *will recognize.*

Reading can have a profound effect on all who experience it. It draws us in, it changes us, it opens our minds, and draws our hearts back to it. Through the use of imagery and irony, these passages offer vivid accounts of the power of books and ideas to shape our lives.

Analysis

This essay reveals the writer's thorough understanding and appreciation of the texts and makes persuasive connections between the writer's controlling idea and the ideas in the texts. It is especially strong in the discussion of theme and irony in both passages. This essay is also a good model of how to use quotes from the passages to develop ideas, and it summarizes the narrative in each work without unnecessary detail.

The organization is clear, with an introduction that establishes the controlling idea and the specific literary elements to be discussed. The discussion of the poem is relatively brief, but it is adequate to support the writer's topic. The discussion of the short story is more fully and persuasively developed; it is especially strong in revealing the writer's own recognition of the ironic tone: "the narrator . . . reports, without comment or judgment . . . " and " . . . the librarian would 'helpfully' offer more books." The reference to works by Orwell and Bradbury also gives authority to the writer's commentary. The conclusion is a strong restatement of the controlling idea, effectively demonstrated in the discussion of the two works.

The language is sophisticated, appropriate, and at times compelling: "[Reading] draws us in, it changes us, it opens our minds and draws our hearts back to it." This writer demonstrates skill in composing sentences to express the complexity of ideas and shows control of the conventions. This essay has all the qualities that merit a high score.

(See pp. 68–71 for a detailed discussion of the rubric for this part of the examination.)

Session Two

Note: See Chapter 4 for review and strategy in responding to this part of the examination.

Part B Sample Student Response Essay

"*The ultimate measure of a man is not where he stands in moments of comfort and convenience, but where he stands at times of challenge and controversy.*" In this statement, Martin Luther King, Jr. is saying that it is not when times are peaceful and easy that a person's character is judged, but rather it is during times of difficulty or moral challenge that a man's true character may emerge. I believe he is correct in this view. Dr. King's observation about human nature serves as a central theme in Arthur Miller's play *The Crucible* and in Harper Lee's novel *To Kill a Mockingbird*. The authors of these works use setting, moral conflict within a community, and strong characterization to develop their themes.

The Crucible takes place in Salem, Massachusetts, during the period of the infamous witch trials. This setting creates an atmosphere of great fear and suspicion. The town is in turmoil after a group of teenage girls has accused several individuals of witchcraft. Frightened at being severely punished after being caught dancing in the woods, the girls accuse a black slave and several old women of the town of bewitching them. As the hysteria grows, other members of the community even begin to accuse neighbors they may have disagreements with. John Proctor, a resident of Salem, is skeptical at first and then later knows for a fact that the girls' accusations are a hoax.

The conflict that John Proctor faces is that in order to prove that the girls' charges are fake, he must reveal his brief affair with Abigail, the leader of the accusing girls. In this Puritan community, adultery is a grave sin and Proctor's admission would lead others to condemn him. However, it is only after Proctor's own wife is accused and arrested that he comes forward with the truth. When Proctor seeks to convince the court that the girls are lying, he too is accused of witchcraft. As the drama concludes, Proctor is faced with the choice to sign a confession he knows to be false or to be hanged as a witch. After struggling with his conscience and a desire to save his life, Proctor decides that he cannot sign his good name to a lie and accepts his death. Another element of Proctor's character to emerge is his feeling that he cannot betray the honor of other innocent victims, who accepted hanging rather than swearing to a lie.

Like *The Crucible*, the novel *To Kill a Mockingbird* by Harper Lee has a main character who is challenged by controversy. This novel is set in the small Southern town of Maycomb during the period of the Depression, when African-American citizens were still the victims of widespread racial prejudice. The story centers on the character of Atticus Finch, a well-respected lawyer in the town, and his two children, Jem and Scout. When a young black man, Tom Robinson, is accused of raping a young white woman, many in the *town assume Tom is guilty and would condemn him even before a trial. Atticus decides to take Tom Robinson's case, and he goes to extraordinary measures to protect Tom and assure that he receives a trial. Atticus not only acts on his beliefs in fairness and justice, he also shows great courage when he spends the night in front of the jailhouse to stand up to a lynch mob. Atticus takes these actions even though he knows he cannot win the case, and he knows that many in the town will turn against him and his children.*

In both of these works, the central character shows courage when challenged by a conflict in a community that forces him to risk disapproval, even death, in order to do what is right. In facing these challenges, Proctor and Atticus show great moral courage. They demonstrate their true character in "times of challenge and controversy."

Analysis

This essay is quite successful in meeting one of the key challenges in a critical lens task: it avoids extensive plot summary yet offers sufficient detail to support an assertion about the nature of the central characters and their actions. This writer has made excellent choices of literary elements as well, offering examples that are relevant and apply to both works equally well. The final sentence of the introduction skillfully specifies those literary elements, which are illustrated in the commentaries that follow.

The organization of the essay is logical and the development is focused on the moral conflict the two central characters face. Both the language and the use of sentence structure are fluent here, showing that this writer has command of the ideas and the means to convey them: "In both of these works, the central character shows courage when challenged by a conflict in a community that forces him to risk disapproval, even death, in order to do what is right." There are no evident weaknesses in the conventions. This essay would merit a high score.

(See pp. 80–83 for a detailed discussion of the rubric for this part of the examination.)

Examination August 2006
English

Session One

Part A

Overview: For this part of the test, you will listen to an account about yellow rice, answer some multiple-choice questions, and write a response based on the situation described below. You will hear the account twice. You may take notes on the page alloted anytime you wish during the readings.

> **The Situation:** Your communications class is studying propaganda. You have been asked to write an essay on one industry's use of propaganda. You have chosen the biotechnology industry. In preparation for writing your essay, listen to an account by Michael Pollan about yellow rice. Then use relevant information from the account to write your essay.

Your Task: Write an essay for your communications class explaining the use of propaganda by the biotechnology industry.

Guidelines:
Be sure to
- Tell your audience what they need to know about the use of propaganda by the biotechnology industry as described by Pollan
- Use specific, accurate, and relevant information from Pollan's account to support your explanation
- Use a tone and level of language appropriate for an essay for a communications class
- Organize your ideas in a logical and coherent manner
- Indicate any words taken directly from the account by using quotation marks or referring to the speaker
- Follow the conventions of standard written English

Note: For this portion of the examination, the teacher will read a passage aloud. You will not actually see the passage reprinted below. Therefore, you are encouraged to have someone read the passage to you, in order to simulate the examination as closely as possible.

Listening Passage

Unless I'm missing something, the aim of the biotechnology industry's audacious new advertising campaign is to impale people like me — well-off first worlders dubious about genetically engineered food — on the horns of a moral dilemma. Have you seen these ads? Over a speedy montage of verdant [green] rice paddies, smiling Asian kids and kindly third-world doctors, a caring voice describes something called golden rice and its promise to "help prevent blindness and infection in millions of children" suffering from vitamin-A deficiency. This new rice has been engineered, using a daffodil gene, to produce beta-carotene, a nutrient the body can convert into vitamin A. Watching the pitch, you can almost feel the moral ground shifting under your feet. For the unspoken challenge here is that if we don't get over our queasiness about eating genetically modified food, kids in the third world will go blind.

It appears that biotechnology, which heretofore had little more to offer the world than plants that could shake off a shower of herbicide, has finally found a "killer app" that can silence its critics and win over journalists. It's working, too: Time magazine put golden rice on its cover, declaring, "This rice could save a million kids a year." Even Greenpeace has acknowledged that "golden rice is a moral challenge to our position."

Yet the more one learns about biotechnology's Great Yellow Hope, the more uncertain seems its promise — and the industry's command of the moral high ground. Indeed, it remains to be seen whether golden rice will ever offer as much to malnourished children as it does to beleaguered biotech companies. Its real achievement may be to win an argument rather than solve a public-health problem. Which means we may be witnessing the advent of the world's first purely rhetorical technology.

If that sounds harsh, consider this: an 11-year-old would have to eat 15 pounds of cooked golden rice a day — quite a bowlful — to satisfy his minimum daily requirement of vitamin A. Even if that were possible (or if scientists boosted beta-carotene levels), it probably wouldn't do a malnourished child much good, since the body can only convert beta-carotene into vitamin A when fat and protein are present in the diet. Fat and protein in the diet are, of course, precisely what a malnourished child lacks.

Further, there's no guarantee people will eat yellowish rice. Brown rice, after all, is already rich in nutrients, yet most Asians prefer white rice, which is not. Rice has long had a complicated set of meanings in Asian culture. Confucius, for example, extolled the pure whiteness of rice as the ideal backdrop for green vegetables. That works fine so long as you've still got the vegetables. But once rice became a monoculture cash crop, it crowded the green vegetables out of people's fields and out of their diet.

Proponents of golden rice acknowledge that persuading people to eat it may require an educational campaign. This begs a rather obvious question. Why not simply a campaign to persuade them to eat brown rice? Or how about teaching people how to grow green vegetables on the margins of their rice fields, and maybe even give them the seeds to do so? Or what about handing out vitamin-A supplements to children so severely malnourished their bodies can't metabolize beta-carotene?

As it happens, these ridiculously obvious, unglamorous, low-tech schemes are being tried today, and according to the aid groups behind them, all they need to work are political will and money.

Money?

More than $100 million dollars has been spent developing golden rice, and another $50 million has been budgeted for advertisements touting the technology's future benefits. A spokesman for Syngenta, the company that plans to give golden rice seeds to poor farmers, has said that every month of delay will mean another 50,000 blind children. Yet how many cases of blindness could be averted right now if the industry were to divert its river of advertising dollars to a few of these programs?

Which brings us to some uncomfortable questions about the industry's motives. In January, Gordon Conway, the president of the Rockefeller Foundation — which financed the original research on golden rice — wrote, "The public-relations uses of golden rice have gone too far." While genetically engineered rice has a role to play in combating malnutrition, Conway noted, "We do not consider golden rice the solution to the vitamin-A deficiency problem."

So to what, then, *is* golden rice the solution? The answer seems plain: To the public-relations problem of an industry that has so far offered consumers precious few reasons to buy what it's selling—and more than a few to avoid it. Appealing to our self-interest won't work, so why not try pricking our conscience? (Do I hear an echo? *Eat your peas — there are children starving in Africa.*)

Ordinarily, evaluating a P.R. strategy in terms of morality rather than efficacy would seem to be missing the point. But morality is precisely the basis on which we've been asked to think about golden rice. So let us try. Granted, it would be immoral for finicky Americans to thwart a technology that could rescue malnourished children. But wouldn't it also be immoral for an industry to use those children's suffering in order to rescue itself? The first case is hypothetical at best. The second is right there on our television screens, for everyone to see.

— from "The Great Yellow Hype"
The New York Times Magazine, March 4, 2001

Notes

Multiple-Choice Questions

Directions (1–6): Use your notes to answer the following questions about the passage read to you. Select the best suggested answer and write its number in the space provided. The questions may help you think about ideas and information you might use in your writing. You may return to these questions anytime you wish.

1 According to the speaker, blindness in Asian children is caused by a lack of vitamin

(1) A   (3) C

(2) B   (4) D   1 _____

2 The new strain of rice gets its ability to produce beta-carotene from a gene originally found in

(1) lilacs   (3) daffodils

(2) dandelions   (4) roses   2 _____

3 According to the speaker, Asians prefer to eat rice that is

(1) wild   (3) brown

(2) sweet   (4) white   3 _____

4 The speaker mentions Gordon Conway, president of the Rockefeller Foundation, in order to

(1) propose a solution

(2) support an argument

(3) support a change

(4) appeal to self-interest   4 _____

5 The speaker asserts that the public relations campaign attempts to persuade based on

(1) facts   (3) morals

(2) logic   (4) emotion   5 _____

6 The speaker accuses the biotechnology industry of attempting to save itself by using

(1) suffering children
(2) generous foundations
(3) well-off first worlders
(4) poor farmers   6 _____

After you have finished these questions, review **The Situation** and read **Your Task** and the **Guidelines**. Use scrap paper to plan your response. Then write your response on separate sheets of paper. After you finish your response for Part A, complete Part B.

Part B

Directions: Read the text and study the time line on the following pages, answer the multiple-choice questions, and write a response based on the situation described below. You may use the margins to take notes as you read and scrap paper to plan your response.

> **The Situation:** Your economics class is studying the effects of consumerism. For a class debate, your teacher has asked you to write a position paper discussing whether consumer culture has had a positive **or** negative impact on society.

Your Task: Using relevant information from **both** documents, write a position paper for your economics class in which you discuss whether consumer culture has had a positive **or** negative impact on society.

Guidelines:
Be sure to
- Tell your audience what they need to know about the impacts of consumer culture
- Discuss whether consumer culture has had a positive **or** negative impact on society
- Use specific, accurate, and relevant information from the text **and** the time line to support your position
- Use a tone and level of language appropriate for a position paper for an economics class
- Organize your ideas in a logical and coherent manner
- Indicate any words taken directly from the text by using quotation marks or referring to the author
- Follow the conventions of standard written English

The Consumer Culture

Steve Brigance joined the throngs of shoppers at the vast Potomac Mills mall in Woodbridge, Va., for one reason: to pick up a pair of shoes for his wife. His mission accomplished, he pushes his young son and daughter in their stroller from store window to store window, checking out the season's offerings. But he's
(5) done his shopping for the day. . . .

And Potomac Mills — with its 230 stores and 1.7 million square feet of space — is the place to go. Indeed, Brigance says, malls like the mammoth emporium literally feed our nation's obsession with acquiring things. . . .

But while the unbridled consumerism symbolized by Potomac Mills worries
(10) Brigance, other shoppers at the bustling mall are untroubled by Americans' embrace of shopping as recreation.

"I don't see anything wrong with it," says Rebecca Michalski, a sixth-grade teacher from Fairfax, Va. "I come to Potomac Mills sometimes with my family, and we find that it's a good way to spend time together." Moreover, she dismisses
(15) the criticism of people like herself who enjoy shopping. "Look, people spend their time the way they want to," she says, "and that's no one else's business."

That may be true, says Michael Jacobson, executive director of the Center for Science in the Public Interest, a consumer advocacy group. But advertising and marketing have become such strong forces in our society, he says, that
(20) consumption for many people has become less a question of personal choice and more a compulsion. . . .

According to Jacobson, [author Mark] Buchanan and other critics of consumerism, the need to buy is literally programmed into us by the media, through advertising and the glorification of material wealth.

(25) "The idea that you can buy fulfillment is repeated constantly in the media, like background noise," says Betsy Taylor, executive director of the Center for a New American Dream, a think tank in Takoma Park, Md., that focuses on "quality of life" issues.

In addition, critics say, consumerism has displaced other, more important
(30) yearnings, such as spending time with our families and in our communities. "Even among religious people I see it," Buchanan says. "They rush out of church on Sunday so that they can go to the mall and shop."

But other observers, economists among them, see the criticism of consumerism as misdirected. They argue that consumers are not brainwashed
(35) slaves to shopping but intelligent people who know what they want and usually purchase things they genuinely feel that they need. . . .

In the final analysis, [economists Diane] Furchtgott-Roth, [Martin] Regalia and others say, consumer spending drives the economy, creating jobs and bringing material prosperity to many millions of Americans.

(40)   "The people who make all of these goods use the money they're paid to do things like buy a house, send their kids to school and build their churches," Regalia says.

Still, the critics contend, society needs to impose some limits on what they see as rampant and harmful consumerism, especially when it's directed at children.

(45)   Many critics of consumerism even say that television advertising aimed at children should be severely limited at the very least, or banned. . . .

"Kids are very susceptible to advertising, and advertisers know it," says Kathryn C. Montgomery, president of the Center for Media Education, a children's advocacy group.

(50)   In addition, Montgomery and others argue, the constant barrage of advertising prods children to frequently ask for things that their parents either can't afford or don't want them to have. . . .

But others argue that it is for parents, not government regulators, to decide what their children watch. "Parents have certain standards, and they impose

(55) those standards on their kids," says Jeff Bobeck, a spokesman for the National Association of Broadcasters (NAB).

Opponents of putting limits on advertising also argue that commercials do not send children pernicious[1] messages or turn them into bad citizens. Indeed, Bobeck and others point out, most of today's adults grew up on television and are

(60) now productive and law-abiding citizens. . . .

Taylor and others argue that the desire to reduce or even replace important needs in our lives with consumption is prompted to a large extent by the media, with their almost relentless barrage of advertisements. Indeed, according to a recent article in *Business Week*, the average American is exposed to 3,000

(65) commercial messages per day, from television and newspaper advertisements to billboards, signs and logos on clothing. . . .

"The message is that you are the center of the universe, that you have needs and that you won't be fulfilled until you buy the right product to fill those needs," Taylor says. . . .

(70)   The problem with this message, Jacobson and others say, is that it's misleading, because happiness and fulfillment are not the natural byproducts of consumption. "It's a quick fix, at best, because while you feel better for a little while, it doesn't last and then you have to go buy something else," says Taylor.

Ironically, Taylor and others say, excessive shopping is not only unsatisfying

(75) but highly impractical.

---

[1] pernicious — highly destructive

"One of the things that consumerism has done is to teach us to value things too little," Buchanan says. "We always want the newest or the best version of a computer or car or whatever even when we really have no need to replace what we have."

(80)   We need to recapture the "sacredness" of things, Buchanan continues, "to appreciate the things we already have and not constantly be lusting after something more."

But others dispute this vision of addicted, unhappy consumers who buy simply to satisfy other needs, arguing that people generally purchase goods and
(85)   services because they think they need them. . . .

For Furchtgott-Roth and others, the beauty of the American consumer economy is that it gives people an array of choices. "On balance, more and better choices make people much happier," says CATO's [Stephen] Moore. "The proof is in the pudding," he adds, referring to the simple economic reality that if
(90)   Americans didn't want more choice, the market wouldn't respond by creating more. "And besides," he says, "you always have the choice not to buy."

Indeed, Furchtgott-Roth and Moore argue that, contrary to what the critics of consumerism say, people are not entirely in the thrall of advertisers and marketers. "I don't believe in the idea that the supply is creating the demand,"
(95)   Moore says, "because a lot of products fail even though they've been introduced with sophisticated promotional and advertising campaigns." For example, he points to failed promotional campaigns for new products, such as the infamously unsuccessful effort to introduce New Coke in the mid-1980's. . . .

Finally, the supporters say, even habitual shoppers who spend most of their
(100)   time in malls shouldn't be criticized or looked down upon. "Shopping is a leisure activity for some people," Furchtgott-Roth says. "If it's something that they want to do, something they get value from, there's nothing wrong with it."

But opponents of consumerism say that rampant buying is inherently wrong and that society has a responsibility to find ways to discourage it. One way,
(105)   according to Robert Frank, professor at Cornell University in Ithaca, N.Y., would be to make it more expensive for people to spend their money, especially on luxury goods. "We need to tax savings less and consumption more, to encourage people to spend less and save more," Frank says. . . .

But CATO's Moore warns the critics to be careful about what they wish for.
(110)   "Our whole economy is based on consumers buying things," he says, "and if we stopped buying as much as we now do, the whole economy would naturally slow down" and the results would be devastating. "For starters, many people would lose their jobs."

A cutback on consuming would cause other, equally devastating results,
(115)   Moore and others say. "Consumerism tends to speed the pace of innovation," says

Debbie van Opstal, senior vice president at the Council on Competitiveness, a nonprofit membership group that seeks to increase public awareness of the value of economic competition. According to van Opstal, highly selective consumers impel companies to constantly work at building better mousetraps for less.

(120) "There's nothing that forces companies to do things better, cheaper and faster than demanding customers," she says. . . .

— David Masci
excerpted from "The Consumer Culture"
CQ Researcher, November 19, 1999

TIME LINE
1900–Present
The rise of radio and TV, then the Internet, spurs consumerism.

1900
Businesses are spending $500 million annually on advertising.

1920
First radio station broadcasts in Pittsburgh.

1948
Commercial television begins broadcasts to larger audiences.

1950
Diners Club issues the first credit card.

1955
First shopping malls appear.

1960
Some 90 percent of American homes have a television.

1978
Federal Trade Commission attempts, unsuccessfully, to ban TV advertising aimed at children.

1990
Average credit card debt for U.S. household is $2,250 (adjusted for inflation).

1991
FCC [Federal Communications Commission] sets some limits on children's advertising on television.

1996
Consumer debt grows 20 percent. Average credit card debt per U.S. household reaches $4,250 (adjusted for inflation).

1998
Individual bankruptcy filings reach a record high.

1999
Average credit card debt for U.S. household is $4,500 (adjusted for inflation). Credit card debt exceeds $500 billion. Internet sales are expected to total $20 billion.

2004
Sales of products on-line are expected to reach $185 billion.

Sources: (excerpted and adapted) "The Consumer Culture"
CQ Researcher, November 19, 1999 and
Federal Reserve Bank of Cleveland
Economic Trends, May 2000

Multiple-Choice Questions

Directions (7–16): Select the best suggested answer to each question and write its number in the space provided. The questions may help you think about ideas and information you might want to use in your writing. You may return to these questions anytime you wish.

7 Consumer critic Michael Jacobson believes that shopping has become

   (1) a primary goal
   (2) a harmless pastime
   (3) an extension of work
   (4) an Internet activity   7_____

8 According to lines 29 and 30, our consumer culture has the effect of

   (1) hampering financial planning
   (2) replacing family activities
   (3) inspiring worthless products
   (4) causing traffic congestion   8_____

9 "Critics of consumerism" believe there should be limits placed on

   (1) spending in malls
   (2) prices for entertainment
   (3) repackaging of products
   (4) marketing to children   9_____

10 An example of the "barrage of advertisements" (line 63) includes endorsements on

   (1) furniture   (3) clothing
   (2) food   (4) appliances   10_____

11 According to Stephen Moore (lines 109 through 113), slowing consumerism would result in

(1) increased inflation   (3) new taxes
(2) rising unemployment   (4) more innovation   11 _____

12 According to Debbie van Opstal (lines 115 through 121), as consumers become more selective, industry is pushed to

(1) generate new products
(2) promote workers faster
(3) offer fewer choices
(4) build customer loyalty   12 _____

13 The time line indicates that the first attempt to respond to the harmful effects of television commercials took place in

(1) 1948   (3) 1978
(2) 1960   (4) 1991   13 _____

14 According to the time line, the most recent contributor to consumerism is the

(1) credit card   (3) television
(2) Internet   (4) shopping mall   14 _____

15 The time line implies that consumerism is a product of

(1) advertising use   (3) population growth
(2) government control   (4) increased wealth   15 _____

16 A valid conclusion that can be drawn from the time line is that since 1950 consumers have increased their

(1) purchases of expensive goods
(2) number of credit cards
(3) money in savings
(4) buying on credit   16 _____

After you have finished these questions, review **The Situation** and read **Your Task** and the **Guidelines**. Use scrap paper to plan your response. Then write your response to Part B on separate sheets of paper.

Session Two

Part A

Directions: Read the passages on the following pages (a short story and a poem). Write the number of the answer to each multiple-choice question in the space provided. Then write the essay on separate sheets of paper as described in **Your Task**. You may use the margins to take notes as you read and scrap paper to plan your response.

Your Task:

> After you have read the passages and answered the multiple-choice questions, write a unified essay about the natural world as revealed in the passages. In your essay, use ideas from *both* passages to establish a controlling idea about the natural world. Using evidence from *each* passage, develop your controlling idea and show how the author uses specific literary elements or techniques to convey that idea.

Guidelines:
Be sure to
- Use ideas from *both* passages to establish a controlling idea about the natural world
- Use specific and relevant evidence from *each* passage to develop your controlling idea
- Show how each author uses specific literary elements (for example: theme, characterization, structure, point of view) or techniques (for example: symbolism, irony, figurative language) to convey the controlling idea
- Organize your ideas in a logical and coherent manner
- Use language that communicates ideas effectively
- Follow the conventions of standard written English

Passage I

It was evening in late March. The sun was nearing its setting, its soft rays gilding[1] the western limestone headland of Rathlin Island and washing its green hills with wet gold light. A small boy walked jauntily along a hoof-printed path that wriggled between the folds of these hills and opened out into a crater-like
(5) valley on the cliff-top. Presently he stopped as if remembering something, then suddenly he left the path, and began running up one of the hills. When he reached the top he was out of breath and stood watching fan-shaped streaks of light radiating from golden-edged clouds, the scene reminding him of a picture he had seen of the Transfiguration.[2] A short distance below him was the cow
(10) munching at the edge of a reedy lake. Colm ran down to meet her waving his stick in the air, and the wind rumbling in his ears made him give an exultant whoop which splashed upon the hills in a shower of echoed sound. A flock of gulls lying on the short green grass near the lake rose up languidly, drifting lazily like blown snowflakes over the rim of the cliff.

(15) The lake faced west and was fed by a stream, the drainings of the semicircling hills. One side was open to the winds from the sea, and in winter a little outlet trickled over the cliffs making a black vein in their grey sides. The boy lifted stones and began throwing them into the lake, weaving web after web on its calm surface. Then he skimmed the water with flat stones, some of them jumping the
(20) surface and coming to rest on the other side. He was delighted with himself, and after listening to his echoing shouts of delight he ran to fetch his cow. Gently he tapped her on the side and reluctantly she went towards the brown-mudded path that led out of the valley. The boy was about to throw a final stone into the lake when a bird flew low over his head, its neck astrain, and its orange-coloured legs
(25) clear in the saffron[3] light. It was a wild duck. It circled the lake twice, thrice, coming lower each time and then with a nervous flapping of wings it skidded along the surface, its legs breaking the water into a series of glittering arcs. Its wings closed, it lit silently, gave a slight shiver, and began pecking indifferently at the water. The boy with dilated eyes watched it eagerly as he turned back and
(30) moved slowly along the edge of the lake. The duck was going to the farther end where bulrushes, wild irises and sedge[4] grew around sods of islands and bearded tussocks. Colm stood to watch the bird meandering between tall bulrushes, its body, black and solid as stone against the greying water. Then as if it had sunk it

---

[1] gilding — covering with gold
[2] Transfiguration — a famous religious painting
[3] saffron   yellow
[4] sedge — a marsh plant

was gone. The boy ran stealthily along the bank looking away from the lake,
(35) pretending indifference to the wild duck's movements. When he came opposite
to where he had last seen the bird he stopped and peered closely through the
gently-sighing reeds whose shadows streaked the water in a maze of black
strokes. In front of him was a soddy islet guarded by the spears of sedge and
separated from the bank by a narrow channel of water. The water wasn't too
(40) deep—he could wade across with care.

Rolling up his short trousers he began to wade, his arms outstretched, and his
legs brown and stunted in the mountain water. As he drew near the islet, his feet
sank in the mud and bubbles winked up at him. He went more carefully and
nervously, peeping through the avenues of reeds and watching each tussock
(45) closely. Then one trouser fell, and dipped into the water; the boy dropped his
hands to roll it up, he unbalanced, made a splashing sound, and the bird arose
with a squawk and whirred away over the cliffs. Colm clambered on to the wet-
soaked sod of land, which was spattered with seagulls' feathers and bits of wind-
blown rushes. Into each hummock[5] he looked, pulling back the long grass,
(50) running hither and thither as if engaged in some queer game. At last he came on
the nest facing seawards. Two flat rocks dimpled the face of the water and
between them was a neck of land matted with coarse grass containing the nest. It
was untidily built of dried rushes, straw and feathers, and in it lay one solitary egg.
Colm was delighted. He looked around and saw no one. The nest was his. He
(55) lifted the egg, smooth and green as the sky, with a faint tinge of yellow like the
reflected light from a buttercup; and then he felt he had done wrong. He left it
back quickly. He knew he shouldn't have touched it and he wondered would the
bird forsake it. A vague sadness stole over him and he felt in his heart he had
sinned. Carefully smoothing out his footprints he hurriedly left the islet and ran
(60) after his cow. The sun had now set and the cold shiver of evening enveloped him,
chilling his body and saddening his mind.

In the morning he was up and away to school. He took the grass rut that
edged the road, for it was softer on the bare feet. His house was the last on the
western headland, and after a mile or so he was joined by Peadar Ruadh; both
(65) boys, dressed in similar hand-knitted blue jerseys and grey trousers, carried
home-made school bags. Colm was full of the nest and as soon as he joined his
companion he said eagerly:"Peadar, I've a nest—a wild duck's with one egg."

"And how do you know it's a wild duck's?"asked Peadar, slightly jealous.

"Sure I saw her with my own two eyes, her brown speckled back with a
(70) crow's patch on it, and her little yellow legs and———"

---

[5] hummock— small hill

"Where is it?" interrupted Peadar in a challenging tone.

"I'm not going to tell you, for you'd rob it," retorted Colm sensing unfriendliness.

"Aach! I suppose it's a tame duck's you have or maybe an old gull's," replied (75) Peadar with sarcasm.

Colm made a puss at his companion. "A lot you know!" he said, "for a gull's egg has spots and this one is greenish-white, for I had it in my hand."

And then the words he didn't want to hear rushed from Peadar in a mocking chant: "You had it in your hand! She'll forsake it! She'll forsake! She'll forsake!"

(80) Colm felt as if he would choke or cry with vexation.[6] His mind told him that Peadar was right, but somehow he couldn't give into it and he replied: "She'll not forsake! She'll not! I know she'll not!"

But in school his faith wavered. Through the windows he could see moving sheets of rain—rain that dribbled down the panes filling his mind with thoughts (85) of the lake creased and chilled by the wind; the nest sodden and black with wetness; and the egg cold as a cave stone. He shivered from the thoughts and fidgeted with the ink-well cover, sliding it backwards and forwards mechanically. The mischievous look had gone from his eyes and the school-day dragged on interminably.[7] But at last they were out in the rain, Colm rushing home as fast as (90) he could.

He spent little time at his dinner of potatoes and salted fish and played none with his baby brothers and sisters, but hurried out to the valley, now smoky with drifts of slanting rain, its soaked grass yielding to the bare feet. Before long he was at the lake-side where the rain lisped ceaselessly in the water and wavelets (95) licked the seeping sides leaving an irregular line of froth like frost on a grey slate.

Opposite the islet the boy entered the water. The wind was blowing into his face rustling noisily the rushes, heavy with the dust of rain. A moss-cheeper, swaying on a reed like a mouse, filled the air with light cries of loneliness. The boy reached the islet, his heart thumping with excitement, wondering did the bird forsake. He (100) went slowly, quietly, on to the strip of land that led to the nest. He rose on his toes, looking over the sedge to see if he could see her. And then every muscle tautened. She was on, her shoulders hunched up, and her bill lying on her breast as if she were asleep. Colm's heart thumped wildly in his ears. She hadn't forsaken. He was about to turn stealthily away. Something happened. The bird moved, her neck (105) straightened, twitching nervously from side to side. The boy's head swam with lightness. He stood transfixed. The wild duck, with a panicky flapping, rose heavily, squawking as she did so, a piece of straw and a white object momentarily

---

[6] vexation— annoyance
[7] interminably — endlessly

entwined in her legs. The egg fell on the flat wet rock beside the nest, besmearing it with yellow slime. A sense of tremendous guilt seized Colm, a throbbing silence *(110)* enveloped him as if everything had gone from the earth leaving him alone. Stupefied, numbed to every physical sense, he floundered across the black water, running wildly from the scene of the disaster.

— Michael McLaverty
"The Wild Duck's Nest"
from *The Irish Monthly*, April 1934

Passage II

In Time of Silver Rain

In time of silver rain
The earth
Puts forth new life again,
Green grasses grow
(5)   And flowers lift their heads,
And over all the plain
The wonder spreads
      Of life,
      Of life,
(10)   Of life!

In time of silver rain
The butterflies
Lift silken wings
To catch a rainbow cry,
(15)   And trees put forth
New leaves to sing
In joy beneath the sky
As down the roadway
Passing boys and girls
(20)   Go singing, too,
In time of silver rain
      When spring
      And life
      Are new.

—Langston Hughes
from *Selected Poems of Langston Hughes*, 1959
Alfred A. Knopf

Multiple-Choice Questions

Directions (1–10): Select the best suggested answer to each question and write its number in the space provided. The questions may help you think about the ideas and information you might want to use in your essay. You may return to these questions anytime you wish.

Passage I (the short story)—Questions 1–5 refer to Passage I.

1 The development of the opening paragraph relies on the use of

  (1) cause and effect
  (2) comparison and contrast
  (3) appeal to the senses
  (4) accumulation of generalizations   1 _____

2 The boy's mood as he walks to get his cow can best be described as

  (1) carefree   (3) unhappy
  (2) confused   (4) cautious   2 _____

3 In line 32, the word "meandering" most nearly means

  (1) pausing   (3) falling
  (2) wandering   (4) dancing   3 _____

4 Colm's initial delight at finding the wild duck's egg is followed quickly by

  (1) amusement   (3) anger
  (2) relief   (4) guilt   4 _____

5 The author uses the dialogue between the two boys to

   (1) intensify Colm's feeling
   (2) provide essential information
   (3) lessen Peadar's hostility
   (4) inject comic relief   5 _____

Passage II (the poem)—Questions 6–10 refer to Passage II.

6 The narrator's use of the word "silver" (line 1) suggests that the rain is

   (1) warm   (3) valuable
   (2) hard   (4) safe   6 _____

7 According to the poem, "wonder" (line 7) is inspired by the

   (1) discovery of truth
   (2) renewal of nature
   (3) flight from reality
   (4) freedom from stress   7 _____

8 The narrator describes the actions of both the flowers (line 5) and the leaves (lines 16 and 17) by using

   (1) alliteration
   (2) hyperbole
   (3) metaphor
   (4) personification   8 _____

9 The actions of the "Passing boys and girls" (line 19) suggest

   (1) celebration   (3) escape
   (2) discovery   (4) denial   9 _____

10 The overall attitude of the narrator toward nature is one of

   (1) disappointment   (3) uncertainty

   (2) appreciation   (4) curiosity   10 _____

After you have finished these questions, review **Your Task** and the **Guidelines.** Use scrap paper to plan your response. Then write your response to Part A on separate sheets of paper. After you finish your response for Part A, complete Part B.

Part B

Your Task:

Write a critical essay in which you discuss *two* works of literature you have read from the particular perspective of the statement that is provided for you in the **Critical Lens**. In your essay, provide a valid interpretation of the statement, agree *or* disagree with the statement as you have interpreted it, and support your opinion using specific references to appropriate literary elements from the two works. You may use scrap paper to plan your response. Write your essay in Part B on separate sheets of paper.

Critical Lens:

> "To gain that which is worth having, it may be necessary to lose everything else."
>
> — Bernadette Devlin
> *The Price of My Soul*, 1969

Guidelines:

Be sure to

- Provide a valid interpretation of the critical lens that clearly establishes the criteria for analysis
- Indicate whether you agree *or* disagree with the statement as you have interpreted it
- Choose *two* works you have read that you believe best support your opinion
- Use the criteria suggested by the critical lens to analyze the works you have chosen
- Avoid plot summary. Instead, use specific references to appropriate literary elements (for example: theme, characterization, setting, point of view) to develop your analysis
- Organize your ideas in a unified and coherent manner
- Specify the titles and authors of the literature you choose
- Follow the conventions of standard written English

Regents Comprehensive Examination in English—August 2006

Chart for Determining the Final Examination Score (Use for August 2006 examination only.)

To determine the student's final examination score, locate the student's total essay score across the top of the chart and the student's total multiple-choice score down the side of the chart. The point where those two scores intersect is the student's final examination score. For example, a student receiving a total essay score of 16 and a total multiple-choice score of 19 would receive a final examination score of 72.

Total Essay Score → (columns) / **Total Multiple-Choice Score ↓** (rows)

MC \ Essay	0	1	2	3	4	5	6	7	8	9	10	11	12	13	14	15	16	17	18	19	20	21	22	23	24
0	0	1	2	2	3	5	7	9	11	14	17	20	23	26	30	33	37	40	44	48	52	56	59	63	67
1	1	1	2	3	4	6	8	10	13	15	18	21	24	28	31	35	39	42	46	50	54	58	61	65	69
2	1	1	2	3	4	7	9	11	14	17	20	23	26	30	33	37	40	44	48	52	56	59	63	67	70
3	1	2	3	4	5	7	10	13	15	18	21	24	28	31	35	39	42	46	50	54	58	61	65	69	72
4	2	2	4	5	6	8	11	14	17	20	23	26	30	33	37	40	44	48	52	56	59	63	67	70	74
5	2	3	5	6	7	9	13	15	18	21	24	28	31	35	39	42	46	50	54	58	61	65	69	72	76
6	2	4	6	7	9	10	14	17	20	23	26	30	33	37	40	44	48	52	56	59	63	67	70	74	77
7	3	5	7	8	10	11	15	18	21	24	28	31	35	39	42	46	50	54	58	61	65	69	72	76	79
8	3	6	8	9	11	13	17	20	23	26	30	33	37	40	44	48	52	56	59	63	67	70	74	77	80
9	4	7	9	11	13	14	18	21	24	28	31	35	39	42	46	50	54	58	61	65	69	72	76	79	82
10	5	8	10	12	14	15	20	23	26	30	33	37	40	44	48	52	56	59	63	67	70	74	77	80	84
11	6	9	11	13	15	17	21	24	28	31	35	39	42	46	50	54	58	61	65	69	72	76	79	82	85
12	7	10	13	14	17	18	23	26	30	33	37	40	44	48	52	56	59	63	67	70	74	77	80	84	86
13	8	11	14	15	18	20	24	28	31	35	39	42	46	50	54	58	61	65	69	72	76	79	82	85	88
14	9	13	15	17	20	21	26	30	33	37	40	44	48	52	56	59	63	67	70	74	77	80	84	86	89
15	10	14	17	18	21	23	28	31	35	39	42	46	50	54	58	61	65	69	72	76	79	82	85	88	90
16	11	15	18	20	23	24	30	33	37	40	44	48	52	56	59	63	67	70	74	77	80	84	86	89	92
17	13	17	20	21	24	26	31	35	39	42	46	50	54	58	61	65	69	72	76	79	82	85	88	90	93
18	14	18	21	23	26	28	33	37	40	44	48	52	56	59	63	67	70	74	77	80	84	86	89	92	94
19	15	20	23	24	28	30	35	39	42	46	50	54	58	61	65	69	72	76	79	82	85	88	90	93	95
20	17	21	24	26	30	31	37	40	44	48	52	56	59	63	67	70	74	77	80	84	86	89	92	94	96
21	18	23	26	28	31	33	39	42	46	50	54	58	61	65	69	72	76	79	82	85	88	90	93	95	97
22	20	24	28	30	33	35	40	44	48	52	56	59	63	67	70	74	77	80	84	86	89	92	94	96	98
23	21	26	30	31	35	37	42	46	50	54	58	61	65	69	72	76	79	82	85	88	90	93	95	97	98
24	23	28	30	33	37	39	44	48	52	56	59	63	67	70	74	77	80	84	86	89	92	94	96	98	99
25	24	28	31	35	39	42	46	50	54	58	61	65	69	72	76	79	82	85	88	90	93	95	97	98	99
26	26	30	33	37	40	44	48	52	56	59	63	67	70	74	77	80	84	86	89	92	94	96	97	99	100

Answers
August 2006
English

Answer Key

Session One, Part A	Session One, Part B	Session Two, Part A
1. 1	7. 1	1. 3
2. 3	8. 2	2. 1
3. 4	9. 4	3. 2
4. 2	10. 3	4. 4
5. 3	11. 2	5. 1
6. 1	12. 1	6. 3
	13. 3	7. 2
	14. 2	8. 4
	15. 1	9. 1
	16. 4	10. 2

Answers Explained

Session One

Part A   (1–6)

Note: Refer to Chapter 1 for review and strategy in responding to this part of the examination.

(1) **1** "[vitamin] A." In the opening passage, the speaker describes the campaign for yellow rice as something to help children suffering from vitamin A deficiency. There are references to vitamin A throughout the passage.

(2) **3** "daffodils." Also in the introduction, the speaker tells us that, "This new rice has been engineered, using a daffodil gene . . . ."

(3) **4** "white." On explaining why there is no guarantee people will eat yellowish rice, the speaker tells us that "most Asians prefer white rice," and that white rice is an important part of Asian culture.

(4) **2** "support an argument." The speaker quotes the remarks by the president of the Rockefeller Foundation to support the argument that ". . . public-relations uses of golden rice have gone too far."

(5) **3** "morals." In the conclusion of the passage, the speaker justifies "evaluating a P.R. strategy in terms of morality" because, he says, " . . . morality is precisely the basis on which we've been asked to think about golden rice." "Emotion" would also be a possible choice, but the specific references to morality throughout this part of the speech make "morals" the most precise answer.

(6) **1** "suffering children." In the closing passage cited above, the speaker asserts that it is "immoral for an industry to use . . . children's suffering in order to rescue itself."

Part A   Sample Student Response Essay

Propaganda can be a powerful tool in shaping how people respond to changes in the world around them. Propaganda may be used by an industry, for example, to gain support for its aims or for a new product. The development of genetically modified foods is an area that generates a great deal of controversy and even fear for many. A recent propaganda campaign from the biotechnology industry offers an excellent example of how propaganda may be used to influence public opinion.

The recent Golden Rice campaign of the biotechnology industry uses propaganda to create feelings of guilt among wealthy first world citizens when they oppose the use of genetically modified foods. By developing and then marketing a miracle product in "golden rice," the biotech industry claims that this genetically modified food will save millions of children from blindness or infection by delivering large amounts of vitamin A, an essential nutrient. The industry is seeking to overcome resistance to its technology by appealing to the consciences of people in the developed world. But is this rice the Great Yellow Hope the industry claims?

Foods that have had their genes altered through complex processes to produce a sort of hybrid, allegedly superior to that found in nature, are called genetically modified foods. The foods have been regarded by environmentalists, scientists, and even governments with wary skepticism. Most people do not feel comfortable supporting an industry that has, in essence, mutated something natural. Moral and health-related questions have been raised by many. Yet through the development and marketing of "golden rice," the biotechnical industry aims to change public opinion by posing an argument to silence even the toughest critics.

Yellow, or "golden," rice is the latest food to emerge from the labs, developed by using a gene from the daffodil to produce a rice full of beta-carotene. This is a good source of vitamin A when synthesized by the body. The biotech industry claims that golden rice will prevent blindness and infection in millions of malnourished third world children. By appealing to an apparent moral question, the industry has been gaining some ground. After all, how could anyone argue against a food that could supposedly save the lives of millions of innocent children? Through specific marketing targeted at the conscience of the consumer, the biotech industry plans to enhance its image and exploit the consumer's sense of moral obligation to make a profit.

Syngenta, the company that developed golden rice and plans to give the golden rice seeds to poor farmers, fails to mention some vital facts about its product. Golden rice may be a source of vitamin A, but the amount is not large. A recent article in The New York Times *points out that an 11-year-old would have to eat 11 pounds of golden rice a day to achieve the recommended daily amounts of vitamin A. Moreover, golden rice benefits only those who are already adequately nourished, because converting beta-carotene to vitamin A is a process that requires fats and proteins as well. Severely malnourished children are not likely to benefit as claimed.*

What Syngenta also fails to mention in their $50 million dollar ad campaign is that there are other more effective solutions to this problem. These dollars and the $100 million dollars spent in development could have been spent promoting brown rice, which is naturally rich in nutrients. Sums of money like this could have been used to encourage farmers to grow vegetables in addition to rice. Even Gordon Conway, president of the Rockefeller Foundation, which funded research on golden rice, now says, "The public relations uses of golden rice have gone too far . . . . We do not consider golden rice the solution to the vitamin-A deficiency problem."

It is evident that the morality-based campaign put forth to Americans by the biotechnology industry is really just propaganda, which cleverly pulls at our hearts. For Michael Pollan, the author of the recent Times' article, this campaign is more an effort to save the company than to save starving children. The lesson here is a reminder that propaganda does not tell the whole truth. Propaganda uses information and images to manipulate our feelings and cloud our judgment.

Analysis

This essay reveals that the writer has taken useful notes and made excellent use of information in the multiple-choice questions to form a response. The introduction also shows how to move from a general statement to a more specific one for the controlling idea: *A recent propaganda campaign from the biotechnology industry offers an excellent example of how propaganda may be used to influence public opinion.*

Development is excellent here, making extensive use of relevant details to explain both the nature of the product and the campaign to support its use. The writer maintains a tone appropriate to the task by showing how the public relations campaign uses techniques characteristic of propaganda. The argument is also strengthened by the use of a key quotation. Transitions are clear, and the rhetorical question at the end of the second paragraph is particularly effective: *But is this rice the Great Yellow Hope the industry claims?* The use of language here is fluent and often sophisticated: *"wary skepticism," ". . . posing an argument to silence even the toughest critics," ". . . propaganda, which cleverly pulls at our hearts."* Finally, this writer demonstrates skill in composing sentences of varying length and structure to convey meaning, and there are no significant errors in the conventions. This essay meets all the criteria for a high score.

(See pp. 31–35 for a detailed explanation of the rubric for this part of the examination.)

Part B   (7–16)

Note: Refer to Chapter 2 for review and strategy in responding to this part of the examination.

(7) **1** "a primary goal." From the beginning of the article, examples of the importance of shopping to many are offered, our "obsession with acquiring things." The tone of the article makes it clear that Jacobson does not consider it a harmless pastime.

(8) **2** "replacing family activities." These lines cite specifically "spending time with our families and in our communities" as being displaced by consumerism.

(9) **4** "marketing to children." At lines 45–46, critics of consumerism are reported to recommend that "advertising aimed at children should be severely limited at the very least . . . ."

(10) **3** "clothing." The list of examples cited at the end of the paragraph ends with "logos on clothing." This passage makes no reference to furniture, food, or appliances.

(11) **2** "rising unemployment." Moore is quoted here as saying that if "we stopped buying as much as we now do . . . many people would lost their jobs."

(12) **1** "generate new products." Debbie van Opstal is quoted as saying that "consumerism tends to speed the pace of innovation," that is, development of new products.

(13) **3** "1978." This is the first reference in the time line to efforts at regulation of advertising.

(14) **2** "Internet." The most recent entries—for 1999 and 2004—show a dramatic increase in on-line sales of products, from $20 billion to $185 billion. The subtitle of the chart also supports this answer.

(15) **1** "advertising use." Because the time line includes citations to show the growth of radio and television as influences on consumerism, it is implied that advertising is responsible for the growth in consumerism.

(16) **4** "buying on credit." The entries for 1000, 1006, and 1999 show the rapid growth of consumer debt in the United States, doubling for individual households in that period.

Part B   Sample Student Response Essay

In today's world, people are consuming products in the market more eagerly than ever before. Society seems to constantly be waiting for the next great innovation to arrive, ready to purchase it. This is especially true in the United States, where the advertising industry relentlessly tries to tell consumers what they want and need. Many argue that consumerism is of great benefit to society, but others feel that it is, in fact, a source of great harm. The benefits of consumerism to our economy are clearly evident, but its negative aspects far outweigh the positive ones.

Those who argue that the effects of consumerism are mostly positive claim that consumer buying is necessary to maintain a healthy and prosperous economy. This view is supported by the fact that consumerism certainly accounts for the employment of countless individuals who would not otherwise have a paycheck. But, for as much economic benefit as a "consumer culture" provides, it also has serious negative consequences. For example, in 1999 credit card debt in the United States exceeded $500 billion, averaging about $4,500 per household, and this total is probably much higher today. Debt of this size can be a real threat to family stability.

Supporters of consumerism also point out that shopping can serve to bring families together, as many view it as a recreational and fun activity. Others, however, see obsession with shopping as a distraction from family life and community activities. Mark Buchanan, another critic of consumerism, says that people "rush out of church on Sunday so that they can go to the mall and shop." As Kathryn C. Montgomery, president of the Center for Media Education, points out, children are constantly demanding that their parents buy things that they see on television advertisements. For many families, these demands lead to conflict or to purchases the family cannot really afford.

Consumer culture has also given individuals the sense that they always need more. Buchanan points out that advertising leads us to "want the newest or the best version of a computer or car or whatever even when we really have no need to replace what we have." Compulsive shopping also seems to come from people feeling the need to buy things for their happiness. Consumerism can be beneficial to our society, but when a society becomes obsessed with shopping, research shows that it harms society more.

Obviously, not all things about consumer culture are bad. Consumerism probably does inspire new innovations, higher-quality products, and it certainly supports jobs for many people. On the other hand, individuals and families need to realize the importance of saving and spending money wisely. Too much time spent enjoying shopping malls, credit cards, and the Internet can put people in financial danger, even bankruptcy. When the negative consequences of consumerism mean families can no longer afford to shop, the entire economy and society can suffer.

Analysis

Though many students chose to argue _tor_ the benefits of consumerism on this task, this essay is successful in presenting an opposing view. This writer is especially skillful in developing the argument by first acknowledging the benefits of consumerism before offering what the writer believes is the stronger evidence for its harmful effects. This strategy is declared in the final sentence of the introduction: _The benefits of consumerism to our economy are clearly evident, but its negative aspects far outweigh the positive ones._ The controlling idea also suggests a thorough understanding of the documents.

Development of the essay is clear and makes use of relevant and specific details from _both_ documents as required. Note how the second and third paragraphs begin with a claim for the benefits of consumerism, which the writer than rebuts with evidence from the texts. The transition to the third paragraph is effective: _"Supporters of consumerism also point out,"_ and the closing sentence is an effective conclusion in capturing a serious, general concern.

The balance of sentence structure is skillful, and the use of language is fluent and appropriate throughout. This writer also demonstrates mastery of the conventions, with few errors. This essay would merit a high score.

(See pp. 48–53 for a detailed discussion of the rubric for this part of the examination.)

Session Two

Part A   (1–10)

Note: See Chapter 3 for review and strategy in responding to this part of the examination.

(1) **3** "appeal to the senses." This paragraph is rich in visual and aural imagery: "hills with wet gold light," "golden-edged clouds," "a shower of echoed sound."

(2) **1** "carefree." The second paragraph of the story reveals that the boy "was delighted with himself"; he is in no hurry, and spends time skipping stones on the lake.

(3) **2** "wandering." To *meander* means to follow an indirect route or course, especially one with a series of twists and turns, or to move in a leisurely way. This is an example of how the Regents exam assesses vocabulary in context.

(4) **4** "guilt." At lines 56–58 the narrative indicates that the boy felt in his heart that "he had done wrong . . . He knew he shouldn't have touched it and . . . wondered [whether] the bird [would] forsake it."

(5) **1** "intensify Colm's feeling." At lines 66–67, the narrative indicates that Colm is proud of having found the nest and is eager to tell his companion about his discovery.

(6) **3** "valuable." The sense of the stanza is that the rain brings forth "new life again" and "the wonder spreads."

(7) **2** "renewal of nature." This theme is developed in images of "new life," "green grasses grow," and "flowers lift their heads."

(8) **4** "personification." This is a form of simile or metaphor in which nonhuman things—in this case flowers and leaves—are given human qualities: flowers lift their heads; new leaves sing.

(9) **1** "celebration." Just as the new leaves "sing in joy," the "passing boys and girls/Go singing, too."

(10) **2** "appreciation." The tone, or general attitude, of the entire poem is one of joy, wonder, and delight, which goes beyond curiosity. There is no sense of disappointment or uncertainty in this poem.

Part A   Sample Student Response Essay

Both the story by Michael McLaverty and the poem by Langston Hughes are a celebration of the beauty and life in nature. Though contrasting in form and in tone, these works dramatize how much there is to appreciate in the natural world. In the story, a curious boy is happily exploring the hills and wetlands near where he lives when he makes a discovery that deepens his love and respect for nature. The poem celebrates the natural gift of rain and the spring renewal of the natural world. Both works serve to reveal the value of the natural world and lead the reader to share in the appreciation of its many wonderful gifts.

The story tells of a young boy's curiosity as well as his deep remorse for the harm he later causes. In the opening paragraph, the rich imagery and sensory detail convey the beauty of the natural world and the boy's delight in it: "The sun was nearing its setting, its soft rays gilding the western limestone headland of Rathlin Island and washing its green hills with wet gold light." The boy is consumed by the beauty of the "golden-edged clouds" and the "reedy lakes." He is also fascinated by the flight of a wild duck and carefully follows to where it has landed. As he wades in the lake, "his feet sank in the mud and bubbles winked up at him." All seems beautiful and peaceful during the boy's exploration as he finally discovers the duck's nest. He admires the nest for several moments and is delighted and surprised to discover a single egg, "smooth and green as the sky, with a faint tinge of yellow . . . ." "And then he felt he had done wrong." At this point, the tone of the story changes, as "a vague sadness stole over him." He knew not to touch the egg, and he regrets the fact that the mother bird might "forsake" it. Colm flees the scene, feeling sadness, regret, and guilt.

When Colm later sees his friend, he is eager to share what he has discovered. When Peadar is finally convinced that this really was a wild duck's nest, he shouts at Colm, "She'll forsake!" The omniscient narrator tells us that Colm feared Peadar was right but in his heart he is determined that she'll not forsake: "She'll not. I know she'll not!"

When Colm returns, hoping to see that the duck is still there, he accidentally startles her and when she takes off, the egg falls and breaks. Colm is overwhelmed to see the "yellow slime" on the rock and flees the disaster filled with guilt and regret. Where once Colm's exploration of nature was filled with golden light and beauty, "a throbbing silence enveloped him as if everything had gone from the earth leaving him alone."

The poem "In Time of Silver Rain" is also a celebration of the natural world and the miracles that emanate from it. In the first stanza, the gifts of nature are expressed through personification and repetition: "the flowers lift their heads," and at the end, the poet voices "of life, of life, of life!" This repetition serves to reflect the wonderful joy of life that rain brings to the natural world. It causes new life to arise, flowers to grow, and spreads happiness everywhere. In the poem, there is no shift in tone as the second stanza continues to celebrate the wonders of nature. Here too there is personification as new leaves "sing." The energy of nature putting forth "new life again" is conveyed in the short lines, rhymes with the word "rain" or "cry" and "sky," and in the repetition of the opening line "In time of silver rain."

Primarily through imagery and tone, the authors of these two passages convey the theme that the natural world is filled with life and beauty. They urge us to appreciate and celebrate that beauty.

Analysis

The second sentence here—*Though contrasting in form and in tone, these works dramatize how much there is to appreciate in the natural world*—both establishes a controlling idea for the essay and reveals the writer's recognition of important literary elements. In the rest of the essay, key themes are developed with specific references to imagery, narration, personification, and repetition.

The introduction demonstrates that the writer has made a thorough analysis of the two works, and the opening of the final paragraph offers an insightful connection between the two: *The poem ... is also a celebration of the natural world and the miracles that emanate from it.* The discussion of the story is the more fully developed, which is justified by its length and greater complexity; the discussion of the poem is brief but captures well its themes and effective use of imagery. Language throughout the essay is precise and engaging, notably in expressing the feelings of the boy in the story: *delighted and surprised; determined; feeling sadness, regret and guilt,* and in describing the meaning of the two works: *Both works serve to reveal the value of the natural world and lead the reader to share in the appreciation of its many wonderful gifts.*

This writer demonstrates skill in using a variety of sentence structures to good effect, and there are no significant errors in the conventions. This essay meets all the criteria for a high score.

(See pp. 68–71 for a detailed discussion of the rubric for this part of the examination.)

Session Two

Note: See Chapter 4 for review and strategy in responding to this part of the examination.

Part B   Sample Student Response Essay

Bernadette Devlin once stated, "To gain that which is worth having it may be necessary to lose everything else." Indeed, through experiencing severe challenges or devastating sorrow and loss, the individual may very well gain insight into the world around him, understanding of others, or possibly embark on a journey of self-discovery and enlightenment. Two literary works that illustrate the meaning of this statement are the novel Great Expectations *by Charles Dickens and the play* The Crucible *by Arthur Miller. It is through characterization and setting that these works develop their most important themes.*

Through the character of Pip, the protagonist, Dickens introduces an individual who is lost and unable to recognize the worth of what he has. Although Joe, Pip's common blacksmith brother-in-law, gives Pip love, guidance, and friendship, Pip is ashamed of Joe's ignorance and lack of fortune. Once Pip comes into a great deal of money from a secret benefactor, whom he believes to be the rich and eccentric Miss Havisham, he abandons Joe and moves to the city. There Pip begins to find delight in attending lavish parties, spending money on material things, and conversing with other shallow members of the London aristocracy. Pip develops into a proud and cold young man, ashamed of his past and mortified by his connection to the innocent and loving blacksmith, Joe. Pip's world of privilege and aristocratic pretensions comes tumbling down when Pip discovers that his secret benefactor is not of social standing but rather is a criminal Pip gave aid to as a child.

Losing his status and respectability in the shallow society he admired, Pip is humbled. He also comes to realize that his relationship with Joe, the only truly good person he has ever known, was nearly destroyed by his own arrogance. As Pip loses everything, he undergoes a personal transformation, recognizing his past transgressions and coming to understand that a life of love and goodness is much more valuable than a life of material wealth and social standing.

Great loss is also dramatized in Arthur Miller's The Crucible. *Set in colonial Massachusetts during the time of the infamous witch trials, this play relates the events of one fateful summer in the Puritan town of Salem. The setting creates the environment of religious authority and hysteria of the times. Although there is great danger in speaking out against the accusations of witchcraft, several brave individuals display courage and strength of conviction in challenging what they believe to be false accusations. One such individual is John Proctor, a flawed character whose conscience is troubled by past infidelity to his wife. Proctor knows that the chief accuser, a young woman named Abigail, is creating stories of witchcraft among some of the women in the town out of fear of punishment for herself and others. It is with Abigail that Proctor had once had an affair.*

When Abigail charges Proctor's own wife, Proctor has the courage to expose Abigail and the fraud of the witch trials. In doing so he must admit to adultery and be condemned by the people of Salem. When Proctor himself is accused and is given the opportunity to save himself by admitting to witchcraft, he refuses. Proctor accepts hanging because he cannot give his good name to what he knows are false accusations and conviction of others who are innocent.

Both works help to illustrate that great loss may be necessary in order to gain something of greater worth. In the case of Pip in Great Expectations *the loss of superficial social position and underserved wealth made Pip a humble and compassionate person, able to appreciate his relationship with people who truly and honestly loved him. John Proctor loses his life but redeems himself of past sins and challenges the injustice of proceedings that condemned innocent victims. These two characters recognize injustice and falsity in their worlds and in suffering great loss, they achieve greater understanding and meaning in their lives.*

Analysis

This writer has made good choices of literary works to develop the controlling idea, an elaboration of the prompt found in the second sentence. The discussion that follows offers examples of the key terms: *insight into the world, understanding of others*, and *self-discovery*. The last sentence in the introduction clearly identifies the literary elements that will be implicit in the development and assures that the essay does not rely on plot summary alone: *It is through characterization and setting that these works develop their most important themes.*

Ideas are fully and effectively developed, and in discussion of both works there is skillful integration of accounts of the characters' actions with references to their respective settings: *"Losing his status and respectability in the shallow society he admired, Pip is humbled." "The setting creates the environment of religious authority and hysteria of the times."* The essay is coherent in a two-part structure and maintains focus on the interpretation of the critical lens through to the concluding sentence: *These two characters recognize injustice and falsity in their worlds and in suffering great loss, they achieve greater understanding and meaning in their lives.*

The writer demonstrates skill and varying sentence structures to enhance meaning and shows control of the conventions. This essay fits all the criteria for a high score.

(See pp. 80–83 for a detailed discussion of the rubric for this part of the examination.)

Examination June 2007
English

Session One

Part A

Overview: For this part of the test, you will listen to an account about the power of books, answer some multiple-choice questions, and write a response based on the situation described below. You will hear the account twice. You may take notes on the page alloted anytime you wish during the readings.

> **The Situation:** To open the local library's book fair, you have been asked to give a speech about the power of books. In preparation for writing your speech, listen to an account by author Gary Paulsen. Then use relevant information from the account to write your speech.

Your Task: Write a speech for the local library's book fair in which you discuss the power of books.

Guidelines:
Be sure to

- Tell your audience what they need to know about the power of books
- Use specific, accurate, and relevant information from the account to support your discussion
- Use a tone and level of language appropriate for a speech at a local library's book fair
- Organize your ideas in a logical and coherent manner
- Indicate any words taken directly from the account by using quotation marks or referring to the speaker
- Follow the conventions of standard written English

Note: For this portion of the examination, the teacher will read a passage aloud. You will not actually see the passage reprinted below. Therefore, you are encouraged to have someone read the passage to you, in order to simulate the examination as closely as possible.

Listening Passage

Books saved my life.

First reading them, then writing them.

As surely as my lead dog Cookie pulled me from the bottom of a lake after I fell through the ice, books are the reason I survived my miserable childhood. As certainly as my sloop Scallywag has safely taken me through storms and huge seas, books have sustained me as an adult.

The awfulness of my childhood has been well covered. But I remember two women who took the time to help me when I was a boy and both women, not so coincidentally, helped me with books.

Because I lived from the age of seven to when I was nearly ten in the Philippine Islands and had a private military tutor, I had never been to a public school.

We came back to the States when I was just short of ten and moved to Washington, D.C., so my father, who was in the army, could work at the Pentagon. My mother promptly enrolled me in public school, took me there the first morning, handed me over to a teacher, and left.

I was painfully shy, terrified at the mob of kids and could not go into the room. It was an old school and at the back of the classroom, there was a cloakroom, a shallow closet the width of the room but closed in except for one door. I went in the closet and took my coat off with the rest of the children but then I could not leave, simply could not make my legs move to walk out into the classroom. I was too frightened.

There were many things the teacher could have done wrong. She could have forced me out, dragged me into the classroom, could have made me leave. Instead she did everything right.

She looked into the closet, saw me sitting back in the corner and disappeared for a moment and said something to the children. Then she came back into the closet and sat down next to me in the corner and put her arm around me.

She had a book, a picture book. I cannot recall the contents of the book except that it had a horse's head on the cover and she sat next to me quietly for a time and read to me softly and let me turn the pages. I was lost in the quiet of the cloakroom, lost in the book so deeply that everything else fell away.

After a time, it could have been ten minutes or an hour or my whole life, she asked me if I thought I could come out into the room and take my seat at a desk. I nodded and she stood and took my hand and led me into the classroom.

A few years later, when I was thirteen, another woman, a librarian, gave me another book and I consider every good thing that has ever happened to me since then a result of that woman handing me that book.

I'd been wandering the streets of the small Minnesota town we lived in one bitter winter evening, waiting for the drunks in the bars to get juiced. I sold newspapers, trying to scrape together a little money so that I could buy better clothes, believing, as kids do, that the right clothes might somehow lift me from my wretchedly unpopular social life. And if I waited for the men who hung around in the bars to get a few drinks in them, I could hustle them for extra change.

I stopped in the library to warm up. The librarian noticed me, called me over, and asked if I wanted a library card. Then she handed me a card with my name on it and gave me a book.

Later that night back at home, or what passed for home—a crummy apartment in the bad part of town—I took the book, a box of crackers, and a jar of grape jelly down to the basement, to a hideaway I'd created behind the furnace where someone had abandoned a creaky old armchair under a bare lightbulb.

I sat in the corner, eating jelly-smeared crackers, plodding through the book. It took me forever to read. I was such a poor reader that, by the time I'd finished a page, I'd have forgotten what I'd read on the page before and I'd have to go back. That first book must have taken me over a month to finish, hunched over the pages late at night.

I wish I could remember the name of that first book—I can't even remember what it was about. What I do remember about that evening at the library was that it marked the first of many nights the librarian would give me a book. "Here," she'd say, handing me a few battered volumes, "I think you'll like these." She would hand select books that she thought would interest me—Westerns, mysteries, survival tales, science fiction, Edgar Rice Burroughs. I would take them home to hide in the basement and read; I'd bring them back and we'd talk about them, and she'd give me more books.

But she wasn't just giving me books, she was giving me ... everything. She gave me the first hint I'd ever had in my entire life that there was something other than my drunken parents screaming at each other in the kitchen. She handed me a world where I wasn't going to get beaten up by the school bullies. She showed me places where it didn't hurt all the time.

I read terribly at first but as I did more of it, the books became more a part of me and within a short time they gave me a life, a look at life outside myself that made me look forward instead of backward.

Years later, after I'd graduated from high school, joined the army, gotten married, had children, and made a career as an electronics engineer working in satellite tracking, books once again changed the course of my life. This time, though, I wrote them.

I was sitting in a satellite tracking station at about nine o'clock at night when suddenly I knew that I had to be a writer. In that instant, I gave up or lost everything that had made up my life until that point—my work, my family, certainly my earning potential.

Writing had suddenly become everything ... everything ... to me.

I stood up from the console, handed in my security badge, and headed for Hollywood. I had to go to a place where I knew writers were; I had to be near them, had to learn from them. I got a job as a proofreader of a men's magazine, going from earning $500 a week to $400 a month, and apprenticed myself to a couple of editors.

These two men gave me writing assignments, and in order to continue receiving their help, I had to write an article, a chapter of a book, or a short story every night, every single night, no exceptions, no excuses, for them to critique. If I missed a single day, they would no longer help me.

I have been writing for over thirty years, spent most of it starving, trying to make it work for me, in my mind; trying to make words come together in the right patterns, movements, what some have called the loops and whorls of the story dance, and it has always been hard. It is, sometimes, still difficult. But I love writing more now, I think, than I ever have. The way the stories dance, the rhythms and movements of them, is grandly exciting to me. ...

— excerpted from *Shelf Life: Stories by the Book,* 2003
Simon and Schuster Books for Young Readers

Notes

Multiple-Choice Questions

Directions (1–6): Use your notes to answer the following questions about the passage read to you. Select the best suggested answer and write its number in the space provided. The questions may help you think about ideas and information you might use in your writing. You may return to these questions anytime you wish.

1 The speaker begins his account by stating that books have the potential to

   (1) excite   (3) rescue
   (2) educate   (4) accommodate   1____

2 At age 13, Paulsen entered the library in order to

   (1) get warm   (3) meet friends
   (2) borrow a book   (4) escape pursuers   2____

3 Paulsen would most likely characterize his home life as

   (1) supportive   (3) enriching
   (2) dull   (4) chaotic   3____

4 Paulsen moved to Hollywood in order to

   (1) forget his childhood
   (2) follow his dream
   (3) improve his health
   (4) increase his salary   4____

5 Paulsen sought to improve his writing through

   (1) a college course
   (2) a personal journal
   (3) an informal apprenticeship
   (4) an enlightening trip   5____

6 According to the account, after thirty years of writing, Gary Paulsen views his craft as

(1) stimulating   (3) distracting

(2) relaxing   (4) predictable   6 ____

After you have finished these questions, review **The Situation** and read **Your Task** and the **Guidelines.** Use scrap paper to plan your response. Then write your response on separate sheets of paper. After you finish your response for Part A, complete Part B.

Part B

Directions: Read the text and study the graphic on the following pages, answer the multiple-choice questions, and write a response based on the situation described below. You may use the margins to take notes as you read and scrap paper to plan your response.

> **The Situation:** As part of a unit on contemporary issues, your science class is preparing a panel discussion on the social responsibility of scientists. In preparing for the panel discussion, your teacher has asked you to write an essay in which you discuss what volcanologists are doing to lessen the dangers of volcanic eruptions.

Your Task: Using relevant information from *both* documents, write an essay for your science class in which you discuss what volcanologists are doing to lessen the dangers of volcanic eruptions.

Guidelines:
Be sure to
- Tell your audience what they need to know about what volcanologists are doing to lessen the dangers of volcanic eruptions
- Use specific, accurate, and relevant information from the text *and* the graphic to support your discussion
- Use a tone and level of language appropriate for an essay for your science class
- Organize your ideas in a logical and coherent manner
- Indicate any words taken directly from the text by using quotation marks or referring to the author
- Follow the conventions of standard written English

Text

...There are about 1,500 active volcanoes, not counting hundreds more under the oceans, and any of them could erupt at any time, said Dr. Tom Casadevall, western regional director of the United States Geological Survey in Menlo Park, Calif[ornia]. Of the 1,500, 583 have exploded within the last 400 years, making
(5) them particularly dangerous. Each year, scientists observe 50 to 60 volcanoes in various stages of eruption, some gently extruding lava like red hot toothpaste down hillsides, others heaving molten rock particles and noxious gases many miles up into the atmosphere.

The number of people living on the sides of volcanoes and in the valleys
(10) below has skyrocketed, said Dr. Stanley Williams, a volcanologist at Arizona State University in Tempe. At least 500 million people live dangerously close to volcanoes, he said. Many dwell in megacities in Asia and Latin America — Tokyo, Manila, Jakarta, Mexico City, Quito — or in cities of at least a million people. Here in the United States, the people of Seattle and Tacoma live in the
(15) shadow of Mount Rainier, a 13,000-foot volcano whose mudflows have swept through the places where the cities are situated....

Most of the time, the people who colonize danger areas do not know any better. And the people who do know better, scientists and civil disaster officials, "are not always listened to," said Dr. Grant Heiken, a volcanologist at the Los
(20) Alamos National Laboratory in New Mexico.

For example, scientists issued a warning when a high volcano, capped with ice, began rumbling in the mountains of Colombia in 1985. On Nov[ember] 13, the icecap exploded above the town of Novado del Ruiz. The eruption melted snow fields that picked up debris and went roaring down the side of the volcano
(25) toward the villages 30 to 40 miles away. The residents were warned that night that a large volcanic mudflow was on the way, Dr. Heiken said. "But it was raining," he said. "People said, 'Why worry, the volcano is far away.' They had only to walk 100 yards to a hill to be safe. That night, 26,000 people died."

Scientists were horrified, said Dr. Chris Newhall, a volcanologist at the
(30) United States Geological Survey at the University of Washington in Seattle. This episode and other natural disasters prompted the United Nations to declare the 1990's the International Decade of Natural Hazard Reduction, he said. "The notion was, look, the world population is growing, the hazards are not getting any less," he said. "People are moving into marginal lands that are more prone to
(35) disasters — volcanoes, floods, earthquakes and hurricanes. The basic idea was to encourage countries to take a hard look at the hazards that their populations were facing and to undertake projects to try and reduce risks."

But the United Nations did not have money for the program, Dr. Newhall said. The International Decade of Hazard Reduction has existed in name only.

(40)   So the scientists began taking action on their own. Under the auspices of the International Association of Volcanology and Chemistry of the Earth's Interior, "we volcanologists got together and scratched our heads for ideas," Dr. Newhall said. "We came up with three."

     First, they made a video that depicts what volcanoes can do to people and
(45) property, with such horrifying accuracy that it is not recommended for children under 15. It is being shown to mayors and other public officials in charge of getting people to evacuate when volcanoes threaten to explode.

     Second, the scientists picked 15 volcanoes around the world to study intensely. These so-called decade volcanoes are near large population centers
(50) and could erupt any time. Workshops have been held at most of them, bringing together scientists and disaster relief officials from the local regions.

     Third, there has been an effort to make better predictions of when volcanoes will erupt, using new scientific instruments and insights.

     Although real progress has been made, volcanologists face a couple of
(55) intractable[1] problems, Dr. Williams said. One is the tendency for people to deny danger even when it is obvious. Also, once a threat is passed, they tend to dismiss it. "They forget that grandma once told a story about how her grandmother was killed by a volcano," he said. And second is the sheer perversity[2] of volcanoes. They may show all the signs and symptoms of erupting and then quiet down,
(60) leading the public to accuse scientists of "crying wolf."...

     The major cause of death in volcanoes is not hot lava or rivers of mud, but rather glowing clouds of super-hot gas and ash particles that silently sweep down the volcano's flank and across the countryside at 60 miles an hour, vaporizing everything in their path. These pyroclastic[3] flows can knock down stone walls 10
(65) feet thick and have killed thousands of people in less than two minutes, he said.

     In the movies, people outrun the flows, but in real life, the flows desiccate[4] the flesh and fry the lungs of everyone in their path. Ninety-eight percent of the people in Guatemala live on the surface of a pyroclastic flow that raced over the countryside 75,000 years ago, Dr. Williams said.

(70)   From watching volcano movies and films of the rather gentle and atypical volcanoes in Hawaii, people think they can walk away from danger, Dr. Heiken said. The volcanologists' video shows otherwise. It is very blunt and shows dead bodies, he said. "When people see it, they gulp and say, 'Could that really happen here? How far did you say the town was from that volcano?'"

---

[1]intractable — not easily managed
[2]perversity — defying reason
[3]pyroclastic — formed as a result of volcanic action
[4]desiccate — dry out

(75)   In 1991, a rough cut of the newly made video was rushed to the Philippines, where Mount Pinatubo was threatening to erupt. The day after it was shown on television, 50,000 people evacuated voluntarily. A few days later, the volcano erupted, spewing 12 cubic kilometers of material. "We are convinced that the video saved tens of thousands of lives,"Dr. Heiken said.

(80)   Getting the word out and convincing people to evacuate is a huge challenge, Dr. Williams said. Ultimately, whether people live or die depends as much on communication as on science. "We try to teach people how not to freak out," he said. "They think falling ash is lethal, but it's not. The problem is that the ash is three times heavier than water so their roof can collapse in hours. We teach

(85) people to get under the strongest table in the room, near the corner. The air is full of static electricity, so radios and traffic lights go haywire and they get scared."

Such public education saves lives, Dr. Heiken said. In September 1994, a volcano at Rabaul in Papua New Guinea destroyed 75 percent of the homes in the city. But because the citizens had been trained in evacuation procedures,

(90) they did not panic and got away safely. Only five people died....

—Sandra Blakeslee
excerpted from"Facing the Peril of Earth's
Cauldrons, Scientists Try to Save Lives"
The New York Times, August 26, 1997

GRAPHIC

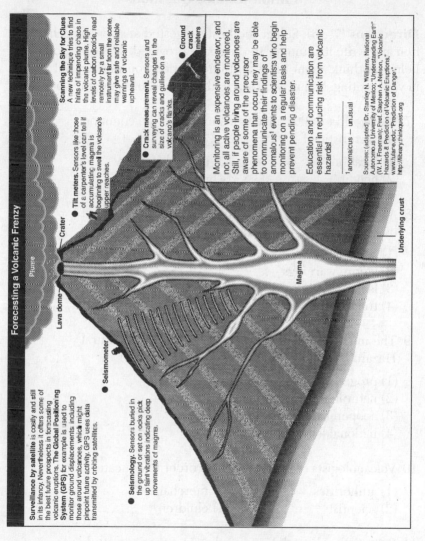

Forecasting a Volcanic Frenzy

Surveillance by satellite is costly and still in its infancy. Nevertheless it offers some of the best future prospects in forecasting volcanic eruptions. The **Global Positioning System (GPS)** for example is used to monitor ground displacements including those around volcanoes, which might pinpoint future activity. GPS uses data transmitted by orbiting satellites.

Seismology. Sensors buried in the ground or set on rocks pick up faint vibrations indicating deep movements of magma.

Tilt meters. Sensors like those of a carpenter's level can tell if accumulating magma is beginning to swell the volcano's upper reaches.

Scanning the Sky for Clues A new technique tries to find hints of impending chaos in the volcanic plume. High levels of carbon dioxide, read remotely by a small instrument far from the scene, may give safe and reliable warnings of volcanic upheaval.

Crack measurement. Sensors and surveying can reveal changes in the size of cracks and gullies on a volcano's flanks.

Ground crack meters

Plume
Crater
Lava dome
Seismometer
Magma
Underlying crust

Monitoring is an expensive endeavor, and not all active volcanoes are monitored. Still, if people living around volcanoes are aware of some of the precursor phenomena that occur, they may be able to communicate their findings of anomalous[1] events to scientists who begin monitoring on a regular basis and help prevent pending disaster.

Education and communication are essential in reducing risk from volcanic hazards!

[1] anomalous — unusual

Sources: (adapted) Dr. Stanley N. Williams, National Autonomus University of Mexico; "Understanding Earth" (W. H. Freeman); Fred, Stephen A. Nelson, "Volcanic Hazards & Prediction of Volcanic Eruptions," www.tulane.edu; "Prediction of Danger," http://library.thinkquest.org

Multiple-Choice Questions

Directions (7–16): Select the best suggested answer to each question and write its number in the space provided. The questions may help you think about ideas and information you might want to use in your writing. You may return to these questions anytime you wish.

7 The world's 1,500 active volcanoes have the common characteristic of

(1) location	(3) unpredictability
(2) height	(4) unattractiveness

7 _____

8 According to the text, people are often victimized by volcanoes because people

(1) believe myths
(2) ignore warnings
(3) lack transportation
(4) treasure valuables

8 _____

9 The mission of the International Decade of Natural Hazard Reduction was threatened by a lack of

(1) program funding
(2) natural disasters
(3) cooperative scientists
(4) national legislation

9 _____

10 Volcanologists created a video in order to educate

(1) authorities	(3) merchants
(2) scientists	(4) children

10 _____

11 Scientists selected 15 "decade volcanoes" to study because these were

(1) less researched	(3) easily accessible
(2) essentially dormant	(4) most threatening

11 _____

12 "Pyroclastic flows" (line 64) are dangerous because of their

(1) weight   (3) noise

(2) speed   (4) unpredictability   12 _____

13 The text indicates that the eruptions of Mt. Pinatubo and Rabaul were unusual because of the

(1) amount of property saved

(2) number of warnings issued

(3) number of residents evacuated

(4) amount of data obtained   13 _____

14 According to the graphic, seismometers measure

(1) distance   (3) fumes

(2) heat   (4) motion   14 _____

15 According to the graphic, satellite monitoring of volcanoes is

(1) temporary   (3) erroneous

(2) promising   (4) traditional   15 _____

16 According to the graphic, where are tilt meters and crack measurement sensors placed?

(1) along the slopes   (3) high in the air

(2) within the crater   (4) under the magma   16 _____

After you have finished these questions, review **The Situation** and read **Your Task** and the **Guidelines**. Use scrap paper to plan your response. Then write your response to Part B on separate sheets of paper.

Session Two

Part A

Directions: Read the passages on the following pages (a fable and an excerpt from an autobiography). Write the number of the answer to each multiple-choice question in the space provided. Then write the essay on separate sheets of paper as described in **Your Task**. You may use the margins to take notes as you read and scrap paper to plan your response.

Your Task:

> After you have read the passages and answered the multiple-choice questions, write a unified essay about lessons learned as revealed in the passages. In your essay, use ideas from **both** passages to establish a controlling idea about lessons learned. Using evidence from **each** passage, develop your controlling idea and show how the author uses specific literary elements or techniques to convey that idea.

Guidelines:
Be sure to
- Use ideas from **both** passages to establish a controlling idea about lessons learned
- Use specific and relevant evidence from **each** passage to develop your controlling idea
- Show how each author uses specific literary elements (for example: theme, characterization, structure, point of view) or techniques (for example: symbolism, irony, figurative language) to convey the controlling idea
- Organize your ideas in a logical and coherent manner
- Use language that communicates ideas effectively
- Follow the conventions of standard written English

Passage I

A man ambushed a stone. Caught it. Made it a prisoner. Put it in a dark room and stood guard over it for the rest of his life.

His mother asked why.

He said, because it's held captive, because it is the captured.

(5)   Look, the stone is asleep, she said, it does not know whether it's in a garden or not. Eternity and the stone are mother and daughter; it is you who are getting old. The stone is only sleeping.

But I caught it, mother, it is mine by conquest, he said.

A stone is nobody's, not even its own. It is you who are conquered; you are

(10) minding the prisoner, which is yourself, because you are afraid to go out, she said.

Yes, yes, I am afraid, because you have never loved me, he said.

Which is true, because you have always been to me as the stone is to you, she said.

— Russell Edson
from *A Stone is Nobody's*, 1961
Thing Press

Passage II

…Once, when I was the only child at home, my mother went to Danang[1] to visit Uncle Nhu, and my father had to take care of me. I woke up from my nap in the empty house and cried for my mother. My father came in from the yard and reassured me, but I was still cranky and continued crying. Finally, he gave

(5)   me a rice cookie to shut me up. Needless to say, this was a tactic my mother never used.

The next afternoon I woke up and although I was not feeling cranky, I thought a rice cookie might be nice. I cried a fake cry and my father came running in.

(10) "What's this?" he asked, making a worried face. "Little Bay Ly doesn't want a cookie?"

I was confused again.

"Look under your pillow," he said with a smile.

I twisted around and saw that, while I was sleeping, he had placed a rice

(15) cookie under my pillow. We both laughed and he picked me up like a sack of rice and carried me outside while I gobbled the cookie.

In the yard, he plunked me down under a tree and told me some stories. After that, he got some scraps of wood and showed me how to make things: a doorstop for my mother and a toy duck for me. This was unheard of—a father *(20)* doing these things with a child that was not a son! Where my mother would instruct me on cooking and cleaning and tell stories about brides, my father showed me the mystery of hammers and explained the customs of our people.

His knowledge of the Vietnamese went back to the Chinese Wars in ancient times. I learned how one of my distant ancestors, a woman named Phung Thi *(25)* Chinh, led Vietnamese fighters against the Han[2]. In one battle, even though she was pregnant and surrounded by Chinese, she delivered the baby, tied it to her back, and cut her way to safety wielding a sword in each hand. I was amazed at this warrior's bravery and impressed that I was her descendant. Even more, I was amazed and impressed by my father's pride in her accomplishments (she was, *(30)* after all, a humble female) and his belief that I was worthy of her example. "*Con phai theo got chan co ta*" (Follow in her footsteps), he said. Only later would I learn what he truly meant.

Never again did I cry after my nap. Phung Thi women were too strong for that. Besides, I was my father's daughter and we had many things to do together.

(35) On the eve of my mother's return, my father cooked a feast of roast duck. When we sat down to eat it, I felt guilty and my feelings showed on my face. He asked why I acted so sad.

"You've killed one of mother's ducks," I said. "One of the fat kind she sells at the market. She says the money buys gold which she saves for her daughters' *(40)* weddings. Without gold for a dowry—*con o gia*—I will be an old maid!"

My father looked suitably concerned, then brightened and said, "Well, Bay Ly, if you can't get married, you will just have to live at home forever with me!"

I clapped my hands at the happy prospect.

My father cut into the rich, juicy bird and said, "Even so, we won't tell your *(45)* mother about the duck, okay?"

I giggled and swore myself to secrecy.

The next day, I took some water out to him in the fields. My mother was due home any time and I used every opportunity to step outside and watch for her. My father stopped working, drank gratefully, then took my hand and led me to the *(50)* top of a nearby hill. It had a good view of the village and the land beyond it, almost to the ocean. I thought he was going to show me my mother coming back, but he had something else in mind.

He said, "Bay Ly, you see all this here? This is the Vietnam we have been

---

[1]Danang — seaport in central Vietnam
[2]Han — Chinese Dynasty

(55) talking about. You understand that a country is more than a lot of dirt, rivers, and forests, don't you?"

I said, "Yes, I understand." After all, we had learned in school that one's country is as sacred as a father's grave.

(60) "Good. You know, some of these lands are battlefields where your brothers and cousins are fighting. They may never come back. Even your sisters have all left home in search of a better life. You are the only one left in my house. If the enemy comes back, you must be both a daughter and a son. I told you how the Chinese used to rule our land. People in this village had to risk their lives diving in the ocean just to find pearls for the Chinese emperor's gown. They had to risk tigers and snakes in the jungle just to find herbs for his table. Their payment for (65) this hardship was a bowl of rice and another day of life. That is why Le Loi, Gia Long, the Trung Sisters, and Phung Thi Chinh fought so hard to expel the Chinese. When the French came, it was the same old story. Your mother and I were taken to Danang to build a runway for their airplanes. We labored from sunup to sundown and well after dark. If we stopped to rest or have a smoke, a (70) Moroccan would come up and whip our behinds. Our reward was a bowl of rice and another day of life. Freedom is never a gift, Bay Ly. It must be won and won again. Do you understand?"

I said that I did.

"Good." He moved his finger from the patchwork of brown dikes, silver (75) water, and rippling stalks to our house at the edge of the village. "This land here belongs to me. Do you know how I got it?"

I thought a moment, trying to remember my mother's stories, then said honestly, "I can't remember."

He squeezed me lovingly. "I got it from your mother."

(80) "What? That can't be true!" I said. Everyone in the family knew my mother was poor and my father's family was wealthy. Her parents were dead and she had to work like a slave for her mother-in-law to prove herself worthy. Such women don't have land to give away!

"It's true." My father's smile widened. "When I was a young man, my parents (85) needed someone to look after their lands. They had to be very careful about who they chose as wives for their three sons. In the village, your mother had a reputation as the hardest worker of all. She raised herself and her brothers without parents. At the same time, I noticed a beautiful woman working in the fields. When my mother said she was going to talk to the matchmaker about this (90) hard-working village girl she'd heard about, my heart sank. I was too attracted to this mysterious tall woman I had seen in the rice paddies. You can imagine my surprise when I found out the girl my mother heard about and the woman I admired were the same.

"Well, we were married and my mother tested your mother severely. She not
(95) only had to cook and clean and know everything about children, but she had to
be able to manage several farms and know when and how to take the extra produce
to the market. Of course, she was testing her other daughters-in-law as well.

When my parents died, they divided their several farms among their sons, but you
know what? They gave your mother and me the biggest share because they knew
(100) we would take care of it best. That's why I say the land came from her, because
it did."

I suddenly missed my mother very much and looked down the road to the
south, hoping to see her. My father noticed my sad expression.

"Hey." He poked me in the ribs. "Are you getting hungry for lunch?" ...

— Le Ly Hayslip with Jay Wurts
excerpted from *When Heaven and Earth Changed Places*, 1989
Doubleday

Multiple-Choice Questions

Directions (1–10): Select the best suggested answer to each question and write its number in the space provided. The questions may help you think about the ideas and information you might want to use in your essay. You may return to these questions anytime you wish.

Passage I (the fable) — Questions 1–4 refer to Passage I.

1 According to the mother, when one takes a prisoner, one becomes

(1) cruel   (3) safe
(2) captive   (4) heroic   1 _____

2 Line 8 reveals that the adult son thinks of himself as a

(1) victor   (3) fool
(2) destroyer   (4) fugitive   2 _____

3 In lines 11 through 13 the mother and the adult son are disagreeing over

(1) jealousy   (3) punishment
(2) debt   (4) control   3 _____

4 The fable is primarily developed through the use of

(1) dialogue   (3) suspense
(2) allusion   (4) description   4 _____

Passage II (the autobiographical excerpt) — Questions 5–10 refer to Passage II.

5 The incidents involving the rice cookies suggest the father's

(1) thriftiness   (3) thoughtfulness
(2) industry   (4) daring   5 _____

6 The father's interactions with Bay Ly reveal his disregard for

   (1) technological farming
   (2) historical fiction
   (3) international relations
   (4) gender roles   6 _____

7 Which words suggest that the story of Phung Thi Chinh influenced the narrator?

   (1) "I was her descendant" (line 28)
   (2) "Never again did I cry after my nap" (line 33)
   (3) "I was my father's daughter" (line 34)
   (4) "I took some water out to him" (line 47)   7 _____

8 The lesson taught in school "that one's country is as sacred as a father's grave" (lines 56 and 57) relates to

   (1) theology
   (2) economics
   (3) literature
   (4) patriotism   8 _____

9 In calling "a bowl of rice and another day of life" (lines 65 and 70 and 71) both payment and reward, the father is emphasizing the

   (1) continuing struggle of the people
   (2) generous benefits of governments
   (3) limited capacity of the land
   (4) appropriate gratitude of farmers   9 _____

10 What characteristic was most important in the arranged marriage of Bay Ly's parents?

(1) their personal happiness
(2) their political connections
(3) her hard work
(4) his social status   10 _____

After you have finished these questions, review **Your Task** and the **Guidelines.** Use scrap paper to plan your response. Then write your response to Part A on separate sheets of paper. After you finish your response for Part A, complete Part B.

Part B

Your Task:
Write a critical essay in which you discuss *two* works of literature you have read from the particular perspective of the statement that is provided for you in the **Critical Lens**. In your essay, provide a valid interpretation of the statement, agree *or* disagree with the statement as you have interpreted it, and support your opinion using specific references to appropriate literary elements from the two works. You may use scrap paper to plan your response. Write your essay in Part B on separate sheets of paper.

Critical Lens:

> "For what does it mean to be a hero? It requires you to be prepared to deal with forces larger than yourself."
>
> —Norman Mailer
> *The Spooky Art*, 2003

Guidelines:
Be sure to
- Provide a valid interpretation of the critical lens that clearly establishes the criteria for analysis
- Indicate whether you agree *or* disagree with the statement as you have interpreted it
- Choose *two* works you have read that you believe best support your opinion
- Use the criteria suggested by the critical lens to analyze the works you have chosen
- Avoid plot summary. Instead, use specific references to appropriate literary elements (for example: theme, characterization, setting, point of view) to develop your analysis
- Organize your ideas in a unified and coherent manner
- Specify the titles and authors of the literature you choose
- Follow the conventions of standard written English

Regents Comprehensive Examination in English—June 2007
Chart for Determining the Final Examination Score (Use for June 2007 examination only.)

To determine the student's final examination score, locate the student's total essay score across the top of the chart and the student's total multiple-choice score down the side of the chart. The point where those two scores intersect is the student's final examination score. For example, a student receiving a total essay score of 16 and a total multiple-choice score of 19 would receive a final examination score of 70.

Total Essay Score → Total Multiple-Choice Score ↓	0	1	2	3	4	5	6	7	8	9	10	11	12	13	14	15	16	17	18	19	20	21	22	23	24
0	0	1	1	2	3	4	5	7	9	11	14	17	20	23	27	31	34	38	41	46	50	54	58	61	65
1	1	1	2	2	3	4	6	8	10	13	16	19	22	25	29	32	36	40	43	48	52	56	59	63	67
2	1	1	2	3	4	5	7	9	11	14	17	20	23	27	31	34	38	41	46	50	54	58	61	65	69
3	1	2	2	3	4	6	8	10	13	16	19	22	25	29	32	36	40	43	48	52	56	59	63	67	70
4	1	2	3	4	5	6	9	11	14	17	20	23	27	31	34	38	41	46	50	54	58	61	65	69	72
5	2	3	3	4	6	8	10	13	16	19	22	25	29	32	36	40	43	48	52	56	59	63	67	70	74
6	2	3	4	5	7	9	11	14	17	20	23	27	31	34	38	41	46	50	54	58	61	65	69	72	76
7	3	3	4	6	8	10	13	16	19	22	25	29	32	36	40	43	46	52	56	59	63	67	70	74	77
8	3	4	5	7	9	11	14	17	20	23	27	31	34	38	41	46	50	54	58	61	65	69	72	76	79
9	3	4	6	8	10	13	16	19	22	25	29	32	36	40	43	48	52	56	59	63	67	70	74	77	80
10	4	5	7	9	11	14	17	20	23	27	31	34	38	41	46	50	54	58	61	65	69	72	76	79	82
11	4	6	8	10	13	16	19	22	25	29	32	36	38	41	46	48	52	56	59	63	67	70	74	77	80
12	5	7	9	11	14	17	20	23	27	31	34	38	40	43	48	50	54	58	61	65	69	72	76	79	82
13	6	8	10	13	16	19	22	25	29	32	36	40	43	46	48	52	56	59	63	67	70	74	77	80	84
14	7	9	11	14	17	20	23	27	31	34	38	41	46	50	54	58	61	65	69	72	74	77	79	82	85
15	8	10	13	16	19	22	25	29	32	36	40	43	48	52	56	59	63	67	70	74	77	80	84	86	88
16	8	11	14	17	20	23	27	31	34	38	41	46	50	54	58	61	63	69	72	76	79	82	84	86	89
17	9	13	16	19	22	25	29	32	36	40	43	48	52	56	59	63	65	70	74	77	80	84	85	88	91
18	10	14	17	20	23	27	31	34	38	41	46	50	54	58	61	65	67	72	76	79	82	85	86	89	92
19	11	16	19	22	25	29	32	36	40	43	48	52	56	59	63	67	70	74	77	80	84	86	89	92	93
20	13	17	20	23	27	31	34	38	41	46	50	54	58	61	65	69	72	76	79	84	85	88	91	93	94
21	14	19	22	25	29	32	36	40	43	48	52	56	59	63	67	70	74	77	80	84	86	89	92	94	95
22	16	20	23	27	31	34	38	41	46	50	54	58	61	65	69	72	76	79	82	85	89	91	93	95	96
23	17	22	25	29	32	36	40	43	48	52	56	59	63	67	70	74	77	80	84	86	91	92	94	96	97
24	19	23	27	31	34	38	41	46	50	54	58	61	65	69	72	76	79	82	85	88	92	93	95	97	98
25	22	25	29	32	36	40	43	48	52	56	59	63	67	70	74	77	80	84	86	89	93	94	96	98	99
26	23	27	31	34	38	41	46	50	54	58	61	65	69	72	76	79	82	85	88	91	94	95	97	99	100

Answers
June 2007
English

Answer Key

Session One, Part A	Session One, Part B	Session Two, Part A
1. **3**	7. **3**	1. **2**
2. **1**	8. **2**	2. **1**
3. **4**	9. **1**	3. **4**
4. **2**	10. **1**	4. **1**
5. **3**	11. **4**	5. **3**
6. **1**	12. **2**	6. **4**
	13. **3**	7. **2**
	14. **4**	8. **4**
	15. **2**	9. **1**
	16. **1**	10. **3**

Answers Explained

Session One

Part A   (1–6)

Note: Refer to Chapter 1 for review and strategy in responding to this part of the examination

(1) **3** "rescue." Paulsen begins his remarks by saying, "Books saved my life." He goes on to say that books are the reason he survived his "miserable childhood." It is only later in the passage that Paulsen talks about other ways in which books shaped his life.

(2) **1** "get warm." Later in the passage, Paulsen recounts how, as a teenager in Minnesota, he would wander the streets in the evening, hoping to "hustle" drunks for small change. On one cold night, he stopped in the library to "warm up," not to meet friends or to borrow a book.

(3) **4** "chaotic." Chaotic means "disorganized, confused, and disordered." Paulsen says the librarian showed him that his life could be "something other than [his] drunken parents screaming at each other...." There is nothing in the passage to suggest that his home life was dull, let alone supportive or enriching.

(4) **2** "follow his dream." Paulsen tells us that suddenly he "knew that [he] had to be a writer. . . . Writing had suddenly become everything . . . everything . . . to me."

(5) **3** "an informal apprenticeship." Toward the end of the passage, Paulsen says that he "apprenticed [himself] to a couple of editors." In order to receive their help, he had to practice by writing an article or story every night, without exception. The passage makes no reference to a journal, nor to a college course or trip.

(6) **1** "stimulating." This choice best captures the feeling in Paulsen's final statement: "But I love writing more now, I think, than I ever have. . . . [It] is grandly exciting to me. . . ."

Part A   Sample Student Response Essay

Today's opening of the library book fair is an opportunity to reflect on how books and literature in general can have an overwhelming influence in our lives. Words, organized creatively and poetically, have the ability not only to change lives but also to define them. Gary Paulsen, a well-known author, has experienced firsthand the significance books can hold in someone's life. His success as a writer shows that in a world with books, all things are possible.

A book is much more than just an arrangement of words, more even than the story within the binding. For Gary Paulsen, books were a means of survival in his painful childhood, and they have sustained him as an adult. In other words, books kept him going when nothing else might have. They have the power to erase fears and worries, shyness and anger. Books allow the unknown to become a little less frightening. Gary Paulsen illustrates this power of books in recounting how, as a 10-year old child, he was forced into public school for the first time and was overwhelmed by fear. It was his teacher who drew him out, literally and emotionally, simply by reading to him. The words, although he can't remember them now, calmed him; as he became lost in the story, his worries and fears fell away. Paulsen's story reminds us of the power of books to rescue us from the difficulties of the outside world.

Not only can books change a life, they have the power to define it as well. Books offer visions that life can be different. This power was one that Gary Paulsen was fortunate enough to experience as a child, and later as a teenager. Growing up with angry, indifferent parents led Paulsen to find refuge in reading. He tells us that after a librarian in Minnesota gave him a library card, he began to spend nights in a secret place in the basement, where he could read as he ate jelly and crackers. He was thirteen at the time, but it was not easy at first because he was not a good reader; he says it took him "forever to read" the first book he took home. The librarian continued to offer the young Gary books to take home, books she thought he would like such as Westerns, science fiction, and survival tales. She would even spend time talking about them with him when he came to return them.

Paulsen emphasizes the importance of this experience in his life by telling us that this librarian had given him much more than books – she had given him an entire world without constant pain, drunken parents, and school bullies. It was this experience that allowed him to look forward. He went on to graduate from high school, serve in the army, and later become an electronics engineer. It was as an adult that Paulsen tells us books again changed the course of his life, but this time because he wanted to write them. After many years as an engineer and raising a family, Paulsen discovered that writing was everything to him. He gave up his work and family to go to Hollywood, where he was determined to learn how to write. Now, after many years of success, he says that writing is as exciting and meaningful to him as ever.

Paulsen's story is a good one for this occasion–the opening of our library's book fair. Gary Paulsen owes his life to the "loops and whirls of the story *dance," and we know many others do as well. This fair is a reminder that books have changed lives, spurred action, and brought comfort and purpose to readers. Have you read a good book lately?*

Analysis

This essay reveals the writer's thorough understanding and appreciation of the passage. It also makes effective use of the Situation to frame the discussion: "Today's opening of the library book fair . . ." "Paulsen's story is a good one for this occasion . . ." The connections between the information and ideas in the text and the task are clearly expressed, and the introduction makes explicit the relevance of Paulsen's story to the occasion.

The development of ideas is good here as the writer elaborates both on the general idea that books can help shape lives and on the specifics of Paulsen's story: the second and third paragraphs begin with universal statements about the power of books, then illustrate with the details of Paulsen's account. The organization is also clear in moving from general statements to specifics, both within paragraphs and in the essay as a whole. The conclusion is effective in connecting the universal assertions to Paulsen's story and to the audience for the speech: "This fair is a reminder that books have changed lives, spurred action, and brought comfort and purpose to readers."

Throughout this essay, the language is strong, clear and often sophisticated: "[Books have] the power to erase fears and worries . . ," "[Living with] angry, indifferent parents led Paulsen to find refuge in reading . . ." ". . . books have changed lives, spurred action, and brought comfort and purpose to readers." This writer also demonstrates skill in composing sentences of varying length and complexity and shows mastery of the conventions. This essay would rate a high score.

(See pp. 31–35 for a detailed explanation of the rubric for this part of the examination.)

Part B (7–16)

Note: Refer to Chapter 2 for review and strategy in responding to this part of the examination.

(7) **3** "unpredictability." The article asserts in the opening sentence that the 1,500 active volcanoes ". . . could erupt at any time." The article makes it clear that there is no significant commonality in the height or location of the world's volcanoes.

(8) **2** "ignore warnings." Beginning at line 17, the passage offers examples of recent eruptions in which many thousands of people died because warnings "are not always listened to."

(9) **1** "program funding." Following disasters such as the ones noted above, the United Nations encouraged countries to undertake projects that would reduce the risks of such disasters, but ". . . did not have money for the program." (line 38)

(10) **1** "authorities." The article indicates that the video had images of "horrifying accuracy" and was shown to "mayors and other public officials in charge of getting people to evacuate when volcanoes threatened to explode." (lines 46–47)

(11) **4** "most threatening." "These so-called decade volcanoes are near large population centers and could erupt any time." (lines 49–50)

(12) **2** "speed." The paragraph beginning at line 61 indicates that these volcanic flows are so deadly because they can "sweep . . . across the countryside at 60 miles an hour . . . and have killed thousands of people in less than two minutes. . . ."

(13) **3** "number of residents evacuated." Beginning at line 75 to the end of the passage, the two examples offered show that because thousands of people evacuated voluntarily, there were almost no casualties; only five people died in the eruption of Rabaul, even though 75 percent of the city's homes were destroyed.

(14) **4** "motion." The graphic indicates that seismometers "pick up faint vibrations indicating deep movements of magma."

(15) **2** "promising." This is the best answer to describe a technology that is "still in its infancy . . . but offers some of the best future prospects in forecasting volcanic eruptions." None of the other choices is supported by information on the graphic.

(16) **1** "along the slopes." The illustration shows clearly that these devices are placed along the slope, not within the crater nor under the magma.

Part B   Sample Student Response Essay

  The men and women who study volcanoes, otherwise known as volcanologists, are coming up with new ways to lessen the disastrous consequences of volcanic eruptions. Because of improved technology, volcanologists have many new resources to research volcanoes and to help educate the public.

  There are about 1500 active volcanoes on our planet. Out of these, 583 have erupted within the last 400 years. Many of these eruptions leave horrible destruction and death in their path. In one recent instance, a volcano in Colombia, exploded and over 26,000 people died, mainly because warnings from scientists were ignored. Since the number of people living "dangerously near" volcanoes has grown enormously, and because "scientists and civil disaster officials are not always listened to," volcanologists are trying to get countries to examine the hazards and take steps to reduce the risks to their citizens. Even though the United Nations declared the 1990's the International Decade of Natural Hazard Reduction, there was no money for the program, so some volcanologists decided to take steps on their own.

  The first attempt to educate people on the hazards of volcanic eruptions came in video form. This video was shown to public officials in charge of evacuating people living near active volcanoes. This video contained horrifying footage of "what volcanoes can do to people and property." Scientists also decided to intensely study 15 "decade" volcanoes located near large population centers. Workshops were held at the sites of these volcanoes where scientists helped to educate disaster relief officials on how to be prepared for eruptions and needed evacuations. A third step was in efforts by volcanologists to make predictions of eruptions more reliable through better technology.

  Information in a recent graphic, "Forecasting a Volcanic Frenzy," illustrates five technological ways to forecast volcanic eruptions. Now that we have satellites, scientists can use surveillance and Global Positioning Systems to monitor ground displacements in the areas around volcanoes. Tilt meters and seismology are also used. These indicate deep movements of magma and can detect if accumulating magma is "beginning to swell the volcano's upper reaches." One of the newest ways to predict eruptions is by using a crack measurement. These are sensors, placed on the slopes of the volcanoes that reveal changes in the size of cracks and gullies. Scientists can even scan the sky to detect unusual levels of carbon dioxide in the area around a volcano.

  Volcanologists are not only working hard to better understand how to predict volcanic eruptions, they are committed to educating municipal and civil disaster officials in ways to protect the increasing numbers of people who live in areas that are threatened by volcanic activity. This is an important example of how scientists meet their social responsibility.

Analysis

This essay meets the requirements of the task very well. Information from the article and the graphic is expressed clearly and accurately, and the discussion is adequately developed with details to support the topic: efforts of volcanologists to educate the public and civil officials on the dangers of volcanic eruptions.

As many of the essays in this part of the examination are, this one is organized by treating the two documents separately: the second and third paragraphs present the key ideas from the article, followed by a paragraph of supporting details from the graphic. The writer makes an effective transition in articulating technology as the linking idea between the two documents. The essay ends with a simple conclusion that reiterates the topic and effectively connects it to the overall concept of the social responsibility of scientists.

This writer shows skill in composing sentences of varying length and complexity; there are a few instances of comma errors, but no significant weaknesses in the conventions. This essay would rate a high score. (See pp. 48–53 for a detailed discussion of the rubric for this part of the examination.)

Session Two

Part A   (1–10)

Note: See Chapter 3 for review and strategy in responding to this part of the examination

(1) **2** "captive." At line 9, the mother says, "It is you who are conquered...," asserting that the man himself is the prisoner because he is "afraid to go out."

(2) **1** "victor." The son declares that the stone is his "by conquest." None of the other choices is implied by the idea of capture and conquest.

(3) **4** "control." The mother points out that the "stone is nobody's," meaning that it cannot truly be possessed; she acknowledges at the end that she has attempted to keep her son captive in the same way he has claimed conquest of the stone. There is no direct suggestion of jealousy or punishment here, and no reference to debt.

(4) **1** "dialogue." This brief fable is developed as a series of exchanges between a son and his mother. Beginning at line 4, each statement is identified as what either "he said" or "she said." The passage is spare in language, with little or no description, and no true suspense or recognizable allusion.

(5) **3** "thoughtfulness." The discovery that the father has placed a rice cookie under the child's pillow reveals that he understood how reassuring a cookie had been for the child on the previous day. None of the other choices is suggested by the incident.

(6) **4** "gender roles." In the passage that begins at line 17, Bay Ly recounts how her father told her stories and showed her how to make things that normally would be shared only with boys. "This was unheard of—a father doing these things with a child that was not a son!"

(7) **2** "Never again did I cry after my nap." This brief paragraph (at line 33) emphasizes how deeply the child was influenced by her father's admiration of the woman ancestor's bravery. Choices 1 and 3 are relevant, but Bay Ly's assertion that she would no longer cry is the strongest of these statements.

(8) **4** "patriotism." These lines introduce an extended recounting by the father of how their country was once ruled by China and more recently colonized by France. He is impressing upon Bay Ly the importance of appreciating and defending one's home land. "Sacred" refers here to fundamental importance rather than to a particular theology; there is no reference to economics or literature.

(9) **1** "continuing struggle of the people." The father's description of the bowl of rice as a "reward" is ironic in that was probably just enough to keep them alive to continue working. The father goes on to remind Bay Ly that freedom is never a gift—it must be won and won again. None of the other choices is implied by the passage.

(10) **3** "her hard work." In the passage beginning at line 86, the father relates how "your mother had a reputation [in the village] as the hardest worker of all." It is clear that was the quality that led his own mother to choose her as the bride for her son.

Part A   Sample Student Response Essay

By teaching their children truths they themselves have learned, parents can help their children realize their potential as adults. In Passage I, a fable, a mother shows her son that by holding something captive, he is the one who is imprisoned; in Passage II, a memoir, a father teaches his daughter about courage and determination. These are also stories about the meaning of freedom.

In the fable, a man "ambushes and captures a stone," as if it were a living thing; he then puts it in a dark place and stands guard over it for the rest of his life. The mother questions her son about why he has made the stone his prisoner, which elicits his childish justification: ". . . because I caught it . . . it is mine." Continuing the personification of the stone, the mother explains that, "the stone is asleep . . . it does not know whether it's in a garden or not." She further explains to her son that while he is occupied with guarding what cannot be owned, he is "getting old" and missing his own life. Despite his protests that he "caught it . . . it is mine by conquest," she shows him that his actions have made him the prisoner: "It is you who are conquered." The irony here is that the lesson applies to the mother as well. The son confesses that he has been afraid to "go out,"—into the world, into life—because "you have never loved me...." And in the final line of the dialogue, the mother acknowledges that her son has "always been to me as the stone is to you." The moral of the fable is that if you try to hold on to something too tightly, you may destroy it; or, it will become a burden and an obligation devoid of joy, as the son has become to his mother.

In the second passage, an excerpt from the autobiography of a Vietnamese woman, Bay Ly recalls her close relationship with her enlightened father. Not only does he "spoil" his daughter with rice cookies when she is sad, but he also teaches her "how to make things" that are by custom taught only to boys. Throughout the passage, we see that Bay Ly's father seemed to reject the typical gender-based roles of Asian society in the way he treated his daughter. His lessons are not about cooking and marriage, but about hard work, love of one's country and its past, and about the value of freedom.

Bay Ly is transformed by her father's stories about her heroic female ancestor, Phung Thi Chinh, who fought against Chinese occupation; she is even more deeply moved by her father's admiration of her mother, whose hard work he credits for all of the land he owns. From her father's stories, Bay Ly learns the importance of hard work and love—for family and for country. She also comes to believe in the power of women.

In the fable, the lesson seems to come too late, for the mother has already imprisoned and stunted her son's life. Bay Ly's father, on the other hand, is eager to encourage his young daughter to value what is most important and to appreciate the exceptional achievements of female ancestors and of her mother. The fable is told in a detached voice, which simply "reports" a dialogue between mother and son. The voice in Bay Ly's memoir, however, is her own, in which she recounts experiences from when she was an only child at home and presents much of what her father says in direct quotes and dialogue with her. Although the two passages are very different in form and tone, each is about a parent teaching a child important lessons about how to live a full and meaningful life.

Analysis

In this essay, the introduction establishes an appropriate controlling idea, which reflects the writer's thorough understanding of the two passages: "By teaching their children truths they themselves have learned, parents can help their children realize their potential as adults." The final sentence of the introduction is justified by the texts, but is only developed implicitly.

The discussion of the fable is clearly developed, capturing the fundamental theme of the story while pointing out elements of irony and personification. Although it is minimally developed in ideas, the discussion of Bay Ly's story is sufficient to show how the father disregards traditional gender roles in teaching his daughter to love her country and to believe in her own potential. The references to dialogue, voice, and to differences in form and tone are also brief, but reveal the writer's understanding of how literary elements contribute to the meaning of these passages.

Language throughout is clear, fluent, and occasionally striking: "...it will become a burden and an obligation devoid of joy, as the son has become to his mother." Sentences are varied, and complex ideas and structures are composed with skill. There are no significant weaknesses in the conventions. Though somewhat brief in development, this essay effectively meets the requirements of the task and would rate a high score.

(See pp. 68–71 for a detailed discussion of the rubric for this part of the examination.)

Session Two

Note: See Chapter 4 for review and strategy in responding to this part of the examination.

Part B   Sample Student Response Essay

Norman Mailer tells us that to be heroic is to "deal with forces larger than yourself." History and literature have shown repeatedly that extraordinary human beings rise and distinguish themselves from the masses, often struggling against the forces of entire societies. Such figures may be recognized as heroes. Two novels in particular, Fahrenheit 451 by Ray Bradbury, and 1984 by George Orwell, depict protagonists who come to recognize the evil in their repressive societies and face overwhelming odds in acting to resist.

In Fahrenheit 451, the reader is introduced to Guy Montag, a fireman in a futuristic world where it is his duty to set fires—to burn books—not to put them out. For most of his life, he has accepted his role without questioning what he is doing or why. As Montag encounters figures who resist the burning of their books, even die, to defend their freedom of ideas and thought, he becomes deeply dissatisfied and troubled by what he and his society represent. Montag even begins to keep some of the books he is meant to destroy and puts his own life at great risk. Because Montag has grown up in a society where books are banned and citizens are urged only to watch television for ideas and information, it is difficult for him to understand what he is secretly trying to read. He seeks out a former English professor named Faber and they imagine a way for Montag to remain a fireman in order to sabotage the firemen's work. But Montag's "treason" is discovered by the Chief, and, with Faber's help, Montag flees the city to join a group of intellectuals who live secretly in the countryside.

Montag's character is further developed as he discovers that these men and women have memorized entire books as a way of preserving them, looking forward to a time when books again will be permitted in society. Montag himself will become one of them and memorize the Book of Ecclesiastes. Bradbury's novel ends with a nuclear war that destroys the entire city. Montag and the "homeless" intellectuals he has joined will continue their heroic struggle and hope to rebuild a better society out of the ashes of the old one.

Orwell's 1984 takes the story of a repressive regime even further. This time it is the entire world in which all thought is controlled and independent thought is suppressed. This is a world in which "Ignorance is Strength," and "War is Peace." In this novel, Orwell created the concept of Big Brother watching over everything we think and do. The central character, Winston Smith, is another example of a figure working within his society who gradually comes to question what he does: rewriting history to fit the Party's dogma. He becomes curious to know more about what "really happened" in the past and struggles to have thoughts and feelings that are his own. Winston also develops a relationship with Julia, a woman whose job is to write novels that comply with Party thought. Winston and Julia meet in a secret place, where the shop-keeper helps them to learn more about the past and to escape surveillance. Toward the end of the novel, we see that this has been a trap and that they have been betrayed by the shopkeeper—Big Brother has seen and heard everything! The novel ends in the utter defeat of the protagonists, who are tortured into betraying each other and are then brainwashed to love Big Brother.

In both 1984 and Fahrenheit 451, the authors have imagined worlds in which freedom of thought has been totally suppressed; they are novels whose theme is the supreme value of individual minds and ideas and that freedom of thought is one we must always be willing to fight and even die for. At the end of Bradbury's novel, we have an image of the possible rebirth of ideas and literature; Montag and his friends may succeed in rebuilding the civilization they have preserved in their memories. They have courageously faced "forces larger than themselves." The characters of Winston and Julia also face such forces, though one might argue that they are simply trying to escape. I think Orwell suggests that their desire to have true knowledge and free thought is also a worthy struggle. Mailer's definition says that it is heroic to "deal with forces larger than ourselves." He does not say that only those who succeed are heroic.

Analysis

This writer meets one of the most important criteria of the task by offering an interpretation of the critical lens that is faithful to its complexity. This interpretation is presented first in the introduction: "History and literature have shown repeatedly that extraordinary human beings rise and distinguish themselves from the masses, often struggling against the forces of entire societies." In the conclusion, however, the writer further refines the interpretation in a way that not only fits the works under discussion, but also suggests a more sophisticated understanding of Mailer's remark: "Mailer's definition says that it is heroic to 'deal with forces larger than ourselves.' He does not say that only those who succeed are heroic."

The topic is developed well, with adequate summaries of the struggles of the protagonists that include relevant and specific details. The essay also develops important similarities between the two works: for example, as Montag and Winston begin to think for themselves, they question the work they do. The writer also develops a common theme in the ultimate value of free thought. The organization is clear, with discussion of one novel following the other, and the statement, "Orwell's 1984 takes the story of a repressive regime even further," creates an effective transition.

This essay is composed with admirable variety and complexity of sentence structure, and the language is suitably strong and precise. There are no significant errors in the conventions. This essay would rate a high score.

(See pp. 80–83 for a detailed discussion of the rubric for this part of the examination.)

Examination August 2007
English

Session One

Part A

Overview: For this part of the test, you will listen to an account about the coffee culture, answer some multiple-choice questions, and write a response based on the situation described below. You will hear the account twice. You may take notes on the page alloted anytime you wish during the readings.

> **The Situation:** Your economics class has been studying the impact of national business chains. In preparation for a classroom debate, you have chosen to write a position paper pointing out the positive impact of national business chains on independent vendors. In preparation for writing your position paper, listen to an account by reporter Lynn Rothenberg about the coffee shop business. Then use relevant information from the account to write your position paper.

Your Task: Write a position paper for your economics class in which you discuss the positive impact national business chains have on independent vendors.

Guidelines:
Be sure to
- Tell your audience what they need to know about the positive impact of national business chains on independent vendors
- Use specific, accurate, and relevant information from the account to support your position
- Use a tone and level of language appropriate for a position paper for an economics class
- Organize your ideas in a logical and coherent manner
- Indicate any words taken directly from the account by using quotation marks or referring to the speaker
- Follow the conventions of standard written English

Note: For this portion of the examination, the teacher will read a passage aloud. You will not actually see the passage reprinted below. Therefore, you are encouraged to have someone read the passage to you, in order to simulate the examination as closely as possible.

Listening Passage
...In Europe, stretching time is an attitude, a culture, even an art. Luxuriating over a cup of coffee while discussing politics, literature or life seems to come more naturally there than in the U.S. But here, some exceptions exist where café culture survives: large cities with European and international influence, college towns, and resort areas like the Berkshires [in Massachusetts]. For the most part, though, American suburban residents often ask themselves, why go out for coffee when they can make it themselves at home? This notion ignores the integral ingredient of coffee culture—the pleasure of connecting with friends, and that most foreign of concepts—slowing down.

The dearth of coffee culture opportunities began to change during the 1990's as American tastes evolved as a result of international influences. More cafés opened in cities, even in the suburbs. But the main force of this change in the landscape was a large publicly owned company from Seattle—Starbucks.

Many have boycotted this gargantuan coffee peddler and remained loyal to the independents, thus supporting a small cadre of distinctive and personal locally owned establishments. Oddly enough, it appears that Starbucks has not been as much of a threat to the local café as initially imagined.

I recently spoke with three successful independent coffee vendors in the capital district: Lee Cohen of The Daily Grind on Lark Street in Albany and Broadway in Troy; Dan Murphy of Uncommon Grounds on Western Avenue in Albany and Broadway in Saratoga Springs; and Frank Figliomeni of Professor Java's on Wolf Road [in Colonie]. They agree that the influence of Starbucks on American culture has been to introduce people to the idea of setting time aside and hanging out over a cup of coffee without guilt. This, in turn, has been good for their business.

Cohen, who has co-owned The Daily Grind since 1980, recently said: "Starbucks has the power to introduce people to coffee, people who would never even think about the concept. They educated the United States on coffee."...

Figliomeni wouldn't mind if Starbucks opened next door, because he has a service they can't provide. "We know every customer that comes in. We have a product made on the premises. We do what Starbucks can't do. We're built into the community; we have a relationship." In fact, Starbucks is nearly next door at the southern end of Wolf Road.

Murphy, who opened Uncommon Grounds in 1992 in Saratoga and 1997 in Albany, is unfazed by the large chain and claims it has not had an impact on his business. "If you have a mediocre shop, and you're the only one in town, if Starbucks comes in you might be in trouble. But if you have a good product, it doesn't matter." In his view, while Starbucks may be a billion dollar company, each store doesn't offer any more than a good local coffee shop, albeit with higher prices.

Cohen explained that prices at Starbucks are always more expensive because the corporation consistently rents prime real estate with high rent. While it's difficult for the independent to raise the price of his product, when the "leader" comes in with the higher prices, "You can raise the price 50 cents and still be under."

Cohen is comfortable with his persona as an independent coffee vendor and says that while Starbucks is accessible from nearly any lane of traffic in large cities, he has elected to remain small. "I think we do better than Starbucks in many ways, but not in volumes of money." He recalled one day when a customer had come in for coffee, then said they forgot their money at home. "I'll get it next time," Cohen told them. "You wouldn't get that at a chain store."

Cohen, Murphy and Figliomeni have met the challenge of being independent in a variety of ways. Murphy's Uncommon Grounds is a half bagels/half coffee shop, which has kept business steady since incorporating the concept in 1997. The three men roast their own beans, providing customers a truly fresh cup of coffee made from beans roasted that day— and in some cases just minutes before.

Like many other small business owners competing in today's marketplace, Cohen has turned to the internet. Now, through his internet sales of coffee machines, as well as coffee, he is in the same ring as the larger companies, like Peet's from California and Starbucks. Previously, Cohen's limitations were Albany, but now he says he's limited only by those who use 220, which refers to European voltage as compared to American at 110.

At Professor Java's, Figliomeni offers conference rooms where neighboring corporate businesses can meet. Also, he ships coffee to customers who initially discovered his café during layovers at nearby Albany International Airport. "One customer at a time. It's a Dean Witter thing," he said. "Business is good. You have to make it good."...

The three coffee houses, Uncommon Grounds, The Daily Grind and Professor Java['s] all offer shade grown, organic, and fair trade coffee. They all agree that if customers ask for it, they'll make a point of carrying it, and indeed, it has become a request they hear more and more.

While many Americans still feel compelled to hurry to everywhere and to nowhere like the Little White Rabbit, it is becoming more common to visit a café and find full tables in the afternoon or evening. The notion of slowing down is still a hard one for our scurrying culture to swallow, but it does appear to be settling in, sip by sip. And if more people are asking for social and environmental qualification of their brew, then perhaps one day the farmers will consistently be paid a living wage and the songbirds will have the distinctive habitat, which they travel so far to find.

— excerpted from "Coffee Culture,"
Capital District Home Style, July, 2004

Notes

Multiple-Choice Questions

Directions (1–6): Use your notes to answer the following questions about the passage read to you. Select the best suggested answer and write its number in the space provided. The questions may help you think about ideas and information you might use in your writing. You may return to these questions anytime you wish.

1 According to Dan Murphy of Uncommon Grounds, the basis for a successful business is a

   (1) national reputation   (3) quality product
   (2) good location   (4) well-trained staff   1 _____

2 According to Lee Cohen, Starbucks must charge more than independent vendors because Starbucks spends more on

   (1) real estate   (3) advertising
   (2) employee salaries   (4) inventory   2 _____

3 Creating a "half bagels/half coffee shop" and roasting "their own beans" are examples of how independent vendors have

   (1) utilized new technology
   (2) reinvested their profits
   (3) influenced Starbucks' techniques
   (4) adapted to competition   3 _____

4 Some independent dealers like Lee Cohen have become competitive with large corporate chains by

   (1) providing in-store computers
   (2) marketing over the Internet
   (3) lowering their budgets
   (4) sponsoring community projects   4 _____

5 Frank Figliomeni's coffee shop, Professor Java's, has
   succeeded by

   (1) featuring a regional decor
   (2) creating a hurried atmosphere
   (3) meeting customer needs
   (4) offering product-related classes   5 _____

6 The account emphasizes that the modern coffee
   shop has encouraged American customers to value

   (1) relaxation   (3) travel
   (2) variety   (4) continuity   6 _____

After you have finished these questions, review **The
Situation** and read **Your Task** and the **Guidelines.**
Use scrap paper to plan your response. Then write
your response on separate sheets of paper. After you
finish your response for Part A, complete Part B.

Part B

Directions: Read the text and study the graphic on the following pages, answer the multiple-choice questions, and write a response based on the situation described below. You may use the margins to take notes as you read and scrap paper to plan your response.

> **The Situation:** Your technology class produces a monthly newsletter for the community on the importance of technology. You have decided to write an article for this month's issue on the history of the voting process and recommend *one* technological change that could improve the process.

Your Task: Using relevant information from *both* documents, write an article for your class's community technology newsletter in which you describe the history of the voting process and recommend *one* technological change that could improve the process.

Guidelines:
Be sure to
- Tell your audience what they need to know about the history of the voting process
- Recommend *one* technological change that could improve the voting process
- Use specific, accurate, and relevant information from the text *and* the graphic to support your recommendation
- Use a tone and level of language appropriate for an article for your technology class's community newsletter
- Organize your ideas in a logical and coherent manner
- Indicate any words taken directly from the text by using quotation marks or referring to the author
- Follow the conventions of standard written English

Text

...A new set of players in the election arena—computer scientists and cryptographers—are now developing systems to let people know that their votes have actually counted. It's a tricky task. The bedrock requirements of any decent voting system are security strong enough to prevent fraud and the anonymity of
(5) a secret vote. This makes verification a challenge, because using a simple digital audit trail to re-create what happened on Election Day would mean revealing who voted for whom (violating the principle of secret ballots). But election geeks are finding ways to help solve these puzzles.

The most-talked-about scheme was first conceived in the early 1990s by a
(10) graduate student named Rebecca Mercuri. It's now called verified voting (to the dismay of those with alternate ideas, who note that *their* schemes involve verification, too). The system is a kind of truth serum for touch-screen systems. After a ballot is cast, the choices are not only summarized on the screen but printed out on a piece of paper. The voter looks at the printout and has an
(15) opportunity to verify that the choices are actually the ones he or she cast. If so, the vote is approved, and the paper goes into a locked ballot box. (The voter isn't allowed to leave the booth with the printout in hand—it's displayed behind a transparent barrier—to prevent someone from running a vote-buying scheme.) If there's a recount, or if officials want to check the accuracy of the touch screen,
(20) the paper ballots are counted. One variation, the VoteMeter, replaces the printout with a readout on a palmtop device that stores ballots securely.

The Mercuri scheme has picked up a lot of momentum. Last year [2003] Rep. Rush Holt of New Jersey introduced a voter-verification bill that is now bottled up in committee. Just two weeks ago [March 15, 2004] New York Sen.
(25) Hillary Clinton and Florida Sen. Bob Graham unveiled a similar bill in the Senate. And California's secretary of State recently mandated that by 2006 all touch-screen systems should include printers that generate ballots for verification. Six other states have jumped on the paper-trail bandwagon, spurred in part by a campaign on the Internet called "The Computer Ate My Vote."
(30) Mercuri herself, who's now at the Kennedy School of Government, is concerned that the scheme might not be implemented correctly, and is now advocating that the actual count should be made not from the computers but from the printed-out ballots. "It's a case of 'Be careful what you wish for'," she says. "I asked myself, 'If these ballots are used to verify the results of machines we don't trust,
(35) why not use the ballots as the actual votes?'"

In 1999 a trio of computer scientists suggested a different method. It involves a doodad called a frog, for no particular reason other than that the term has no association with elections. A frog in this sense is a cheap form of digital storage

that records votes. It might be a business-card-size piece of plastic with a bit of
(40) digital memory. After proving you're eligible to vote, you get a frog from an
election official, who initializes it with the ballot appropriate to your precinct.
(Bonus: there's no reason you can't get your home ballot if you're at some other
location. It's possible to store information on a single CD that could generate any
ballot in the country.) If you like, you could get the frog well in advance of
(45) Election Day, and use any computer you like to enter the votes. On Election Day
itself, you take your frog into the booth and insert it into the official voting
terminal, which reads the frog's content and displays your choices on the screen.

Then comes an "Is that your final answer?" moment: if you're happy with the
selection, you press a button to make your vote official. If for some reason the
(50) readout did not reflect your choice, or you change your mind, you can reprogram
the frog. (This ability to alter the frog means that no one can give you a
preprogrammed frog with the assurance that you'll stick with the choices.) After
the vote is formally cast, the frog, well, croaks—the memory freezes, and the
device takes no changes. You'll leave it behind in case a recount is necessary, but
(55) it couldn't be used to revote. Though no one has yet identified many warts in the
system, the frog idea seems like a long shot. "It's an attractive method, but no
one's picked up on it yet," says co-inventor David Jefferson.

The most sophisticated systems deliver verifiability without a cumbersome,
possibly vulnerable, set of printed-out ballots (or discarded frogs). With clever
(60) cryptographic algorithms[1] and innovative viewing devices, it's possible to envision
a process that provides specific proof *after the fact* that your vote was included in
the total—without compromising the privacy of your selection.

Cryptographer David Chaum, who wrote the first papers on computer-based
anonymous voting in the early 1980s, has been experimenting with such schemes.
(65) (He's behind the aforementioned VoteMeter.) His latest iteration is Votegrity,
involving a device in addition to standard technology (like a touch screen). When
you cast your vote, this device generates three images, or "stripes"—bar-code-like
objects with encoded information. Each stripe contains your vote in encrypted
form, but by some form of mathematical magic, when overlaid on top of each
(70) other, the stripes display your selections in plain language. As you vote, this
readable output is projected on a small screen inside the voting booth so you can
check it for accuracy. Then the paper is divided to separate the stripes, and voters
may choose which one to take with them. That same image is stored digitally, and
officials will use it to register the actual vote. The decryption process involves
(75) techniques to ensure that the votes counted are the same ones the voters saw in
the booth.

---

[1]cryptographic algorithms — coded procedures

Where's your verification? The codes are all posted to the Web, and using the encoded receipt and a serial number also printed on the paper, you can go online to check that your encrypted vote was tallied. (Of course, since the image is
(80) encrypted, no one can know how you voted.) "The Chaum system is the better ballot box," says Mercuri. "It's the first solution that proves to someone that his or her vote counts."...

Some say that the final frontier of elections is Internet voting. About 46,000 participants in this year's Michigan primary actually pulled virtual levers from
(85) cyberspace to cast their votes. But another much publicized venture, the Department of Defense's SERVE program (which would have allowed up to a million armed forces members and expats[2] to choose a president via a Web browser this year), was put on hold after a formal study by top computer scientists pretty much outlined the reasons that the Internet isn't nearly as good a place to
(90) vote as it is to buy books or Google one's blind date: the security is dicey, votes aren't secret (computers aren't closed off like voting booths) and, in a pinch, someone could screw up an Internet election by a denial-of-service attack. Most computer scientists interested in voting think that the foreseeable future still lies in polling places....

—Steven Levy
excerpted from "Ballot Boxes Go High Tech"
Newsweek, March 29, 2004

---

[2]expats — people who live in a foreign country

GRAPHIC

Voting Through the Ages

Choosing leaders is as old as democracy itself. While elections have become a lot more accurate over the centuries, today's systems are far from fail-safe, as the 2000 Florida recount revealed. A brief history:

ballots. If they don't press hard enough, the cards are difficult to interpret, producing the kind of disputes that plagued the 2000 Florida recount.

500 B.C.
ATHENS Ancient Greeks voted by dropping clay balls into pots designated for each candidate.

tiality, but remained popular into the 19th century. This 1852 painting shows a typically chaotic county election.

1800s Paper Ballots
Looking for increased privacy, more voters began

50 B.C. ROME
Romans used beans or small balls to vote. The word ballot comes from the Italian for "little ball." The Roman Senate (above) submitted votes on writing tablets.

marking their choices on pieces of paper. The government later created

Inspecting a punch-card ballot, Florida, 2000

standardized ballots. Politicians like Boss Tweed (below left) were notorious for rigging counts.

1892 Lever Machines
These mechanical booths are tougher to tamper with than ballot boxes. But they leave no paper record of how people vote, so it's hard to go back and recount contested elections.

1600s NORTH AMERICA
Early settlers voted with corn kernels or beans. Public meetings, in which voters shouted out their choices, didn't offer much confiden-

Butterfly punch ballot

1960s Optical Scans
Voters pick candidates by filling in blanks, as they would on a standardized test. The method has one of the best track records for reliability among voting technologies.

2004 Electronic Voting
Millions of voters will use these modified PCs in the November elections. They guard against voter mistakes, but don't all provide a paper trail to double-check accuracy.

– JOSH ULICK

1960s Punch Cards
Voters punch holes near their candidates' names on these machine-read

Sources: (adapted) Douglas Jones, University of Iowa; PBS/ *Newsweek*, March 29, 2004

Multiple-Choice Questions

Directions (7–16): Select the best suggested answer to each question and write its number in the space provided. The questions may help you think about ideas and information you might want to use in your writing. You may return to these questions anytime you wish.

7 According to the text, two important considerations for any voting system are

(1) speed and accuracy
(2) honesty and privacy
(3) convenience and cost
(4) simplicity and efficiency   7 _____

8 The "truth serum" (line 12) in touch-screen voting systems is provided by

(1) voter signatures   (3) paper records
(2) fingerprint identities (4) curtained booths   8 _____

9 According to the text, one result of "The Mercuri scheme" (line 22) has been an increase in

(1) legislative action   (3) voter participation
(2) candidate debate   (4) voter education   9 _____

10 The "frog" (line 37) voting system takes advantage of

(1) easy text manipulation
(2) environmentally safe components
(3) quick voter recognition
(4) inexpensive memory capacity   10 _____

11 David Chaum incorporated "stripes" (line 67) into his voting system both to assure that the vote has been counted and to

(1) enhance screen visibility
(2) protect voter identity
(3) facilitate manual use
(4) speed vote tallies   11 _____

12 According to the text, one hindrance to the development of Internet voting is

(1) expensive software
(2) computer inaccessibility
(3) complex programs
(4) security concerns   12 _____

13 The primary focus of the graphic is that voting

(1) has a long history
(2) began in America
(3) was seldom successful
(4) is now widely practiced   13 _____

14 According to the graphic, the word "ballot" originally referred to a

(1) popular politician   (3) campaign strategy
(2) famous country   (4) polling method   14 _____

15 According to the graphic, one of the most reliable voting methods utilizes

(1) mechanical booths   (3) optical scans
(2) punch cards   (4) electronic voting   15 _____

16 According to the graphic, lever machines present difficulties in

(1) verification   (3) transportation

(2) storage   (4) confidentiality   16 _____

After you have finished these questions, review **The Situation** and read **Your Task** and the **Guidelines**. Use scrap paper to plan your response. Then write your response to Part B on separate sheets of paper.

Session Two

Part A

Directions: Read the passages on the following pages (an essay and a poem). Write the number of the answer to each multiple-choice question in the space provided. Then write the essay on separate sheets of paper as described in **Your Task**. You may use the margins to take notes as you read and scrap paper to plan your response.

Your Task:

After you have read the passages and answered the multiple-choice questions, write a unified essay about accomplishment as revealed in the passages. In your essay, use ideas from **both** passages to establish a controlling idea about accomplishment. Using evidence from **each** passage, develop your controlling idea and show how the author uses specific literary elements or techniques to convey that idea.

Guidelines:

Be sure to

- Use ideas from **both** passages to establish a controlling idea about accomplishment
- Use specific and relevant evidence from **each** passage to develop your controlling idea
- Show how each author uses specific literary elements (for example: theme, characterization, structure, point of view) or techniques (for example: symbolism, irony, figurative language) to convey the controlling idea
- Organize your ideas in a logical and coherent manner
- Use language that communicates ideas effectively
- Follow the conventions of standard written English

Passage I

Two days before my first novel was to be published, while I was packing to leave the small Vermont town in which I live to go to New York, the telephone rang, and when I snatched it up irritably and said, "Hello," a sweet old lady's voice answered me, "Hello, who's this?" which is a common enough Vermont
(5)   telephone greeting.

"This is Shirley Jackson," I said, a little soothed because my name reminded me of my book.

"Well," she said vaguely, "is Mrs. Stanley Hyman there, please?"

I waited for a minute and then, "This is Mrs. Hyman," I said reluctantly.
(10)   Her voice brightened. "Mrs. Hyman," she said, pleased, "This is Mrs. Sheila Lang of the newspaper. I've been trying to get in touch with you for *days*."

"I'm so sorry," I said. "I've been terribly busy—my book, and all."

"Yes," she said. "Well, Mrs. Hyman, this is what I wanted. You read the paper, of course?"
(15)   "Of course," I said, "and I've been sort of expecting—"

"Well, then, surely, you read the North Village Notes column?"

"Yes, indeed," I said warmly.

"That's *my* column," she said. "I *write* that column."

"Of course, I'm a North Village resident," I said, "but I rather thought that
(20)   for a thing of this importance—"

"Now, what I'm doing is this. I'm calling up a few people in town who I thought might have items of news for me—"

"Certainly," I said, and reached for one of the numerous copies of the book jacket lying around the house. "The name of the book—"
(25)   "*First* of all," she said, "where exactly in town do you live, Mrs. Hyman?"

"On Prospect Street," I said. "*The Road Through the Wall*."

"I see," she said. "Just let me take that down."

"That's the name of the book," I said.

"Yes," she said. "Which house would that be, I wonder?"
(30)   "The old Elwell place," I said.

"On the corner of Mechanic? I thought the young Elwells lived there."

"That's next door," I said. "We're in the *old* Elwell place."

"The old *Thatcher* place?" she said. "We always call that the old Thatcher place; he built it, you know."
(35)   "That's the one," I said. "It's going to be published the day after tomorrow."

"I didn't know *anyone* lived there," she said. "I thought it was empty."

"We've lived here three years," I said, a little stiffly.

"I don't get out much any more," she said. "Now, what little items of local news do you have for me? Any visitors? Children's parties?"

(40)   "I'm publishing a book next week," I said. "I am going down to New York for my publication day."

"Taking your family?" she asked. "Any children, by the way?"

"Two," I said. "I'm taking them."

"Isn't that nice," she said. "I bet they're excited."

(45)   "You know," I said madly, "I've been asked to do the Girl Scout column for your paper."

"Really?" She sounded doubtful. "I'm sure you'll enjoy it. It's such an *informal* newspaper."

"Yes," I said. "Would you like to hear about my book?"

(50)   "I certainly would," she said. "Anytime you have any little newsy items for me, you be sure and call me right up. My number's in the book."

"Thank you," I said. "Well, *my* book —"

"I have so much enjoyed our little talk, Mrs. Hyman. Imagine me not knowing anyone was living in the old Thatcher place!"

(55)   "*The Road Through the Wall*," I said. "Farrar and Straus."

"You know," she said, "now that I don't get out any more, I find that doing this column keeps me in touch with my neighbors. It's social, sort of."

"Two-seventy-five," I said. "It'll be in the local bookstore."

"You'll probably find the same thing with the Girl Scout column," she said.

(60)   "Thank you so much, Mrs. Hyman. Do call me again soon."

"I started it last winter," I said.

"Goodbye," she said sweetly, and hung up.

I kept the column that appeared as the North Village Notes of the newspaper the next day. Several people remarked on it to me. It was on the last page of the

(65) four!

NORTH VILLAGE NOTES

Mrs. Royal Jones of Main Street is ill.

Miss Mary Randall of Waite Street is confined to her home with chicken pox.

One of the hooked rug classes met last evening with Mrs. Ruth Harris.

(70)   Hurlbut Lang of Troy spent the weekend with his parents in North Village, Mr. and Mrs. R. L. Lang.

The food sale of the Baptist Church has been postponed indefinitely due to weather conditions.

Mrs. Stanley Hyman has moved into the old Thatcher place on Prospect

(75) Street. She and her family are visiting Mr. and Mrs. Farrarstraus of New York City this week.

Mrs. J. N. Arnold of Burlington spent the weekend in town with Mr. and Mrs. Samuel Montague.

Little Lola Kittredge of East Road celebrated her fifth birthday on Tuesday. (80) Six little friends joined to wish her many happy returns of the day, and ice cream and cake were served.

—Shirley Jackson
"Fame"
from *Writer*, August 1948

Passage II

Soybeans

The October air was warm and musky, blowing
Over brown fields, heavy with the fragrance
Of freshly combined beans, the breath of harvest.

He was pulling a truckload onto the scales
(5)   At the elevator near the rail siding north of town
When a big Cadillac drove up. A man stepped out,
Wearing a three-piece suit and a gold pinky ring.
The man said he had just invested a hundred grand
In soybeans and wanted to see what they looked like.

(10) The farmer stared at the man and was quiet, reaching
For the tobacco in the rear pocket of his jeans,
Where he wore *his* only ring, a threadbare circle rubbed
By working cans of dip and long hours on the backside
Of a hundred acre run. He scooped up a handful
(15) Of small white beans, the pearls of the prairie, saying:

Soybeans look like a foot of water on the field in April
When you're ready to plant and can't get in;
Like three kids at the kitchen table
Eating macaroni and cheese five nights in a row;
(20) Or like a broken part on the combine when
Your credit with the implement dealer is nearly tapped.

Soybeans look like prayers bouncing off the ceiling
When prices on the Chicago grain market start to drop;
Or like your old man's tears when you tell him
(25)   How much the land might bring for subdivisions.
Soybeans look like the first good night of sleep in weeks
When you unload at the elevator and the kids get Christmas.

He spat a little juice on the tire of the Cadillac,
Laughing despite himself and saying to the man:
(30)   Now maybe you can tell me what a hundred grand looks like.

—Thomas Alan Orr
from *Hammers in the Fog*, 1995
Restoration Press

Multiple-Choice Questions

Directions (1–10): Select the best suggested answer to each question and write its number in the space provided. The questions may help you think about the ideas and information you might want to use in your essay. You may return to these questions anytime you wish.

Passage I (the essay) — Questions 1–6 refer to Passage I.

1 According to the passage, the narrator calls herself "Shirley Jackson" on the phone to emphasize pride in her

(1) marriage   (3) wealth

(2) career   (4) children   1 _____

2 The caller, Mrs. Lang, is seeking information for a

(1) brief biography

(2) neighborhood census

(3) community database

(4) newspaper column   2 _____

3 The passage's main conflict is based on the characters'

(1) different motives   (3) varied education

(2) mutual jealousy   (4) similar ages   3 _____

4 As used in the passage, *The Road Through the Wall* refers to a

(1) newspaper   (3) novel

(2) play   (4) movie   4 _____

5 Mrs. Lang's reference to the builder and original
owner of the house (lines 33 and 34) emphasizes
her

(1) respect for historic architecture
(2) interest in modern literature
(3) knowledge of town history
(4) appreciation of local art　　　　　　　　　5＿＿＿

6 The passage is primarily developed through the use
of

(1) description　　　　　　　(3) argument
(2) example　　　　　　　　(4) dialogue　　　　6＿＿＿

Passage II (the poem) — Questions 7–10 refer to Passage II.

7 The purpose of the first stanza is to

(1) establish setting　　　　(3) introduce conflict
(2) explore character　　　　(4) create rhyme　　　7＿＿＿

8 The description of "a man" (lines 6 through 9)
emphasizes the man's

(1) humility　　　　　　　(3) prosperity
(2) intolerance　　　　　　(4) jealousy　　　　8＿＿＿

9 In stanza 3, the contrast between the farmer and
the man is best established by which phrase?

(1) "reaching for the tobacco" (lines 10 and 11)
(2) "*his* only ring" (line 12)
(3) "a hundred acre run" (line 14)
(4) "small white beans" (line 15)　　　　　　9＿＿＿

10 Stanzas 4 and 5 make the reader aware of the

    (1) size of the family
    (2) struggles of the farmer
    (3) growth of the soybeans
    (4) effects of the drought   10 _____

After you have finished these questions, review **Your Task** and the **Guidelines.** Use scrap paper to plan your response. Then write your response to Part A on separate sheets of paper. After you finish your response for Part A, complete Part B.

Part B

Your Task:

Write a critical essay in which you discuss *two* works of literature you have read from the particular perspective of the statement that is provided for you in the **Critical Lens**. In your essay, provide a valid interpretation of the statement, agree *or* disagree with the statement as you have interpreted it, and support your opinion using specific references to appropriate literary elements from the two works. You may use scrap paper to plan your response. Write your essay in Part B on separate sheets of paper.

Critical Lens:

> "You must take life the way it comes at you and make the best of it."
>
> —Yann Martel
> *Life of Pi*, 2001

Guidelines:

Be sure to

- Provide a valid interpretation of the critical lens that clearly establishes the criteria for analysis
- Indicate whether you agree *or* disagree with the statement as you have interpreted it
- Choose *two* works you have read that you believe best support your opinion
- Use the criteria suggested by the critical lens to analyze the works you have chosen
- Avoid plot summary. Instead, use specific references to appropriate literary elements (for example: theme, characterization, setting, point of view) to develop your analysis
- Organize your ideas in a unified and coherent manner
- Specify the titles and authors of the literature you choose
- Follow the conventions of standard written English

Regents Comprehensive Examination in English—August 2007
Chart for Determining the Final Examination Score (Use for August 2007 examination only.)

To determine the student's final examination score, locate the student's total essay score across the top of the chart and the student's total multiple-choice score down the side of the chart. The point where those two scores intersect is the student's final examination score. For example, a student receiving a total essay score of 16 and a total multiple-choice score of 19 would receive a final examination score of 71.

Total Multiple-Choice Score	Total Essay Score																								
	0	1	2	3	4	5	6	7	8	9	10	11	12	13	14	15	16	17	18	19	20	21	22	23	24
0	0	1	1	2	2	3	5	7	9	12	14	18	21	24	28	31	35	39	42	47	51	55	58	62	66
1	1	1	2	2	3	4	6	8	10	13	16	19	23	26	30	33	37	40	45	49	53	57	60	65	68
2	1	2	2	3	3	5	7	9	12	14	18	21	24	28	31	35	39	42	47	51	55	58	62	66	69
3	1	2	3	3	4	6	8	10	13	16	19	23	26	30	33	37	40	45	49	53	57	60	65	68	71
4	1	2	3	5	5	7	9	12	14	18	21	24	28	31	35	39	42	47	51	55	58	62	66	69	73
5	2	2	4	5	6	8	10	13	16	19	23	26	30	33	37	40	45	49	53	57	60	65	69	71	75
6	2	3	5	6	7	9	12	14	18	21	24	28	31	35	39	42	47	51	55	58	62	66	71	73	77
7	2	3	5	7	8	10	13	16	19	23	26	30	33	37	40	45	49	53	57	60	65	68	73	75	78
8	2	4	6	8	9	12	14	18	21	24	28	31	35	39	42	47	51	55	58	62	66	69	75	77	80
9	3	5	7	9	12	14	18	21	24	28	30	33	37	40	45	49	53	57	60	65	69	71	77	78	81
10	3	6	8	10	13	16	19	23	26	30	31	35	39	42	47	51	55	58	62	66	69	73	78	80	83
11	4	7	9	12	14	18	21	24	28	31	35	37	40	45	49	53	57	60	65	68	71	75	80	81	85
12	5	8	10	13	16	19	23	26	30	33	37	39	42	47	51	55	58	62	66	69	73	77	81	83	86
13	6	9	12	14	18	21	24	28	31	35	39	40	45	49	53	57	60	65	68	71	75	78	83	85	88
14	7	10	13	16	18	21	24	28	31	35	39	42	45	49	53	57	60	65	68	73	77	80	83	86	89
15	8	12	14	18	21	24	28	31	35	39	42	45	49	53	55	58	62	65	69	73	77	80	83	86	91
16	9	13	16	19	23	26	30	33	37	40	45	47	51	55	58	62	65	68	71	75	78	81	85	88	93
17	10	14	18	21	24	28	31	35	40	45	47	49	53	57	60	65	68	71	73	77	78	83	87	89	94
18	12	16	19	23	26	30	33	37	40	45	49	51	55	58	62	65	69	73	75	78	80	85	89	90	95
19	13	18	21	24	28	31	35	39	42	47	51	53	57	60	65	68	71	75	77	80	83	86	90	91	95
20	14	19	23	26	30	33	37	40	45	49	53	55	58	62	65	68	73	77	78	81	85	87	91	93	96
21	16	21	24	28	31	35	39	42	47	51	55	57	60	65	68	71	75	78	80	83	86	89	93	94	97
22	18	23	26	30	33	37	40	45	49	53	57	58	62	66	69	73	77	80	81	85	87	90	94	95	98
23	19	24	28	31	35	39	42	47	51	55	58	60	65	68	71	75	78	81	85	86	89	93	95	96	98
24	21	26	30	33	35	40	45	49	51	55	60	62	66	69	73	77	80	83	86	87	90	94	95	97	99
25	23	28	30	33	37	42	45	49	53	57	60	65	68	71	75	78	81	85	87	90	93	95	96	98	99
26	24	28	31	35	39	42	47	51	55	58	62	65	69	73	77	80	83	86	89	91	94	96	97	99	00

Total Essay Score →

Answers
August 2007
English

Answer Key

Session One, Part A	Session One, Part B	Session Two, Part A
1. 3	7. 2	1. 2
2. 1	8. 3	2. 4
3. 4	9. 1	3. 1
4. 2	10. 4	4. 3
5. 3	11. 2	5. 3
6. 1	12. 4	6. 4
	13. 1	7. 1
	14. 4	8. 3
	15. 3	9. 2
	16. 1	10. 2

Answers Explained

Session One

Part A   (1–6)

Note: Refer to Chapter 1 for review and strategy in responding to this part of the examination.

(1) **3** "quality product." The speaker quotes Murphy as saying that Starbucks had no impact on his business because, ". . . if you have a good product, it doesn't matter."

(2) **1** "real estate." Cohen explains that Starbucks is more expensive because the corporation "consistently rents prime real estate with high rent." The passage makes no reference to salaries, advertising, or inventory.

(3) **4** "adapted to competition." This point is made when the author says that the independent owners ". . . met the challenge of being independent in a variety of ways."

(4) **2** "marketing over the Internet." The speaker points out that "Like many other small business owners . . . Cohen has turned to the internet . . . [and] he is in the same ring as the larger companies."

(5) **3** "meeting customer needs." Among the services Figliomeni's shop offers are a conference room for business meetings and mail order service for out-of-town customers. None of the other choices is suggested in the passage.

(6) **1** "relaxation." In concluding, the speaker claims that "the notion of slowing down [in coffee shops and cafés] appear[s] to be settling in, sip by sip." This answer is suggested both in the conclusion and in the introduction, in which the speaker describes the European coffee culture as ". . . the pleasure of connecting with friends—[and] slowing down."

Part A   Sample Student Response Essay

Public opinion regarding the effects of large chain businesses often tends to be negative. Many think of large chains as being the "bad guys," out to destroy any local competition, interested only in large profits. While in many cases this may have been true, chains in some industries actually propel the success of their smaller competitors. In the coffee business, or more specifically coffee café business, chains like Starbucks have actually helped independents by providing them with a larger customer pool. The Starbucks vs. the independent café example not only works very well to describe the positive effects a chain can have on one area of American business, this example also illustrates the benefits more generally of nationally owned chain businesses in the US.

Until the 1990's, what we call the coffee culture was prevalent in the United States only in areas with European influences, like large cities, or in resort areas where people seek opportunities to relax. College towns have also long provided what we call the coffee house, a place to spend extended periods of time reading or talking. Not until the 1990's, however, did coffee become a "hot" commodity nationally. With the advent of Starbucks, a chain that penetrated nearly every city and suburb in the nation, designer coffee became a luxury that everyone had access to. Lee Cohen of the independently owned Daily Grind in Albany said of Starbucks' influence, "Starbucks has the power to introduce people to coffee." Starbucks offers lattes, frappacinos, coffees adorned with whipped cream and chocolate shavings, European luxuries the average American had little knowledge or experience with. Starbucks educated Americans in the pleasures of café culture, the slow paced relaxation in sharing gourmet coffee with friends. This in turn provided independent cafés with a much larger pool of customers interested in what they had to offer.

As independent coffee vendors enjoyed more customers, Starbucks also made it easier for these shops to make a profit. Starbucks tends to rent locations in highly priced areas and therefore must charge high prices for their drinks. Independent cafés could then raise their own prices, by 50 cents for example, but still be the less expensive café in town. This increased profits for them by not only increasing the number of customers but also by increasing profit on the drinks they sold.

Independent coffee vendors like to point out that their cafés are truly local. The owners are also members of the community who often know their customers and may feel a more personal relationship with them. Many people prefer this more personal atmosphere over that of a Starbucks, where cafés often look the same and those serving never know you. Smaller cafés often strive for superior quality in their products. They roast their own beans daily to provide the best tasting coffee they can. They also cater specifically to their customers' needs to keep up with the competition. Professor Java's, near Albany airport, for example, provides meeting rooms for local businesses; the store also has coffee available for shipping to accommodate travelers who dis-

cover their coffee during layovers. Many of these shops also provide organic, fair trade, and shade grown coffees as more and more customers are demanding these.

It is evident from the effects of Starbucks on independent cafés in the US, not all chains are harmful to independently owned smaller businesses. Chains provide larger customer bases and highlight the advantages of a more personal atmosphere. In turn, the independents cater directly to the local customer and often offer a higher quality product. The arrival of large chains may even have the effect of leading people to value the small businesses that are already invested in their community. The example of the development of a coffee culture in the US is a reminder of a principle all businesses should heed: provide a superior product at a good price and the customers will come!

Analysis

The sense of voice and tone in this essay is one of its greatest strengths. The task requires students to take a particular position on a controversial issue, and this essay is an especially good response because the writer conveys a feeling of genuine belief in what he or she is saying. The response makes insightful connections between the information in the text and the controlling idea: ". . . chains in some industries actually propel the success of their smaller competitors." Examples are clearly and effectively developed, and the organization of the essay remains focused on the positive effects—however unintended —of a large chain on one particular kind of business.

Coherence is also achieved in the logical cause and effect structure of the argument: "Starbucks educated Americans in the pleasures of café culture . . . . This in turn provided independent cafés with a much larger pool of customers interested in what they had to offer." "As independent coffee vendors enjoyed more customers, Starbucks also made it easier for these shops to make a profit." The language is precise and appropriate to the subject: "They roast their own beans daily to provide the best tasting coffee they can. They also cater specifically to their customers' needs to keep up with the competition." The concluding statement indicates that this writer has fully understood and appreciated the task. With regard to the conventions, there are no significant errors other than inconsistent use of present and past tenses. This essay would rate a high score.

(See pp. 31–35 for a detailed explanation of the rubric for this part of the examination.)

Part B   (7–16)

Note: Refer to Chapter 2 for review and strategy in responding to this part of the examination.

(7) **2** "honesty and privacy." These terms represent another way of expressing the requirement that a voting system be secure enough "to prevent fraud and to [preserve] the anonymity of a secret vote." (lines 4–5)

(8) **3** "paper records." This paragraph outlines a process in which a voter's "choices are not only summarized on the screen but [also] printed out on a piece of paper . . . if officials want to check the accuracy of the touch screen, the paper ballots are counted."

(9) **1** "legislative action." This paragraph lists several efforts on the federal and state levels to pass voter-verification bills. None of the other choices is suggested in the passage.

(10) **4** "inexpensive memory capacity." This is another way of saying that, "A frog in this sense is a cheap form of digital storage."

(11) **2** "protect voter identity." In the following paragraph, the author points out that in Chaum's voting system, ". . . since the image is encrypted, no one can know how you voted." (lines 80–81)

(12) **4** "security concerns." This is the best choice since it expresses an important <u>hindrance</u> or obstacle to be overcome. In the final paragraph, the author remarks that on the Internet ". . . security is dicey, votes aren't secret . . . ."

(13) **1** "has a long history." The title of the graphic is "Voting Through the Ages" and the sections illustrate voting practices from 500 B.C. to 2004. None of the other choices is supported by the text.

(14) **4** "polling method." The origin of ballot is from the Italian word for "little ball." In ancient Greece "voters dropped small clay balls into pots designated for each candidate."

(15) **3** "optical scans." In the section labeled 1960's, the graphic states that the optical scan method has "one of the best track records for reliability . . . ."

(16) **1** "verification" In the final section of the graphic, 2004, the text declares that lever machines "don't all provide a paper trail to double-check accuracy." None of the other factors is mentioned in the text.

Part B   Sample Student Response Essay

Voting has been part of human society for thousands of years, dating as far back as 500 BC in ancient Greece. However, voting has never been a perfect institution, with issues of security and verification arising even in very recent presidential elections in the United States. Voting methods have evolved over the centuries, and even now in the 21st century we are still seeking ways to make the ballot secret but completely verifiable for every individual.

Stretching back to the times of antiquity, polling has existed in many different forms. In ancient Greece and Rome, a very rudimentary form of voting was practiced as voters dropped balls into pots designated for each candidate. In fact, it is from this practice that we have the word "ballot," which originally meant "little ball." History also tells us that in the 1600's in America, the early settlers gathered in meetings and simply shouted out their preferences. The results were often chaotic and very unreliable. By the 19th century, however, paper ballots and lever voting machines were in wide use. These methods also presented problems: paper ballots resulted in vote buying scandals, and the results in lever machines cannot be fully verified.

The 1960's witnessed the advent of punch cards and optical scans, while the 21st century saw the introduction of electronic voting. Although these recent methods have increased voter security, they have not really aided in very precise verification. A recent article in Newsweek *magazine points out "computer scientists and cryptographers are now developing systems to let people know that their votes have really counted."*

One of the new systems being developed, the Chaum System of voting, is one that would dramatically increase the validity in voting. Developed by cryptographer David Chaum, the system uses encryption to ensure security along with an ingenious "stripe" or electronic image technology. When voting, the individuals can see clearly whom they voted for and also take a record with them, which only they can de-code to verify later. Votes are recorded digitally and officials use those images to register the actual vote. Though this may sound very complicated, experts feel that some form of encrypted record of voting is the most reliable way to provide accuracy and verifiability without compromising secrecy for the individual.

The 2000 US presidential election made many people aware of the need to assure all voters that their votes have been counted. It is only through advancing technology that this assurance will be granted.

Analysis

The difficulty for most students on this task was to be able to summarize one of the technological advances outlined in the article. This essay is an example of an adequate response in that regard. The discussion of the Chaum system is brief, but offers a general understanding of the process. This writer also captures the two-part nature of the task in an excellent topic assertion: "Voting methods have evolved over the centuries, and even now in the 21st century we are still seeking ways to make the ballot secret but completely verifiable for every individual."

Organized chronologically, the discussion of the history of voting methods is well done: there are several details, explained clearly and fully. The organization of the entire response is also coherent, with an introduction, history, and discussion of the needs for new technology. The conclusion is also brief but adequate to the task. The writing is fluent and the writer has made effective use of language and phrasing from the two texts.

There are no significant errors in the conventions. This essay would rate a high score.

(See pp. 48–53 for a detailed discussion of the rubric for this part of the examination.)

Session Two

Part A   (1–10)

Note: See Chapter 3 for review and strategy in responding to this part of the examination.

(1) **2** "career." Shirley Jackson says, ". . . my name reminded me of my book."

(2) **4** "newspaper column." Mrs. Lang points out that it is she who writes the North Village Notes column: "That's *my* column." "I'm calling up a few people in town who . . . might have items of news for me—"

(3) **1** "different motives." It is evident throughout the passage that Mrs. Lang is interested only in local matters, such as parties, illness, or visits; Shirley Jackson, on the other hand, wants Lang to be excited by the news of the publication of her novel and is frustrated when she shows no interest.

(4) **3** "novel." Shirley Jackson tells us in the opening line that this conversation took place just before publication of her first novel; she makes several efforts in the conversation to point out its title to Mrs. Lang.

(5) **3** "knowledge of town history." Mrs. Lang seems to know all about who lived in which house and when. She makes no mention of architecture or local art, and—unfortunately—she shows no interest in Shirley Jackson's novel.

(6) **4** "dialogue." Jackson's renders this experience by recounting the entire phone conversation with Mrs. Lang. The author's frustration and the two women's failure to fully understand or appreciate each other emerges in the dialogue itself.

(7) **1** "establish setting." The first three lines are composed entirely of images of the air, the fields, and the fragrances of harvest. There is no rhyme here, and character and conflict are introduced only in the following stanzas.

(8) **3** "prosperity." The specific details of the man who drives up in a Cadillac, wearing a three-piece suit and pinky ring—are classic, almost clichéd—images of wealth and prosperity. None of the other choices is suggested in these lines.

(9) **2** "*his* only ring." The stress on *his* emphasizes the contrast between the wealthy man in the car and the farmer who toils long hours on the land and whose only "ring" is a threadbare pocket on the back of his jeans.

(10) **2** "struggles of the farmer." To show what soybeans "look like," the farmer offers the man a series of images of the difficulties farmers face: bad weather at planting time, uncertain incomes and low prices, and the knowledge that selling the land would be more profitable than farming it. The reference to the number of children the farmer has makes the image more vivid, but it is the catalogue of his struggles that makes the greatest impression on the reader.

Part A   Sample Student Response Essay

People may believe that feeling accomplished must have to do with great achievements and large sums of money. Many may also think that when a significant accomplishment is achieved, the world will notice and be impressed. But life around us suggests that accomplishment takes many forms and may be felt only by the individual. The accomplishments of a simple, hardworking man make him a success in his own eyes and in the eyes of his family while the rest of the world takes no notice; and the worldly success of a creative artist may fail to impress the neighbors in her own small town. In the essay by Shirley Jackson and the poem by Thomas Alan Orr, we observe several examples of individual accomplishment and the ironic way in which these accomplishments are unrecognized by others.

In the essay entitled "Fame," Shirley Jackson recalls an incident when she was living in a small town in Vermont and preparing for a trip to New York to mark the publication of her first novel. The phone rings, and the caller is a columnist from the local newspaper, who wants to speak only to Mrs. Stanley Hyman (Jackson's married name). Believing that the call is about an interview regarding her novel, Jackson tries to impress upon the caller both her professional name and the name of the book. Mrs. Lang, however, takes no notice because her interest is in homey personal items for her social column; Mrs. Lang is also eager for Jackson to know about her role at the newspaper and her knowledge of town history. The entire conversation proceeds at cross-purposes, neither woman really interested in what the other wants to talk about. As a result, Mrs. Lang's column will indicate that Mrs. Hyman and her family have recently taken a trip to visit Mr. and Mrs. "Farrarstrauss" in New York City.

The poem "Soybeans" is also about an ironic encounter between two people whose lives and "accomplishments" are dramatically different from one another's. The scene is set with images of warm October air and "brown fields, heavy with the fragrance . . . of harvest." A farmer is bringing in his crop of soybeans for sale when an evidently wealthy man arrives in his Cadillac, dressed in a fine suit and wearing a pinky ring. The rich man, who says he has just invested a hundred thousand dollars in soybeans, symbolizes material success. This figure is juxtaposed with the farmer who grows soybeans. The farmer is described as wearing worn jeans and "his only ring" is the worn patch on his pocket formed by a tin of tobacco. When the investor says he just wanted to see what soybeans "look like," the farmer responds in a series of metaphors in which the soybeans look like all the uncertainties and hardships small farmers survive from year to year. The farmer concludes with an image of his accomplishment when he says, "Soybeans look like the first good night of sleep in weeks/When you unload at the elevator and the kids get Christmas." The farmer seems to appreciate the irony of the situation when he laughs and asks the man, "Now maybe you can tell me what a hundred grand looks like."

Both passages are developed primarily through dialogue. In the first passage, the two women are talking but not really listening to each other. Shirley Jackson tries to turn the conversation to her book and in a final effort to

impress Mrs. Lang, Jackson adds that she will be writing the Girl Scout col-
umn in the same paper. Mrs. Lang simply does not "hear" what Shirley
Jackson says. Shirley Jackson's accomplishment is outside Mrs. Lang's ability
to appreciate, and Mrs. Lang's must seem trivial to the novelist. In contrast,
the farmer is amused by how different his world of actually growing soybeans
is from the world of the investor for whom soybeans are abstract commodi-
ties. We are left to wonder if the businessman now appreciates what soybeans
"look like." We do know, however, that the four characters represented in
these passages have their own sense of satisfaction in accomplishment.

Analysis

This is an especially good response to the task because the writer has established a controlling idea that reveals an in-depth understanding of the irony in the two passages, which is developed in the common theme of accomplishment ". . . we observe several examples of individual accomplishment and the ironic way in which these accomplishments are unrecognized by others." Throughout the essay we see insightful connections between the controlling idea and ideas in the passages: "The poem *Soybeans* is also about an ironic encounter between two people whose lives and 'accomplishments' are dramatically different from one another's"; "Shirley Jackson's accomplishment is outside Mrs. Lang's ability to appreciate, and Mrs. Lang's must seem trivial to the novelist."

The development is well illustrated with relevant details, and the integration of quotes for emphasis is nearly seamless. Organization is also clear in the pattern of introduction, separate discussion of the two passages, and a conclusion that gathers common elements from the two and links them to the controlling idea. Note too that the discussion remains focused on the "disconnect" between characters. Finally, this writer uses sophisticated language to show how the literary elements of character, irony, image and metaphor contribute to the meaning of the passages: ". . . the farmer is amused by how different his world of actually growing soybeans is from the world of the investor for whom soybeans are abstract commodities. We are left to wonder if the businessman now appreciates what soybeans 'look like.' " There are no evident errors in the conventions. This essay would rate a high score.

(See pp. 68–71 for a detailed discussion of the rubric for this part of the examination.)

Session Two

Note: See Chapter 4 for review and strategy in responding to this part of the examination.

Part B   Sample Student Response Essay

Yann Martel once declared, "You must take life the way it comes at you and make the best of it." Simply stated, this observation means that it is up to each person to do his best with the circumstances of his or her life. Martel's quote might be saying that we should be resigned to accept whatever comes our way and "make the best of it." But I believe that Martel is saying that it is up to the individual to find a fulfilling life in even difficult or challenging circumstances. Two literary works that illustrate such an affirmative view are Jane Eyre *by Charlotte Bronte and* The Woman Warrior *by Maxine Hong Kingston.*

In the novel Jane Eyre, *the central character is a young woman living in Victorian England. Orphaned at a young age, Jane lives several years with her harsh aunt, and for several years after that she lives in a boarding school where the headmaster is cruel and abusive. Jane's circumstances become better after a more kindly headmaster takes over and she later becomes a teacher at the school. Seeking to broaden her horizons, Jane accepts a position as a governess at a mansion where she will fall in love with her dark and brooding employer, Mr. Rochester. Throughout these experiences, Jane remains an intelligent and spirited young woman who is convinced of her worth as an individual. Like many other young women of her time, she might have simply become a bitter old maid, living day to day just to survive; or, she might have married the first man to show interest in her to escape the fate of a spinster. Jane, however, is courageous and true to herself.*

The setting of Jane Eyre's *story is especially significant. Victorian England was a place of rigid social standards and was a harsh place for women outside the wealthy and upper class. Women were not expected to think for themselves, but were expected to marry and care for a husband and family. It was not customary to think of women as capable in their own right. Jane Eyre, however, maintained her ability to think for herself and even more important, she demonstrated an ability to overcome the cruelty of her childhood and the period of poverty and hunger she faced after fleeing Thornfield. Jane's happy (and highly unforeseen) marriage to Mr. Rochester at the end of the novel confirms her ability to make the best of her circumstances.*

Maxine Hong Kingston's memoir The Woman Warrior *recounts her experience as a young Chinese girl growing up in America, where she must assimilate while retaining traditional Chinese culture. She is confronted with an ongoing predicament that plagues her entire existence: she was born a girl and not a boy. Traditional Chinese culture expects females to be subordinate to males. Kingston portrays herself as an emotional and awkward young girl, yet she is also openly rebellious and determined. At one point, she even taunts another young Chinese girl for conforming to tradition and remaining silent.*

Although she does not want to accept a traditional Chinese feminine role, she does want to make the best of her circumstances as a Chinese–American.

Much of this work is in the form of storytelling, or what the Chinese call "talk-stories." Kingston recalls from her mother a story of her aunt, known as the "No Name Woman," abandoned by her family for having a child out of wedlock. In retelling this story, Kingston uses flashbacks to remember a woman somewhat like herself. She was always on the defensive yet determined to survive and make a life for herself. Throughout The Woman Warrior *there remains a defiant tone and subtle sense of pride in who she is as an individual. The culture in which she is growing up is a powerful force, but Kingston also wants to be comfortable with herself. Maxine Hong Kingston's story is truly one of a woman who has "made the best" of her life's circumstances.*

The fictional Jane Eyre *and the writer Maxine Hong Kingston tell stories of bold, independent young women who face the circumstances of their families and societies and struggle to achieve happy and fulfilling lives.*

Analysis

This writer offers a thoughtful interpretation of the critical lens and reveals an understanding that is faithful to its complexity: "Martel's quote might be saying that we should be resigned to accept whatever comes our way and 'make the best of it.' But I believe that Martel is saying that it is up to the individual to find a fulfilling life . . . ." The choice of two works about strong, independent young women also gives unity to the discussion that follows.

The development of ideas is clear and supported by relevant details from the lives of the two central characters. The writer avoids excessive plot detail in the discussion of *Jane Eyre* while offering an outline adequate to support the argument. The details of Kingston's life are less developed, but details of the tension between American and Chinese cultures that she experiences are sufficient to support the topic: "Although she does not want to accept a traditional Chinese feminine role, she does want to make the best of her circumstances as a Chinese–American."

This writer articulates the importance of setting and character in the meaning of these works, and there are several instances in which the language is especially effective: "It was not customary to think of women as capable in their own right"; "[Kingston] is confronted with an ongoing predicament that plagues her entire existence: she was born a girl and not a boy." The organization of the essay is conventional and perfectly clear; the conclusion is sufficient to bring the discussion to a close but adds little otherwise. Sentence structure is varied to good effect, and the overall composition suggests mastery of the conventions. This essay would merit a high score.

(See pp. 80–83 for a detailed discussion of the rubric for this part of the examination.)

NOTES

NOTES

NOTES